SHAKESPEARE

SHAKESPEARE

Michael Wood

A Member of the Perseus Books Group
New York

The emblems at the chapter headings and on the contents page are taken from Geoffrey Whitney's *Choice of Emblems* (1586), and other Elizabethan emblem books.

This book is published to accompany the television series
In Search of Shakespeare
produced by Maya Vision and first broadcast on BBC2 in 2003

First published in Britain by BBC Worldwide Ltd. 2003.

British ISBN 0 563 53477 X

First published in the United States in 2003 by Basic Books,
a member of the Perseus Books Group,
387 Park Avenue South, New York, NY 10016-8810.
Basic Books' edition is published by arrangement with
BBC Worldwide, Ltd.

A cataloging-in-publication record for this book
is available from the Library of Congress.
ISBN 0-465-09264-0

Set in Garamond Simoncini by BBC Worldwide Ltd

03 04 05 / 10 9 8 7 6 5 4 3 2 1

Contents

To my teachers
Bert Parnaby and Brian Phythian

PROLOGUE:

'The Revolution of the Times'

THIS AGE KNOWS GOD

In the winter of 1563, four or five months before William Shakespeare was born, his father was called upon by the corporation of his home town to oversee a troubling task. John Shakespeare had served Stratford diligently as constable and ale-taster, and was now the chamberlain or treasurer, responsible for the town accounts. And on a cold day in the darkest time of the year it was his job to hire workmen, with ladders, scaffolding poles and pots of limewash, to desecrate the town's religious images: to destroy the medieval paintings that covered the walls of the guild chapel, next door to the guildhall and the school.

In the old days, before King Henry's time, the chapel of the Guild of the Holy Cross had been the centre of Stratford's civic life and ceremonies. The guild had endowed and run the grammar school, held feasts, disbursed charities and run the town's almshouses. Inside the chapel, every inch of wall was covered with splendidly gaudy paintings depicting tales loved by all English people, stories rooted in the fabric of the nation's culture for nearly 1000 years. There was St George and the Dragon, the Vision of the Emperor Constantine, and St Helena and the Finding of the True Cross, the subject of Old English poetry 700 years earlier and more recently retold in Caxton's *Golden Legend*, one of the first books to be printed in English. Near the door were images of local female saints, familiar friendly intercessors, such as Modwenna, whose sacred well at Burton-on-Trent was still much visited by traditional folk in Warwickshire. There was a

depiction of the murder of Thomas Becket, whose great pilgrimage had been immortalized by Chaucer. Over the nave arch was a painted wooden crucifix, the Holy Rood, and behind it a great mural of the Last Judgement: Christ seated on a rainbow, the world as his footstool, with souls on their way to heaven, hell or purgatory, red-hot chains encircling the damned, alongside the seven deadly sins and devils blowing horns and wielding clubs: images of warning and consolation, of fear and bliss.

These were the stories of John Shakespeare's childhood and youth in the first half of the sixteenth century. Like most countrymen of his age, his mental world had been shaped by the traditional Christian society of England: the old rhythms of the farming seasons and the religious calendar, and the feasts and holy days that accompanied them. But such things were now officially condemned as childish superstition. At the start of Elizabeth's reign a royal injunction had instructed town councils to enforce 'the removal of all signs of idolatry and superstition, from places of worship, so that there remain no memory of the same in walls, glasses, windows, or elsewhere within their churches and houses'. The aldermen of Stratford had put it off for five years, but now the time had come. Whatever his private feelings, it was John's duty to vandalize images that represented a world of encoded memories built up over the centuries. These were the familiar and beloved observances of his parents and grandparents, a vast and resonant world of symbols that linked him to the ancestors and to the old idea of the community of England.

How had it come to this? It's the kind of thing we associate with the religious conflicts that mar our modern world, the rage of iconoclasts – but this was in England. It had been Elizabeth's father Henry VIII, back in the 1520s and 1530s, who had begun the revolution that would turn England from a medieval Catholic society into a modern Protestant state. Henry's Reformation had begun with his

love for Anne Boleyn and his desire for a divorce from his first wife, Katherine of Aragon. A battle for supremacy resulted: who was the ultimate authority in his kingdom, the king or the pope in Rome? Eventually this led to the breaking of the link with Rome, which had been maintained steadfastly by the English since the mission of St Augustine in 597 to convert them to Christianity. In pursuit of his divorce, the king made himself supreme head of the Church of England, in place of the pope. Henry had intended change to stop there; and so it might have done, but for two things. First, in 1536 Henry's money troubles led to his seizing the lands, buildings and treasures of the monasteries, many of which went back to the beginnings of English Christianity. The second major factor was the influx of new Protestant ideas from Germany, where Martin Luther had defied pope and emperor and become a national hero. For Luther the way to God was a matter of individual conscience grounded in scripture, that did not need either the institution of the Catholic Church or its 'superstitious'

OPPOSITE: *The guild chapel today, showing the remains of the wall painting of Christ and the Last Judgement.* ABOVE: *The mural as uncovered in 1804. This was one of the images whitewashed by Shakespeare's father in the winter of 1563.*

Above: *The burning of a Protestant martyr under Bloody Mary. Religious conflicts marked Shakespeare's lifetime: born of a Catholic family, in his writing he often took an oppositional stance between both sides.*

doctrines, which he perceived as chains to bind the simple-minded. The dissolution of the monasteries and the Protestant Reformation that followed inaugurated a permanent shift of power in England, the creation of an absolutist state and a new landed class that would have a vested interest in supporting the new regime and its state religion. Out of these convulsions, involving religion, class conflict and civil war, modern secular Britain would emerge.

But at grass-roots level in towns such as Stratford, and in the countryside round about where John Shakespeare grew up, little had changed by the time of Henry's death in 1547. In the years after the break with Rome a half-Protestant, half-Catholic Church with a Protestant prayerbook had been established. It was in the short reign of Edward VI, Henry's son from his third marriage, to Jane Seymour, that the real revolution began. Edward was a pious, cold-hearted swot, who was surrounded by a tight-knit group of politically motivated men. Now the fury of destruction that had visited the monasteries fell on all churches, cathedrals and chapels, which he ordered to be stripped of their screens, statues and paintings. In many places, however, the pace of such change was slow, and when Edward died in 1553, still in his teens, his half-sister Mary, daughter of Katherine of Aragon and an ardent Catholic, became queen. Greeted with a burst of enthusiasm on her accession, Mary soon lost public goodwill because of her intolerance. She attempted to reverse Henry's revolution, to turn the clock back, and in her brief time on the throne she earned the name Bloody Mary by burning Protestants up and down the land. In this story, terrible things were done in the name of God by England's rulers on both sides of the religious divide.

So when Mary died and Elizabeth, daughter of Henry's second wife, Anne Boleyn, came to the throne in 1558 the country was caught between old and new. Elizabeth was a convinced but not zealous Protestant. This brilliant, vulnerable and psychologically damaged monarch gambled that she would outlive the troubles she had inherited, and with her advisers set out to return the country to the path of her father's and half-brother's 'reformation' of religion.

Back in Stratford in that winter of 1563, then, they had gone through three changes of religion in less than twenty years when John's workmen began to cover up the great cycle of medieval paintings. With that the story was supposed to be over: in Elizabethan terms it was the end of history, or of one version of history. Such at least was the government's intention. The town was to lay its past aside, put its best foot forward and walk into a brave new Protestant future. Its children, the next generation such as John's son William, were to be obedient citizens of Elizabeth's reformed state.

But was that really how it was? It is generally believed that the defacing proves Stratford was by then a Protestant town, and John himself a conforming member of the Church of England – even a zealous one. But scrutiny of the town minutes reveals a rather different story. The corporation of Stratford and their treasurer in fact left all the stained glass in place and refused to sell off their finely embroidered vestments and cloths. They left wall paintings untouched where they thought they could get away with it, and even partitioned off the chancel so that none of the paintings there was destroyed – they were still visible on the eve of the Civil War in 1641. And as for those images defaced that day, they were so thinly covered over that they were still vivid and intact when discovered centuries later. The work, then, was reversible, and surely deliberately so. After all, no one in Stratford at that moment knew which way history would go.

So here's a parable at the start of our tale, but one full of ambiguity. What lies under the whitewash? What lies behind actions and words in an age when covering up, concealment and dissimulation became the order of the day? Such questions are as relevant to the life of the greatest poet of all time as they are to untangling the tale of his father and his neighbours in his home town.

This is the tale of one man's life, lived through a time of revolution – a time when not only England, but the larger world beyond, would go through momentous changes. In one of her most famous painted portraits, Elizabeth stands on a map of little England with her foot on Ditchley in Oxfordshire – a huge figure on a small country. And when Shakespeare was born her England was a small place, nothing compared with the great contemporary powerhouses of civilization: Moghul India, Safavi Iran, Ottoman Turkey and Ming China. When the Persian Shah and the Great Moghul stand on their map in another emblematic picture of the age, the world beneath their feet spreads from China to the Mediterranean, embracing the old heartlands of civilization. England, with a population of less than 3 million, was an old-fashioned, backward place out on the fringe of Europe. But as the centre of gravity of history began to

RIGHT: *'The Ditchley Portrait' of Elizabeth I by Marcus Gheeraerts the Younger, c. 1592. Elizabeth gambled that she would outlive the bitter religious divisions bequeathed by her predecessors.*

shift, as the old civilizations of Asia were outflanked by the new maritime states of the Atlantic seaboard, England's moment was about to arrive.

Shakespeare, then, was lucky to be born on the cusp of history. If he had been born in his parents' generation, two or three decades earlier, his mind might not have been open to the challenges of the modern world; a few decades later and he would not have been in touch with the old world view, the imaginal universe of the medieval Christian civilization of England and Europe. Shakespeare may be, as has been claimed in our time, the first modern man, the creator of our modern idea of personality, the 'inventor of the human', but he was also the last great product of the Gothic Christian West. If great writers are made by their times, then to be born in 1564 was to be born in very interesting times indeed.

Such dramatic changes would provide the raw material for the artists, poets and thinkers of Shakespeare's lifetime, a time that would lead to civil war and the execution of the king. And from the macrocosm to the microcosm, these ideas run through Shakespeare's works. New worlds are discovered, old worlds are lost; the people rise up; kings are overthrown; women speak up for equality with men; black people find a voice in England. Ships sail across the world loaded with people, spices and ideas; potatoes rain out of the sky; tales are told of Lapland sorcerers, Persian emperors and embassies to the Pigmies. Off Sierra Leone, African dignitaries watch *Hamlet* on a British ship; the Native American princess Pocahontas attends a masque in London. Then as now, globalization means that ideas are globalized too.

The winter light is falling over Chapel Street as the last lime is sloshed over Christ's rainbow throne and drips down the face of Jesus. The workmen untie the ropes on the scaffolding, looking forward to their wages and a jug of ale in Burbage's tavern in Bridge Street. John Shakespeare stamps his feet to keep warm in the chilly chapel. The job is done, to be entered into his January account along with repairing the vicar's chimney and mending the bell rope: 'Item payd for defaysing ymages in the chappell iis' (years later, uncannily, his poet son would write of 'defacing the precious image of our dear Redeemer'). At this moment, in Stratford in the winter of 1563–4, John Shakespeare might not have been able to see it yet, but the world was poised between old and new, between no longer and not yet; or, as his son would put it, between 'things dying and things newborn'.

DRATON

CHAPTER ONE

Roots

Look Backwards and Forwards

Stratford-upon-Avon in Warwickshire, where Shakespeare was born in April 1564, was a rural market town 100 miles from London – not so far in physical distance, perhaps, but a long way in terms of mental horizons. The best place to get an idea of the lie of the land today is outside the town, at Welcombe, where low winter sunlight sharpens the patterns of ridge and furrow etched long ago by the medieval ox teams: the faint skeleton of Shakespeare's England. From the ridge above, where the wind, as they would say, comes 'rowling and gusting' across the valley, you can see the Avon like a silver ribbon snaking down from the hills of Northamptonshire. To the south in his day were arable fields; to the north the Forest of Arden. Stratford itself, the crossing point on the river, was where the produce of the two regions was bartered and sold in its markets and fairs. Even including outlying hamlets the town had a population of less than 2000, with no more than 100 good houses. A small place, then, ranked below the county town of Warwick and the urban centre of Coventry, now decaying as a result of the mid-century recession.

In those days it took three days and nights to get there from London. The roads were bad, and infested by robbers at lonely spots: it was safest to travel in a group, or on horseback with the regular packhorse trains. Every two weeks the Stratford carriers, the Greenaways, took goods for sale in London – country produce, such as linen shirts, bespoke gloves, wool, cheeses and linseed oil – a small contribution to the

Opposite: *Stratford on a sixteenth-century tapestry. Shakespeare grew up with the image of Warwickshire as the heart of England.*

flood of rural wealth that poured into the markets at Smithfield to feed the conspicuous consumption of the capital. On the return journey they carried the kind of imported luxuries that went down well in Warwickshire on middle-class tables, or at sheep shearings and other country feasts: dates, sugar, rice, figs, raisins and almonds. After crossing the river at Clopton Bridge, the homebound pack trains unloaded in the Greenaways' yard near the Market Cross, a few doors from the Shakespeares' house in Henley Street, where it is thought the poet was born.

Shakespeare's Family and Ancestors

The story of a person's life begins before he or she is born. It is our family that shapes our values and our ways of seeing, that gives us our deepest fund of tales and images: stories at our mother's knee; our observations of the way the family works; the relationship between our parents; the way they resolve conflicts or tell jokes; their attitude to work and play, to life and love, to public success and failure, and to the law.

On both sides of the family William Shakespeare came from farming stock: old families rooted in the Warwickshire countryside, families who, like all English people in the mid-sixteenth century, went through the traumatic religious crises out of which Britain's modern secular, capitalist society emerged. Contrary to the myth of the poet's lowly origins, the Shakespeares were an aspiring lower middle-class family – they were people with money, and his father later became mayor of Stratford. But both his parents were descended from husbandmen, small to middling yeomen with a peasant house and 100 acres, horses, barns and an ox team; people grounded in the penny-pinching realism of a class who laboured to build themselves up. Many of his relatives continued to live that life: Aunt Joan and Uncle Harry stayed farmers to the end.

The search for Shakespeare starts not in Stratford, then, but a short way to the north, for both sides of his family originated in a tiny cluster of villages in the Forest of Arden. His mother's name, indeed, was Arden. Warwickshire poets liked to call Arden the heart of England. Today, south of Birmingham and west of Warwick, only fragments of woodland remain alongside the roar of the M42 motorway. In the sixteenth century it was still a vast tract of forest, all part of what the Normans, who had hunted there, called Beaudesert, 'beautiful wild country', and a completely

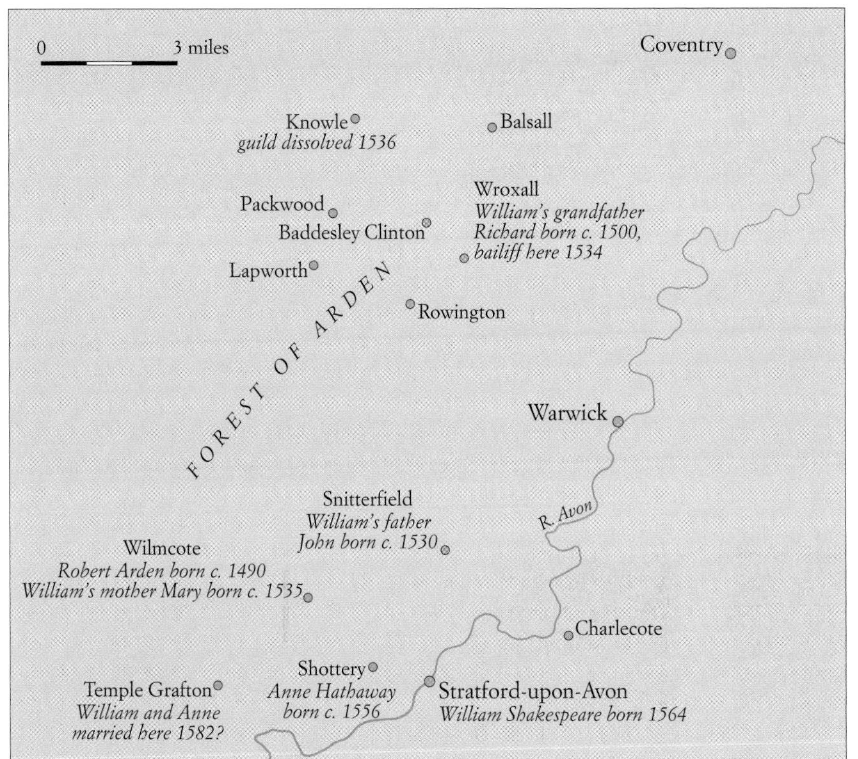

Opposite: *A country woman of Shakespeare's class: both his mother and his wife were the daughters of well-off farmers.*
Left: *The villages around Stratford where Shakespeare's family farmed for generations.*

different world from the crowded streets of London where Shakespeare would spend so much of his life.

This was a place to fire the imagination. Unlike the works of most of his urban or university-educated contemporaries, Shakespeare's plays are full of images of flowers, trees and animals. His linguistic roots are here too – not in the more socially acceptable speech of London or the court. Shakespeare spoke with a Warwickshire accent, like Brummie today: more Lenny Henry than Laurence Olivier. The veneer of high culture and high society would come later, but in his plays the Warwickshire boy would still constantly betray his origins in the easy way he slipped into rural custom and country talk. Indeed, he would use it deliberately as an imaginal world to counterpoint with that of kings and nobles: Joan blowing her nails, frozen pails, the shepherd's son with his tods of wool and rice and dates for the fair. Long into his fame he still used idiosyncratic phonetic spellings of Warwickshire words, which perplexed his London printers; he would drop in minutely observed Midlands images, in dialect words still used well into the twentieth century, to describe the turn at the top of a furrow made by a plough team ('hade land'), the wheat sown in Gloucestershire at the end of

August ('Red Lammas'), Cotswold apples ('redcoats' and 'caraways') or the kind of grass with which kids make whistles ('kecksies' – a word still known in Warwickshire). Shakespeare would use 'breeze' in a memorable image when describing the Egyptian queen's flight from the battle of Actium in *Antony and Cleopatra*:

> The breeze upon her, like a cow in June,
> Hoists sail and flies

'Breeze' here has nothing to do with wind; it is an Anglo-Saxon word that was still used in Midlands dialect in Tudor times. It refers to the gadflies that, in summer, trouble cows, who all at once lift their tails high in the air and stampede away. That's the kind of knowledge you don't get at Oxbridge, or in a rich man's house.

This rich seam of peasant vocabulary in Shakespeare's language survived in the West Midlands into our own time. As late as the 1930s in the Cotswolds, you could still hear Shakespeare's 'mazzard' for head, 'lush' for rich, 'plash' for pool, 'twit' for blab, 'slobberly' for sloppy and 'orts' for the leftovers of food. More specifically, farming people still used 'reeds' for thatch, and 'pleaching' or 'plushing' for laying a hedge. In the village of Compton Abdale at this time one seventy-five-year-old farmer still used 'on a line' for in a rage and Iago's 'speak within doore' for speak softly.

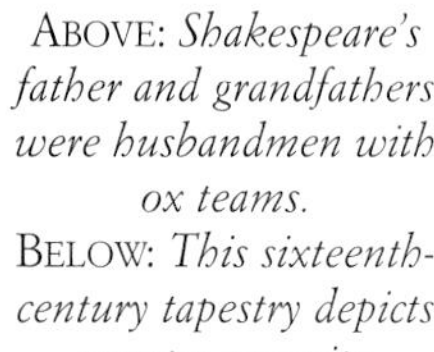

ABOVE: *Shakespeare's father and grandfathers were husbandmen with ox teams.*
BELOW: *This sixteenth-century tapestry depicts country pursuits.*

So although the poet was born in a small country town, his forebears were of farming stock. The Shakespeares' ancestors came from around the village of Balsall, with its old chapel and hall of the Knights Templars. Nearby, down Green Lane, shrouded by thickets of ash and silver birch, across a ford that runs deep in winter, there is still a red-brick farm where one Adam of Oldeditch lived in the fourteenth century. Rewarded by the king with land for service in war, his son gave himself the surname 'Shakespeare', perhaps to denote his deeds on the battlefield. There were still Shakespeares at Oldeditch 100 years later, in early Tudor times, and almost certainly the clan descended from them.

By the sixteenth century Shakespeares were thick on the ground and had spread to four villages: Rowington, Wroxall, Knowle and Packwood, with its moated hall and church surrounded by ancient yew trees. The Shakespeares at Packwood were business partners of William's father John, and probably his kinsmen. (Interestingly enough, the historian Raphael Holinshed passed his last days here as steward until 1580. Shakespeare would later use his *Chronicles* (1577) as the main source of his history plays – might he perhaps have known Holinshed in person?)

A Sense of History

All families have tales about their past. Today, they might be about the Second World War or the Depression, centred on an old box of photos, service medals and cuttings. One particular tale suggests that the Shakespeares were like that too. In 1596, when William was thirty-two and famous, he and his father went to London to try to obtain a coat of arms for John, to gain him the status of a gentleman. In the files of the Royal College of Arms their submission survives, including a rough draft with the herald's notes. That day Shakespeare claimed that long ago an ancestor had won reputation and 'lands and tenements' when he had done King Henry VII 'valiant and faithful service'. That meant deeds in war, and implies that William's ancestor had fought with Henry Tudor against Richard III at Bosworth in 1485.

Of course, it may have been pure fantasy, a family myth that had lost nothing in the retelling. But maybe the tale was true: handed down from the grandparents, or gleaned from a crumbling old title deed bearing the king's name in the family box under the bed. This particular ancestor has never been traced, but the likeliest candidate is Thomas Shakespeare of Balsall who, with his wife Alicia, affirmed his status by joining the well-to-do guild of the chapel at Knowle in 1486. Perhaps Thomas had been in the army, in the retinue of his local lord, and was rewarded with a small parcel of land in the victor's share-out, which included the Warwickshire estates of Richard and his supporters. The real

point here, though, is not whether the tale is true or not, but that it was a family tradition. Because it comes from words spoken and jotted down that day in 1596, it enables us to say confidently that history – national history, indeed – was part of the Shakespeares' family story.

As an adult Shakespeare would be fascinated by English and British history: the national narrative of the past two centuries with its good kings and bad kings; the sacredness of monarchy; the struggle between justice and might, power and conscience; the relation of poor people to the mighty; and what constitutes patriotism. All this was of particular fascination because the national narrative was up for grabs in Elizabeth's day as history was being rewritten root and branch. His early fame would rest not on comedy or tragedy, but on history.

There are many ways in which history is important. It shapes our identity; it gives reality and authenticity to our family and communal life; it creates for us a sense of a shared past; and, not least, it fashions our sense of justice. The Shakespeare family motto – composed, it would seem, by William for that meeting with the herald, and intended to sum up the family and their ancestry – makes precisely that point: 'Not without right'.

Religious Roots: The Society of Arden

Warwickshire was a focus for the ideological struggles of the time in the clash between Elizabeth's new elite and the old gentry of the shire. Elizabeth's enforcer Robert Dudley, Earl of Leicester, who drove her Protestant revolution in these parts, was a new man, as were his local agents, such as the influential Lucy family at Charlecote. But old families like the Ardens, the poet's mother's kin, who were Catholic, resented the power of Dudley and his henchmen. The head of the Ardens, Edward Arden, called him an upstart and an adulterer; and he pointedly refused to wear Dudley's livery on the queen's visit to Kenilworth in 1575. From Henry VIII's day wills survive of these old-fashioned stalwarts of the shire – Underhills, Throgmortons and Ardens – which give a sense of this deep-rooted, almost medieval culture: the last gasp of the Old Religion, still rebuilding churches, leaving pious bequests and making provision for good works, all out of affection for the old saints and the 'dear familiar place'. In 1526 John Arden, for example, left Aston church 'my best black damask gown to be made into a cope … my suit of armour to dress an image of St George to be placed over the pew where I was accustomed to sit … and two two-year-old heifers to help towards the maintenance of the church bells'.

In the Stratford area many families of this class kept loyal to the Old Faith right into the seventeenth century – the Treshams, Winters, Catesbys and Throgmortons prominent among them. The wooded countryside hereabouts was dotted with their isolated houses: Huddington, Packwood, Bushwood and 'moated granges' like Baddesley, with its moat, priest holes and secret tunnels. These places were safe houses for the Catholic underground in the 1580s and 1590s, and the scene of open warfare in the aftermath of the Gunpowder Plot, when members of eminent Warwickshire families, well known to Shakespeare, would die fighting, clinging hopelessly to their older version of English history.

Below the gentry, many of the husbandmen in the villages of the Forest of Arden were of the same persuasion. Twenty-five years into Elizabeth's reign a Rowington man told friends that, given a free choice, only one in ten of his village would attend Protestant church. He was probably right: government surveys and interrogations reveal the strength of such loyalties well into Shakespeare's adulthood.

Just before Henry VIII dissolved the monasteries Shakespeares and Ardens were associated with the local gentry in the guild book of the chapel at Knowle, which survives in Birmingham Public Library. The entries for 1526 include Shakespeares from Packwood and Rowington, among them a Richard who is probably the poet's grandfather, alongside the old names of the shire:

> Domina Jane Shakespeare
> Robert Catesby and his wife Jane
> George Throgmorton, knight, and his wife Katherine
> Edward Ferrars, knight, and Constance his wife
> William Clopton, knight, and Elizabeth his wife
> Richard Shakespeare and Alicia his wife
> William Shakespeare and Alicia his wife
> John Shakespeare and Joanna his wife

There we have an image of the old community of the shire, the local farmers and gentry of Arden, as they were on the eve of Henry VIII's revolution: rooted in the soil, deferential to the old landed families, devoted to the local shrines and guilds. This is an image in microcosm of the early sixteenth-century society of Arden into which Shakespeare's parents were born, and out of which his view of England, and its history, emerged.

Moving Out and Up

Although these family connections do not by themselves prove anything about William's own allegiances, they give precious hints about the world view handed down to him by his parents and grandparents. His was a traditional society in which such loyalties were valued and remembered. In our modern world we

tend to think of close family in terms of no more than three generations, and our view of kinship can be quite narrow. Tudor people had a much wider sense of family relations; 'cousin', for example, meant something even when once or twice removed. And people had a bigger picture of their place in the family tree.

Yet even in a traditional society this kind of rooted local culture has many strands. The Shakespeares, like all families, could thrive only by means of work, enabling them to achieve practical and material advancement. William's paternal grandfather, Richard, struck out from the family roots around Wroxall and Rowington and, as a young man in the 1520s, leased land at Snitterfield, a village five miles northeast of Stratford off the old Warwick road. Here he farmed for the next thirty-five years.

The site of the Shakespeares' house has recently been identified. Richard had an 80-acre plot on the corner of Bell Lane, running down the hill to the ford over Snitterfield brook, and the present house incorporates part of a Tudor farm building. The land was originally leased from the local branch of the Ardens – a family of similar sturdy farming stock, with the same kind of holding, the same kind of outlook on life, and the same faith. In that house in Snitterfield Richard's wife bore him two sons, John and Henry. Henry – the poet's Uncle Harry – stayed on the land as a farmer all his life; an outbuilding of his house survives by the church. But John, born perhaps in the late 1520s, made the move to become a townsman and to rise above his peasant status. Ambitious, charming and hard-working (but also canny and litigious), John could have stayed a farmer but had different ideas. Working partly on some land he leased in Snitterfield and partly in town, he apprenticed himself for seven years to a glover in Stratford.

The Rise of John Shakespeare

> The towne of Stratford standithe apon a playne ground on the right hand of Avon, as the water descendithe. It hathe 2 or 3 very lardge stretes, besyde back lanes. One of the principall streets ledithe from est to west, another from southe to northe. The bishop of Worcester is lord of the towne. The towne is reasonably well builded of timbar. There is once a year a great fayre at Holy-Rode Daye. The parish church is a fayre large peace of worke, and standith at the southe end of the towne.... The church is dedicated to the Trinitie.

Opposite: *The Henley Street house as it was in 1769 and (below) the rear view today. It is likely, but not certain, that Shakespeare was born here.*

Riding into the town in the late 1530s or 1540s, during the days of John Shakespeare's apprenticeship to Dixon the glover, this is how the traveller John Leland described the place with all the accuracy of a modern guidebook. He also mentioned the fine stone bridge, the grammar school, the almshouses and

the 'right goodly chapel' with its murals of the Dance of Death. Despite development and tourism, his portrait is recognizable today: the guild chapel, the Clopton Bridge and the almshouses (still occupied by poor people, but now administered by the local authority), the guildhall and the grammar school (refounded in 1553), and many of the half-timbered houses remain, although the 'pretty house of brick and timber', where Shakespeare died, is long gone.

Sixteenth-century Stratford was a small but thriving town of 1500 people. The fair held every 14 September was where hired labour was recruited and paid; where freelance dealers – 'higglers' – bought up eggs and poultry to sell at a profit in the big towns. It was where well-off country 'broggers' – illegal wool merchants – came to buy bricks and tiles, and ironwork from the smiths in Henley Street. There was plenty of business for tradesmen and craftsmen working in small-scale industries as the economy slowly picked up after the recession of the 1540s and 1550s.

Even luxury goods were to be found now. On their boards shopkeepers sold goods imported into London and carried here by the Greenaways' pack trains: fruit and nuts from the Mediterranean and soon potatoes from Virginia.

ABOVE: *The reconstructed parlour of the Shakespeare house. Painted cloths on the wall, pewter on the table and napery were the marks of an aspirant Tudor family.*

The growth of a new middle class encouraged specialized trades: people were beginning to covet smart clothes, for instance. The opportunities were here, not driving an eight-ox team up and down a piece of ploughland at Snitterfield. And it was here that John Shakespeare made his career as a glover.

The earliest record of John in Stratford is in a document of 1552, the first case in a long career of litigation that seems to have run in the Shakespeare family. He was fined for leaving a 'dung heap' – a rubbish tip – in Henley Street; perhaps a rotting heap of leather shavings and offcuts. Once he had done his apprenticeship, John became a bespoke glover who sold his work on a stall with the other glovers at Market Cross. He would have cut and worked the leather in his own home – quite a cottage industry, perhaps, with outworkers, and with women in his outhouse doing the sewing.

As late as 1561 he appeared in the Snitterfield post-mortem of his father as *agricola*, a farmer, but by then he had risen in social status in Stratford and become a town councillor, justice of the peace, constable and ale taster. By then, this 'merry cheeked man who durst have cracked a jest at any time' had become part of the town's ruling elite and was clearly a popular and respected man of good judgement and capacity. So the Snitterfield farmer was now a member of Elizabeth's new civic order, part of what they called the 'commonwealth' of England. It seems he never learned to write: he always signed with a mark depicting the glovers' compasses or the 'donkey' on which leather was stretched. But he must have had basic reading skills simply to fulfil his civic role, let alone to keep his account books.

English local government was part of a very old tradition of consultation and representation; looking after what, even three centuries before, had been known to well-to-do peasants as 'the welfare of the community of the realm' – a national community personified by the monarch, who was the focus of their allegiance provided that he or she was sensitive to local feelings. John's twenty-four fellow-councillors or aldermen were middle-class propertied sorts: glovers, hatters, haberdashers. Meetings were held behind closed doors in the guild rooms. The job of the council was to run the town: to supervise education and ensure cleanliness; to look after the poor, sick and unemployed; and to keep order and resolve conflicts. Its members were reimbursed for expenses, but not paid. They were not expected to refuse office, nor could any of them resign their appointment; it took a serious misdemeanour or a dramatic falling out to be struck off, as John would eventually be.

His role as town councillor is significant for his son's story, for he and his colleagues were compelled to engage with national politics and history. As representatives of central government they had to control, to encourage conformity and to identify dissent. They were the people whose fate it was to negotiate change, to guide the town through the dangerous times of the Catholic Queen Mary and her Protestant successor Elizabeth; times in which England would be changed for ever.

The Ardens: Shakespeare's Mother's Family

In the late 1550s – at the end of Queen Mary's reign – John was probably getting on for thirty. The average age for a man to marry in Tudor England was twenty-eight, and twenty-six for a woman. So off he went to seek a wife. She was the daughter of his father's old Snitterfield landlord, a girl he might have known since childhood: Mary Arden.

Shakespeare's mother adds another dimension to the poet's biography, in terms of his cultural and social background. For Mary came from a family of real status in Warwickshire, with links to some of the powerful Catholic families in the shire. For a start – and how could this not have impressed itself upon a child? – they bore the ancient name of the forested region of Warwickshire north of Stratford. According to seventeenth-century local antiquarians, the Ardens traced their ancestry back to the Anglo-Saxon lord Thurkill of Arden

ABOVE: *The Arden family house in Wilmcote, originally an open Tudor hall of 1514.*

(and, according to *Domesday Book*, their land at Curdworth was indeed held by Thurkill in 1066). But tradition took them back further still to legendary figures such as the hero Guy of Warwick, who figured in poems of the sixteenth century that William Shakespeare certainly knew. The Ardens' ancestry reinforced the family's sense of national history. Thomas Arden had fought for the Barons and Simon de Montfort in the civil war of the thirteenth century; Robert Arden, who had fought for the Yorkists in the Wars of the Roses, had been executed in 1452. More recently John Arden, Mary's great-uncle, had been in service at the court of Henry VII as an Esquire of the Body. The family even had a room in Park Hall, their house at Curdworth 20 miles away, called the King's Chamber – perhaps Henry had actually stayed there.

There is still some uncertainty over Mary Arden's exact relation to the Park Hall Ardens, but the evidence suggests she was descended from Thomas Arden, one of several younger sons of Walter Arden of Park Hall, who recovered the family estates during the Wars of the Roses. Thomas had land in Warwickshire at Wilmcote and Snitterfield. His son Robert, who farmed in both places, was called a 'gentleman of worship' by Shakespeare in his submission to the Royal College of Arms in 1596. That was to rewrite history a little. In reality Robert was just a well-to-do local farmer who called himself a husbandman. But he came from an ancient family, and he was the father of Mary, the poet's mother.

Mary Arden's Childhood Home: A Place of Substance

Thanks to a fascinating piece of archival detective work, the house in which Mary lived up to her marriage was identified in 2001 as Glebe House in Wilmcote, four miles north of Stratford. The house has a Victorian brick skin, but up on the second floor is Tudor lath and plaster, and beams whose tree rings reveal they were cut in 1514. It started life as a plain hall house 55 feet long with an open hall in the middle, and a chamber with a bedroom floor at one end and the kitchen at the other; outside was a workshop. In the yard stood cattle and hay barns, a stable, a well and a privy. Mary's father had about 135 acres, with another holding of 30 acres called Asbies and further land at Snitterfield. It was a sizeable holding for a husbandman of the day.

So Mary, one of seven sisters, grew up as the daughter of a prosperous farmer and bearer of the oldest name in Warwickshire. By a great stroke of luck Robert Arden's will, dated November 1556, survives in Worcester Record

Office. Mary, then still unmarried, was the executrix: a clear sign of her ability. The document gives a picture of traditional rural society only a few years before William was born, and is thoroughly Catholic with its appeal to the Angels and the Virgin Mary 'and all the blessed company of saints'. Henry VIII's Reformation had so far touched this part of Warwickshire only lightly. In keeping with most of her class and neighbours, Mary Arden would have been brought up in a highly ritualized, old-fashioned English country Catholicism.

Attached to the will is an inventory of Robert's goods, which enables us to imagine the house as it was furnished in the year before Mary married. The list of possessions reflects the changing world of the Tudor lower middle classes and includes eight painted tapestries, tables, chairs, benches, a cupboard, beds and bed linen. No plate is mentioned: as was customary in some places even until the nineteenth century, the Ardens would have eaten out of wooden bowls. In the kitchen were pots, skillets, a frying pan, a cauldron and pewter candlesticks; and there was 'bacon in the roof'. In the outhouse Robert kept a good kit of carpentry tools – he was obviously a skilled woodworker. The barn housed a cart, harness and gear, a heavy plough and an eight-ox team of the kind that had been traditional since pre-Conquest days. The inventory also lists cattle, sheep, pigs, horses, beehives and sown wheat in the fields. Quite an extensive holding, it suggests a well-off middle-class landowner of the sixteenth century who would have employed both permanent workers and seasonal labourers. Although not rich enough to possess woven tapestries, the family was still able to afford painted cloths of the kind Shakespeare would later describe in his works (Falstaff talks of being 'frightened by a painted cloth', referring to cloths with religious themes; in *The Rape of Lucrece* the poet mentions a painted cloth depicting the story of the siege of Troy).

Shakespeare's grandfather's inventory is fascinating because it reveals the material culture of the class out of which William came; it anchors us in his reality as a child. Not only the cloths on the wall, with their frightening and fascinating images, but the skillets, iron crows, pails, mattocks, cauldrons, augers, querns, handsaws, joint stools, cupboards, benches, bolsters, pillows and diapers – words that all appear in his plays – have their documented counterparts in his mother's home. This house, with its furnishings, represents the world into which William would be born: solid, down-to-earth, practical.

The Accession of Elizabeth

After her father's death Mary became a woman of property with her acres in Wilmcote and her portion in Snitterfield. She married John Shakespeare a few months later in early 1557, when she was at least seventeen and maybe even in her

early twenties. The wedding is likely to have been solemnized at the parish church of Wilmcote at Aston Cantlow; and, given the date and the history of the families, it would have been a Catholic service followed by a mass. Then the couple moved into a new house in Henley Street, where they could look forward to a prosperous middle-class provincial lifestyle, with some pewter on the table, good linen in the cupboard, hangings on the wall, a table laid for guests, and a servant or two. In Queen Mary's Stratford this was what it meant to have standing in the world.

But their world was about to change. Scarcely more than a year after John and Mary's marriage, the queen died. In her short reign she had reinstated Catholicism as the national religion and bitterly persecuted Protestants, some of whom had been burnt at the stake in nearby Coventry. On 17 November 1558 Mary's half-sister Elizabeth came to the throne. The daughter of Henry VIII by Anne Boleyn, Elizabeth instituted a return to the stalled Protestant Reformation of her father and her half-brother Edward VI. With the nation already in a state of deep anxiety over recent changes of rulers and religion, people braced themselves for the next phase in the war for English hearts and minds.

Like all parishes, Stratford celebrated the coming of a new ruler with the traditional rituals. The following Sunday, the first in Advent, the leading townsmen, including John Shakespeare, would have processed to church to proclaim the new queen and to pray for a happy and prosperous reign; but they would have recited 'Our Father' and 'Hail Mary' for her prosperity, sung with the Latin litanies and collects for a Catholic ruler. The mood of the congregation that day was probably nervous. Some neighbours and friends were Protestants, and one or two perhaps leaned towards Puritanism; but most were old Catholics, and traditionalists in the town (although they might have been horrified by the Coventry burnings) would have agreed with the churchwardens in one Berkshire parish that under Henry and Edward 'all godly ceremonies and good uses were taken out of the church ... all goodness and godliness despised and in manner banished ... [when] devout religion and honest behaviour of men was accounted and taken for superstition and hypocrisy'. For them, Mary's reign had been a time when 'the church was restored and comforted again'. In this part of Warwickshire many would have agreed with that. Even twenty-five years later a Rowington villager spoke on behalf of his community when he said of the Old Faith, 'This is our religion here.'

So what did the future hold? After mass, across England the parishes rang bells and lit bonfires at church gates, with a dole of cheese, bread and beer for the poor. But the fires of Elizabeth's accession ceremonies were to be the funeral rites of Catholic England. A year later in July 1559, the government brought in measures 'to plant true religion'. What this meant was the suppression of all Catholic ceremonial and imagery: the destruction of altars and images, rood lofts, wall paintings, stained glass and ritual vestments. Parish priests (who were still mainly of Queen Mary's Church) were instructed to adopt new rituals, a new prayerbook and the authorized Protestant Bible. In many parts of the country churchwardens were required to prepare a document containing an inventory of all the 'church goods', together with 'all the names of all the houselling people in the parish and the names of all them that were buried there since midsummer and was twelvemonth Christened and wedded'. 'Houselling' – a word Shakespeare puts into the mouth of Old Hamlet's ghost – designated those who took Catholic communion.

So the process was beginning by which the government would gradually cast a net round all the adherents to the Old Faith. A battle had begun between power and conscience which would take the best part of half a century to resolve itself. Broadly speaking, historians now see the process in four phases: in the first dozen or so years of Elizabeth's reign an uneasy equilibrium was maintained; then, from around the time Shakespeare started school in 1571, the storm gathered; not long after he left school in 1580 the crisis began with the missions of the Catholic Counter-Reformation, and the ensuing repression; and finally, from the beginning of the 1590s, the establishment gained the ascendancy. This period of cultural revolution spanned most of Shakespeare's lifetime and is crucial to an understanding of his mind and thought.

ABOVE: *Stained glass in the church at Wroxall, an important place in the family memory. William's grandfather Richard was bailiff here and Shakespeare women were prioresses at the nunnery, including Jane who died when William was a boy.*

Two Funerals and a Christening

Although she purged the universities, the powerhouses of ideology, early in her reign, Elizabeth did not at first set out to persecute her subjects. She was a sincere Protestant, but not a zealous reformer and had no desire, as she put it, to 'open windows into men's souls'. This laissez-faire attitude must for a time have kept most ordinary people happy. For who could tell, at this moment, what they might be called on to believe in the future? So in Stratford they didn't rock the boat but just got on with their lives. Under the new queen the town was still run by the old regime, and John Shakespeare rose fast to become borough treasurer, a member of the town corporation. He was a man who could be trusted to assess a situation: the property of a deceased neighbour, the standard of workmanship on corporation property, or the quality of brewers' ale.

Meanwhile, in his private life John was hoping to become a father. Mary had got pregnant quickly but their first child, Joan, born in September 1558 and

baptized as a Catholic, died in infancy. As was the custom, the name would be used again. A second daughter, Margaret, was born in December 1562 but died within five months. Infant mortality was high in those days: in the big cities nearly a third died before their first birthday and even in the kinder air of Stratford, child deaths reached the same grim level in the 1560s. Another daughter, Anne, would die at the age of seven.

The death of their first two children must have hit the parents hard, but Mary conceived again in the summer of 1563. It would be interesting to know if they resorted to any particular prayers or rituals to safeguard this special baby. There is some evidence that John's patron saint was Winifrid of Holywell, whose shrine was a place of pilgrimage for old Warwickshire families like the Throgmortons and the Fortescues of Alveston. The intercession of such accessible female saints, who were painted on the nave in the guild chapel in Stratford, was often sought in matters of childbirth.

John and Mary's first son, William, was born in late April 1564, and within a day or two was christened in Stratford parish church by John Bretchgirdle, a humanist scholar with Catholic sympathies, whose curate had drawn up Catholic wills and who had performed old-style baptisms for parishioners. The date of the baptism was 26 April and the birth date is traditionally held to be the 23rd. But this is only supposition. Usually children were baptised within five days of birth, which means he could have been born as early as the 20th. In traditional belief, which would largely die away over the next couple of generations, it was important to have a baby baptized as soon as possible: being born with original sin, a child who died unbaptized was believed to go not to heaven but into limbo. The boy's name has no more significance than any other: he was presumably named after his godfather who may have been William Smith, a haberdasher and Henley Street neighbour who headed a very aspirant family – all five of his sons were literate, and one went to university. The vicar's entry in the register, copied by a slightly later hand, says simply: '26 April William son of John Shakespeare.'

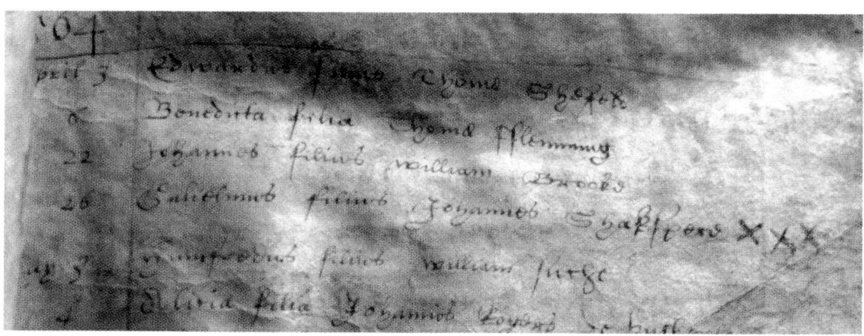

Right: *The original entry in Latin for William's baptism, 26 April 1564.*

CHAPTER TWO

A Child of State

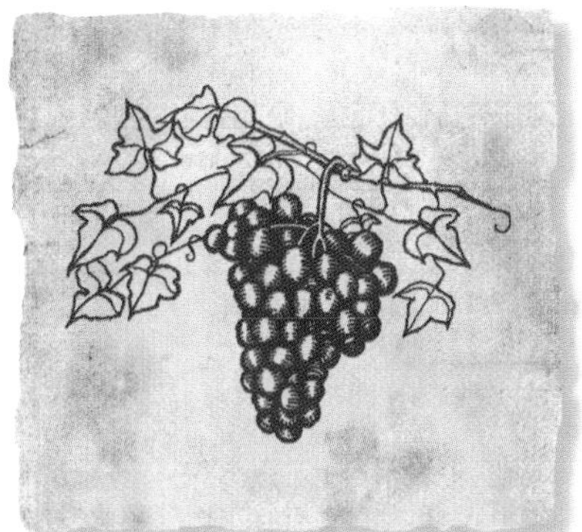

Things Ripen in Time

It was a hot summer in 1564. Under Clopton Bridge the strong current of the river Avon eddied around the stone piles where the children liked to swim to cool off; at lowest water they could stand on the old Roman ford which gave the town its name. The tall spire of Holy Trinity Church peeped over rows of elms – there were said to be 1000 of them – which gave shade to the lanes that led into the town. Indeed, the countryside came right to the town edge: fields butted on to the back gardens along the Gild Pits behind the Shakespeares' house in Henley Street, and a stream, the Meeres brook, ran across the road and along a gulley through the market place.

But even in small-town Tudor England such as this, a 'Great Rebuilding' of domestic housing was under way, accompanied for the middle class by a significant rise in the standard of living. In the old world into which Shakespeare's parents had been born, each family had lived in a communal hall where they all slept on straw pallets with 'a good round log under the head', as one contemporary observed; pillows were just 'for women in childbed'. But old habits were changing: privacy was now much sought after and possessions were becoming a mark of status. For those who were old enough to remember the days of Henry VIII, 'three things are marvellously altered in England within their sound remembrance', wrote William Harrison in 1587: 'the multitude of chimneys' needed for private rooms, the accumulation of furniture and possessions in houses, and the variety that middle-class people now expected on the table.

Right: *Stratford's Holy Trinity Church in 1870: an Old English minster which by William's time had been the focus of a deep-rooted and stable local society for nearly 900 years.*

Of course, all this came at a cost: inflation, the growth of usury and the oppression of tenants by landlords were the common grouses of Shakespeare's childhood, and there was a huge increase in poverty as peasants were driven off the land in the break-up of the last vestiges of the medieval feudal order. These things were on people's minds right across the Midlands, and no doubt they were remarked on in Burbage's tavern in Bridge Street, too. Young Shakespeare's parents, then, were part of a new rising middle class, in every respect poised between old ways and new.

'In Feasting of This Sort They Do Exceed'

Tudor birthing manuals prescribed a month's lying-in for the new mother before a purification or 'churching', an old Catholic ceremony that continued for some time in Protestant churches of Elizabeth's day (and still hung on in some places until the twentieth century). The idea was that a woman who had given birth should be kept in isolation during this time so that she and the infant could gain strength and avoid infection. In Stratford in 1564 nearly two-thirds of all babies died in their first year: easy to see why, then, those first few weeks were viewed as the most dangerous in a child's life.

Mary's churching on Sunday 28 May would have been conducted by the vicar, John Bretchgirdle, in Holy Trinity Church. Then, as was customary in the countryside, the family would have held a feast in Henley Street for friends and neighbours, with a table full of 'fruit pies, game birds, cheese and butter'. Country people were said to be much better at this sort of thing than the townsfolk: 'in feasting of this sort they do exceed after their manner especially at bridals and purifications of women, where it is incredible to tell what meat is consumed and spent, each one bringing such a dish, or so may, as his wife and he do consult upon'.

Such country feasts were thought not only to be more generous, but also more fun than those given in towns; full of 'scurrility and ribaldry', as opposed to the 'great silence' at the tables of the 'wiser sort' who would not get drunk. 'Sir Sullen and Sir Solemne are seldom welcome to any place,' said a Worcestershire contemporary of Shakespeare's father. The Henley Street house is unlikely to have been a silent one, and the baby was no doubt welcomed with an overflowing table. Six weeks later, however, when William was not yet three months old, the town was rocked by a tremendous blow.

Plague Strikes Stratford

The almanac for 1564 had correctly predicted a hot summer and a late harvest, accompanied by 'fevers and tertians [which] shall grieve many people'. Over the

previous twelve months London had lost a tenth of its population to the plague, and that summer the disease was carried from the teeming streets of the capital by soldiers of the Earl of Warwick, returning to Coventry and Stratford from the siege of Le Havre. On 11 July the Stratford burial register tersely marks the moment when the apprentice Oliver Gunne died: '*Hic incepit pestis*' (here the plague began). Before it was over more than 200 people would have died in Stratford, up to one-sixth of the population. In late August the council, reeling at the town's losses, held an emergency meeting in the fresh air of the garden behind the guildhall (plague was believed to circulate in indoor 'infected air', as Shakespeare later wrote in *Timon of Athens*). The corporation minute book records their deliberations over the money to be given out to the plague-stricken townspeople: 'At the Hall holden in oure garden the 30 daye of auguste anno 1564. Moneye pd towardes the releffe of the poore.' As the richest men in the borough, the aldermen were expected to fork out for the poor and alleviate the mounting distress among their neighbours. John Shakespeare was among those who dug into their own pockets; as acting chamberlain he was also responsible for the distribution of the money.

Like most epidemics, the plague hit in particular the old, the infirm and the very young. For a small, tight-knit community where everyone knew each other,

BELOW: *Fingers clinging to the frogging on a mother's bodice evoke the fragility of the family in William's time; three of his female siblings died in infancy or early childhood.*

it must have been horrendous. Richard Symons, the town clerk, lost two sons and a daughter. The victims also included four children of the Shakespeares' neighbours the Greens, three doors down in Henley Street – but not their own son William. Having already lost two babies, maybe Mary took him back across the fields to Wilmcote, where she and John had recently built a small house. By the end of the summer Stratford had been devastated, but Wilmcote escaped without a single death.

Old Ways, New Demands

What were the prospects for a child in a small town early in Elizabeth's reign? Then, much more than now, everything depended on money and class. Had William's parents stayed in the countryside, he would have been a farmer – perhaps on the 80 acres at Wilmcote that he would have expected to inherit from his mother. But because his father had moved into the town and risen to be an alderman he would have the right to a decent education, and with it the chance to better himself. With good Latin he might become a clerk, working in a law office; or he might decide to enter his father's business as a glover. Alternatively, he could become an apprentice in a bigger town or city – Coventry, say, or even London, as quite a few Warwickshire boys did. Among his Stratford contemporaries, one, Richard Field, became a London printer, and another, Alderman Smith's son William, went to university. We know Shakespeare became an actor and a playwright, but exactly how he made the leap is, as we shall see, still mysterious.

Like anyone, though, the young Shakespeare was shaped by family, work, church and environment. And although we have few details of the poet's early life we can access these influences through other sources. Like so many places in provincial England, Stratford was wary of the new and sympathetic to the old. In Shakespeare's childhood and youth, this part of Warwickshire was viewed by the government, and by the ecclesiastical authorities in Worcester, as an ungodly region, a stronghold of Catholicism and notoriously reluctant to implement the wishes of Elizabeth's ministers. A report made to the Privy Council in the year of the poet's birth says that half of the shire's forty-two JPs were 'adversaries of true religion' and only eight were 'favourers' of Protestantism. One Warwickshire Protestant writer had Stratford and the big neighbouring parishes of Arden in mind when he spoke of 'great parishes and market towns … utterly destitute of God's word'.

This was still true twenty years later, as is revealed in a fascinating document compiled by Elizabeth's religious spies. In 1585 a government inquisition concluded of Warwickshire, 'How miserable the state of the Church is for want of a godly learned ministerie.' Astonishingly, even at that late date, fewer than half the parishes possessed the authorized Bishops' Bible of 1568; of 186 priests, 120 were said to be 'dumbe' and 48 certain or suspected Catholics. Humfrey Style, vicar at Spernall until 1607, gave the commissioners a typically curt response: 'our bible is not Authorished by the sinod of Byshopps ... I have no degree in the universities and doe not preache ... to the Rest of the Articles I can say nothinge.' But nearly one-third of the shire's sixty-five parishes ignored the inquisition and sent no replies at all. Among these were twelve parish priests directly accused of still being papists, who officiated in the big old parishes west and north of Stratford in the Forest of Arden. Geoffrey Heath, vicar of Oldbarrow, was reported to be 'popish and useth incantation'; Hugh Bate at Packwood was 'an old priest and a massemonger, a drunkard and dumbe and it is thought a sorcerer'. These were the kind of priests and friars whom Shakespeare would write about in his plays with persistent affection and nostalgia. And it is interesting that the list included John Frith of Temple Grafton, who may have conducted the poet's marriage ceremony. He was described as 'an old priest, unsound of religion', much resorted to by locals for his skill in cures, recalling the old friar in *Romeo and Juliet* with his medicines and potions.

This picture of the survival of Catholic beliefs alongside the rituals of the Protestant Church, and of the continued use of masses for the dead, exorcism and incantation, we now know was paralleled up and down the country. Even in Shakespeare's late twenties, it was said by government informers of England in general that 'most of the common people are still papist at heart, given to saying it was a good world when the old religion was, because everything was cheap then, and a man eats his maker in the Sacrament, and we might swear by our Lady ...'. Men like Frith were not superstitious throwbacks; loyal to their parishioners and their locality, they were the link between old and new.

Such stories help us to understand the first twenty years of Shakespeare's life. This complex, gradual shift and interaction between the old world and the new is what shaped him. The Reformation is no longer seen as a broadly consensual matter, contested only by extremists. That long-entrenched idea is merely another example of history told by the winners. Here, in the persons of John Frith and his fellow clergy, was the reality on the ground. In the end, from the 1550s to the 1580s the old generation helped make possible the marriage of the old ways and the new. This was the reality of historical change in many parts of England, and especially in Warwickshire. And it is a picture to bear in mind when looking not only at the broad changes that occurred during Shakespeare's lifetime, but at his personal life too. For he too would have a foot in both

worlds; and as a writer he too would be a bridge between old and new, carrying down something of the pre-Reformation past into his children's and grandchildren's generations – and into our own.

'A Fart of Ons Ars for You'

So how did the citizens of Stratford feel about these changes? The corporation records from the time of Shakespeare's childhood reveal most by what they *don't* say. They offer none of the tell-tale signs of precocious Protestant enthusiasm found in East Anglian towns, or even in neighbouring Coventry. There are no accounts of official hospitality towards visiting Protestant preachers, of anxious debates about church attendance or Sabbath-breaking, or of wheedling investigations of newcomers and strangers. This makes sense in a community in which many aldermen and their wives were avowed Catholics. The Wheelers were firm adherents, who, in 1592, would be accused of being recusants ('refusers of Protestant communion') along with John Shakespeare; as late as 1606 Hamnet and Judith Sadler, godparents of Shakespeare's twins, were arraigned in the church courts for their Catholicism; the Debdales of Shottery, who also appeared in the 1592 list of recusants, had a son who died on the scaffold as a Jesuit martyr.

In such a community the women were perhaps especially important in terms of holding on to the old beliefs and customs. In 1580 Elizabeth's Privy Council were alarmed by reports that 'women in their ordinary meetings among themselves very irreverently speak of the religion now established in this realm'. As the Shakespeares' old friend and neighbour Elizabeth Wheeler memorably told the Puritans on the benches of the church court in 1592: 'Godes woondes, a plague of God on you all, a fart of ons ars for you!' (God's wounds … a fart of one's arse for you!)

A Well-to-do Family of Church Papists

Like many English people in those uncertain early years of Elizabeth's reign, Shakespeare's parents were most likely what were called church papists. John, as a leading townsman, would have gone to church when he had to, on Sundays and holy days, but would have drawn the line at taking communion. At home Mary would have privately brought up their children with the old prayers, rituals, beliefs and stories, as is borne out by the numerous references to such things in William's plays and by his palpable affection for the medieval English Christian past. This suggests that from the start young Shakespeare was brought up in a world of conflicting viewpoints and that by the time he left school he knew what it was like to be an outsider.

In the Stratford house of Susanna Hall, William's daughter, there hangs a

haunting Flemish picture of a middle-class family of the period. Painted perhaps in the last years of the sixteenth century, it gives a vivid impression of what the Henley Street house might have looked like. The family – the father and mother, their hands together in prayer, along with their young sons and daughters, perhaps a grown-up son and daughter-in-law – are saying grace before a meal. All are soberly dressed, the adults in black, the women with ruffs, pearls and lace headdresses. Their clothing, stiff bearing and religious poses suggest a mercantile family influenced by Calvinism, a more silent household than those of the English country middle classes; John and Mary's home, one imagines, would have been more relaxed, their table more jolly.

Nevertheless, the painting gives an idea of what the Shakespeares' domestic environment would have been like. The family are sitting on wooden stools around a table, in front of which stands a big glazed earthenware water jug. On the table is fine linen, a pewter dish, plates and cups, salt cellars, a big joint of meat and a loaf of bread. A woman servant enters from the right. Beyond the wooden screen is a view out to a mulberry tree in the garden. In the foreground are two boys aged about eight, in brown jerkins, striped red breeches and short leather boots. One of them turns to look directly at the viewer: with his cropped hair, big almond eyes and intent look he is perhaps something like the young William.

John and Mary had more children in the late 1560s: first Gilbert, then Joan, followed by Richard and Edmund. Another sister, Anne, was born when William was seven. The house was filling up. Throughout this time John Shakespeare was doing very well for himself. In 1569, when William was five, his father was elected bailiff of Stratford, the equivalent of mayor, 'the Queens Officer and cheffe of the town'. No longer a peasant farmer like his father, John could now call himself 'Master Shakespeare'. How proud the family must have been to watch him walk in procession down Chapel Street to the guildhall, in his ermine and red wool robes topped off by his alderman's cap, escorted by the buff-coated serjeants bearing their maces before them.

John the Brogger and Moneylender

In recent years several documentary discoveries about Shakespeare's father have cast fascinating new light on his son's early days. John had a barn and outbuildings behind the house in Henley Street, and his glover's workshop would have been inside the house, just over the passage from the parlour. Gloving is a highly skilled trade which demands great attention to detail; then, as now, the fine stitching was usually done by women, and it may well be that Mary worked with her husband alongside hired workers and apprentices.

As a child in Henley Street, William no doubt saw these things. In his plays he uses unusual gloving metaphors: when he talks about a wit, or a conscience, which can 'stretch like a piece of chevril' (goatskin), it is clear that he must have watched chevril being stretched by hand. No mere wearer of gloves would have known about this process. He uses the big round glover's paring knife as a rather unlikely simile for a beard (how many of his audience would have got that?). It is unlikely that John had animals killed on the premises; presumably he got his skins from the Taylors' slaughterhouse near by. But young William no doubt saw that part of the trade too: not only the act of killing, a running metaphor in his plays, but also the way that blood flows is very closely and disturbingly observed.

In William's first few years his father bought more property and seems to have been making more money than might be expected of a small-town glover. How did he do it? There is a seventeenth-century story that John was a 'considerable' dealer in wool on the side. This tale was often dismissed by early modern authorities as an unreliable oral tradition, even though in the nineteenth century wool waste was found under the floor of the birthplace house in the room long known as 'the Woolshop'. Subsequently the record was discovered of a court case involving an alderman in Marlborough, Wiltshire, who had bought wool from John in Stratford in 1569 but had never paid him; but the full significance of this find was not realized until a fascinating recent discovery in the Public Record Office that may cause the experts to look again at other aspects of the Shakespeare 'myth'.

The Elizabethan government employed a network of informers, spies and bounty hunters, who pried into every aspect of people's business affairs, their religion and even their sex life. When Shakespeare was six, his father was twice shopped for breaking the stringent laws on usury; and then, when the boy was eight, John came before the courts on two charges of illegal wool dealing. The latter cases confirm the old tradition: the two purchases were of a couple of tons of wool, purchased for £210 in cash at a time when a good house cost £60. One lot had been bought from a Warwickshire sheep farmer at the Wool Staple in Westminster, where John had evidently pretended to have a licence. The money-lending case involved a shepherd called John Mussem, from Walton, a village near Stratford, to whom John had lent two sums of £80 and £100, on each of which he had charged £20 interest – much higher than the 10 per cent permitted by law.

So we now know that the poet's father was a brogger, a freelance wool dealer working illegally without the necessary licence from the London Wool Staple. This was a very competitive business of high risk and fast profit in an uncertain economic climate. The discovery of these court appearances gives a

Right: *A Flemish Protestant family of the middle class in the late sixteenth century. This was the kind of material life to which Shakespeare's parents aspired.*

key to the many legal cases involving John Shakespeare during William's childhood. Put them together and John's contacts, loans, debts, sales and purchases make a picture. He clinches deals with sheep farmers in Worcestershire and Warwickshire – at first, probably, for skins for leather; later, as he diversifies, for wool. He works with friends and kinsmen in several places close to Stratford – his distant relatives in Packwood, the Mussems in Walton, Walter Newsham in Chadsunt, the Catholic Grants at Northbrook, Thomas Such over the border in Worcestershire. Some of these men are evidently financial partners: John Mussem at Walton looks like one, as does the Stratford glover John Loxley. But other contacts spread further afield. The clothier from Marlborough, a glover in Banbury and a hatter in Nottingham may also have been partners. John's web of dealings might even explain a cluster of Cotswold references that crops up in Shakespeare's play *Henry IV* Part 2, in which he mentions one George Vizor, an 'arrant knave' from Woncot (Woodmancote) in Gloucestershire, in a court case with Clement Perkes of Stinchcombe Hill. Tax documents and parish records show that the Vizors and the Perkeses were real people; the Vizor family, of Flemish descent, worked in the wool industry in Dursley and Woodmancote, where there were thirty Tudor woollen mills along the Cotswold escarpment looking out over Berkeley (a view that Shakespeare mentions in *Richard II*).

Things Seen, Things Overheard

The life of a brogger supplies another hint of the world Shakespeare knew as a boy. He would have seen wool bagged up in tods (of 28 pounds) in the woolshop or stored in the barn behind the house in Henley Street. Perhaps he also accompanied his father on business trips – in traditional societies the eldest son helps the father as soon as he is big enough, and certainly by the time he is eight. Operating on the shady side of the law, broggers usually combined their wool dealings with farming or a respectable trade like John's. They would arrange their buying in April or May, when sheep farmers could estimate the year's clip reasonably well. The broggers would collect the wool in June after shearing, and then resell, perhaps taking it to regional markets where they had contacts. Thame in Oxfordshire was one – even today fleeces are graded and priced there in the old barns by the church.

This world is vividly brought to life in a Warwickshire wool brogger's account book which has survived from the 1540s and 1550s. The entries in Peter Temple's ledger give an idea of how John's business worked, and name people he might have known; for example, 18 tods 'Bought of Richard Quiney of Fleckenhoe at 21sh the tod'. This is the world that Shakespeare later vividly

described in *The Winter's Tale*: 'Let me see – every 'leven wether tods; every tod yields pound and odd shilling; fifteen hundred shorn, what comes the wool to?'

Temple's account book also details payments for packing the wool and carrying it to London, either to Leadenhall Market or to the Wool Staple in Westminster. In return dealers sent back goods to meet special needs in sheep farming, as well as fish and exotic groceries. The brogger's book mentions 'Half a hundred of allam; 6 lb almonds; 2 lb rice; 4 lb sugar; 2 tapnets [baskets] of figs'. And again in *The Winter's Tale* Shakespeare has the shepherd's son shopping for the same edible luxuries for his shearers' fair:

> Let me see; what am I to buy for our sheep-shearing feast? [*He takes out a paper.*] Three pounds of sugar, five pound of currants, rice – what will this sister of mine do with rice? But my father hath made her mistress of the feast, and she lays it on… I must have saffron, to colour the warden pies; mace – dates – none; that's out of my note; nutmegs, seven; a race or two of ginger – but that I may beg; four pound of prunes, and as many of raisins o' the sun.

All this close observation might suggest that in his childhood Shakespeare got to know quite a lot about the gloving trade and the hard-nosed business conducted between country shepherds and wool dealers from the towns.

So there was no sheltered upbringing for young Shakespeare. Through his father's wheeler-dealing the child was brought into contact with every level of society, with the world of business and of profit and loss, and it would come out later in his language. As a mature writer he would be particularly good at social interaction, especially between men. Even the gaps in colloquial speech, the things left out, are very precisely observed.

This rich rural vocabulary, full of dialect words that Shakespeare was to use to such great effect in his plays and poetry, has already been mentioned. Sometimes contemporary records give us precise parallels to his language. For example, the itinerant labourers and others who came through Warwick and Stratford were recorded in the 1580s in the books of the magistrate John Fisher, still kept in Warwick Town Hall. Here we meet cattle drovers, sheep stealers, unemployed labourers, discharged veterans from the Irish wars, pickpockets, coney catchers and 'bawdy baskets'. Wonderful tales they are too, such as the saga of Ursula Reddish at the Sign of the Unicorn in Warwick, and her lover, a womanizing bigamist wool-carder from Manchester, an 'evil fellow and a shifter'.

This is the raw, unmediated life of small-town Warwickshire in Shakespeare's youth. People from all over the country, from as far as Berwick and

especially Lancashire and Yorkshire, with their different accents and stories, are interviewed here. All the lower-class characters in Shakespeare's plays work so well because they speak authentically. The Warwick town books show us their real-life counterparts, people like 'Henry Carre with his wife or woman and a pedlar's pack' (Autolycus from *The Winter's Tale*?) and Dorothy Grene, whipped for the theft of a fine woman's overskirt on the road from Stratford and summonsed under her alias 'coosyning doll' (Doll Tearsheet from *Henry IV* Part 2?).

Even in the nineteenth century, the colourful Warwickshire dialect had changed very little since Shakespeare's time. Take the arrival of the itinerant workforce at pea-picking time (a time to date things by, as Mistress Quickly does in *Henry IV* Part 2), 'with long black coats and black beards and black tea cans a dangling in my face and shoes that looked as if they'd been tramped to the end of the earth and back ... and strange names they was an all, like feet hitting gravel: Dag and Lop and Clommer and Grauncher and Dink'. It is hard to believe that this world survived into Victoria's day, but here, recorded from a near-centenarian in late twentieth-century Stratford, is the world of Autolycus's sheep-shearings in the mouths of Autolycus's descendants:

> Their tales came straight from fairy-land: strawberries big as taters, cider apple country, fields upon fields of lilies, all colours of the rainbow, as far as the eye could see, an army of wapses, each one as fierce as a ferret, man traps, wading through peppermint 'till you stank o' nothin' else! Mothers on Waterside shouted their kiddies indoors and such a clucking started up you's thought the old fox was in the hencoop.

Crisis in the North

But at peascod time in 1569, when William was five, grimmer news came with the newcomers along the road from Warwick and Coventry: rumours of a rebellion that shook Elizabeth's still precarious hold on power. In Stratford the corporation would find itself caught up in the growing momentum of events, which would eventually upset the uneasy equilibrium in the town and force change willy-nilly.

The crisis had begun over the border in Scotland. Early in the year the Catholic Mary Queen of Scots, daughter of James V of Scotland and widow of François II of France, had fled into England after her forces' defeat at the Battle of Langside and had thrown herself on Elizabeth's 'hospitality'. Some English and foreign Catholics saw Mary as a potential successor to Elizabeth, so the English government acted with extreme caution, fearing they were 'holding a wolf by the ears'. In February 1569 Mary was brought down to the Midlands;

Left: *Mary Queen of Scots, c. 1578. Her presence cast a shadow over the first thirty years of Elizabeth's reign; the aftermath of the Northern Rebellion of 1569 saw the beginning of the end for the old order in Stratford.*

the High Sheriff of Warwickshire ordered a watch on all roads and the interrogation and punishment of vagabonds. Monthly searches for strangers were carried out in all the boroughs; unlawful or riotous games were banned. On 27 June Sir Thomas Lucy, the leading JP in the Stratford area, raised a levy of 640 men from the shire, including 'honest and habell men' from Stratford. The corporation minutes tell of archery practice at the butts by the river; Robert Locke was paid to clean the armour and harness; Robert 'the joiner' was put to work on new gunstocks; and Simon Biddle dressed two pikes and a bow.

Rumours spread of a rising in the north, and of a secret marriage between Mary and the Catholic Duke of Norfolk. On 8 October the Spanish ambassador wrote to his king, Philip II: 'the Earls of Northumberland Westmorland, Cumberland and Derby and the whole body of the Catholics will take forcible possession of Mary and make themselves masters of the Northern Counties and re-establish the Catholic Faith'. The rebellion broke out in November with echoes of earlier northern revolts against Tudor rule, in particular the Pilgrimage of Grace at the time of Henry VIII's dissolution of the monasteries in 1536. On 14 November Charles Percy, the Earl of Northumberland, called on 'all true and faithful subjects' to restore 'the ancient customs and liberties to Gods Church'. Then the rebels entered Durham and celebrated Catholic mass in the cathedral. The news came south like wildfire. Mary was taken for safety to Coventry,

while the Warwickshire levies prepared to march north. For a moment Elizabeth's hold on power seemed uncertain.

But the alarm quickly subsided. On the approach of Elizabeth's army, the rebellion collapsed. Stratford, with its leanings to the Old Religion, felt the fall-out. The vicar, curate and schoolmaster all left, the vicar in the middle of the crisis in November, the schoolmaster at Christmas. The curate was pointedly described in the town minutes as *fugitivus*, a fugitive who had apparently sympathized with the rising.

Aftermath: The Town 'on the Blind Side of the Diocese'

The town books for the following year disclose signs of a reaction in Stratford. A retainer of Sir Thomas Lucy was now installed as steward. During 1570 the corporation were required to remove the stained glass from the guild chapel, and a year later, at the first meeting chaired by the new mayor, Adrian Quiney, it was resolved that the Catholic copes and vestments should be sold off: 'First, one suit of blue velvet vestments being three in number ... one suit of white damask, three in number, two copes of tawny velvet, one cope of white damask, one cope of blue velvet, three stoles, and three gloves or manuaries for the hands [for handling relics]'.

And so, thirteen years after the Protestant queen's accession, the corporation finally lost their treasured vestments, what Puritans liked to call 'the relics of the Amorites'.

In February 1571 Elizabeth was excommunicated and declared illegitimate by Pope Pius V, a pivotal moment for the ensuing tragedy. From now on the conflict of loyalties would become intense, and many faithful English Catholics would soon find their position intolerable. Elizabeth's local men, such as Robert Dudley, would put increasing pressure on local gentry who stuck by the Old Faith – people like Edward Arden. And, as the 1570 town minutes suggest, more pressure to come into line would be placed on local communities, especially one as notorious as Stratford, that 'ungodly town ... on the blind side of the diocese'. The times were beginning to change.

Such events, no doubt, were the topic of conversation behind the closed doors of the council chamber at the guildhall, and in Henley Street. Every alderman knew the meaning of what had happened, and if the six-year-old William was listening at home, he would have understood something too: a first lesson, perhaps, in the way that great national events impinge on local affairs; in the way that ordinary people can be swept up in the whirlwind of history. When seen in the eyes and heard in the whispers of one's parents, such struggles of power and conscience are things a child never forgets.

CHAPTER THREE

Education: School and Beyond

KNOWLEDGE MUST BE SOUGHT AFTER

John Shakespeare, as bailiff of Stratford, was entitled to send his son to the town's free school, once attached to the guild, but now, in the mid-sixteenth century, a grammar school financed by the corporation. Boys normally started grammar school at the age of seven, by which time they were already expected to be able to read and write basic English, and to have basic reading skills in Latin. So William would have begun his tuition at home, or at petty school, when he was about five years old.

'MY MOTHER GAVE IT TO ME'

In Stratford the petty school for both boys and girls was held in the guild chapel, and perhaps a special teacher came round to hold handwriting classes on particular days. Shakespeare's style of writing is what was called the 'secretary's hand', which appears among the thirty-seven styles illustrated in the first English book on handwriting, published in 1570 by Beau Chesne, a French schoolmaster living in London; the poet's writing closely resembles Beau Chesne's example. Most likely he learned basic letter forms at petty school from a handwriting teacher who used that book.

But it is just possible that he received some tuition at home. Although, as mentioned earlier, his father probably never learned to read and write, his mother may have had some ability. She was competent in legal matters, serving

as an executrix and a juror, and her mark on documents has all the appearance of someone who knew how to use a pen: her elegantly formed 'M' uses the edge and then the flat of the quill, with a stylish decorative circle reminiscent of her son's flamboyant habit with his own initials. She also employed a personal seal of a running horse (her father bred horses), which again suggests someone who was literate and accustomed to handling her own affairs.

So could Mary have been Shakespeare's first teacher? In her childhood in Wilmcote in the late 1540s did she have access to chapbooks and prayer books? At any rate, it was not uncommon for women to teach their children, particularly in rural Catholic homes. *Titus Andronicus*, possibly Shakespeare's earliest play, contains one of those throwaway remarks that he seems to put in for no apparent reason:

> TITUS: Lucius, what book is that she tosseth so?
> YOUNG LUCIUS: Grand Sire, 'tis Ovid's Metamorphosis; *my mother gave it me.*

The poet's mother, Mary, is one of the figures in his life we could wish to know better.

Myth and Magic: Stories at His Mother's Knee

But in trying to get a sense of Shakespeare's early education we shouldn't exaggerate the importance of books. The household in Henley Street might have possessed the odd book: a Bible, for example, an old prayer book or a primer. In a culture where women were expected to be doctor and apothecary as well as housekeeper, Mary might also have had an almanac to ascertain the best time for blood-letting, and a herbal to augment her countrywoman's knowledge of the medicinal uses of plants. But in Stratford, book-owning families were still a rarity: house inventories of the day tend not to mention books. And although the English were beginning to be fascinated by the possibilities of books and print, this was still above all an oral culture. Telling stories was the key; hearing them was the first stage in a child's education.

In his plays Shakespeare alludes to tales, retold by almost every Tudor writer on Warwickshire, that appear in the folk plays, songs and ballads of his day. Every child would have been familiar with them, and one in particular, the tale of Guy of Warwick, may serve as an example of the rich popular culture of the region in the mid-sixteenth century.

Guy was a legendary Saxon hero who fought the invading Danes, overthrew the giant Colbrand, went on crusade to the Holy Land to do battle with

the Saracens, and finally returned to Warwickshire to live as a hermit in the Forest of Arden. There on his deathbed he was reunited with his childhood sweetheart, who had thought him long dead. A tale of adventure, monsters and fairy-tale mishaps, this medieval romance is also a story of redemption and has some curious resonances in Shakespeare's works. As a boy he may even have been told that Guy of Warwick was his kinsman: his mother's family claimed him as their ancestor.

To Warwickshire writers, the Arden of these tales was the mythic heart of England, a wilderness, a place of refuge from powerful enemies, which also gave access to the world of magic and fairies. 'The land is uncanny and enchanted – it is called Arden the great,' declares one fourteenth-century poem. Shakespeare would put that magical Arden into his pastoral comedy, *As You Like It*.

The legend's portrayal of Arden as a fairyland also recalls the fantastically rich portrayal of the fairy world in Shakespeare's plays, which surely harks back to tales heard in his childhood. Although *A Midsummer Night's Dream* is set in Athens, the wood and its spirits – Puck or Robin Goodfellow, Cobweb, Moth, Mustardseed and Peaseblossom – are English through and through. They are all part of the pre-Reformation imagination. For the Protestants, fairies, like ghosts, had been devised by popish priests from an earlier era to 'keep the ignorant in awe'; Protestants saw the fairy kingdom as 'a mixt religion, part pagan part papistical'. It is easy to forget Shakespeare was old-fashioned even in his own day for his love of fairyland, and it is no accident that in his greatest plays he chooses the form, and sometimes the substance, of fairy tales.

'Small Latin and Less Greek'

In due course young William moved on to the grammar school: for seven years from 1571 he attended Big School (as opposed to petty school) in Church Lane, between the almshouses and the guild chapel. Given the controversy that still surrounds the authorship of the plays, and the persistence of the myth that Shakespeare must have been an uneducated provincial, that last sentence may seem over-confident. But it can be stated for near certain, even though the early records of King Edward VI Grammar School in Stratford have not survived, because this is one instance where direct biographical evidence from the plays is indisputable. Their author, as we know from the contemporary testimony of his friends and colleagues, was William Shakespeare of Stratford-upon-Avon. In these plays, the patterns of his quotation and his remembered reading betray the fact that the author was steeped in the Tudor grammar school curriculum. Although this does not prove that the school was in Stratford, it does offer very strong circumstantial evidence that he went to grammar school; and since

John Shakespeare was entitled to send his son to the one in Stratford, and lived in that town for the whole period in question, it is as good as certain that this was the school that William attended.

Education was chiefly in the language of authority, church and the law: Latin. Years later, in a back-handed compliment, Ben Jonson said Shakespeare had 'small Latin and less Greek'. This is often quoted as if to dismiss Shakespeare's education, but Jonson's remark needs to be taken in perspective. Jonson himself was a very good Latin scholar. What would be 'small Latin' in his day was much more than is mastered by many a classics graduate now. Even in country grammar schools from Devon to Cumbria, boys were expected to 'speak Latin purely and readily'. The quotes in Shakespeare's plays show that he started with the nationally prescribed text Lily's Latin Grammar (which he sends up in *The Merry Wives of Windsor*), then books of 'Sentences', before moving on to Dialogues and, at eight or nine, to full texts of writers such as Ovid.

As Jonson tells us, Shakespeare also knew some Greek; this was indeed part of the curriculum. As far away as Bangor in Wales in 1568, it was declared that 'nothing shall be taught in the said school but only grammar and authors on the Latin and Greek tongues'. At Harrow in Shakespeare's day the boys started Greek grammar in the fourth year. If the regime at Stratford was similar, he might have been able to follow, with a crib, a Greek text such as *Aesop's Fables*.

The end product was a poet who could and did sit down and read a book or play in Latin – although, like most people then and now, he preferred a translation for speed. Late in his career, in *The Tempest*, he gives the correct translation of a word in Ovid omitted in the English version by Arthur Golding.

If all this is a surprise, remember that Tudor England was probably the most literate society that had yet existed in history; Thomas More, in his *Apologye*, estimated basic literacy to be 60 per cent. This may seem unbelievable in a country where half the population was living below the poverty line. But England's first literacy revolution, in the thirteenth century, had brought basic reading down into the peasantry for simple mortgages, legal cases and prayers. In land documents relating to the medieval ancestors of the Tudor yeoman class, the use of limited literacy with a personal seal is commonplace as early as the 1200s. So the dramatic Tudor expansion of literacy was the culmination of a long period of growth. By the 1550s, many grammar schools had sprung up all over England, and 160 more would be opened in Elizabeth's reign. Some were the foundations of rich philanthropic benefactors; but many, like the one in Stratford, were the direct descendants of the guild school. In the generation educated as a result of this great burst of grammar school

foundations in the 1560s and 1570s, the literacy figures shot up. Shakespeare, then, was a child of the English Renaissance, who was lucky to be born in a privileged generation.

ROTE LEARNING, DEBATE AND DEFERENCE

It started at the crack of dawn. A grammar school boy got up at five, said his morning prayers, then departed for school at six in summer, seven in winter. Schoolchildren took only a small breakfast: the main meals in the Tudor age were dinner (at midday) and supper (at six o'clock for a tradesman like John, eight for farmers like his brother in Snitterfield who worked a longer day). In the schoolroom there were two classes at opposite ends of the room, sometimes separated by a screen. The younger boys were supervised by the usher, the older ones by the master; those young ones who needed to catch up may have had special writing lessons with an outside tutor. In winter, when the weather was cold, the schoolroom was warmed by a brazier. Parents were expected to provide their child with ink, paper, quill pens and wax candles.

The regime was strict: boys learned by rote, and beating was the norm. Later, in his plays, Shakespeare paints a picture of lessons as a grind; but in

LEFT: *Sixteenth-century woodcut of an Elizabethan school. Birching was the rule in Tudor schools, but learning by rote stuck with you.*

As You Like It he talks of the schoolboy going to school with his 'shiny morning face', recalling chill, dark Stratford mornings and the unquenchable optimism of childhood.

Shakespeare was the product of a memorizing culture in which huge chunks of literature were learned off by heart. Today we no longer live in such a culture, but learning by rote offers many rewards, not least a sense of poetry, rhythm and refinement – a feel for heightened language. It forms habits of mind too: what they called the 'art of memory' was an invaluable tool when it came to composing speeches. Teachers also used classroom debate to improve Latin and develop rhetorical skills. The Harrow school statutes of 1580 required every schoolmaster there to hear debates for an hour each day with the third, fourth and fifth forms (that is, those aged about nine to eleven). Each boy in turn stood in front of the class and defended a proposition, for example, whether Brutus was right to assassinate Caesar. (The school textbook on composition, Thomas Wilson's *Art of Rhetorique*, which urged the importance of writing about English matters in English, also suggests that boys could make comparisons from English history, for instance between Richard III and Henry VI.) All this would come out later in Shakespeare's plays: in *The Merry Wives of Windsor* he sends up a Latin class with a Welsh headmaster (his own Mr Jenkins?) and quotes the textbook that bored him and his classmates to death, Lily's Grammar, with terrible jokes about focatives, genetivos, horums and harums. Schoolboy humour never changes.

Politeness and deference were drummed into pupils by Elizabethan schoolmasters: 'to thy Parents duty yield, Unto all Men be courteous, and mannerly in town and field'. This reverence for parents is expressed in a letter of the time, written in Latin as a school exercise by an eleven-year-old Stratford schoolboy, Richard Quiney, to his father, a family friend of the Shakespeares: '*Patri suo amantissimo Magistro Richardo Quinye*,' it begins; 'With all respect – but even more with filial affection towards you, my father, I thank you for all the kindnesses which you have bestowed upon me ...' After a dozen lines of formal Latin, culled from the style manual of Cicero's letters, the boy's missive ends (in translation): 'Although I could never repay your kindnesses, I wish you all prosperity from my heart of hearts ... Your little son most obedient to you Richard Quiney.'

Filial devotion and civic-mindedness: such was the style of Tudor education. The letter shows what an eleven-year-old Stratford grocer's son could do after four years at grammar school; William would no doubt have had to write the same sort of model letter to his own proud father. Such sentiments of politeness are expressed in the plays time and again: they recall descriptions of 'gentle' Shakespeare's character in later life, his 'civil and honest' demeanour, his 'facetious grace'. That was what a good provincial school education gave you.

Schoolmasters of the Old Faith

The room where he was taught is still above the guildhall, still used for teaching, and the boys still call it 'Big School'. It is an atmospheric place with rows of eighteenth-century desks covered with carved initials and doodles blackened with age. On the ground floor fragments of Tudor wall paintings are still visible on the lath and plaster wall of the old guildhall; this is where the corporation met and where travelling players performed throughout Shakespeare's childhood; here in 1586 the packed townspeople almost lifted the roof off when the greatest stand-up comic of the age, Richard Tarlton, stuck his head through the curtain and began to pull the most famous face in English drama.

Stratford council paid their schoolmaster £20 a year and provided a house and removal expenses. It was a good salary for the time – better than that of the headmaster of Eton, although at Eton there were more perks. The names of the incumbents at Stratford going back to the refounding of 1553 are painted on a wooden board in Big School. They were good Oxford graduates, selected by the senior men of the corporation, and in the town book is the wording of the oath sworn by every new master to be a 'trusty and wellbeloved bachelor of arts … lawful and honest man learned in grammar and in the law of god' (the old connection made by medieval educators). He was 'henceforth diligently to employ himself with such godly wisdom and learning as God hath and shall endue him with: to learn and teach in the said grammar school all such scholars and children as shall come together to learn godly learning and wisdom being fit for the grammar school or at the least-wise entered or ready to enter into the accidence and principles of grammar'.

That contract demonstrates the importance of the religious dimension in Tudor education. The statutes of Tudor schools all included instruction in the chief points of faith, the aim being to produce good conforming members of the Protestant state; and in the government's eyes Shakespeare's was the target generation. He would already have known the Lord's Prayer, the Creed and the Catechism, and at school he would have spent considerable time on the main articles of the Protestant faith. But in the early years

BELOW: *Stratford's fifteenth-century guildhall today, with the schoolroom above and the hall below. This is where William must have seen his first plays.*

ABOVE: *The schoolroom with its eighteenth-century desks. Here young William studied from the age of seven, and at nine was introduced to Ovid's poems by Master Hunt.*

of Elizabeth's reign such things were not cut and dried, even at school: in Stratford at least four of the six teachers in Shakespeare's time had Catholic leanings. Two of them came from Oxford colleges with especially strong connections: St John's (the Jesuit martyr Edmund Campion's college) and Brasenose (known until recently for its links with Lancashire Catholicism). Of these masters, Simon Hunt would have taught William in his upper school from about 1573. Hunt was a private Catholic, or at least Catholic in sympathies, who in 1575 retired to the seminary at Douai and became a Jesuit.

Nor was this situation unique to Stratford, as the government was well aware. In June 1580, not long after Shakespeare had left school, Elizabeth's Privy Council sent a letter to all dioceses detailing their continuing concerns about Catholic influences in education and urging the bishops 'to have regard to the daily corruption grown by schoolmasters both public and private in the teaching and instructing of youth'. In April 1582 this would stretch to intervention on the kind of books used at school, especially 'the poets as are commonly read and taught in grammar schools'. The Privy Council recommended a new verse book of Protestant history with an appendix on the 'peaceable government of the Queenes Majesty' in place of 'some of the heathen poets now ... publicly read and taught by schoolmasters'.

In the light of such evidence, the presence of so many sympathizers with the Old Faith at Stratford grammar school in the 1570s is interesting. The corporation had vetted and hired these teachers for their 'learning and godliness', and they clearly preferred to hire their own kind of teacher. Simon Hunt was recruited a year or so after the Northern Rebellion, when John Shakespeare was deputy bailiff. Was it a deliberate political act by an old-fashioned corporation? The times, after all, could still change.

Street Theatre and Plays in the Guildhall

But there was more to life for a boy than religion. Every year the streets of Stratford hosted a pageant of St George and the Dragon (the sword that dispatched the beast is still kept in the town hall). In small-town Warwickshire it was one of many shows, pageants and folk plays based on local history and legends such as Guy of Warwick, the Dunsmore Cow and the Boar of Callidon. The Hoke Day pageant in Coventry, for instance, celebrated battles in which the English had defeated the Danes, ending with the invaders 'led captive by our English women'; typically, it was attended by much junketing and brawling by rowdy young men. Shakespeare must have seen this sort of entertainment from very early in his life. Performance, acting and declaiming were at the heart of English culture in those times: from a king to a plain alderman, you had to be able to speak up in public and argue a good case. And great performances of the day, whether on the stage, in the pulpit or on the scaffold, were held up as models of style as well as of courage, constancy or virtue.

Puritans, of course, viewed such fripperies as stage and street theatre with distaste. For them, actors were 'schoolmasters of vice and provocations to corruption', and many wanted to protect the young and impressionable by banning plays altogether: 'What great care should be had in the education of children,' wrote one old fogey, 'to keep them from seeing spectacles of ill examples and hearing of lascivious or scurrilous words, for that their young memories are like fair writing-tables.' Such censorship would come, but not in Shakespeare's life. Yet again, he was lucky in his time.

Even before he went to school, Shakespeare had surely already encountered the magic of the theatre. In 1569 the town accounts record that Shakespeare's father, as mayor, welcomed players to Stratford and paid donations from the borough purse:

> Item payd to the Quenes Pleyers ix s
> Item to the Erle of Worcesters Pleers xii d

A contemporary, Robert Willis, born in the same year as Shakespeare, describes a similar show in Gloucester:

> As in other like corporations, when players of interludes come to town they first attend the Mayor to inform him what nobleman's servants they are, and so to get licence for their public playing; and if the Mayor likes the actors ... he appoints them to play their first play before himself and the aldermen and the common council; and that is called the Mayor's Play, where every one that will goes in without money, the Mayor giving the players a reward as he thinks fit to show respect unto them. My father took me with him, and made me stand between his legs, as he sat upon one of the benches, where we saw and heard very well. This sight took such an impression in me that when I came towards man's estate it was as fresh in my memory as if I had seen it newly acted.

'Bear Witness ... That There Are No Gods'

Once Shakespeare went to school, plays and acting, which were regarded as an important element in the education process, would have been a regular part of his experience. Indeed, early in the Reformation, in the 1550s, educators wrote didactic Protestant school plays such as *Ralph Roister Doister*, which taught a moral lesson and included patriotic songs and prayers for the queen.

At school Shakespeare also did plays in Latin. This is perhaps where he first encountered the Roman comedies of Plautus, which inspired his own comedies of mistaken identity, *The Comedy of Errors* and *Twelfth Night*. More important still was the Roman dramatist Seneca, a vast presence who shaped the imagination of Renaissance Europe. By now Greek drama was well known among European intellectuals in Latin versions such as Erasmus's translations of Euripides, but, writing as they did in an age of despotism, the Elizabethan dramatists felt their greatest affinity was with Seneca, the philosopher-poet at Nero's court who died by suicide – the fate of a writer in an age of tyranny. Seneca had been translated into English in the 1550s, but was still studied in Latin at school. And to schoolboys his work must have been shocking: a theatre of cruelty, whose terrible images of human beings brought to the ultimate point of endurance matched the judicial atrocities performed as exemplary and theatrical punishments on the public stage of Elizabethan England. The great Greek dramatists measured human suffering in the balance of divine justice, but Seneca rejected any evidence of such justice. Indeed, to him the gods were hardly more than names for the inscrutable and remorseless forces of history

and the self-destructive urges of humanity itself: 'Go on through the lofty spaces of high heaven,' cries Seneca's Jason to Medea. 'And bear witness where you ride that there are no gods.' In his art, as in his life, Seneca placed in opposition to these blind malignant forces the power of rationality, the Stoic affirmation of a kingdom of the mind, unshaken by tyranny and unmoved by horrors:

> Not riches makes a king …
> A king is he that hath laid fear aside,
> And all affects that in the breast are bred …
> It is the mind only that makes a king
> The kingdom each man bestows upon himself.

Shakespeare never forgot this. The young are sponges, and style is one of the most important building blocks in forming a young person's taste. However confined his palette, however wearing his repetition of horrors, Seneca has style in spades. Shakespeare's first youthful tragedy, *Titus Andronicus*, was pure theatre of cruelty: a young man's exercise in Seneca as stylish and derivative as a Quentin Tarantino film script.

Genius, of course, is not explicable simply in terms of the accumulation of influences. Roman comedy and tragedy were part of Shakespeare's diet at school, and with his fabulous memory he made ample use of them in his professional life. But there was also another dramatic influence from his childhood, which had a more all-embracing effect on his emotional view of his art. The roots of the public theatre in Tudor England lay in a centuries-old vernacular and popular tradition of tremendous dramatic and spiritual power, which was still accessible to Shakespeare in the first fifteen years of his life: the mystery plays.

The Coventry Mysteries

Eighteen miles from Stratford – an easy day's trip on horseback – lay the great medieval wool city of Coventry. From a distance it still bore the marks of its fourteenth-century boomtime: three miles of city walls with twelve gates and thirty-two towers, and the dramatic cluster of church spires and towers – Holy Trinity, St John's and St Michael's, whose 300-foot spire soared over the houses, gardens and orchards inside the walls.

In the late 1560s, when William first rode in as a boy, perhaps sitting on the front of his father's saddle, the place was on its uppers. The third largest city in England, in its heyday it had been home to more than 10,000 people, but after the recession of the 1520s, and the collapse of its old industries, it had seen

RIGHT: *Players at a country fair in Flanders in the mid-sixteenth century. Such shows were common in Tudor England: perhaps Shakespeare acted in Davy Jones's Whitsun pastoral in Stratford in May 1583?*

bitter times. Now local balladeers in the market place sang of 'dearth and idleness, and little money'. As one Tudor commentator said, 'This city which was heretofore well inhabited and wealthy ... is now for lack of occupiers fallen to great desolation and poverty.'

But in Shakespeare's childhood, Coventry was still the proud centre of one great civic tradition. Every year its famous cycle of medieval plays was performed by the guilds, until in Shakespeare's teens they were discontinued, denigrated as 'papist superstition' by an increasingly Puritanical town council (who ended up banning the maypole and even football). Judging by the numerous echoes in his plays, young Shakespeare certainly saw the mysteries; indeed John, as a traditionalist, may have taken the family every year. In the popular *Hundred Merry Tales* (a book that Shakespeare knew), a Warwickshire priest advises his parishioners to go to the mysteries in Coventry as a learning experience: he felt there was more to be learned from the drama than from the preacher in his pulpit.

The Coventry mysteries were Christian folk drama, ten substantial mystery plays enacting New Testament tales, which were performed on wagons in conjunction with the annual Corpus Christi procession. They were a matter of considerable expenditure, civic pride and effort, and in their heyday they drew huge crowds. The seventeenth-century antiquarian William Dugdale reported that 'the confluence of people from farr and neare to see that Shew was extraordinarily great, and yielded noe small advantage to this Cittye'. During her 1567 visit to Kenilworth, Elizabeth herself saw the smiths' pageant of Christ's trial before Herod.

The mysteries were written by ordinary folk for ordinary folk. And their plots had everything: myth and history; love, passion and betrayal. They had bawdy and knockabout humour, and at the same time sublimity, terror and tremendous pathos. Their tales and symbols were known to all: simple parables that opened up the deepest human feelings. In the plays tragedy existed alongside low jesting – even sometimes in the same scene, as when the rude mechanicals make farting jokes as they work a bellows to cast the nails for Christ's crucifixion. Here was earthy life even at the moment of cosmic anguish. It was a lesson Shakespeare never forgot.

In later life the poet had a soft spot for old-fashioned things, and he clearly loved the mysteries – references to the cycle abound in his works. For example, when he has Judas greeting Christ with 'All hail', he is quoting not the New Testament but the Coventry mystery plays. The tale of Herod and the massacre of the innocents must have particularly affected him, as well it might any child. He mentions it in several plays; and when Hamlet famously complains about a ham actor tearing a passion to tatters he chooses Herod to underline his point ('It out Herods Herod. Pray you avoid it'). This suggests that young William had seen the Coventry shearmen and tailors' play, of which the Tudor text survives. What Hamlet was referring to was the scene in which Herod 'rages in the street and on the pageant wagon' (as the stage direction puts it) because the baby Jesus has slipped through his grasp. To appreciate its full flavour, the text has to be seen in its original language:

> HEROD: Owt! Owt! Owtt!
> Hath those fawls traturs done me this ded?
> I stampe! I stare! I look all abowtt!
> Myght I them take, I schuld them bren at a glede!
> I rent! I rawe! And now run I wode!
> A, thatt these velen trayturs hath mard this my mode!
> They schalbe hangid yf ma cum them to!

Wonderful pantomime villainy over-egged by an amateur cast. But Shakespeare's knowledge of these plays was not just a matter of jokes about acting style. He echoed and plundered them to powerful emotional effect in themes, images, words and staging, knowing that their old imaginal world was still there in the minds of so many of his audience.

Opening the Door to the Classical World

One day in class, when Shakespeare was about nine, his schoolmaster Simon Hunt introduced him, in Latin, to the Roman poet Ovid. (We don't know exactly what the curriculum was at Stratford, but this was the age boys started Ovid at Rotherham Grammar School in Yorkshire, for example; at Ashby de la Zouche in Nottinghamshire they began Ovid and Virgil in the third form, at the age of nine or ten; at Harrow it was Ovid in the third form and Virgil a little later.) The book was the *Metamorphoses*, the 'book of changes'; the story of the gods and myths of the ancient world, and the principle of the universe – change itself:

> Of bodies changed to other forms I tell;
> You Gods, who have yourself wrought every change,
> Inspire my enterprise and lead my lay
> In one continuous song from nature's first
> Remote beginnings to our modern times.
> Ere land and sea and the all-covering sky

Were made, in the whole world the countenance
Of nature was the same, all one, well named
Chaos…

Everyone knows the feeling of excitement on discovering a book that unlocks the imagination; it enables us to inhabit another world – of heightened language, thought and ideas. Great literature holds the seed of a kind of liberation that remains with us throughout life – all the more so if it is learned by heart. Shakespeare's older contemporary, the French philosopher Michel Montaigne (here in John Florio's translation), described his own discovery of this Roman poet: 'the first taste or feeling I had of bookes, was of the pleasure I tooke in reading the fables of Ovids Metamorphosies; for being but seven or eight yeares old, I would steale and sequester my selfe from all other delights, only to reade them'.

Ovid is one of the key poets in Western culture: elegant, witty, sexy, impassioned, a great storyteller, a teacher – and a delightful companion, too, in the confiding way he talks to the reader:

The elements themselves do not endure;
Examine how they change and learn from me ….
Nothing retains its form; new shapes from old
Nature, the great inventor, ceaselessly
Contrives. In all creation, trust me,
There is no death – no death, but only change
And innovation; what we men call birth
Is but a different new beginning; death
Is but to cease to be the same ….

This long poem on the Greek myths was probably Shakespeare's best-loved book. He had other favourites – among vernacular poets he loved Chaucer and had a soft spot for old John Gower – but to Ovid he went back time and again. Here he read the stories of Jason and Medea, of Pyramus and Thisbe and of the siege of Troy with its great heroes Hector, Achilles and Ulysses. To a child it was perhaps the Tudor equivalent of *The Chronicles of Narnia*, *The Lord of the Rings* or *Harry Potter*, but demanding a higher and deeper level of engagement, drawing as it does on an ancient tradition expressed in heightened poetic language – and a foreign language to boot. These were tales that unlocked a door to the incomparably rich universe of the classical world, and had the capacity to lift a child's mind beyond the claustrophobic conformities of 1570s' education.

Shakespeare would have worked on the Latin text with Simon Hunt at

school, of course, reading it aloud, parsing and explaining. But it is conceivable that his family might have bought him Arthur Golding's recent translation (as Young Lucius says in *Titus Andronicus*, 'My mother gave it me.') As a professional writer in London, he used Golding, but he also worked direct from the Latin text, which he presumably also possessed. (Interestingly enough, a sixteenth-century Latin Ovid survives in Oxford with an abbreviated signature on the title page which may just be his, and a seventeenth-century note that it was Shakespeare's copy which had come through a Mr Hall – perhaps his son-in-law, Dr John Hall.) Shakespeare grew to know the *Metamorphoses* extremely well, and it is one of a small number of books that he used throughout his career – chief among them the Bible, Holinshed's *Historie of England*, Cinthio's *Hundred Stories* and Plutarch's *Lives* – amid thousands of texts browsed, skimmed, plundered or read intensively. In his last play as a solo author, *The Tempest*, he transmutes Ovid's fantastic description of Medea mixing her magic herbs into Prospero's valediction, his renunciation of magic. This speech is often taken to be Shakespeare's farewell to his art, and if it is, its source could not be more appropriate. Shakespeare the poet was obsessed by concealment, role-playing and illusion. Ovid too delights in showing his readers their own image, playing with them, pointing out the intellectual reality that a text is just a text, and yet forcing us to believe in the parallel reality of the world created in the text. In Ovid, the supreme poet of illusion found a soulmate for life.

Humanist Allegory Versus Puritan Literalness

But there was another dimension to the reading of a Tudor child that had nothing to do with literal comprehension. Ovid's *Metamorphoses* is not just a book of good tales. And no more than with his experience of the mystery plays did Shakespeare's reading of Ovid come down simply to stories, images and words mechanically borrowed. It was about ways of seeing. This was acknowledged directly by Golding on his title page in a kind of spiritual health warning to the reader. First published in Protestant England in 1567, the book was described as 'A worke very pleasaunt and delectable'; nonetheless, said Golding, 'with skill, heede, and judgement, this worke must be read, For else to the Reader it standes in small stead'. Shakespeare's Ovid teacher, the Oxford graduate Hunt, had a background in old-fashioned humanism; and Renaissance Christian humanism was frankly pagan in colour. For university-educated humanists like Montaigne, or John Colet in England, the works of Ovid and Virgil were a kind of profane Bible. In other words, God's eternal revelation had been given to the pagans, too. These were not just dry texts; in their great themes of mutability and the gods they offered an alternative mental world to

the post-Reformation universe. The key is the relationship between literalness and allegory, as Erasmus says in his *Handbook*: 'more profit is perhaps to be derived from reading pagan literature (*poetica*) with its allegorical content in mind than from the Scriptures taken merely literally'.

Not surprisingly, Puritans and the stricter Protestants regarded ideas like these as dangerous and even heretical. Allegory was not acceptable; literalness was everything. Luther vehemently condemned those moralizers of Ovid 'who would turn Apollo into Christ and Diana into the Virgin Mary'. In England Puritans would attempt to ban the pagan poets; and a Privy Council memo of April 1582 called for 'the removing of such lascivious poetes as are commonly read and taught in grammar schools ... as Ovid de arte amandi, or such lyke'

The whole of Shakespeare's writing career shows that he supported the humanist rather than the Puritan view of Ovid. In his late romances he would use this late medieval allegorical tradition and bring the pagan gods on stage: for example, in *Pericles* he uses Diana to evoke the Virgin Mary. The destruction of this medieval tradition would be a great blow to the richness of English literary culture, and Shakespeare's plays were so successful in part because he drew on it, incorporated it into his work and handed it down to us.

So the books that Shakespeare closely studied tell us more than simply what he read. At school he learned whole chunks of great literature off by heart; he got inside Latin well enough to be able to invent words from Latin stems; he also encountered heightened language, refinement of expression, the sound and rhythm of language, and respect for tradition. But most of all he absorbed tales and myths, and discovered allegory and the topography of another universe – one of the most exciting gifts for a young person's imagination. His childhood reading experiences matched his experience of the outer world, and he would always observe life from multiple viewpoints. In the famous epigram of the ancient Greek satirist Archilochus, the fox knows many things, the hedgehog one big thing. Shakespeare learned early to be a fox.

Prospects: Life After Grammar School

So what were the prospects for the boy William? What could a bailiff's son in 1570s' Warwickshire have expected from life after school? By the time he was approaching his thirteenth birthday, in the normal course of events he might have expected his future life to be mapped out for him. In a Tudor town there were plenty of job opportunities for a former mayor's son with a good Latin education. After all, his father, now in his late forties, had been a pillar of local society for twenty years and had money, status and influence. But over the winter of 1576, when Shakespeare was twelve, a dramatic change came over the family fortunes.

CHAPTER FOUR

John Shakespeare's Secret

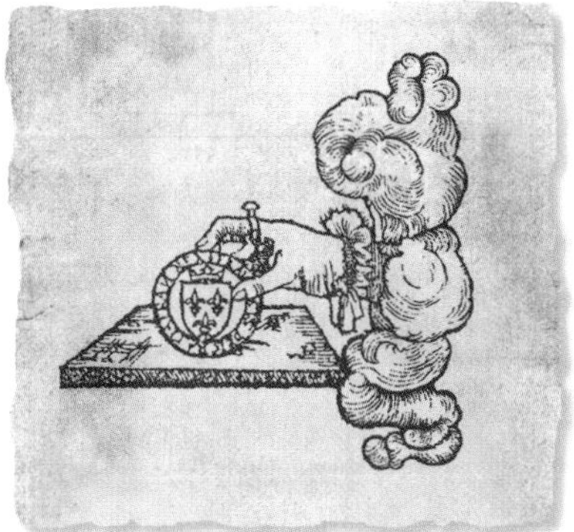

THUS FAITH IS TO BE TESTED

Until the mid-1570s John Shakespeare was still doing well and had bought more land and two more houses in Stratford. It was at this time that he applied to the College of Arms in London for a coat of arms, hoping to become a gentleman. For some reason it didn't happen; whether they refused him, or whether he dropped the matter, is unknown. Maybe he saw the writing on the wall, for his fortunes were about to turn.

Brogging, illegal dealing in wool, was a risky business: you worked on credit, so you had to trust your supplier. Broggers no doubt always lived with occasional bad debts, like the Marlborough clothier whom John pursued fruitlessly for payment over twenty years. The court case in 1572 had been a warning: John had laid out £210 to purchase wool in Westminster and in Snitterfield, only to be shopped by an informer for contravening the laws protecting the monopoly of the Staple of Wool Merchants. (Some of the government's undercover army of informers were very nasty characters: James Langrake, who caught John, was later jailed for raping his maidservant and blackmailing his victims.) This time John got away with a fine because it was his first offence, and most likely he got off further charges by doing what people normally did – making a private settlement with the informer out of court.

THE COLLAPSE OF THE WOOL TRADE

Things were not good in England in that winter of 1576–7. The economy was in trouble, and disillusionment with Elizabeth's rule was widespread. In the new

year the Privy Council noted with alarm the seething state of the realm, 'tending as it seemeth to some seed of rebellion'. And then came the first indication that all was not well in the Shakespeares' affairs. On the corporation's account day, 23 January, John failed to appear at the council meeting; nor, after thirteen years with only one absence, did he attend any other meeting in 1577. The next year the pattern continued. Soon the family started mortgaging off their property, and John appears to have run into debt.

What triggered this financial slide is still unknown. But in the autumn of 1576 there was a growing crisis in the wool industry because the raw material was in short supply, and this led to a countrywide recession, especially in the Cotswolds. The following summer the Privy Council instructed the mayor of the Wool Staple to canvas 'skilful clothiers' about 'the cause of the said dearth and how it may be remedied'. Their answer was the old refrain: the broggers were to blame. So in July the Privy Council issued orders to the shire authorities to clamp down on them. Obviously it didn't work, because eventually, in September 1580, the government ordered the broggers to be 'identified, and proceeded against in the law' – they were to be run out of town once and for all. By then, however, John's troubles were altogether more serious.

A Grand Commission Ecclesiastical

Just when the broggers were being squeezed, the authorities initiated a witch-hunt against the followers of the Old Religion. In the first ten or fifteen years of Elizabeth's reign there had been a degree of live and let live in religious observance. But now the war for hearts and minds entered a new phase. In April 1576 the queen appointed a Grand Commission to inquire into offences against her 1559 statutes of supremacy, which made the monarch, not the pope, supreme governor of the Church of England. The commission's aim was to 'order correct, reform and punish any persons wilfully and obstinately absenting themselves from church and service'. Fines against Catholics were to be levied by the churchwardens of each parish for the benefit of the poor; in serious cases heavier fines and imprisonment were to be imposed by the commissioners, with bonds or sureties taken for the appearance of offenders. Anyone who held civic office now had to take the oath of allegiance to the queen in matters of religion. The investigations were conducted throughout the second half of 1576, coinciding with John's last appearance at a Stratford town council meeting.

The next year the Privy Council appointed commissioners to recruit armed forces from landowners, gentlemen and freeholders in each shire. This move was as much about political and religious control as about military assessment. In October the musters commissioners came to Stratford, among them Sir

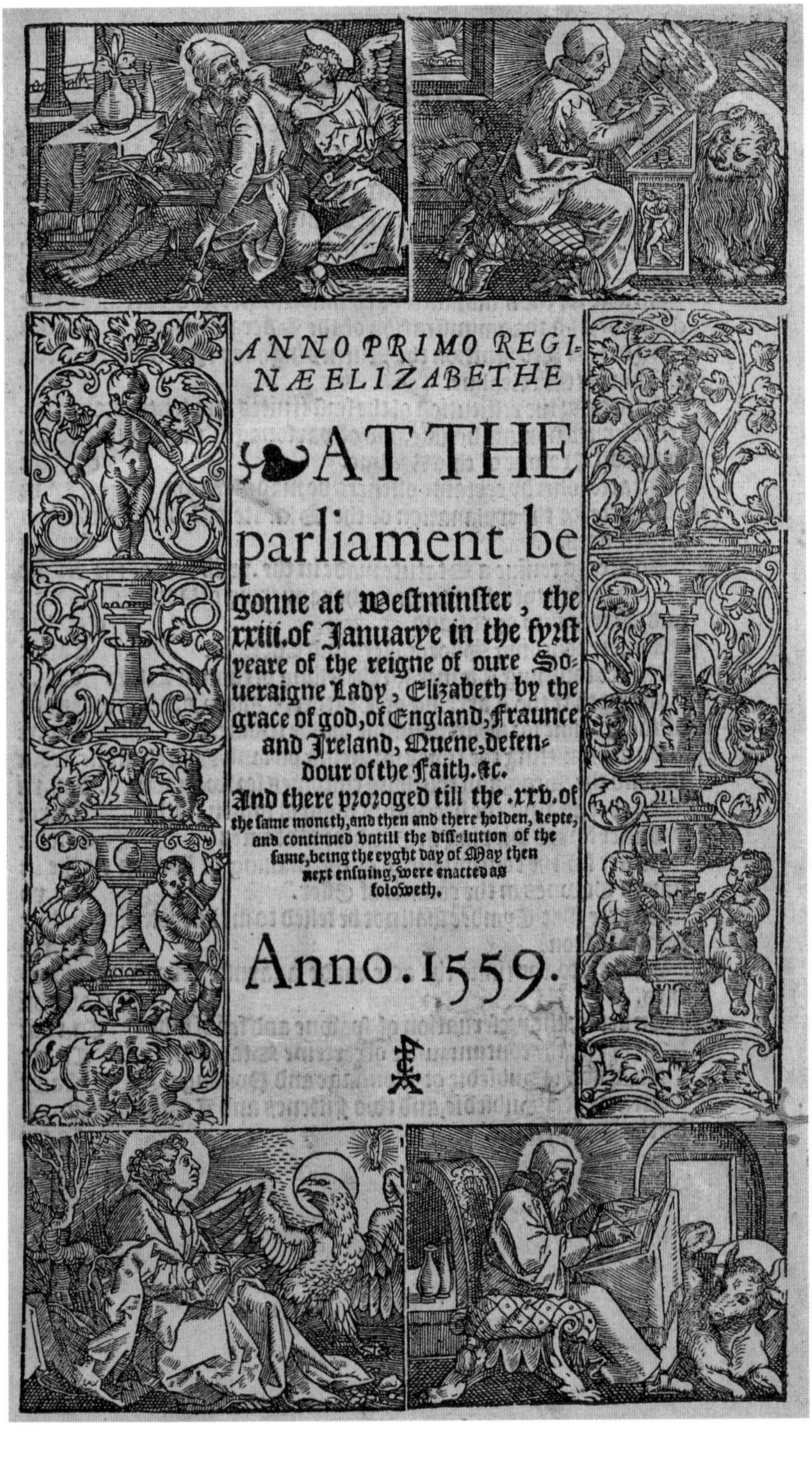

ANNO PRIMO REGI-
NÆ ELIZABETHE

AT THE
parliament be-
gonne at Westminster, the
xxiii. of Januarye in the fyrst
yeare of the reigne of oure So-
ueraigne Lady, Elizabeth by the
grace of god, of England, Fraunce
and Ireland, Quene, defen-
dour of the Faith. &c.
And there proroged till the .xxv. of
the same moneth, and then and there holden, kepte,
and continued vntill the dissolution of the
same, being the eyght day of May then
next ensuing, were enacted as
foloweth.

Anno. 1559.

LEFT: *Elizabeth's statutes of 1559 enforcing religious uniformity. In Stratford it was live and let live for the first fifteen years of her reign: sanctions only began to bite after William left school in the mid-1570s.*

Thomas Lucy of Charlecote, the anti-Catholic enforcer for the local area. At the same time an order was sent to all bishops to 'certify the name of all persons in his diocese who refused to come to church, together with the values of their lands and goods'. A concerted effort was to be made to demand loyalty under the threat of fines and confiscation of land. But in south Warwickshire this proved hard to implement. The bishop of Worcester was unpopular, many of the landowners, burghers and clergy were sympathetic to their Catholic neighbours, and the lists of recusants remained incomplete.

In January 1578 a levy was made in Stratford itself for the strengthening of the militia (to be used against possible uprisings, but also to enforce anti-Catholic measures). In this list John Shakespeare appears with a 3s 4d assessment – half that of the other aldermen. But he refused to pay. Among those reported for non-payment along with him were George Badger, one of the staunchest Catholics in town; Thomas Reynolds, another Catholic and the father of a friend of William's; and Thomas Nashe, the father of another friend of the poet. Interestingly enough, however, the corporation excused John payment of the levy, and also his fine for non-attendance on election day in September 1578. In fact there is no record that he ever paid the fines imposed for his absence.

The Family's Troubles Mount

So although John was unwilling or unable to pay his levies and fines, he was being protected by friends on the council. It was at this point, in autumn 1578, that John and Mary began to dispose of their land and other property. In November they transferred 86 acres to Thomas Webbe and Humphrey Hooper, who may have been distant relatives of the Ardens. The lease contained a strange condition: it stipulated that the tenant for twenty-one years was to be George Gibbes, a friend of the Ardens, who was to pay 'a quarter of wheat and a quarter of barley annually'. This peppercorn rent strongly suggests that the real object of the transaction was not to raise cash but to temporarily transfer ownership of the land. (Subletting property, handing it over to friends or family, was a common tactic, especially among Catholics, to thwart government attempts to locate their land and goods.) Two days later John and Mary mortgaged their newly built house at Wilmcote with upwards of 80 acres to Mary's brother-in-law Edmund Lambert in Barton-on-the-Heath. Again, it seems to have been a short-term ploy, for a year or so later John tried (unsuccessfully) to retrieve the property.

It was a terrible winter in 1578, with a long, hard frost and heavy snow 'whose drifts in many places, by reason of a North-East wind went so deep that the mere report of them may seem incredible', according to one observer. The thaw, when it came, caused widespread flooding: in London, for instance,

Opposite: *Elizabeth c. 1574: brilliant, vulnerable, psychologically damaged. She was portrayed by her poets as the goddess Astraea, symbolizing the rule of universal peace and justice. In reality her job was to keep the lid on sometimes unresolvable tensions.*

the Thames burst its banks and flooded Westminster Hall. With such a wet spring everywhere, there was much sickness among both people and livestock. At the start of April, William's seven-year-old sister Anne died. The church accounts show that John paid an 8d fee 'for the bell and pall' – clearly a high-status funeral for a family anxious to keep their heads up in the community. But the Shakespeares were being hit hard from every side. When troubles come, as their eldest son would say, they come not in single spies but in battalions.

That October John and Mary made their last sell-off, giving up their interest in Mary's share of her father's property in Snitterfield to their kinsman Robert Webbe – only this time for far more than it was worth. During this period John had also accumulated debts, for which he was being sued by his creditors. In other documents he is shown as being exempted from the levy for poor relief: evidently there were still men on the corporation who stood by their old friend and colleague. Still only in his late forties, he had effectively given up his civic position. For ten years, until he was finally expelled in 1586, he did not attend meetings except on one occasion to vote for the son of an old and close friend, John Sadler. After twenty years of service to the town, John had bowed out.

William Leaves School

Seeing his popular, successful father go down a slippery slope, hounded for money, selling off all his carefully acquired parcels of land, and being publicly humiliated, might well be thought to have left its mark on William. Certainly, in his adult life the son would work hard to restore the family's land, property and fortunes in Stratford – even acquiring for his father the gentlemanly status to which he had aspired unsuccessfully just before the crash.

William would have expected to leave school at about sixteen in 1580, possibly even later if he had wanted to go on to university. But an early eighteenth-century source, Nicholas Rowe, asserts that he was taken out early from school, that his father's circumstances 'and the want of his assistance at Home, forc'd his Father to with draw him from thence'. Given the family's problems, this is plausible. Very likely William left school when he turned fourteen in 1578. With five children under twelve, his parents needed the eldest, able-bodied son to become another breadwinner.

What did he do next? A job as a scrivener in a local lawyer's office has been suggested, but there is no evidence for this beyond his very good working knowledge of legal terminology, which might simply have come from living with a litigious father. One tradition has it that Shakespeare was a country schoolmaster for a while, but surely not yet – at fourteen he would have been too young. By far the likeliest answer is that to begin with he worked for his father,

as both Rowe and the seventeenth-century diarist John Aubrey say. But two years later an extraordinary event took place which had repercussions right across England and which left its mark on the Shakespeare family and their Warwickshire friends and neighbours. It puts John Shakespeare's problems in the late 1570s in an entirely different light.

'Rome Has Her Musters in England'

In 1580 the simmering religious divisions within Elizabeth's realm were still a source of deep concern to her government. The Privy Council minutes from the spring of that year reveal these and other anxieties. The threat of foreign invasion was always at the back of their minds, and the council called for coastal defence forces in Suffolk from Aldeburgh to Lowestoft. Victualling the English forces in Ireland, who were protecting Protestant settlers there, was another headache forever compromised by the shambolic and corrupt system of supply. And amidst all this, strange tales of sorcery were reported from Shropshire, Worcestershire and the Welsh borders, among other places. There were dark whispers of witchcraft with graven images and wax dolls, and in Essex a wax figure of the queen herself had been stabbed with pins. Up and down the land government agents and justices of the peace were reporting a 'falling away of religion ... people who conform but secretly use the Popish service'. It is not surprising, then, that the Privy Council were in a panic about losing the hearts and minds of the next generation, given the ongoing failure to control schools and schoolmasters and the seepage of books and 'unlawful stuff' brought in from overseas though England's porous coastline.

That spring, too, news came that a small force of papal troops and refugee English Catholics intended to land in Ireland. At the same time Elizabeth's spies in the Jesuit colleges in Rheims and Rome spoke of a planned attempt to send priests to England, the spearhead of a spiritual underground to revive the Old Faith. It was a dangerous moment, rumoured by some to be the prelude to a new Spanish attempt to invade England, to overthrow Elizabeth and re-establish the Catholic religion.

Obsessed with enemies internal and external, the government began to compile new lists of freeholders to distinguish those on whom they could rely for military help and those who were suspected of Catholic sympathies. On 18 March 1580 military commissioners were appointed for musters throughout England 'in defence of her Majesty, Crown, Realm and Good Subjects against all attempts both inward and outward'. Writing to the sheriff of Lancashire on 14 April, the Privy Council clearly associated the recusants with the musters, letting him know 'Her Majesty's intention being to terrify the offenders'.

John Shakespeare appeared in the Stratford lists among the 'gentlemen and freeholders', then, a few weeks later, he suddenly ran up against the power of the state, bound over with many others to present himself at the Queen's Bench in Westminster on a specified day in June with sureties that he would 'keep the peace towards the queen and her subjects'. The list of co-defendants numbered over 200 and included gentlemen, hatters, tailors, glovers, drapers, silk weavers, vintners and grocers; there were many yeomen and husbandmen, and even a couple of Middle Temple lawyers; both men and women were named. Among them is this entry:

> John Shakespeare Stratford upon Avon Warwickshire Yeoman £20
> John Audeley of Nottingham, in the county of Nottingham, hatmaker surety of John Shakespeare £10
> Thomas Cooley Stoke Staffs yeoman surety of John Shakespeare £10

On the same sheet John Audeley stood for £40; his sureties were Shakespeare and Cooley for £20 each, along with two more men from the local area: Nicholas Walton from Kidderminster and William Lonley, a yeoman from Elmley, both in Worcestershire.

What was the significance of this mysterious web of contacts in a central government document? At a critical moment in national politics, it concerned the peace and security of the realm. Clearly something other and deeper than neighbourhood must have united them. Circumstantial evidence suggests that religion was the key. 'Rome has her musters in England, intestine and inward,' the lord keeper of the Great Seal, Sir Nicholas Bacon, had written to the queen. A survey of the inmates of London's jails in April 1580 produced lists of Catholic prisoners who had been 'covenanted' on sureties. The next year the system was put on the statute books: every person above the age of sixteen who did not obey the requirements of Elizabeth's Act of Uniformity would be fined 'twenty pounds by the month exacted of such as are able to pay it', rising to 'all their goods and the third part of their lands'. Those who had not attended church for twelve months were, in addition to the fine, 'to be bound with sufficient sureties in the sum of £200 at the least to good behaviour until their conformity'.

John Shakespeare was now a marked man in the eyes of the government. Yet despite his apparently dire financial situation, he failed to turn up in London on the appointed day for his sureties case. He was therefore fined £40: £20 as pledge for Audeley, and another £20 for his non-appearance. This was big money – it was what John had raised on the Wilmcote property – and especially so for a man supposedly in debt who had gone to the trouble of selling off his

wife's share of one property to raise a mere £6. Just why did he decide to stay away and pay up?

The Mission of Edmund Campion

On 12 June, right in the middle of the sureties affair, a well-dressed stranger landed at Dover. He sported the black coat and hat of a gentleman, but his dark hair was cropped unfashionably short and the sharp-eared listener might have picked up the faintest hint of an Italian accent. After the phoney war of the first ten years of Elizabeth's Protestant revolution, and the gathering storm of the last ten, the crisis had come in the form of the Catholic Counter-Reformation. This was the start of the Jesuit mission of Edmund Campion.

The government had been expecting him. Reacting like any modern regime, they had provided customs officials at the Channel ports with artist's impressions of Campion done from descriptions supplied by double agents who had been posing as theological students in the seminaries in Rheims and Rome. The first Jesuit undercover operators had in fact entered the country six years before. But Campion was the biggest fish: the most gifted scholar of his generation, in his Oxford heyday he had declaimed in Latin in front of the queen. Now, re-entering the country at Dover, he was detained for a while and underwent a routine interrogation by the mayor, but was then released. Others were not so lucky; one of his companions was arrested and charged with bringing 'books from overseas'. Shaking with nerves, Campion disappeared gratefully into the darkness and headed on foot for London.

Below: *Edmund Campion, whose 1580 mission was a turning point in the ruin of the English Catholic community. It appears to have sucked in Shakespeare's father.*

Intending to meet up with him were three other Jesuits who had close connections with the Stratford region. Thomas Cottam was a former schoolmaster and the brother of William's Stratford teacher. Robert Debdale, a relative of Shakespeare's mother, came from the nearby village of Shottery and had probably been educated at the grammar school. And lastly there was Robert Persons, who, luxuriantly moustached, had already landed in the flamboyant disguise of an army officer. He counted Edward Arden, another of Mary Shakespeare's kinsmen, as a friend, and would use his house as a base.

Campion found refuge in a safe house in the bustling London suburb of Southwark, and there

announced the opening gambit of his mission. From now on it would no longer be acceptable for Catholics to be church papists and to go to Protestant church; to do so was the 'greatest iniquity that can be imagined'. Like the excommunication of Elizabeth, it was a disastrously misjudged step and only hastened the destruction of the English Catholic community.

Alarmed at the Protestant regime's growing grip on education and the care of souls as the old generation of Queen Mary's priests faded away, the Jesuits hoped to organize an underground movement to succour the Catholic population. They knew that conformity and accommodation would mean the death of the Catholic tradition in England. 'What on earth would Gregory the Great and St Augustine think if they could see their country now,' asked one, 'which they evangelized in the name of God in 597?' A new generation was growing up which had known nothing else; which believed the pope to be the antichrist, the mass a mummery, and hell and purgatory tricks to awe the simple-minded: a generation that did not look back to Catholic England as their own.

In the language of such battles everywhere, then as now, the authorities saw the Jesuits as terrorists, but to the Catholics they were freedom fighters. After a few weeks the newcomers left London. In July Campion went to Northamptonshire, Oxfordshire and East Anglia; Persons to the West Midlands, Worcestershire and Gloucestershire. Their portable altars and surplices hidden in packs, they told travellers whom they met on the road that they were merchants. Persons headed into Warwickshire. Cottam too had planned to come this way, and Debdale wrote a letter, commending him to his parents at Shottery. But the letter was intercepted and Cottam captured. More heat was drawn on to Stratford: the net was tightening.

From the government's inquisitions we can piece together Persons' route that summer. He stayed with the Grants, business partners of John Shakespeare, at Northbrook, close to the Shakespeare family farm at Snitterfield. He was received by the Skinners at Rowington, then went on to Lapworth Hall and perhaps to Bushwood, the home of Sir William Catesby and a famous refuge for recusants; Campion himself stayed there the following year. The Ferrars' house at Baddesley Clinton was another: 'a very safe refuge which we had nearly always used previously for our meetings', wrote one of the Jesuits later. The government's informers also reported that Campion was entertained 20 miles north of Stratford at Park Hall, the residence of Shakespeare's mother's kinsman, Edward Arden. This was never proved, but a letter written by the Jesuit Robert Southwell confirms that Edward Arden was an active supporter, 'a friend of Father Persons, in whose house he generally used to hide'.

The only one of the 1580 mission to escape execution, Persons claimed that the Jesuits were received by thousands of people that summer. For Campion, too, it had been 'a joyous harvest'. At their secret meetings, loyal families came to meet them and celebrate mass together. They were drawn from right across the social spectrum: gentry, gentlemen freeholders, yeomen and local priests. Swimming against the tide of history, although they perhaps did not yet know it, the old community of the shire turned out in force for the missionaries.

But the Jesuits were not there merely to celebrate mass. They had promised not to engage in politics (and protested that they intended no harm to the queen), but the agenda that Campion had set in Southwark was of course political in the extreme. He wanted people to be not church papists, but recusants. And the missionaries' letters suggest that to do this they hoped to get lapsed Catholics to reaffirm their faith by swearing an oath of loyalty, a testament of faith to set against the oath of allegiance required by Elizabeth's government.

In one letter Campion referred to old Catholics and new converts 'signing their names'. But to what? Were Campion and Persons carrying some form of written testament of faith? Such testaments were in the air at this time. Shortly after the mission a Worcestershire man, William Bell, wrote just such a testament, in the form of a will, with a confession of faith affirming the tradition that 'England first received the Christian religion from Joseph of Arimathea that buried Christ and came after to England'. The Jesuits certainly brought pamphlets with them, for one of Campion's party had been arrested at Dover carrying printed material from abroad. Writing back to Rome from Rheims that year, the Jesuit controller William Allen said the mission was proving so popular that Persons 'would like 3 or 4000 or more of the *testamenta'*. The Latin word can mean either a form of will or the New Testament. But although the Catholic Rheims Bible was completed later that year, it seems unlikely that Allen was letting them know in Rome that Persons would like so many copies of an as yet unpublished 800-page book put together in Rheims. There is a much more plausible explanation, which takes us to what may be the most sensational and controversial of all the Shakespeare family documents.

The Secret Testament of John Shakespeare

In April 1757, some men working in the Shakespeare birthplace in Henley Street discovered, concealed between the eaves and the joists, a six-page handwritten Catholic testament of faith, in English, each page signed in the name of John Shakespeare. There were several witnesses to the find, including the foreman, members of the Hart family (descendants of Shakespeare's sister Joan), the vicar of Stratford and a local alderman. Most importantly, though, the document

was examined by the great eighteenth-century Shakespearean scholar Edmond Malone, in whose opinion it was written in a late sixteenth- or early seventeenth-century hand. Malone later came to believe that it could not have been written by John or any of his family, but he was 'perfectly satisfied' about its authenticity as a late Tudor document.

Unfortunately the manuscript is now lost, but it was printed by Malone in 1790: 'I John Shakspeare, do protest that I am willing, yea, I do infinitely desire and humbly crave, that of this my last will and testament the glorious and ever Virgin Mary, mother of god, refuge and advocate of sinners (whom I honour specially above all other saints) may be the chief Executresse, together with these other saints, my patrons ....' Further on, John prayed and beseeched 'all my dear friends parents and kinsfolks, by the bowles of our Saviour Jesus Christ ... to do masses for my soul after my death'. Here the document touched on one of the most contentious tenets of the English Reformation: the denial of prayers and masses for the dead. Crucially, he also made a solemn promise 'that I will patiently endure and suffer all kind of infirmity, sickness, yea and the pain of death itself' rather than let go of the Catholic faith. Here, it might appear, is the oath of loyalty that the members of the 1580 mission were demanding.

The document is so strange, so wordy, so un-English in its baroque Catholic rhetoric that for a long time it seemed impossible to attribute such a creed to a good English burgher and former mayor of Stratford, let alone the father of the national bard. Malone died in 1812 and after his time the testament tended to be dismissed as a forgery, a verdict made easier by the fact that the first page had been lost, and restored ham-fistedly by a well-known Stratford antiquarian with an absurd pastiche quoting Hamlet's ghost (which has nonetheless fooled several modern biographers). But the real point was that for most nineteenth-century scholars it was simply unthinkable that the bard's family should have been tainted by Catholicism.

In the twentieth century, however, first a Spanish version and then a printed English translation of 1634 were discovered. They prove beyond doubt that what was found in the roof of the Henley Street house was an accurate sixteenth-century English translation of a spiritual testament composed in Latin in the 1570s by Cardinal Borromeo of Milan. Campion and Persons had stayed with Borromeo on their way to England – in one letter from England Persons asks to be remembered to the cardinal, whom he calls his patron. Unquestionably, what lay behind the discovery was a genuine sixteenth-century text.

BELOW: *The 1634 printed English version of the Testament of the Soul. A mysterious hand-written version, bearing Shakespeare's father's name, was found in the roof of the birthplace house.*

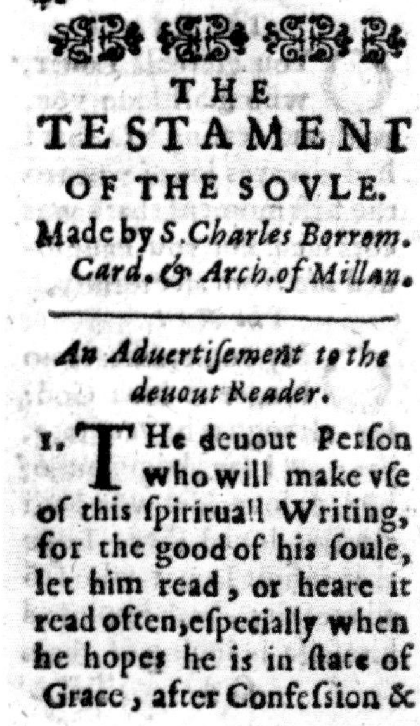

42

THE TESTAMENT OF THE SOVLE.

Made by S. Charles Borrom. Card. & Arch. of Millan.

An Aduertisement to the deuout Reader.

1. THe deuout Person who will make vse of this spirituall Writing, for the good of his soule, let him read, or heare it read often, especially when he hopes he is in state of Grace, after Confession &

But how did this extraordinary document find its way into the roof of the Shakespeares' house? And how did the poet's father's name come to be on it? Could John have received it from Campion or Persons? He could, of course, have come into contact with the testament at any time in the next twenty years through friends and neighbours hand-copying the text and disseminating it. But the impetus to sign such a formal document is much more likely to have come from the direct influence of the missionaries. There remains, of course, the faint possibility that it was an eighteenth-century forgery, but what possible motive could there have been at that time for falsely attributing it to John Shakespeare, when the question of his Catholicism was not remotely an issue?

The available evidence makes it virtually certain that the document was genuine. The missionaries used such things because they touched on crucial aspects of the battle of spirits in the sixteenth century: allegiance to the Catholic Church, prayers for the dead, resistance. Whilst complete certainty is impossible, it is likely that limited numbers of a printed version of the testament were among the 'books brought in from overseas' in June 1580. At the Jesuits' secret masses copies were given out, and proved so popular that they needed to get more of them printed. Most likely, printed copies were handed out by Persons and supplemented by hand-written ones when they ran out.

On balance, then, it is probable that John Shakespeare, the former bailiff of Stratford, really did receive the testament – perhaps through a local priest, or through friends, but most likely from the hands of Robert Persons himself, as a curious later tradition asserts. John was in dire financial straits, deprived of civic office, and his daughter Anne was only a year dead. Inspired by the mission's charismatic preaching, at this moment the church papist and lapsed Catholic reaffirms his faith. Perhaps he attended mass at the Catesbys' house at Bushwood, or at Park Hall with the Ardens, his wife's family. This in turn might suggest that the document itself was no mere copy at third hand made by a friend or neighbour, but treasured because it had been written at the time of his profession of faith. Then subsequently, perhaps under some kind of threat, John was forced to get rid of it, significantly choosing to hide it in his roof rather than destroy it.

Dramatic as its implications are, the testament does not materially alter our view of John's religion. If genuine, it simply tends to confirm what is already suggested by other sources. Two Stratford recusancy returns for 1592 have survived, the first drawn up after Easter, the most important church festival for Catholics and therefore the one on which they would least wish to worship in a Protestant church. Among the names of those who had failed to take Protestant communion were well-known resisters, 'obstinate papists, shelterers

of seminaries'. Appearing in both lists, among those who had excused themselves from church on the grounds of debt, was the poet's father.

Modern scholars have tried to cast doubt on this testimony. But John's excuse, that he couldn't be seen in a public place such as a church for fear of being arrested by his creditors, was a very common story among Catholics; and it certainly was an excuse – that summer he appeared in town conducting public business as an assessor on two deceased friends' estates. John may still not have wished to come out as a recusant, but it appears he had crossed the line from being a church papist.

The final clue was only discovered in the episcopal records in Maidstone in 1964. In the aftermath of the Gunpowder Plot, in May 1606, in a list of avowed Catholics and church papists who 'did not appear' at Protestant Easter communion in Stratford is 'Susanna Shakespeere', the poet's daughter and John's granddaughter. The sureties case, the mysterious testament in the eaves, the recusancy list, and now the granddaughter. There is happenstance, and then there is coincidence. But this is surely one coincidence too many. This looks very much like family loyalty.

When he reaffirmed his faith in these dangerous circumstances John Shakespeare solemnly beseeched his nearest and dearest – among whom his eldest son would have been the most important – to have masses said for him after his death, and to pray for his soul in purgatory. To consider that in the light of the ghost's speech about purgatory in *Hamlet* is to experience a little shiver. By the time he wrote that play, around 1600, Shakespeare had long been a leading light of London's theatre world and was probably no longer a Catholic. But he never sounds like a Protestant. And if William's upbringing was set against these underground battles of conscience and power, it surely casts his later life in a very interesting light.

To the Scaffold: The End of Campion's Mission

Campion remained at liberty for a year. A massive manhunt through the winter of 1580–1 tried to track him down. In the south, he used a secret printing press at Stonor House in the Chilterns to print his anti-government tract *Decem Rationes*. Then he moved up into Lancashire and stayed with the Hoghton family at Lea Hall and Hoghton Tower, where he was for Easter and Pentecost 1581. But in June Robert Debdale was captured, followed by Campion and Cottam. Taken under armed escort to London, Campion arrived beneath a banner reading 'Campion the Seditious Jesuit'. His lengthy interrogation was reinforced by starvation, thumbscrews, needles under his fingernails, compression in the metal frame known as the Scavenger's Daughter, and eight days in the

Pit, a dank and dark wellshaft. On 30 July warrants were issued to use the rack. Eventually he gave in and began to provide his torturers with names.

On 14 November the trial began in London of Campion and Thomas Cottam, the first of the great Jesuit dramas of conscience. Evidence against Campion came from a double agent called Anthony Munday, who had posed as a Catholic student in Rheims and published a lurid bestseller on doings in Jesuit seminaries. Campion, of course, was doomed. Despite the intellectual strength of his defence and the way that, despite his badly weakened physical state as a result of his torture, he discredited all the witnesses, he was found guilty and sentenced to death. He responded with prophetic words that resonate all the more powerfully given the obsession with history in Elizabeth's England: 'In condemning us, you condemn all your ancestors, all the ancient bishops and kings, all that was once the glory of England.'

Campion's contacts were investigated, including all those fingered by informers or by hearsay as having attended their masses. All the houses where he had stayed were searched. Some leading figures in the north bit the dust: Alexander Hoghton, mysteriously, died that autumn, and Sir Thomas Hesketh was jailed in Manchester, where he too died. The inquisitors also followed Campion's trail in the Stratford area. At Bushwood Catesby was arrested and interrogated by Sir Thomas Lucy, and it may be no coincidence that that autumn John Cottam left his post at Stratford Grammar School and returned to Lancashire. His brother, after all, was one of the two main defendants in the most sensational treason trial of the era. Back home, Cottam and his wife ran private tuition for Catholic children and were frequently fined as recusants. He was replaced by Alexander Aspinall, another Lancastrian, but, outwardly at least, a conforming Protestant. Amazingly, it had taken over twenty years of Elizabeth's reign before the corporation had finally wished to appoint, or been forced to appoint, a more orthodox master.

On 1 December Campion was hanged, drawn and quartered at Tyburn – the place of punishment or crucifixion for Shakespeare's generation, depending on their point of view. Relics of the butchery, including a bloodstained cloth, a knife and a finger, are still preserved by loyalists in shrines in Lancashire.

The End of Childhood

Sometimes childhood can be over in an instant, following one traumatic event. The gradual collapse of John's fortunes had taken more than four years. But the sureties case and the contact with the 1580 mission, however it happened, were perhaps the final step into adulthood for young William. For here was the stark reality of power and conscience. And with it the golden childhood was gone.

Not long afterwards, he disappears from our view in what have become known as the 'lost years' of his life. What happened? Back in the summer, the news of the Jesuit leader's arrest had spread like wildfire among the many Catholics who had sheltered him and were now, of course, in danger themselves. On 13 August 1581 in Lancashire Alexander Hoghton hastily made his will. In it he rewarded many of his servants and staff, among whom he recommended two men called Fulk Gillom and William Shakeshafte to his brother Thomas at Lea Hall; and, failing that, to his neighbour and kinsman Sir Thomas Hesketh. Shakeshafte and Gillom are assumed to be players or musicians, as the will mentions musical instruments and 'play clothes' in connection with them. Hesketh was a renowned patron of players and Hoghton hoped he would either employ Shakeshafte and Gillom or 'help them find a good master'.

Alexander Hoghton's will, it is now claimed, is the key to those missing years in Shakespeare's life. Many scholars now believe that Shakeshafte was the seventeen-year-old Shakespeare. His last Stratford schoolmaster, John Cottam, was a Hoghton man, and, it is argued, might perhaps have recommended his former pupil to the Hoghtons as a private tutor. Some authorities have gone further and imagined young Shakespeare being recruited by the Campion mission from among the sons of Catholic gentlefolk, and going up north to be trained as one of the spearheads of the next generation.

Far-fetched as this may seem, there are certainly some curious coincidences in this tale. Shakespeare's trustee and backer at the Globe nearly twenty years later, Thomas Savage, was also from this part of Lancashire and his wife was a Hesketh; so the Shakespeare connection may not be pure fantasy. But was Shakeshafte Shakespeare? Shakeshafte was, and still is, a very common name in Lancashire – the Preston guild records are full of them in that year of 1580–1, one John Shakeshafte even being a glover. On the face of it, then, a man in a Hoghton will bearing a Preston name ought to be a local and with that, hard evidence for the young Shakespeare's Lancashire connection evaporates. On this, as on numerous other details of Shakespeare's early biography, the jury is still out.

But on the immediate events in his life at this moment there is no doubt; at the end of August or early September 1582 he reached a turning point. Another young Stratford man, the Jesuit Robert Debdale, was still in prison in London, where his father had sent him food parcels – 'two cheeses, a loaf of bread and five shillings in money' – via William Greenaway, the Stratford carrier. But three weeks later he was discharged – maybe the terrified youth had offered to take Protestant communion – and he was able to come home to Shottery, in time for a wedding.

CHAPTER FIVE

Marriage and Children

LOVE, THE MOST POWERFUL OF EMOTIONS

About a mile outside Stratford lies the hamlet of Shottery, in Shakespeare's day a pleasant walk from Henley Street through the marketplace and into Rother Street, from where a track led northwards to Shottery brook. Along the stream there are now allotments encroached on by a housing estate, but in the sixteenth century he would have passed through cornfields on either side before reaching a cluster of half-timbered thatched houses. The eighteen-year-old Shakespeare perhaps took that walk frequently during the summer of 1582. Back in Henley Street, William would have been sharing a room with his three younger brothers. As with all teenage boys, no doubt his thoughts were on love and sex – and in particular on a woman from Shottery eight years older than himself. As the popular song of the day went, youth is the time for love, and it goes fast away.

One of the houses there, with a garden and a fine apple orchard, belonged to the family of Richard Hathaway, a husbandman and sheep farmer who had sold fleeces to Shakespeare's father. Richard, a widower, had died the previous summer, leaving a daughter, Anne, and her brother, Bartholomew, who now shared the family home. It was a well-appointed place with good furniture, including two 'joyned beds' (four-posters); so, although pre-marital sex among the young usually took place in the open air in those days, the Hathaway home must have been especially attractive to William and the mistress of the house. Towards harvest time, in late August or early September, Anne became pregnant.

ABOVE: *The Hathaway house in Shottery, where the family lived until the nineteenth century. It still contains Tudor furniture, including perhaps William and Anne's marital bed.*

'A DALLIANCE AND BUT A TOUCH OF YOUTH'

It was a common story. It is estimated that a third of all Tudor women were pregnant when they married. The records of the church courts, the so-called bawdy courts, show that extra-marital sex took place at every level of society: our permissive age has nothing on the Elizabethans. Official homilies against 'whoredom and uncleanliness' were read on Sundays in every parish church when there was no sermon. Puritans and stricter Protestants, of course, railed against it particularly vehemently: 'Great swarms of vice,' spluttered one homilist, 'outrageous seas of adultery, whoredom, fornications and uncleanliness have overflowed the whole world, so much so that this vice among many is

counted no sin at all, but rather a pastime, a dalliance and but a touch of youth; not rebuked but winked at; not punished but laughed at.'

So although William and Anne may already have held hands in front of their relatives in his father's parlour, and spoken the beautiful words of the troth plighting, 'foresaking other friends' for each other, it is just as likely that their affair was 'a touch of youth'. Later diaries suggest that to avoid conception, 'mutual pleasuring' among the young did not always go as far as full intercourse. Younger girls often wouldn't have sex unless the man had plighted his troth; and sex was thus more likely to be forthcoming from an older, more experienced woman. Anne was not exactly on the shelf at twenty-six, which was around the average marriage age for women in Tudor England; but perhaps her age was becoming a cause for concern in a rural community where they tended to marry a little younger. As for William, though, at eighteen he was still a minor and would need his parents' permission to marry.

The Riddle of the Marriage

The couple didn't make any move in that direction, however, until the very end of November. Church law forbade marriage between Advent Sunday (which was 2 December in 1582) and mid-January, by which time Anne would be heavily pregnant. At the very last minute, then, on 27 November, two of her father's farmer friends, presumably taking William with them, rode to Worcester to apply for a special marriage licence from the consistory court. The episcopal archive in Worcester still preserves a note of the licence (but not the licence itself) and the marriage bond. These two documents are as intriguing as any in the poet's story.

The special licence gives Shakespeare's name correctly, but names his bride as Anne *Whately*; and it also says she was resident not in Stratford but in Temple Grafton, four miles to the west. The second document, dated the 28th, is the bond entered by the two farmers from Shottery, John Richardson and Fulk Sandells. It states that William Shakespeare was marrying Anne *Hathwey*, and that the couple were both of Stratford. Now we know that Shakespeare's wife was called Anne Hathaway and came from Shottery, which was indeed part of the parish of Stratford; but how to explain the other name for the bride? Over the years a huge industry has been generated by these admittedly confusing entries. Some authorities have even suggested that Anne Whately was the girl William had really wanted to marry, but, with the other Anne pregnant, his hand had been forced. Sadly, however, Anne Whately seems simply to have been the product of a scribal slip by an overworked clerk who had been dealing with a long-running case involving another Whately on the same day.

Once that is accepted, a story emerges. Clearly there was a rush to obtain the licence and have the marriage banns read out in double-quick time. Usually three readings of the banns, on Sundays or holy days in succeeding weeks, were stipulated. But the only valid day for marriage left now was St Andrew's Day, 30 November, the Friday before Advent Sunday when the marriage season closed. That was why they had gone to Worcester on the Tuesday with the paperwork, which would have included Shakespeare's parents' permission and an 'allegation' giving the bride and groom's addresses and their reasons for seeking a special licence.

But was the couple's haste the only reason for the special licence? The law obliged them to marry in one or other of their home parishes. Both parties came from the parish of Stratford, but chose not to marry there, so the licence was needed for that reason too. Interestingly enough, a later memorandum by Bishop Whitgift, in

ABOVE: *Is this Anne Hathaway? A 1708 sketch from a Tudor portrait.*
RIGHT: *A seventeenth-century marriage bowl. To some, wedlock was a fall; to the philosopher John Case it was an equal partnership rooted in Christian-Platonic love – a recurring debate in many of Shakespeare's plays.*

whose name Shakespeare's marriage licence was issued, justified the solemnization of marriages in a different parish on grounds that included 'reasonable secrecy' – for example, if the families wanted a quiet wedding because the bride was pregnant, because there was a difference in social status between bride and groom, or because they simply wanted to save money. What, then, of the bride's place of residence as given in the licence – Temple Grafton? Marriage allegations that have survived in other parts of the country give the domicile of both bride and groom, which suggests that Temple Grafton was not a slip. Anne was either living there at the time (was it her mother's village?) or had chosen to stay there for fifteen days to fulfil the necessary conditions of marrying in another parish (a rule that still applies today).

'An Old Priest and Unsound in Religion'

So why Temple Grafton and not their own parish church? Was this an instance of Bishop Whitgift's 'reasonable secrecy'? Perhaps one or both of the parties did not want to make a fuss because the bride was pregnant; perhaps the Shakespeares even considered the marriage a social mismatch, although this is less likely. But there are other kinds of secrecy, too. On the face of it, Anne and William seem to have gone to some length to avoid marrying in Stratford, where the vicar at that time, Henry Haycroft, was a strong Protestant. His counterpart in Temple Grafton, however, crops up in a government spy's report written four years after Shakespeare's wedding, and clearly he was a very different kettle of fish: 'John Frith vicar an old priest and Unsound in religion, he can neither preach nor read well, his chiefest trade is to cure hawkes that are hurt or diseased, for which purpose many do usually repair to him.'

So 'Sir' John Frith was an old priest from Queen Mary's time, a man who had been a vicar in the days of Catholic England nearly thirty years before. Still accused by informers of papistry, he was typical of the rural Warwickshire clergy we have already encountered: men who stayed loyal to their flock, baptizing, marrying and burying them according to the old rituals if so desired; taking some elements of the Protestant Church on board but still holding on to traditions, such as churching new mothers and praying for the dead.

In the copious archives of the Elizabethan state there is more on Frith. For example, he witnessed, and probably wrote, the will of Richard Smart of Luddington, a Catholic who in 1571 bequeathed his soul 'unto almighty God and to all the company of heaven'. And most pointedly, only two years before Anne and William's wedding, Frith had been reported for solemnizing marriages illicitly outside the times laid down by the Protestant Church and without proper reading of the banns. So there must be a strong suspicion that Frith was

resorted to because he bent the rules and performed the old ceremonies. Anne and William – or more likely their families – probably wanted a marriage in the traditional English style, ending with a Roman mass.

Shakespeare's First Poem?

So after Shakespeare, Richardson and Sandells got back to Stratford there was only the one day left for reading the banns: St Andrew's Day. As it happens, Temple Grafton church is dedicated to St Andrew, a saint who traditionally protected unmarried women and especially those who hoped to become mothers; an old country superstition asserted that if a woman prayed to him and slept naked on St Andrew's Eve she would see her future husband in a dream.

Most likely the banns were read out by Frith just once at the church door that Friday, and the wedding ceremony took place the same day. There is no surviving record, for the early parish registers of Temple Grafton have been lost. But there is one tantalizing clue. Nearly thirty years later, in 1609, Shakespeare, now a famous writer in London, published a collection of sonnets describing his passionate relationship with a beautiful young man, and his obsessive sexual desire for a woman who was not his wife. Near the end he slipped in a poem so juvenile that until recently scholars refused to believe it was by him. But, intriguingly, in the penultimate line, it seems to contain a pun on his wife's surname:

> Those lips that Love's own hand did make
> Breath'd forth the sound that said, 'I hate,'
> To me that languish'd for her sake:
> But when she saw my woeful state,
> Straight in her heart did mercy come,
> Chiding that tongue, that ever sweet
> Was used in giving gentle doom;
> And taught it thus anew to greet:
> 'I hate' she alter'd with an end
> That follow'd it as gentle day
> Doth follow night, who like a fiend
> From heaven to hell is flown away.
>   'I hate' from hate away she threw,
>   And sav'd my life, saying 'not you.'

The pun depends on the Warwickshire pronunciation of Hathaway. In the last line, the listener might also have also heard 'Anne saved my life'. The poem is

not very good, but there is growing consensus that William composed it for his marriage day and that it is his earliest surviving work. If this is so, it reveals something more at this time about Shakespeare the poet as well as the lover. For the teenager had obviously read Thomas Watson's collection of sonnets, *Hecatompathia or The Passionate Century of Love*, which had been published only that year. Watson, who had Warwickshire connections, wrote the book partly as a model of metrical form: a teaching manual for aspiring poets, a 'perfectly pathetical' reference book of Petrarchan themes (that is, as first developed by the medieval Italian poet Petrarch). Watson's sonnets demonstrated the different ways of prettifying classical history and myth in extended conceits. And in his hyperbolical complication of thought, his self-conscious exaggeration of emotion, he set a tone for the sonnet boom of the next twenty years. These were songs for Elizabethan lovers: 'If 't be not love I feel, what is it then? If love it be, what kind of thing is love?'

So young Shakespeare was already ambitious to be a versifier. He had bought or borrowed Watson's book and, like any young lover, he used it to sonnet his lady love. Did the nervous teenage groom recite it to his pregnant new wife at the marriage feast in Henley Street, over the fruit pies and gamebirds and country ale? He would write better, more powerfully, more passionately, about others – both men and women – apparently in an autobiographical way. But there is no more touching or personal poem in all his works.

There is one other point to make about this first surviving work, and it concerns the strange prickle in the second line: the use of the words 'I hate'. Similar jokes by the despised lover appear in Watson. But had Anne rejected William at first? The conundrums of their marriage have given rise to endless speculation ever since: the birth of their last children when William was only twenty-one (why no more?), the lives spent apart (why did they not live together?), the curt and enigmatic bequest in the poet's will (why no affectionate word?). But one can never judge a relationship from the outside. William was eighteen, his innocence lost, his father ruined. He was vulnerable. Anne was twenty-six and knew the world. Reading between the lines, she would be the rock on which he relied through his life, supporting his career in London. Perhaps he really did mean that she had 'sav'd my life'. Years later, those words stood when he published the poem. And later still Anne would desire to be buried with him. Perhaps that poem is the key to the mystery of their marriage.

Be that as it may, a shotgun wedding is perhaps not the best start to married life. In those days, too, for a man, marriage precluded going to university or even taking up an apprenticeship to learn a trade. It was probably not what William's father would have wished for his eldest son.

ABOVE: *The Arden-Somerville Plot. Somerville is arrested (left) and strangles himself in prison (right). The plot touched Shakespeare's family, but William remained proud of his Arden links and he was friends with Somerville's brother in later life.*

TERROR STRIKES THE FAMILY: THE SOMERVILLE PLOT

In May 1583 William and Anne's first child was born. They christened her Susanna. Anne and her baby presumably lived with John and Mary and William's younger brothers and sister, all together under one roof in the Henley Street house. With John nervous of ambush by enemies, creditors and informers, it cannot have been easy, although Tudor people were much less demanding of privacy and personal space than we are today.

That autumn, less than a year into their marriage, the atmosphere in the crowded household took another turn for the worse. Important national events now began to unfold which would affect a number of leading Warwickshire people, including the family's own kinsmen, in a gruesome and terrible manner. Around this time, the government began to receive 'informations' about an alleged Catholic plot against Elizabeth, linked, it was rumoured, with the Throgmorton family who lived close to Stratford. In an increasingly paranoid atmosphere informers and spies were everywhere, and loose words were seized upon. On 25 October a young man called John Somerville from the village of Edstone, near Stratford, was apprehended in a roadside inn at Aynho, between

Banbury and Bicester on the road to London. It was alleged, incredible as it may seem, that he had waved a gun about, declaring that it was Queen Elizabeth who was the real heretic, that it was her head that should be stuck on a spike on London Bridge. Somerville, it was asserted, had then declared that he intended to assassinate her. Whether this unlikely scene ever took place has been doubted, and the opinion at the time was that Somerville was in any case mentally ill. Somerville's father-in-law, however, was none other than Edward Arden, the head of Shakespeare's mother's family.

Arden, of course, was a prominent Catholic who kept a priest disguised as a gardener and was rumoured to have sheltered members of Campion's mission. He had enemies, especially Robert Dudley, the Earl of Leicester. Dudley, suave and handsome, was one of the new men in Elizabeth's body politic: if the queen loved anyone, it was Dudley. But he was hated by the old community of Warwickshire. Back in 1575, when Elizabeth had visited Kenilworth, Arden had publicly insulted Dudley. Now Somerville had given him and his local allies a chance to crush Arden and his friend and relative Robert Throgmorton.

On 31 October a warrant was issued for the apprehension of 'such as shall be in any way kin to all touched, and to search their houses'. On 2 November the clerk to the Privy Council, Thomas Wilkes, arrived at Thomas Lucy's house at Charlecote, just outside Stratford, which he would use as his base for the next fifteen days. The next day Wilkes and Lucy, accompanied by Lucy's retainers, mounted an armed raid on the Ardens' house 20 miles away at Park Hall.

Although well known in Elizabeth's time – it is marked on Saxton's 1575 map of Warwickshire – the site of Park Hall has vanished from today's maps. Where the M6 motorway skirts the industrial landscape northeast of Birmingham, a little belt of countryside appears around Coleshill Hall and Water Orton. Then the motorway curves westwards into the valley of the river Tame, and a strip of woodland can be seen above the river. This is Park Hall Wood. The site of the house lies in the flood plain between the M6 and the railway, where a huge sewage works now straddles the river. A stony track winds down a 100-foot escarpment into a narrow strip of water meadow. Arden's house was still standing, though derelict, in the 1960s and was only demolished at the end of the twentieth century. The site is now overlooked by huge electricity pylons beyond which high-speed trains compete with the incessant roar of the motorway.

Richard Chattock, a local man who knew the place in the 1820s, described the house as 'a fine old residence which could not be surpassed for beauty and

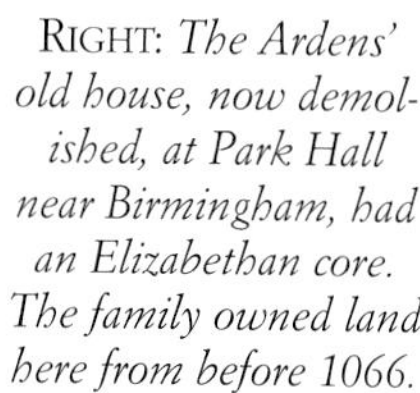

Right: *The Ardens' old house, now demolished, at Park Hall near Birmingham, had an Elizabethan core. The family owned land here from before 1066.*

romantic interest ... the hill opposite studded with wild cherries, roses and honeysuckle. The river as clear as crystal, ran by the garden wall below woods which were then filled with gigantic oak, beech, ash, and fir, completely overhanging and darkening the stream.' His family had lived in the hamlet of Park Hall before the sixteenth century, and he records a family tradition that Shakespeare stayed there. Old photographs show a pretty brick farmhouse, its windows and gables modified in the eighteenth century but with a Tudor core. All that remains now, below the motorway and the wood, is an overgrown heap of debris, a cluster of ancient fruit trees, and the traces of a large walled garden with the tell-tale signs of thin, flat Tudor bricks.

The Ardens had lived here since the eleventh century and had distinguished themselves in the Wars of the Roses, but they belonged to the Old Religion, and since the Reformation had become objects of deep suspicion. In the shifting politics of Elizabeth's reign, newcomers like Dudley were ranged against old families like the Ardens. The Ardens were doubly vulnerable now because of their links to the great Catholic family of the Throgmortons. Edward Arden had been a ward of the Throgmorton family as a child and had married their daughter Mary. It was this link that proved fatal, for the agents of the Secretary of State Sir Francis Walsingham were tracking the movements of Francis Throgmorton, the alleged instigator of another plot in these paranoid

times, when they heard the story of Somerville's boast of wanting to kill the queen. That was enough for the government, and it doomed Edward Arden.

A Tower Diary

Somerville was taken to the Tower of London, and a diary written by a priest imprisoned there captures the tension and fear of the time: '30 October. John Somerville, lay gentleman, son-in-law of that famous man Edward Arden, as he was a Catholic, was thrown into the Tower accused of plotting to kill the queen.' Arden was indicted at Warwick and escorted to London by Henry Rogers, the town clerk of Stratford, with 'seven or eight boxes of evidences'. (His accommodation bills survive: as in all authoritarian states, the Elizabethan government was a stickler for detail.) The Tower diary's next entry shows how the government was working to connect Arden and Somerville with the alleged Throgmorton plot: 'Francis Throgmorton a famous and richly endowed young man was arrested and accused of plotting on behalf of the Queen of Scots and was placed into the torture chamber called Little Ease on the first day'; this was a stone box so cramped that its occupant could neither stand up nor lie down. A week later Arden's wife Mary, their daughter Margaret and Somerville's sister were all thrown into the Tower along with Throgmorton's brother George.

Meanwhile, in Warwickshire, government agents raided the Somervilles' house at Edstone; Bushwood, the home of the Catesbys; Shelfield Lodge in Rowington, where the Skinners lived; the home of the Grants – John Shakespeare's business partners, who were linked by marriage to the Somervilles – near Snitterfield; and the house at Idlicote belonging to the Underhills, an old recusant family from whom Shakespeare would buy his own house, New Place, in 1597. At the Underhills' house Arden's priest, Hugh Hall, was arrested.

But the government found it hard to pin anything on Arden. On 7 November Thomas Wilkes wrote from Charlecote to Walsingham: 'Unless you can make Somerville, Arden, Hall the priest, Somerville's wife and his sister, to speak directly to those things which you desire to have discovered, it will not be possible for us here to find out more than is found already, for that the papists in this country greatly do work upon the advantage of clearing their houses of all shows of suspicion.'

Purge in Warwickshire

The atmosphere of those days is dramatically revealed by the records of interrogations in Warwick, where Lucy was a justice of the peace and Dudley the most powerful figure. The town clerk's book, which is still preserved by Warwick Town Council, shows that on 1 November, the day after the warrants were

issued, several strangers were arrested, including a sawyer from Preston in Lancashire, a man called Robert Chadborne, who under questioning revealed he had not been to Protestant church for several years. What follows crystallizes the battle of conscience faced by many people at that time:

> And being asked why he would not come to the church he saith it was because his father and mother brought him up in the time of King Henry the Eighth and then there was another order. And he mindeth to observe that order and to serve the Lord God above all things.
>
> Being asked what is in the church that he mislikith … he praith the hearers to pardon him for he will say no more.
>
> Being demanded whither the queen's majesty ought to be obeyed in those laws that she makith … as well in matters ecclesiastical as temporal, he answereth that first he is afraid to displease god above all things. And then afraide to displease his mighty prince.
>
> Being demanded whither the order set down and agreed upon and commanded by the queen's majesty to be and that is now commonly used in the Church of England is according to god's institution, or as it ought to be, he answereth that it is against his conscience.
>
> Being offered to be set at liberty upon condition that he will this night go to the church and report to the church in the time of divine service and sermons upon the Sabbath and holy days, he utterly refusith it and will not do it.

The Execution of Edward Arden

While government agents and town clerks feverishly searched and questioned in Warwickshire, in London the interrogation of the Ardens and Somerville continued. The accelerating momentum of the tragedy comes out grippingly in the Tower diary, which was now being written in cipher, for this was dangerous stuff: '13 November Francis Throgmorton arrived in the Tower.' On the 18th Walsingham sent a note to Wilkes asking him to come 'to witness the racking of Francis Throgmorton'. Five days later the diary noted: 'Francis Throgmorton severely tormented on the rack and cast into the Pit in the same day.' (This was a disused well-shaft under the White Tower.) 'On the same day Edward Arden was also subjected to the rack.' The diary continues: '24th Hugh Hall priest also tortured on the rack … 2nd December Francis Throgmorton again subjected to the rack, twice in the same day.' (Finally tried in 1584, he would be hanged, drawn and quartered.)

Events now moved with a terrible inevitability. On the 16th Arden, Somerville, Hall and Mary, Arden's wife, were tried at the Guildhall in London and sentenced to death. Mary was to be hanged and burned, but was then reprieved. For the men, however, there was no reprieve. On the evening of the 19th they were moved to Newgate ready for execution, but within two hours Somerville was allegedly found dead in his cell, as the Tower diary explained: 'John Somerville, who was hardly of sane mind, was transferred to another prison and the following night was found strangled in his prison cell whether by his own hand or by others was not established.' The last diary entry that year runs: '20 December. Edward Arden was led to the scaffold and there hanged, protesting his innocence of that of which he was accused and claiming that his real crime was profession of the Catholic faith, with his usual high spirit, protesting to the last his innocence of anything save of being a Catholic.'

ABOVE: *The spymaster Francis Walsingham, Elizabeth's Secretary of State. External threats led to a war against the enemy within. Control of drama was crucial: Walsingham founded the Queen's Men in 1583 as a propaganda tool.*

The brevity spares us the full horror. Following custom, Arden was dragged on a hurdle behind horses from Newgate through the waking city to the place of execution at Smithfield. Capital punishment in the Elizabethan state was long drawn out, savage, humiliating and very public. When sentenced, you were told by the judge to prepare to be 'hanged by the neck, and being alive cut down, and your privy members to be cut off, and your bowels to be taken out of your belly and there burned, you being alive'. This meant they would castrate and disembowel you while you were still alive, burning your insides before your own eyes. Then your heart would be cut out and displayed to the crowd, before your body was carved up with a butcher's knife. To send a message to the people, this theatre of cruelty took place on a public stage, often in a market or meeting place, such as Tyburn, Smithfield, Cheapside or St Giles.

Arden's end sent shock waves through the Catholic community, especially in Warwickshire, where for sixty years tales persisted that he had been framed, and had only been killed because he was a leading Catholic in the shire and an enemy of Dudley. Circumstantial stories of how Arden was trapped came down

to William Dugdale, the great seventeenth-century historian of Warwickshire, who concluded:

> The woefull end of this gentleman, who was drawne in by the cunning of the priest, and cast by his testimony, was commonly imputed to Leicester's malice. For certaine it is that he had incurred Leicester's heavie displeasure, and not without cause, against whom he had rashly opposed himself in all he could, had reproached him as an adulterer, and detracted him as an upstart.

'Search Their Houses'

Throughout December 1583 and January 1584 Thomas Lucy's investigation of the Arden–Somerville plot widened to the villages north of Stratford: Lapworth, Baddesley Clinton and Rowington. In the Public Record Office are preserved state papers detailing, for example, the interrogations of the leading Catholic family in Rowington, the Skinners, who were believed to have sheltered priests on the Campion mission and since. Among those questioned were house servants, the vicar, the village clerk, the tanner, the old schoolmaster at the nearby grammar school at Solihull, and several local farmers who were 'suspected to be papists, friends of Mr Skinner'. The old order in the countryside outside Stratford was still in place.

Out of these interviews came the stuff of the Privy Council's nightmares: confessions about the sheltering of priests, a defence of Mary Queen of Scots' title, denials of Elizabeth's supremacy and talk of the 'trewe succession'. There were tales of masses said in house and garden, of Latin books and secret schoolmasters. One telling piece in direct speech in a Midlands accent underlines the difficulty that Lucy experienced in getting anywhere with straightforward interrogation: 'this is our religion here amongst us, and therefore if yow will know anything of our secret yow must wring it from us by another means than by oaths, or else yow shall know very little'. Skinner himself, a 'deadly enemy to the gospel these twenty years' according to informers, was dogged and cunning; it was said he had 'great friends and money' and was reported to be 'in good hope that religion wold turne or else that there wolde be a decree that every man shoold live as he list'. 'Thou are a fool to think this religion is the truth,' Skinner had said; given a choice, 'thinkest thou how many would come to church? Less than ten in our parish.' Astonishing given the date, but it may well have been true.

Such, then, was the political and religious climate in this part of Warwickshire when the newly married Shakespeare was nineteen. But was the

family itself touched? Did Lucy and his men search the house in Henley Street? Arden's trial had been preceded by raids on many Warwickshire Catholics' homes, but especially on the kinsmen of the Ardens. The instructions from London to Wilkes and Lucy were that they should 'apprehend such as shall be in any way akin to all touched, and to *search their houses*'. William was a distant kinsman of Edward Arden, but Tudor families were much more aware of their extended family than we are today. Arden and he shared a great-great-grandfather, and the Shakespeares' later submission to the College of Arms reveals that William and his parents were proud of the connection. He would, then, have seen himself as Arden's 'cousin'. And as John Shakespeare, a former mayor of the town, was actually married to an Arden, this made the family an obvious target, especially perhaps given John's surety case three years earlier. Operating with Wilkes from the Privy Council, it would have been Sir Thomas Lucy who was responsible for enforcing any search.

In the Stratford district Henry Rogers, town clerk and Lucy's agent, assisted these two in their search for 'books and writings' of an incriminating character – for which services Rogers was later paid sixty shillings from the government purse. If the house in Henley Street was indeed searched, it was perhaps at this point that John Shakespeare felt he must get rid of the incriminating testament he had received from Persons. But as he had promised to keep it with him and not destroy it, perhaps it is not too fanciful to conjecture that John hid the booklet in the eaves of his house, where, with its startling profession of undying loyalty to the old ways, it was found in the eighteenth century.

Conscience and Power

So before the poet was out of his teens the state's machine of terror and the taint of treason had touched his family. And the cost of conscience was all too plain in the spectacle of their kinsman's tarred head displayed, as was the grim custom, on London Bridge, and his quarters on the gates of Warwickshire towns. Next summer there would be more searches as Cecil retrospectively tried to prove there really had been a plot. Following up the patterns of kinship and friendship, and the whispers of informers, the government now searched suspected houses in London. Printers too were investigated for 'books tending to papistry': at the house of Gabriel Cawood, a printer of well-known Catholic sympathies, a son of Edward Arden was detained. On the same day, during a search of Southampton House in the Strand (the London home of the Catholic earl whose son would later be Shakespeare's patron), one Robert Arden was found, 'who had likewise been lately imprisoned'.

The move against printers was inevitable. On the eve of Arden's execution the government had felt the need to publish a propaganda justification of their treatment of such plots, Cecil's *On the Execution of Justice in England*. But such was its bias that it provoked a pamphlet war, with rebuttals rolling off secret presses in England and coming in from abroad. The ironical *Leicester's Commonwealth*, published abroad the following year, broadcast incriminating gossip against Dudley. Then, from Douai, William Allen offered his *True Sincere and Modest Defence of the English Catholics*, which included a character sketch of Arden, a detailed refutation of the charges against him and bitter allegations over 'certain shameful practises about the condemnation and making away of the worshipful, valiant, and innocent gentleman, M. Arden ... which brought him to his pitiful end, to the great regret of the whole nation'.

There is a strange Shakespearean footnote to the Somerville Plot. In his plays Shakespeare often drops in the names of real people, which perhaps only he would ever notice. All writers do this: Dickens, for instance, uses an amazing plethora of names from real life for his minor characters. But Shakespeare's choices sometimes seem uncannily pointed. Bardolph and Fluellen, for example, in *Henry V* are both Stratford names which appear on the 1592 recusant list with his father. Another example occurs in one of his earliest plays, *Henry VI* Part 2. The mayor of Coventry is standing on the city walls with the Earl of Warwick, who doesn't know that it is a two-hour march from Southam to Coventry. Shakespeare then brings on a character who provides one of those snippets of local Warwickshire detail that sometimes crop up in the plays. Warwick looks in the wrong direction for his enemy Clarence, and is corrected:

> It is not his, my lord. Here Southam lies.
> The drum your honour hears marcheth from Warwick.

The character has no other role in the play. The name Shakespeare gives him is John Somerville.

CHAPTER SIX

The Lost Years

FATE WILL FIND A WAY

Now the trail goes cold. This is the time when the aspiring teenage poet became a skilled playwright, who ten years later would suddenly appear as a star on the scene in London. But how did Shakespeare do it? These have become known as the 'lost years', a time whose opacity has only added fuel to the fantasies and conspiracy theories that have come to surround his life. Frustratingly, between his marriage in 1582 and his first definite mention in the London theatre in 1592, the only sure evidence of his continued existence is the baptism records of his children and a court case of September 1587, when he and his parents tried to recover their lost inheritance in Wilmcote. No wonder there is a Shakespeare mystery!

THE TWINS ARE BORN

Around Easter 1584 Anne became pregnant again. The twins were christened in Holy Trinity Church, Stratford on 2 February 1585, and named after their neighbours Hamnet and Judith Sadler, old Catholics who presumably were the godparents. Twins, of course, are special children, and Shakespeare would put twins into his plays – they appear in *Twelfth Night*, for example, and, bewilderingly, there are two sets in *The Comedy of Errors*.

Why, though, did he and Anne have no more children? The English middle class were tending to have smaller families in his time, but still, only two births is unusual in a sixteenth-century family. Anne was nearly thirty – but not beyond child-bearing age by any means. Had giving birth to the twins caused

her gynaecological problems? Or did the physical side of their marriage soon die away?

The Poaching Myth

As for what happened next, and when and why Shakespeare left Stratford, myths abound. But, as we have already seen in this story, myths have a knack of proving true. So let's start the 'lost years' with the myth.

The story told around Stratford since the seventeenth century goes like this. Shakespeare was driven away from his home town by the enmity of Sir Thomas Lucy of Charlecote, who had been active in the government interest against Edmund Campion and the Somerville Plot. Their enmity began, so it was said, with William poaching Lucy's deer and rabbits, for which he was beaten and thrown into prison. To get his own back, Shakespeare penned a bitter satirical ballad full of personal insults, which he stuck up on Lucy's front gate. That was the final straw and William was forced to leave town.

These days the poaching story is dismissed out of hand. But the story comes in no fewer than three seventeenth-century versions, which suggests that it should be taken more seriously. There is no question that the family would have known Lucy: an important landowner and JP, he would on occasion have been entertained by Stratford borough officials with the customary pint of sack. And John Shakespeare rented Ingon meadow in Hampton Lucy parish, right next to Lucy's land.

BELOW: *This sixteenth-century tapestry depicts a rural hunting scene.*

But to be beaten just for poaching? The idea has been derided by scholars, but it is not totally implausible. In the sixteenth century the Lucys had no deer, but they did have coney warrens; and in the terrible conditions of the early 1580s, with famine and destitution across Warwickshire, people certainly poached. John Fisher's local stories from the Warwick town book, for example, include from the summer of 1581 an account of a case of rabbit poaching that led to a violent beating and a fracas in the streets of Warwick, after which the poachers were bonded to appear at the next general sessions of the peace in front of local magistrates, one of whom was Sir Thomas Lucy.

A local landowner called Brome had complained that a young man named Reynolds had, with two friends, poached 'three or four couple of coneys'. The tale he told the magistrates takes us right into a Warwickshire country

lane on a summer's night. Reynolds denied he had been on Brome's land but admitted the following, as Fisher records it:

> In a lane not farre from Mr Bromes ground he had pitchid his hey [trap] and killid conyes. And that being about to tak up his hey and conyes Mr Bromes man came leapeng over the hedge with a long staff and askid what they did there, and bycause they woold not go with him Mr Bromes man strake at him with his straff and strok him upon the hed that he fell to the ground and being downe beat him with many stripes. And Mr Bromes man having striken down Reynolds so as he could not stirre ran at another of Mr Grenes man And strok him downe also and beat them both and took away the conyes and the heye....

This is evidence from just the right time that physical violence could be meted out even over rabbits. But is such a tale really a likely cause of Shakespeare's quarrel with Lucy? Given what is now known about the background of the Shakespeare family, it is perhaps more to the point that Lucy was a JP and a Puritan, and that, in the dramatic events of 1583–4, as Elizabeth's local enforcer he had pursued Edward Arden to the scaffold and searched the houses of all Arden's kin in the neighbourhood.

Could there, then, be some truth, after all, in the tale that Lucy was the enemy of the Shakespeares – but for this much more serious cause? Where the poaching myth is concerned, it is interesting that two of the seventeenth-century sources say Shakespeare baited Lucy with a slanderous ballad, and insist that he was imprisoned for a time. Later tradition, of course, may have defused the religious and political element in the original events. Poaching and a little gentle satire, after all, could be put down to the exuberance of youth. But if the persecutions of 1583–4 were the real cause of their enmity, then perhaps the libelling of Lucy was of a more offensive nature. The Warwick quarter sessions for these years are missing, so we will never know for sure, but perhaps the poaching tale is another of those Shakespeare traditions that may contain a germ of truth after all.

A Year of Executions

The year after the twins were born was a crucial one in national politics. In this time of plotting and framing, conspiracy theories and religious hatred, 1586 was the year of the Babington Plot, which culminated in the execution of Mary Queen of Scots. The plot perhaps never really existed: the government was by now adept at setting traps to snare unwary and gullible Catholics in order to bring the disaffected out into the open. They used *agents provocateurs*, men

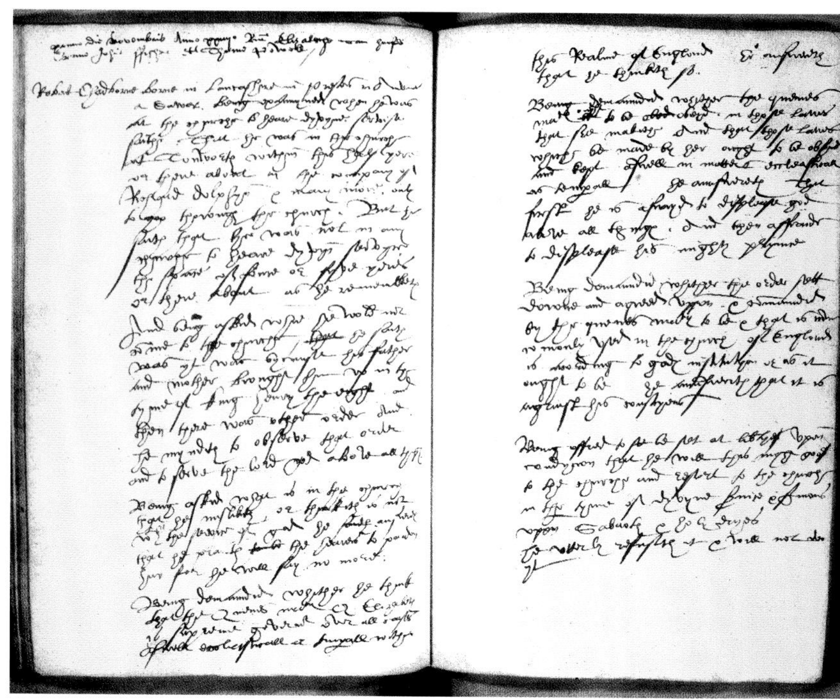

Right: *The book of John Fisher, the Warwick town clerk: a little-known source for the time of anxiety in the 1580s, which led to the execution of Mary Queen of Scots (below).*

rather like Shakespeare's Iago, who pretended to be one thing but were another, and watched as their victims were led to destruction, or even destroyed themselves. The most sinister was Robin Poley, who would later be involved in the murder of Shakespeare's fellow dramatist Christopher Marlowe. Poley was like a Cold War double agent in that no one – not even the government who paid him – ever knew for sure what he really was; whether, for example, he was Protestant or Catholic. He was simply 'like himself', as the priest and poet Robert Southwell memorably put it. Poley's was, it seems, a motiveless malignity. A truly Shakespearean villain, he perhaps just took pleasure in destroying people.

Elizabeth asked for a new and even more horrible way to kill the plotters to ensure that they endured the maximum suffering. But she was assured that, applied with skill, hanging, drawing and quartering would satisfy her on that score. The punishments were so cruelly applied to the victims of this latest sting that, in revulsion after the first few had been butchered, the crowd spontaneously called for the hangman to let them die on the rope before he cut them down.

News of the Babington Plot came back to Henley Street. The Jesuit priest Robert Debdale, Shakespeare's wife's former neighbour in Shottery, his mother's kinsman, and also, like Shakespeare, a former Stratford Grammar School boy, was captured and tortured in the aftermath. His contacts were interrogated, among them a serving girl called Sara Williams, a very touching personality, who revealed the story of the exorcisms conducted by Debdale at Denham in Buckinghamshire; years later her testimony was published verbatim, and would be carefully studied by Shakespeare when he was writing *King Lear* (see page 275).

The Babington plotters, it was claimed, had intended to murder Elizabeth and put Mary Queen of Scots on the throne in her stead. Mary was tried, and in December sentenced to death. In the fall-out from her trial lesser people were killed too, and this time Robert Debdale did not escape. Twenty-six years old, he was publicly executed in London on 21 December 1586 'as a seminary priest and practiser of magic' (that is, of exorcisms – a charge often made against Catholic priests). Debdale's body was quartered and the parts sent to be hung on the gates of provincial towns with placards detailing his crimes. Many among his friends and neighbours in Shottery and Stratford, people like the Hathaways, must have felt that a member of their community had been done to death only for his conscience.

The Old Order Changes

That same year, times were changing in Stratford. John Shakespeare finally lost his position as an alderman, along with John Wheeler, another old Catholic, because they 'doth not come to the halls when they be warned'. At the same

meeting Alderman William Smith also refused to serve any longer and left the corporation. So John's career as a prominent Stratford figure was over. Distraints on his goods followed, and not long afterwards John and Mary would describe themselves in a legal case as people of 'small wealth and very few friends and alliances'. For their eldest son, the attractions of Stratford and the crowded house in Henley Street (with his 'merry cheeked' father perhaps feeling more than a little embittered) must have seemed less and less appealing.

And at this time the atmosphere in south Warwickshire now began to change subtly. The mid-decade was a kind of watershed in the culture of the time; the old world was becoming more distant and new forces were beginning to take control, as they would do across much of the region by the 1590s. The old fabric of society was disintegrating. In Coventry, where the population had slumped by a half, street singers told of hard times in the 'Ballad of Nowadays', and the Puritans, new in power, were rooting out ungodliness and suppressing the old rituals that had once bound the community together. In a single parish, the Warwick clerk John Fisher counted nearly 250 adults and children in the almshouses and on parish aid; many of them were jobless itinerants who had often come from far afield. On the roads around Coventry, Warwick and Stratford that winter such people represented a cross-section of Elizabeth's England. Thomas Wilson, a thirty-year-old Yorkshireman, lived in Warwick with no wife and four children; his jobless teenagers, Tom and Peter, were reduced to begging. William Orchard, eighty, had no support and was unable to work. Anne Iseham, with only one leg, had to provide alone for her small child because her husband, Henry, had disappeared as 'a fugitive'. John Harbet and his wife, aged seventy, and their eighteen-year-old 'idiot' child were whipped and told to find a master. Roger Asplyn of Stratford was fifty and had no wife but four children: Robert, aged sixteen, Cycely (who was blind), fourteen, Ursula, twelve and Isabell, eleven; 'all the children do beg', said Fisher. All had been born in Stratford but had been driven out by the corporation. Roger was whipped, and with his four children sent back down the road to Stratford.

These were the kind of people and the kind of stories that Shakespeare would draw on in his works. They offer a snapshot of the dramatic changes that came over the English commonwealth at this time – the decline of the old order, social and psychological. The Reformation touched everything because it affected the core beliefs that made society tick, the glue that bonded society and maintained it. Even the massive medieval industry of organized civic charity was on the point of collapse. As Roger Asplyn and his four children trudged back towards Stratford in the rains of November 1586, a new age was dawning.

And for William? He was twenty-two now, and the family's main breadwinner. He had a wife and three children to support, in addition to his five siblings and his now ageing parents. If he had not already gone, it was time to do so.

THE MOMENT OF DEPARTURE

But when did Shakespeare leave Stratford? How did he join the theatre, and when and how did he get to London? Unfortunately there is no hard evidence; unless and until more documents come to light, we are likely to remain in the dark. These years were the key time in his development, but we have no idea where he was. It is assumed that Anne remained in Henley Street – but it is not even certain that she conceived the twins in Stratford. In reality William could have left his home town at any time after his marriage in 1582, and could have done a variety of jobs before he established himself in London, presumably at the end of the 1580s. It is only from 1592 that the chronology of his life starts to feel a little more secure.

But a few reasonable conjectures can be made. Shakespeare was twenty when the twins were born and baptized in Stratford. Four years or so later he was surely working in a professional theatre company, and very likely, though not certainly, in London. At some point, then, he had decided he wanted to be a poet. He had already learned to write verse; the marriage sonnet was a halting beginning, with its nod to the new fashions in poetry, but he must have written other verse, and maybe even plays. A late seventeenth-century visitor to Stratford heard a tale that he had gone to London for the first time 'as a serviture, in a very mean rank' in the theatre – a runner, a prompt boy, or an ostler holding horses for wealthier members of the audience. Although this is generally viewed as part of the myth, it is plausible. And he would have had plenty of opportunity to meet theatre companies in Stratford: Berkeley's Men and Leicester's Men performed there around this time; whilst Strange's Men, for whom he worked in his late twenties, did shows in nearby Coventry.

BELOW: *The baptism register of William's twins Hamnet and Judith, who were named after his Catholic neighbours, the Sadlers. In 1585 William had not abandoned the old social and religious loyalties of his family.*

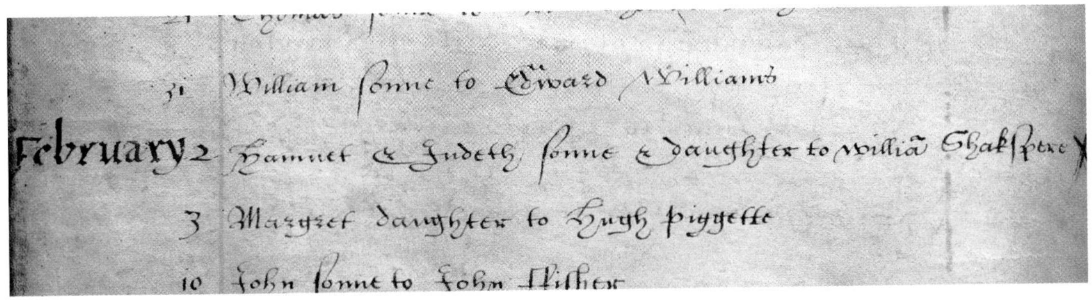

31 William sonne to Edward Williams
February 2 Hamnet & Judeth sonne & daughter to William Shakspere
3 Margret daughter to Hugh Piggette
10 John sonne to John Fisher

Those are possibilities, none of them mutually exclusive. But one theory stands out above the rest, and has recently become something more than mere hypothesis. It suggests that, aged around twenty-two, Shakespeare joined the leading company of the day, the Queen's Men.

A Murder in Thame

In mid-June 1587, in fine summer weather, the Queen's Men were on tour in Oxfordshire, rolling their wagon of props and costumes into the wool town of Thame on the old road to London. In Elizabeth's day, at the time of the sheep clip in June the place was packed with wool buyers and others; it was a good time to play, and it was visited by many travelling companies. The main street still has a long marketplace lined with big timber-framed houses. There were inns for travellers at the east end where the London road points towards the low green ridge of the Chilterns. Here the Queen's Men played on 13 June, in the late afternoon or early evening, in the yard of an inn called the White Hound.

The Queen's Men were the biggest draw of the time. There were riots in some towns when the crowds became too great for everyone to get in; local records note payments for broken benches and cracked windows in town halls across the Midlands when the Queen's Men came through. William Knell played their juvenile leads, such as Prince Henry in *The Famous Victories of Henry V*, the patriotic tale of the battle of Agincourt and the precursor of Shakespeare's play. Knell was remembered even thirty years later as a star of the generation of actors just before Richard Burbage and Edward Alleyn. He was young, physical and fiery – and he was certainly fiery that night in Thame. Perhaps he had been drinking after the show. Between nine and ten in the evening, so the Thame coroner's jury were told, Knell chased a fellow actor into the close behind the inn, raging in his fury and brandishing a sword. The tale is told in the deathless prose of the Elizabethan coroner:

> John Towne late of Shoreditch, yeoman, was in a close called White Hound in Thame when William Knell came and had in his right hand a sword and jumped upon John Towne intending to kill him. Towne in fear and despairing of his life and of the mutilation of his limbs by the aforesaid Knell, drew back to a certain mound of earth which he could neither cross nor ascend without peril of his life. William Knell continuing his attack as before, so maliciously and furiously, and Towne on the hillock, to save his life drew his sword of iron (price five shillings) and held it in his right hand and thrust it into the neck of William Knell and made a mortal wound three inches deep and one inch wide.

Within half an hour, as the midsummer sun set over Oxford and the last light faded from the sky, Knell's life ebbed away. And the next day, as the company headed on towards Abingdon and Stratford, where the town accounts show they played that year, they found themselves a man short.

It has long been noticed that Shakespeare had interesting connections with the Queen's Men. Some of them had previously been the Earl of Leicester's Men, based in Warwick; and among them was James Burbage, the key link in Shakespeare's professional career (James's son Richard would take the lead roles in his greatest plays). And after this 1587 tour one of the company, John Hemmings, married Knell's widow, Rebecca. Hemmings would be another life-long friend of Shakespeare's. A Droitwich man, chubby and stuttering, it would be Hemmings, along with Henry Condell, who would publish Shakespeare's plays after his death. So when the tale of Knell's murder was unearthed some years ago, the suggestion was made that Shakespeare was recruited at that time to replace him. It is a nice thought that the nucleus of the greatest acting company in the history of the theatre might have come about as a result of that night in Thame. But to work for such a prestigious company a young man must have had some kind of apprenticeship as an actor: they would hardly have hired an unknown. Shakespeare's connection with the Queen's Men, however, doesn't just rest on the shaky foundation of Knell's murder in Thame.

Shakespeare and the Queen's Men

The greatest performing art of its day, theatre was also the most political. The Queen's Men had been founded in 1583 as a deliberate act of policy, amalgamating the best players from other leading companies by none other than Sir Francis Walsingham, Elizabeth's spymaster – not for entertainment but for a political purpose. They were intended to spread Protestantism and royalist propaganda through a divided realm. Their repertory was to be based on English themes. The English history play, already present in the drama of the sixties and seventies, now came to prominence. Plays such as *The Famous Victories of Henry V*, *The True Tragedy of Richard III* and *The Troublesome Reign of King John* were Tudor royalist propaganda, strongly Protestant in tone, often virulently so. King John, for example, is built up as a national hero because he fought against the control of Rome. These kinds of story were put on stage because they could be presented as tragedies that were 'true' rather than 'poetical'. They were perceived as popular entertainment that people across the land would enjoy while being constantly reminded of the ideology of God, queen, Protestant Church and nation on which the government depended – an ideology that was being strongly pushed in schools and in church sermons in the

ABOVE: *The comic Richard Tarlton, with tabor and pipe. 'A wondrous plentiful pleasant extemporal wit', Tarlton drew packed crowds in town halls up and down the land; the queen herself was a fan.*

tense years overshadowed by the threat of Spanish invasion, which culminated in 1588 in the Armada.

The core of the Queen's Men had worked with James Burbage in Leicester's Men. Some were famous. Shakespeare's friend Thomas Heywood, for instance, remembered the best actors of the previous generation: John Bentley, William Knell, Tobias Mills, John Singer, Robert Wilson and, of course, the great clown Richard Tarlton, who became a legend with his comic routines, improvisations, dancing and fencing. As the stage keeper recalls in Ben Jonson's *Bartholomew Fair*: 'I kept the stage in Master Tarlton's time, I thanke my starres. Ho!, you should ha seene him ha' come in, and ha' beene coozened I' the Cloath–quarter, so finely And Adams, the Rogue, ha' leap'd and caper'd upon him ...'.

So the Queen's Men formed an important part of Shakespeare's dramatic upbringing; theirs were the hits of his early adulthood. And their shows had a big influence on him as a professional writer. Six or seven of his plays are closely related to the plots of the Queen's Men. His *King John* follows their *Troublesome Reign* almost scene for scene (although he took pains to defuse its anti-Catholic rhetoric); his *King Lear* and *Richard III* cover the same stories as their old *Leir* and their *True Tragedy of Richard III*. Shakespeare's sequence of plays on *Henry IV* and *Henry V* elaborates material used in their *Famous Victories*. His *Two Gentlemen of Verona* was perhaps also modelled on a lost Queen's Men play.

Of course, he could simply have got hold of their scripts through theatre contacts. But some people in the contemporary publishing industry were under the impression that he actually had a hand in writing them. Take the case of *The Troublesome Reign of King John*. The second edition of the play, published in 1611, put Shakespeare's initials on the title page, and the third, in 1622, gave his name in full. This might just have been an unscrupulous sales pitch, but no fewer than four separate publishers of Queen's Men material thought they were dealing with plays by Shakespeare. Maybe they knew something we don't. Perhaps Shakespeare really did have a hand in the Queen's Men's plays.

His connection with the Queen's Men's scripts, then, seems close and deep

– and early. So how did Shakespeare come to know them if not by acting in them? Or even by being involved as one of their group of scriptwriters? Not only did Shakespeare have an unusual and sustained knowledge of their plays, but there are no echoes of Shakespeare's mature style in their plays. Theirs came first. So did Shakespeare begin his career with them? These tantalizing hints for his first steps as a theatre professional are now beginning to add up to something more than a tale of murder in a small Oxfordshire town.

So his professional career might have begun as a jobbing actor and general dogsbody. Some years later Robert Greene (a Queen's Men scriptwriter) would attack Shakespeare as a 'jack of all trades' who had had the audacity to write blank verse of his own and, what is more, 'borrowing our plumes'. Maybe this is what happened. Throughout his career Shakespeare was a magpie who borrowed or stole as much as he could decently get away with. Perhaps he began as an actor, who then moved on to writing as a collaborator in a team, contributing here and there to the joint project, in the way most plays were written at that time. He was not yet a principal writer, like Wilson or Greene: that would only come when he had the confidence and experience to strike out on his own at the end of the 1580s.

Working for the Queen's Men, he would have had to write to their house style, a literal but forceful verse with jigging rhymes. Shakespeare at this stage would have subordinated his talents to their principal writers and actors, to the showmanship of Tarlton or the booming leads of Wilson. And, of course, as far as their anti-Catholic propaganda went, he would have had to keep his own feelings to himself.

The 'Lost Years' Found?

On this reading, then, Shakespeare could have been with the Queen's Men through the late eighties – perhaps even before they came to Stratford in 1587. They were above all a touring company, going as far as Scotland and Dublin. Through provincial town accounts their tour itineraries in those years can be traced. Some venues still survive: Leicester guildhall, the common halls in York and Norwich, Church House in Sherborne. They liked the prosperous towns of East Anglia and the south coast. In eight out of their first eleven seasons they toured the north, playing at the residences of big Lancashire families such as the Stanleys at Knowsley and New Park, and Lord Strange at Lathom – important stops on politically motivated tours. Even a theatre company could help Walsingham keep an eye on families whose loyalty was suspect. (And could that be how Shakespeare first made the Lancashire connection that would be important later in his career?)

The Queen's Men played Coventry and Stratford in the winter of 1587. After Christmas they entertained the queen at her palace in Greenwich, then went into Kent towards Easter and, as rumours grew of the impending Spanish invasion, they moved along the south coast town by town – Dover, Hythe, Romney, Lydd, Rye – entertaining packed houses with their patriotic 'true' histories. By early June they were in Lyme Regis, and in mid-June had reached Plymouth where they would have seen the watchers on the coast, the beacons readied and Drake's galleons patrolling off the Sound. The Armada was approaching. If Shakespeare was there that day, it must have been an exciting time to be with the main propaganda company. Some of their politics may have stuck in his throat; but for a young writer with ambition, what an apprenticeship.

BACK TO THE MYTH

The Queen's Men connection is intriguing and, if true, a revelation for our understanding of Shakespeare's early career. But of course this is a tale held together by a chain of conjectures: plausible, suggestive, but no more. Shakespeare's deep knowledge of their plays is clear, but as yet we cannot prove he was with the company. As so often with Shakespeare, we are left with ambiguity. The 'lost years' are, for the moment, still lost. But here again, the much derided Shakespeare traditions may be able to help us: his father's illicit wool dealing, the enmity with Lucy, even the poaching, have something in them. So before we follow him to London, with or without the Queen's Men, let's remember what the tradition says: that Shakespeare left Stratford as a young man and got a menial job in the London theatre, where he worked up from the bottom, starting off holding horses, or working as the prompt boy holding 'the book'. This story is not often taken seriously. But it is how things happen in real life.

Such breaks usually come about through personal contacts. And Shakespeare's primary relationships in the theatre through his entire professional life were with the Burbage family: James, the entrepreneur responsible for the first custom-built public theatre in the modern world in 1576; his sons Cuthbert, later the manager of the Globe, and Richard, the great actor. So how and where did they meet? Their earlier connection has never been discovered, but it could go back to Warwickshire. James Burbage is first found with Robert Dudley's players in Warwick, and, curiously enough, there were Burbages in Stratford: one of them was mayor in 1555. At Michaelmas 1588 the Court of Common Pleas in London heard a case between William Burbage of Stratford and John Shakespeare, the poet's father; it dragged on for four years until it was

arbitrated by John's old friends Nick Barnhurst and William Badger. Some time in or before 1582 John had leased to Burbage a house in Stratford, possibly in Greenhill Street, and subsequently they had fallen into disagreement about monies owed by John. It is at the least an interesting coincidence that a Burbage should have been a tenant of John Shakespeare at the very time when the myth says William went to London where he teamed up with James Burbage and his sons.

There is another strange twist to the story. Many years later, in December 1598, James Burbage and his men dismantled their Theatre in north London and removed its timbers from the property of their landlord. Present that night in the snow with Burbage and his workmen as they tore down the building was a friend 'of some fourteen years' called William Smith, a gentleman of Waltham Cross. By a strange coincidence an exact contemporary of Shakespeare's at Stratford was William Smith, who went to the University of Oxford, became a schoolmaster in Essex and is known to have lived in Waltham Cross in the 1580s. Smith's father William, haberdasher and alderman of Henley Street, was a friend of John Shakespeare, and perhaps the poet's godfather. Coincidences sometimes invite us to pay attention, and this is one of those instances. Is it too fanciful to imagine that young William Shakespeare's professional career might have begun in Stratford in 1584 with a deal over a table at Burbage's tavern in Bridge Street, with his godfather and James Burbage?

So the 'lost years' have involved a long search with many blind alleys – but none, I think, are fruitless. All are revealing about his times. For now, what we can say is this. At some point around the age of twenty, William decided he was going to be a poet. Whether he joined the Queen's Men, or whether he went straight to London and worked in menial jobs at Burbage's Theatre in Shoreditch (and he could of course have done both), at some point at the end of the 1580s he began to make his name in London as a writer. In the late eighties, around the time of the Armada, the old-fashioned and politically motivated Queen's Men would cease to be the cutting edge in the theatre. The focal point for ambitious artists became London itself, where a new kind of drama was emerging, whose writers and stars were bringing huge audiences into great wooden theatres that could hold up to 3000 people for a show. It was now open to a poet from the provinces to write the kind of dramas and the kind of verse he wanted. Everything we know suggests that around 1588–9 Shakespeare based himself in London. And there his talent immediately made its mark and he rapidly rose to fame.

CHAPTER SEVEN

London: Fame

Opportunity

On 17 November 1588 the church bells rang out as usual across the land for Queen Elizabeth's accession day, but this year's commemoration took on a new meaning with lavish public celebrations of the defeat of the Spanish Armada. This was the defining event that brought the religious conflicts of the previous thirty years of her reign into sharp focus. That summer the country had been under arms: beacons at the ready, watchers set up along the coasts. Even in towns far from the sea, such as Stratford, men were called up to fight. Along with their fellow countrymen, Stratford's recruits marched to the port of Tilbury, but they were not needed: the Armada had already lost the gun battles waged along the south coast from Plymouth to Kent. Then came the grim night when fireships were sent in to wreak havoc among the Spanish ships anchored off Gravelines, after which there was nothing left for the demoralized remnants but to attempt to return home the long way round the north of Britain, only to be battered to destruction on the rocks of Galway and Donegal. To loyal English Catholics, just as much as to the Protestant majority, the defeat of the Spanish invasion force was a deliverance, and it inaugurated a brief surge of optimism throughout the land.

So in London that morning the queen and all her councillors made their way down Cheapside to St Paul's for a particularly heartfelt service of thanksgiving. The day was bright, the rain held off, and the peals of the bells floating over the city were audible

Opposite: *The 'Armada portrait' of Elizabeth. Victory over Catholic Spain finally marked the triumph of the Protestant establishment.*

miles away. Arriving from the north of England or the Midlands at that time, heading for one of the northern gates, Aldersgate or Bishopsgate, the traveller would have seen London in all its splendour: a capital now fast on the way to becoming a world city.

The best view was from the windmills across Finsbury Fields. From here the eye could take in the entire three-mile stretch of the city from Westminster to St Leonard's Church in Shoreditch. And from this viewpoint an almost photographic panorama was drawn by an artist some time in the first few years of Shakespeare's theatrical career. If, as is thought, he arrived here from Stratford at this time, this is the London he would have seen.

Camera Obscura: A View of the City

Far away to the right, across the loop of the Thames at Lambeth, are the Surrey hills, and in the foreground the huge roof of Westminster Hall and the Abbey, finials and weathervanes glinting. In front of the Abbey lies the smart suburb of Westminster, with its royal buildings, grace and favour apartments, tennis courts and tilt yards. The wooden palings of the garden of Gray's Inn help to date the image: they were rebuilt in brick in the late 1590s. Closer still, travellers are moving out of Gray's Inn Road, and the covered wagons of long-distance carriers from Smithfield are setting out for the Midlands. A cluster of men are practising at archery butts; on Moorfields the stainers are laying out their dyeing frames, and laundry women are emptying their 'flaskets' and laying out their washing to dry on fields where cows graze.

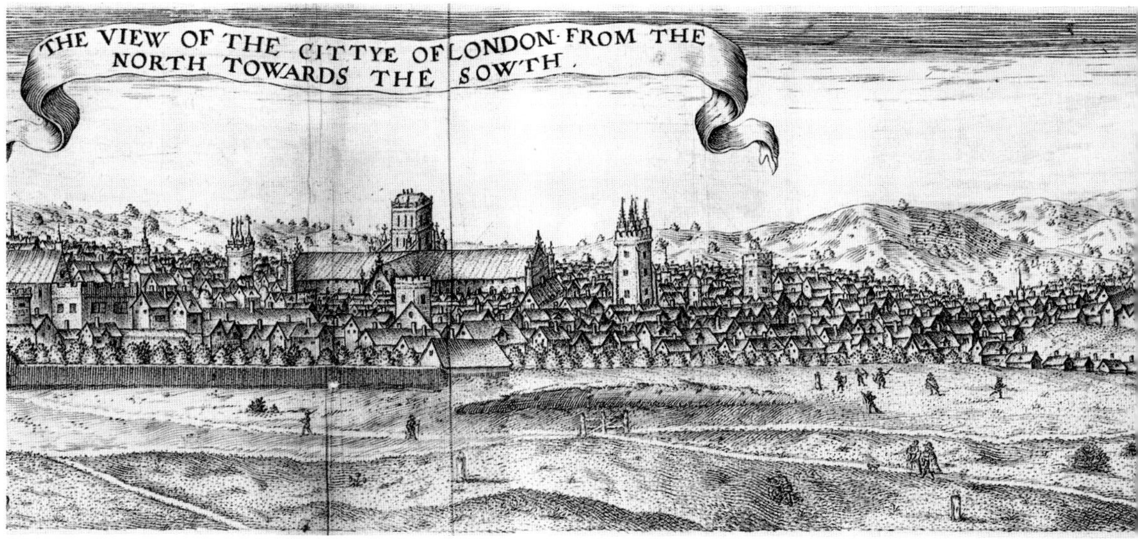

Beyond them in the distance the eye is taken to the towers of the archbishop's palace over the river, and then to the great halls of the lawyers in the foreground. Gilded lanterns, sundials and stained glass catch the early light at Gray's Inn (where Shakespeare would play his *Comedy of Errors*), Arundel House and the Middle Temple (future venue for a memorable *Twelfth Night*). Now the red roofs of the western end of the city come into view, the great private mansions around Holborn and the Strand, and the undulating expanse of tiled rooftops sloping down the Fleet valley and up to St Martin's Ludgate. To see such a magnificent sight in the twenty-first century, one would have to go to Assisi, Toledo or Cuzco.

From the forest of brick chimneys smudges of smoke rise from fires of wood and seacoal. As the gaze shifts eastwards, the suburb of Clerkenwell comes into view, and behind it the huge bulk of St Paul's with its great Gothic gable and tower, still 300 feet high, even though the spire, which took it well over 500 feet, has been gone for nearly thirty years now. Further on lies the mass of the late medieval city: the towers and spires of twenty-five churches, many going back to Anglo-Saxon times; and the huge mansions of the rich, sunlight occasionally catching their vermilioned crests and painted campaniles. Over the jumble of rooftops around the Guildhall and the Royal Exchange we can make out the weather-stained turrets of the Tower of London. Looking east again, Greenwich and the hills of Kent come into view, clear and blue. And everywhere, rising with the smoke into the still air, is what we can never hear now with all the traffic noise: the human roar of a great pre-modern city.

BELOW: *A panorama of London viewed from the north in the 1580s or early 90s: from Westminster Hall (far right) past the lawyers' halls (centre) to St Paul's (left).*

To visitors from home and abroad, Elizabethan London was a phenomenon. Its population was nearly 200,000 and rising fast. The great livery companies, the goldsmiths, merchants, mercers and clothiers, had grown in power and ostentation: their civic rituals and processions were grand public occasions on which fountains ran with wine, and cherubim with gilded wings and trumpets saluted the genius of the city. And in the last twenty years the suburbs had spread in every direction, filling up with tenements for the new urban poor.

With such wild extremes, the city itself would soon become the focus of a whole new genre of city comedies. In one memorable contemporary image London was likened to a 'perspective picture' which, depending on the viewpoint, yielded beauty and ugliness, peace and war, charity and aggression: prodigiously overflowing with wealth, yet sucking the life blood of the countryside as thousands of immigrants poured in to sustain its conspicuous consumption. Yet it was a place of tremendous opportunity, especially to an aspiring playwright in the autumn of 1588.

Back at the windmills in Finsbury Fields, the sounds of the city are still rising. Close by, wheels are rumbling and creaking up the rutted track towards Holloway as covered wagons head north with armed guards to fight off the robbers who haunt the wooded hills around Highgate. Looking east, there are two more windmills in open fields by the road leading down to Aldersgate, their sails turning as they grind flour for London's bread. Beyond them are yet further windmills, half hidden among the suburban sprawl of Shoreditch. Here was London's first theatre district.

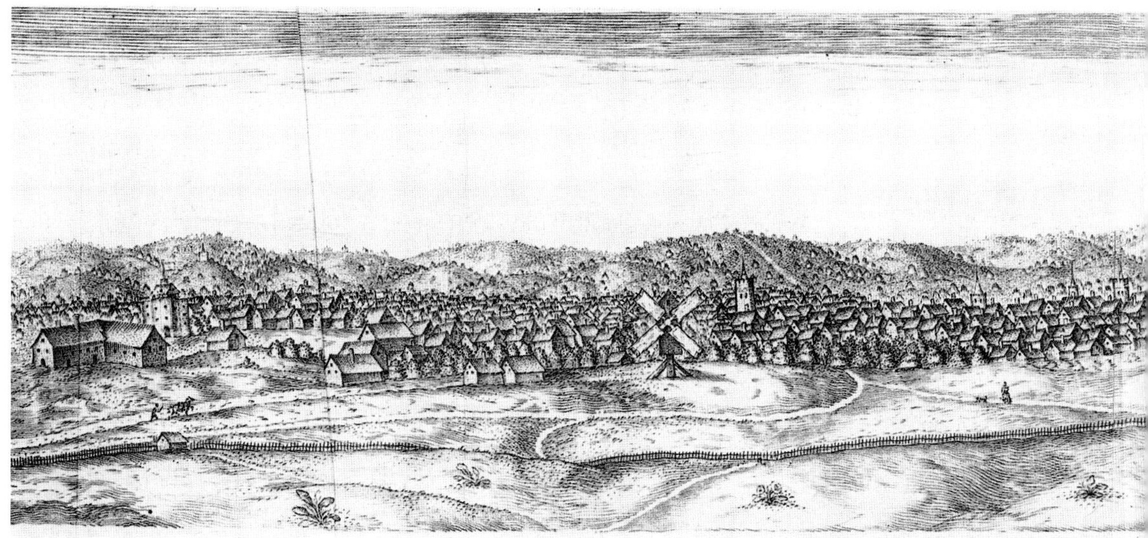

Shoreditch had expanded hugely in the last fifty years, the result of an uncontrolled growth of unlicensed infills by landlords who used every available space to capitalize on the huge influx of unemployed people from the impoverished countryside. And the theatres were in the middle of it. Just over Moorfield ditch the Curtain peeps over the rooftops in our panorama, and 200 yards to the north is a great wooden octagon topped with a huge flag. This is the Theatre, the first custom-built professional playhouse in the modern world. Here in the autumn of 1588 the audience would have been able to see some of the most popular shows of the early Elizabethan drama. From our vantage point in Finsbury Fields, carried on the wind, you can imagine the distant roar of the crowd.

The English Drama

When this eternal substance of my soul
Did live imprison'd in my wanton flesh.
Each in their function serving other's need,
I was a courtier in the Spanish court
My name was Don Andrea ....

So begins the first great verse tragedy of the Elizabethan new wave. With its dark mix of courtly grandeur and corruption, its vistas of eternal torment and its hints of bloody revenge to come, Thomas Kyd's *Spanish Tragedy* caught the anxious mood of the time. It was probably written the year before the Armada,

Below: *Continuation of the panorama: from St John's Clerkenwell (right) across the City to Shoreditch. Visible on the far left, behind the big L-shaped barn or house, is the Theatre, with its flag.*

Above: *Middle Temple Hall, where Shakespeare played* Twelfth Night, *is still used by lawyers for feasts and plays.* Opposite: *Shakespeare's London, showing the sites of the main theatres and the theatre inns.*

as was Marlowe's explosive first play, *Tamburlaine*. What an exciting time for a young man with ambitions to be a writer.

Drama had always been an important element of English vernacular culture, and it is no coincidence that the end of the medieval mystery plays was followed by the swift rise of the professional theatre. London was at the heart of this new venture, which started with the Red Lion in 1567, followed by Newington Butts in 1575, then Burbage's Theatre in 1576 and the Curtain the next year. These were the famous theatres of Shakespeare's early career. The grander Rose, Swan and Globe on the south bank would follow later, as would the Fortune in the north of the city. There were also many inn yard theatres, some specially adapted as permanent stages, such as the Bull in Bishopsgate, the Bell and the Cross Keys in Gracechurch Street and the huge Bel Savage outside Ludgate. All these were public venues for audiences of both sexes and the widest social background. For a higher-class clientele there would soon be indoor auditoria, such as the Blackfriars and the Cockpit. Many private institutions also regularly staged plays in magnificent settings, such as the great lawyers' halls of the Middle Temple and Gray's Inn. And of course Shakespeare's company would regularly provide entertainment at grand festivities in royal palaces, such as Hampton Court, Whitehall, Richmond and Greenwich.

The English drama came out of the medieval tradition. But the professional theatre – with its mass audience, its specialized urban venues, its new and often demanding scripts and its fast turnover – was a new phenomenon. The first professional, custom-built acting arena, Burbage's Theatre, was the model for the big wooden amphitheatres that followed, the largest of which could accommodate up to 3000 people. Foreign visitors, such as Thomas Platter from Switzerland, give us an idea of what they were like:

> These places are built in such a fashion that the players perform on a raised stage so that every one can see what happens. Nevertheless there are different gangways and places where one sits more comfortably, but then you have to pay more. If you stand below you pay one English penny, but if a seat is required you have to go in through another door and pay an extra penny. If you wish to sit on cushions in the most comfortable seat, so that you can not only see everything but can be seen yourself, you enter by yet another door and pay a further penny.

In just a few years the theatre had become the major public art, the single most effective platform for entertainment, ideas and debate. It was the subject of tremendous interest at home and abroad, and the constant object of attention from the authorities, secular and religious; and, for that reason, strictly subject to the censor. In late 1580s' England history was at stake, and theatre was political in the widest sense.

Burbage's Theatre: Shakespeare's Workplace

The Curtain and the Theatre, where Shakespeare first worked, lay a mile north of the city wall, outside city jurisdiction. This was an important consideration in a time when Puritans were making moves against any kind of stage performance,

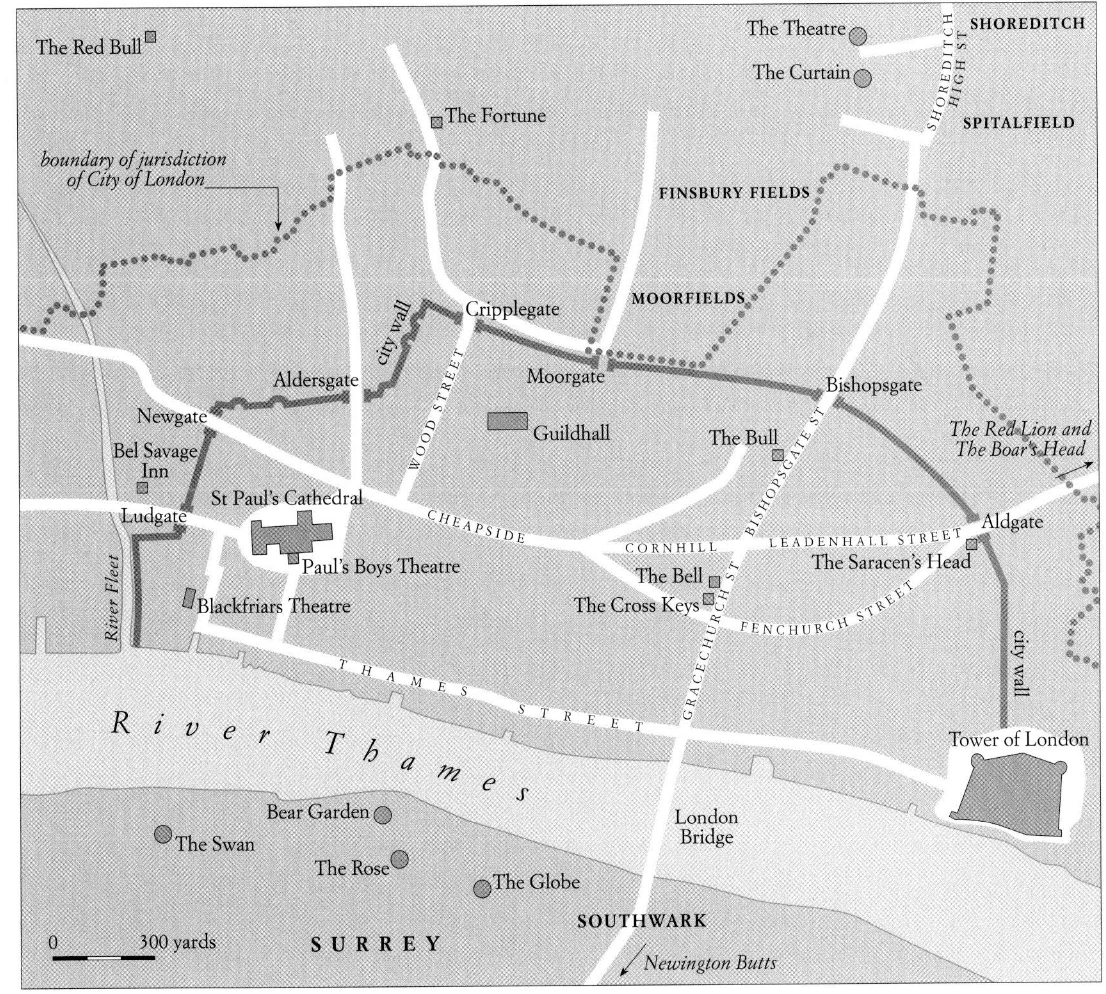

which they regarded as an encouragement to immorality and a threat to the most basic principles of the Protestant religion. The road to Shoreditch from the city at the end of the 1580s was, as the antiquarian John Stow's guidebook notes, lined with houses, 'many of them recently built with alleys backward, and too much pestered with people (a great cause of infection) up to the bars'. There were many lodging places here, including houses owned by the actor Edward Alleyn and his brother. Further north, closer to the theatres, lived the Bassanos, a family of Venetian musicians who had arrived in the days of Henry VIII: they owned three houses by St Mary's Spital, just before the bars crossing the road, which marked the end of city jurisdiction.

Burbage's Theatre was built inside the precinct of a medieval nunnery at an ancient 'holy well'. Sold off by Henry VIII back in the 1540s, the abbey church and buildings had been quarried for building stone, and the granary and brew-houses were now occupied by smallholders. The old stone perimeter wall still stood, enclosing gardens and the former convent orchard, which was now the private garden of Burbage's landlord, Giles Allen. The Theatre itself was a half-timbered, three-storey lath and plaster building with a tiled roof and two external staircases. Nearly 100 feet across, it was squashed in between an allotment garden on the north, the Great Horse Pond to the east, and the Great Barn, part cattle pen and part slaughterhouse, on the south. On the west side, towards Finsbury Fields, along the common sewer ran a brick perimeter wall in which a hole had been broken to give spectators access. To this unprepossessing place audiences rode out from the city up Bishopsgate, leaving their mounts tethered at the Great Horse Pond. Until it was demolished in December 1598, when its timbers were removed to build the new Globe on Bankside, this was Shakespeare's main London workplace.

Shoreditch was a rough area. Like all his class, Shakespeare wore a sword and not just for show: some of his fellow playwrights and actors – Knell, Spencer and Porter – were killed in duels, and several – Towne, Day, Marlowe and Ben Jonson – killed other people. The records of the Middlesex Sessions include constant reports of riot, affray and murder associated with the playhouses, whose 'lewde jigges songs and daunces' were felt to be dangerously attractive to 'cut-purses and other lewde and ill disposed persons'. Already by February 1580 the authorities had become alarmed by

> unlawful assemblies of the people to hear and see certain interludes called plays exercised by the said James Burbage and divers other persons unknown at a certain place called the Theatre in Holywell in the aforesaid county. By reason of which unlawful assembling of the

OPPOSITE: *The Shoreditch theatre district. According to the diarist John Aubrey, this was Shakespeare's first London home – possibly in the actors' rentals in Holywell Lane or Norton Folgate, where Christopher Marlowe lodged.*

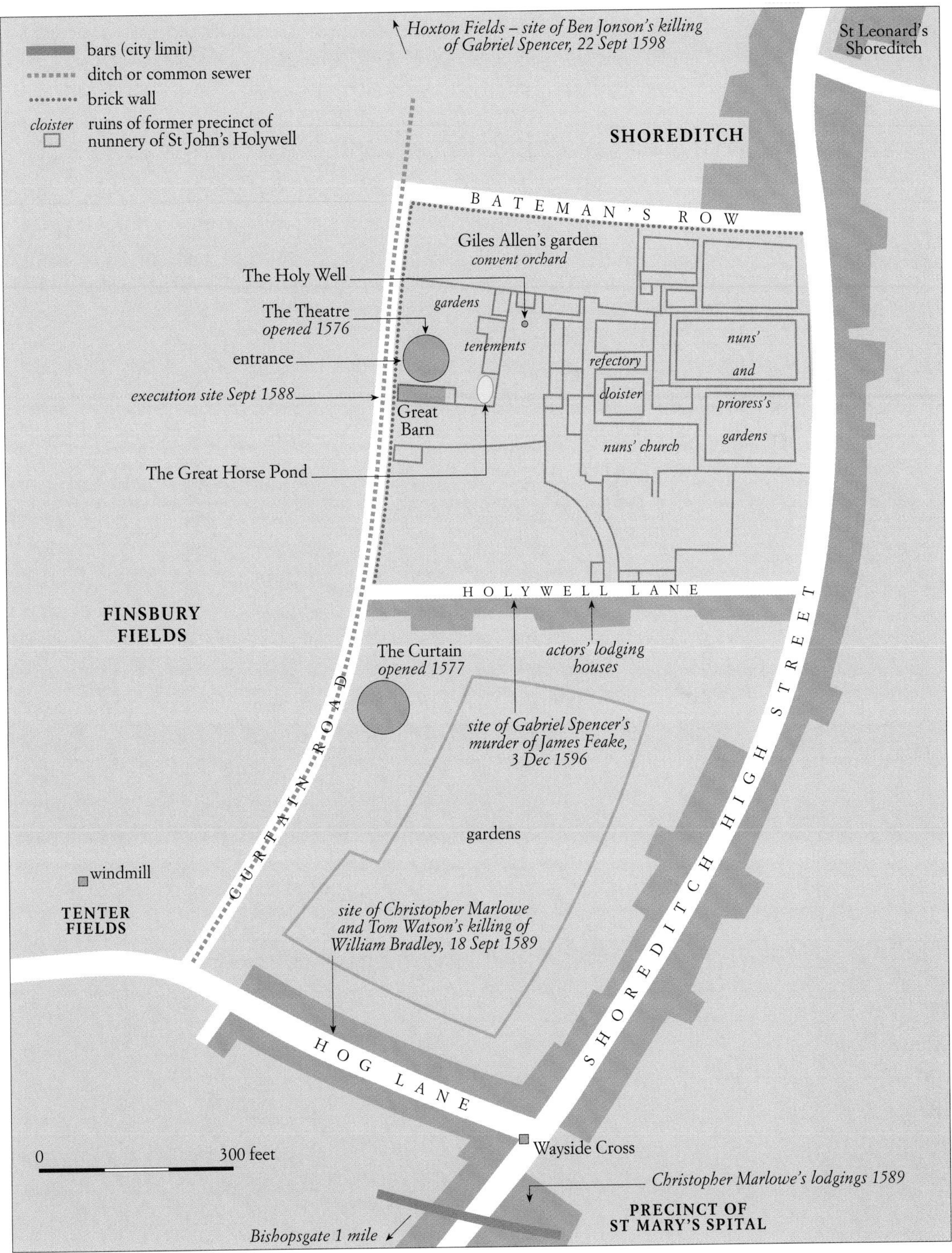

bars (city limit)
ditch or common sewer
brick wall
cloister
ruins of former precinct of nunnery of St John's Holywell
Hoxton Fields – site of Ben Jonson's killing of Gabriel Spencer, 22 Sept 1598
St Leonard's Shoreditch
SHOREDITCH
BATEMAN'S ROW
Giles Allen's garden
convent orchard
The Holy Well
The Theatre opened 1576
gardens
tenements
entrance
execution site Sept 1588
Great Barn
refectory
cloister
nuns' and prioress's gardens
nuns' church
The Great Horse Pond
HOLYWELL LANE
FINSBURY FIELDS
The Curtain opened 1577
actors' lodging houses
site of Gabriel Spencer's murder of James Feake, 3 Dec 1596
CURTAIN ROAD
SHOREDITCH HIGH STREET
gardens
windmill
TENTER FIELDS
site of Christopher Marlowe and Tom Watson's killing of William Bradley, 18 Sept 1589
HOG LANE
0
300 feet
Wayside Cross
Christopher Marlowe's lodgings 1589
PRECINCT OF ST MARY'S SPITAL
Bishopsgate 1 mile

> people great affrays assaults tumults and quasi-insurrections and divers other misdeeds and enormities have been then and there done by very many ill-disposed persons to the great disturbance of the peace...

Fuelled by drink, prostitution and crime, then, the stage crackled with low life and buzzed with the language and edginess of the street. To be sure, it often churned out mindless drivel, sentimental pap or blatant government propaganda, seamed with bigotry, jingoism and racism. But at its best it could be elevated, explosive and oppositional, and it would leave its mark on the culture of England and the world from that day to this.

Theatre as Propaganda, Theatre as Investment

The government cottoned on early to the potential importance of the theatre for the dissemination of ideas. In her first year as queen Elizabeth had issued a decree controlling the performance of plays; all scripts were subject to censorship, and patronage of the main companies usually depended on leading noblemen with strong government links. It had been Elizabeth's spymaster Walsingham, for example, who had set up the Queen's Men, taking the best talent from everywhere: not because he loved the theatre – there is no evidence he ever went to a play – but because he wanted to put the most influential medium of the day to his own use.

Little is known of Shakespeare's first patrons, his early contacts and friendships – the obvious things that lead a person to a particular place or employment; but it is certain that at some point in the late 1580s he came to work in London. In the previous twenty-five years there had been a revolution in dramatic style. The plays of his schooldays had been either the traditional mysteries and moralities, or academic tragedies and comedies; in the mid-1580s the rhyming verse of the Queen's Men had become all the rage. But the rise of a new kind of blank verse during that decade would soon turn the drama into an effective mass medium with appeal across the board. And when Shakespeare hit London the trendsetters were Thomas Kyd and above all Christopher Marlowe.

Marlowe and the Revolution in Language

Marlowe was the same age as Shakespeare, and from the same class. But, unlike Shakespeare, he had been to university. His Cambridge portrait gives you the man: the gold buttons, the expensive slashed doublet with firelicks of red silk, the folded arms and the faintly superior look. Most eye-catching of all is the motto: 'What nourishes me destroys me.' A boast, and a forecast. Recruited as

LEFT: *A presumed portrait of Marlowe at Cambridge in 1585, aged twenty-one. The superb padded doublet with its bossed gold buttons suggests a flashy undergraduate 'ruffed out in his silks in the habit of a malcontent'.*

a secret agent at Cambridge, Marlowe was a young firebrand with an indiscreet tongue. There are hints, too, of a dangerous and unstable character; described by those who knew him as a man 'liable to sudden and privy injuries', he had been implicated in the killing of a man in the streets of Shoreditch. But he was a dazzling talent. A classical translator and poet with a fabulous, effortless lyric sense, a dark irony and black humour, Marlowe was sadistic, iconoclastic, hip. And though Kyd's *Spanish Tragedy* launched the new wave, it was Marlowe

who ran with it. In 1587 the twenty-three-year-old Marlowe captivated London audiences with *Tamburlaine*, the story of an oriental Napoleon. He wrote in the new form of blank verse rather than the 'jigging' rhymes of the Queen's Men, at which he sneered in contempt. The new style was a ten-syllable line so flexible and interesting that foreign visitors – even the French! – would compare it favourably to their own: 'Their plays are in a kind of blank verse which suits an ordinary language better than our metre, and makes some melody. They think it irksome to have the ear continually tickled with the same cadence, and say that listening to heroic verses spoken for two or three hours is not so natural or so pleasing.'

Blank verse had come out of native poetry, but was influenced by the Latin line in rhythm and syntax, and loaded with classicisms with which university types like Marlowe couldn't resist larding their lines:

> As when the seaman sees the Hyades
> Gather an army of Cimmerian clouds

Only the nobs in the boxes would have known that the Hyades were the seven stars that presaged rain, and that Cimmerian simply meant black (the classical Cimmerii lived in perpetual darkness). But it sounded great.

So a revolution was taking place not only in the acting companies and the professional playhouses, but in the verse itself. The English language at this time went through a sudden expansion, borrowing from everywhere. And with that came a vision appropriate to such an expansionist time, when ships sailed back to Tilbury and Deptford loaded with bounty looted from Spanish carracks: Yucatan gold and Potosi silver. The stage now could embody the whole globe 'from the farthest equinoctial line … into the Eastern India'; writers piled on exotic names willy-nilly, plundering their Ovid, and their new maps, for 'Cubar, where the negroes dwell' and 'the wide, the vast Euxine sea'.

As befitted a violent age, the theatre was full of casual cruelty. But there was empathy in it, too. Although a classic Shakespearean quality, it was possessed by all the great writers of the period and came from their education. Marlowe, for example, allows the penny punters to get inside the head of the Scythian tyrant Tamburlaine with his implacable love and cruelty, and even to feel for his religion:

> By sacred Mahomet, the friend of God,
> Whose holy Alcoran remains with us,
> Whose glorious body, when he left the world,

> Clos'd in a coffin mounted up the air
> And hung on stately Mecca's temple roof ....

Above all this, though, are the great set-pieces of the world conqueror. This is what Ben Jonson called Marlowe's 'mighty sounding rhyme':

> Now clear the triple region of the air,
> And let the majesty of heaven behold
> Their scourge and terror tread on emperors.
> Smile, stars that reign'd at my nativity,
> And dim the brightness of their neighbour lamps;
> Disdain to borrow light of Cynthia
> For I, the chiefest lamp of all the earth,
> First rising in the east with mild aspect,
> But fixed now in the meridian line,
> Will send up fire to your turning spheres
> And cause the sun to borrow light of you.

It was the sound that everyone wanted, and that all other artists sought to imitate: the standard by which any aspiring young playwright in London in the late 1580s had to measure himself.

A Young Man's Game

The late Elizabethan theatre was an industry with high pressure and a quick turnover. There was a different show every afternoon, and a play might only get three performances before a company pulled it off. Only big hits might get a decent run and perhaps even a revival. So there was a tremendous demand for scripts. It is interesting that during a modern run of 150 shows at the Royal Shakespeare Company only four plays are presented. The theatre impresario Philip Henslowe's diary reveals the same number of performances in an Elizabethan season but with twenty-eight different plays, half of them new. His players could do as many as fifteen different shows in one month. Obviously, this was only possible in a memorizing culture – so all that learning by rote at school in Stratford would have come in useful.

So it was a young man's game with a demanding routine. Rehearsals for the next show took place in the morning, followed by a quick lunch (but no drink – actors' contracts show that turning up on stage drunk was a sacking offence). The current show would then start at two and ended around five, earlier in winter; with make-up, wigs and costumes off, actors made their way back into town to eat at six or seven in the evening in their lodgings or in an 'ordinary', a simple eating and drinking place where they could relax. Along the road back to Bishopsgate there were several ordinaries, of which the Three Tuns at number 39 was typical: long and narrow, with a stable yard stretching back from the road, a small kitchen, a snug in front with a fire and a big shared garden.

Bishopsgate and the Theatre Inns

Shakespeare's first known address was close by, just inside the city walls in the parish of St Helen's Bishopsgate. Here he probably lived through the early to mid-nineties, and perhaps for some time before. It was a tiny parish, a mere 300 yards long with only seventy-three rateable households, conveniently placed for work in Shoreditch. Most of his London is irretrievably gone now, of course, but this area was not destroyed in the Great Fire of 1666, and many of the buildings Shakespeare knew survived into the 1850s. Victorian photographs still show sixteenth-century cityscapes, and from this rich archive, together with Tudor and seventeenth-century maps and the detailed guide to the city published by John Stow in 1598, it is possible to bring to life the area of London in which Shakespeare first lodged.

Walking back in the evening from Shoreditch, just outside the old city on the right you passed the Bedlam hospital for lunatics (the site is now under Liverpool Street Station). Next door was the church of St Botolph (the patron of travellers) with 'a fair churchyard adjoining the town ditch', says Stow, 'upon the very bank but enclosed by a comely wall of brick'. Next to the church gate was 'a fair inn', the White Hart, built in 1480 with three storeys overhanging the street. Over the road, on the corner of Houndsditch was the famous Dolphin inn, the London base for carriers from Suffolk and Norfolk and typical of those inns described by William Harrison in 1587, that could 'lodge and with ease feed two or three hundred people and their horses at short warning, in a manner which would seem incredible'.

Against the outside wall of the Dolphin second-hand clothing stalls were set up on the stone-paved street of Houndsditch, along with a metal foundry and 'many shops for brokers, joiners, braziers and such as deal in old linen clothes and upholstery'. A recent influx of 'baptised Jews' traded as clothiers and pawnbrokers. They attracted some hostility and were denigrated in one contemporary account as 'a base kind of vermin'. But the area remained a Jewish quarter, and London's oldest synagogue still stands nearby. The year after he left Bishopsgate, Shakespeare would write a play about Jews.

Here outside the gate the sharp growth in population had led to new

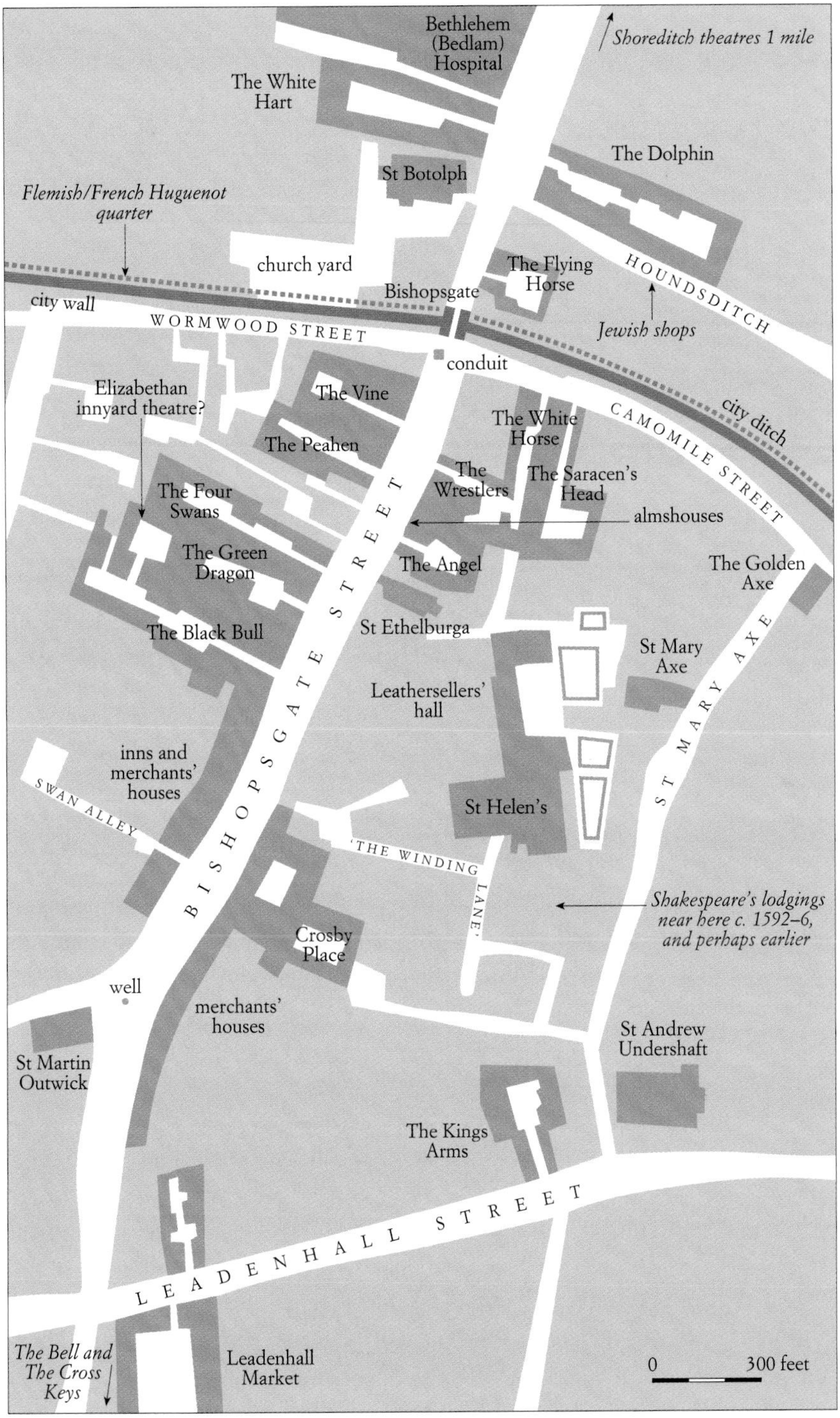

London: Fame

Left: *Bishopsgate and the theatre inns: Shakespeare's first known address. He lived close to St Helen's until 1596. Among his neighbours were the madrigalist Thomas Morley, the poet Tom Watson and the sinister spy Robert Poley.*

ABOVE: *A meal in a high-class inn. When Shakespeare earned good money did he use such places for writing? Food, ale and music were on tap, and candles were free.*

building encroaching on the ditch: next to St Botolph's churchyard a causeway led alongside the brick wall to what had recently become known as Petty France. Here lived a community of French Huguenot refugees, crowded into tenements from where (so their neighbours accused them) they polluted the ditch 'with sewage of the houses and with other filthiness cast into the ditch water which was now forced into a narrow channel and almost filled up with unsavoury things, to the danger of impoisoning the whole city'. So with the billowing smoke from the braziers, the joiners' dust and clamour, and the smell of sewage, it was perhaps best to cover your nose as you walked through the gate into the city.

Inside the gate, Bishopsgate Street was filled with a tide of wagons, pack animals and jostling crowds. Lined with three-, four-, and five-storey jettied houses, no street in London was so well furnished with inns, eating places and houses of entertainment. Facing you, says Stow, were 'divers fair innes, large for receipt of travellers', the biggest of which were the Wrestlers and the Angel. You entered through a long passage into a big yard surrounded with stables on the ground floor and chambers above. This was the pre-modern system in every town and large village: your horse would be taken from you, unsaddled, walked, rubbed down, fed and watered; you were given your own room key by the chamberlain, who unloaded your bags and in winter kindled your fire.

Your room was 'well furnished with bedding and tapestry' and you slept in 'clean sheets wherein no man hath been lodged since they came from the laundress'. For food, you were free to inspect the kitchens and could eat with the host, at common table, or in your private chamber. London inns also had a wide choice of foreign wines, complemented by local beers with weird and wonderful names: 'huffecap' (a 'heady ale'), 'angels' food', 'dragon's milk', 'mad dog' (clearly to be avoided) and, most mysteriously, 'left leg'.

It was best to choose a place you knew, or one that had been recommended by a reliable source, however, for London inns had a bad reputation for 'cozening' or cheating. Country visitors were warned to be on their guard against conmen and cheats, and hosts or room boys who might be in league with robbers. This low-life culture Shakespeare would later bring to life in the tavern scenes in Cheapside in his *Henry IV* plays: Falstaff's robbery of travellers at Gadshill is planned from his inn. In a great city, of course, criminality always thrives around places of rest and entertainment. And in just such an inn the country boy from Stratford may have first lodged, paying a penny a night for food and bed without stabling.

The Bishopsgate inns were also centres of theatrical shows. Most famous was the Black Bull, which Shakespeare would have known and where he may have acted. Early in Elizabeth's reign it was converted into a theatre inn with a permanent stage, which was still to be seen a century later. Although shows could be staged indoors in the hall or 'great chamber', a seventeenth-century plan suggests that here the players used an inner yard. Shows started at around

LEFT: *Private entertainment with topless hostesses. No wonder Nicholas Bacon's mother feared that lodging near the Black Bull might lead her son astray, or at least 'corrupt his servants'.*

ABOVE: *Next door to the Bull was the Green Dragon, a base for Suffolk carriers. This photograph was taken c. 1880.* OPPOSITE: *The end of the 'winding lane' up to St Helen's, in 1886: a walk Shakespeare must have known well when he lived here.*

four o'clock, and were announced by the actors with drums and trumpets in the main street, literally drumming up business. The Black Bull had become such a well-known venue when Shakespeare was a boy that John Florio mentions it in his English-Italian phrase book of 1578 ('Where shal we goe? To a playe at the Bull'). In 1583 it was licensed as a regular London venue for the Queen's Men and they played here 'oftentimes'. So if Shakespeare was indeed with the Queen's Men in the late 1580s, this is where he would have played in London. A little way down Bishopsgate in Gracechurch Street, opposite the main fish, meat and herb markets, were two other famous actors' inns well known to Shakespeare. The Bell, like the Black Bull, was licensed as a venue for the Queen's Men from 1583, and the shows of Tarlton and 'his fellowes' were long remembered there too. Next door was the Cross Keys, Shakespeare's most

important London venue inside the city, where he may have played with Lord Strange's Men in 1589, and certainly did with the Chamberlain's company in 1594.

So, though almost forgotten now, the Bishopsgate area is entitled to be seen as another of Shakespeare's theatre neighbourhoods. It was very different in character from the better-known ones of Shoreditch and Southwark. The streets and properties here were clean, well built and well ordered, with good facilities. There was fresh water from a conduit flowing in from the hills above Clerkenwell. Tucked away in the warren of lanes east of the main street were (and still are) the Leathersellers' hall and the company almshouses. These abutted St Helen's, Shakespeare's local church and a former nunnery. Around its courtyard were great merchant houses, of which the grandest was Crosby Place, built in the 1460s. Richard III once lived here, as did Sir Thomas More when writing both his *Utopia* and his book on that king. Shakespeare, working on his *Richard III* late in 1592 and using poetic licence rather than historical fact, treats Crosby Place as Richard's London base, the centre of his plots and secret machinations. He sets two scenes in the house: the death of Henry VI in 1471 and Richard's marriage to Lady Anne in 1473. Neither event actually took place here: it is just one of those instances where the locality in which Shakespeare lived gave him an idea for scenes in a play.

Although audiences were smaller here, there were many advantages over Shoreditch: not least that theatregoers were spared the mile walk or ride out of the city on cold winter afternoons when it was dark by the time the show was over. In bad weather the unheated Theatre, situated as it was between the common sewer and the Great Horse Pond, was perhaps a little bleak. Also the resident population of Shoreditch included many poor; here in Bishopsgate were audiences with disposable income. And, not least, the inns could offer better facilities for spectators, including of course access from private rooms in the galleries within easy reach of food, drink, music and the other and varied pleasures of the Elizabethan world.

How different it must all have seemed from Stratford. A country town could be busy, to be sure, especially on market days and when the big seasonal fairs were held, but this was a great city. Every day from early in the morning the place was full of noise, smell, colour and life as carters delivered their loads of coal, wood, beer, milk and hay, shopkeepers and street vendors drummed up custom, and carriages and the regular pack trains created a Tudor traffic jam as they blocked the streets. This was the cityscape that we can imagine the young Shakespeare encountering when he dropped his bags and settled into his room close by the Bull in Bishopsgate, with the hum of city life rising outside. The

start of his London career was propelled not only by the excitement of a new art form, but by the sheer exhilaration of the city itself.

A PORTRAIT OF THE ARTIST AS A YOUNG MAN?

Years later, in his sonnets, Shakespeare appears to look back in very revealing words on the days when, a diffident provincial from the yeoman class, he first came to London to make his name:

> How careful was I, when I took my way,
> Each trifle under truest bars to thrust,
> That to my use it might unused stay
> From hands of falsehood, in sure wards of trust

Shakespeare was a guarded person, who protected himself and those he knew. And here he tells us that he did so from the very start of his career. His character, as we have seen, was shaped by his background, although this is perhaps characteristic of artists for whom outward life is often distanced, subordinated to the intensity of artistic endeavour and expression. But this sonnet also offers a picture of a provincial wary of the sophisticated society in which he now has to move and work, and other examples of this guardedness will emerge later in this story.

It is even possible that an image of the young Shakespeare has survived. In the John Rylands Library in Manchester is a painting found in a house in Darlington in 1906. It is the portrait of a man done in Armada year, 1588, at the age of twenty-four – the same age as Shakespeare. The young man is not a noble: his doublet is plain pink-red with slashing and there are no fine buttons or ruff: he is plainly of the Tudor middle class. Nothing can be safely said about the personality of the anonymous sitter beyond a suggestion of diffidence and the fact that the face bears a very close resemblance in looks and proportions to the only certain portrait of Shakespeare, the Folio frontispiece. What makes this more than mere conjecture is that the painting came originally from the village of Grafton in Northamptonshire, close to Abington where Shakespeare's granddaughter Elizabeth died. Elizabeth had inherited the poet's possessions through her mother, Susanna, and the last inventory mentions not only books but 'goods and lumber' from Stratford. It is enough of a hint to make it possible that this is indeed the twenty-four-year old William Shakespeare at the start of his career.

Having a portrait painted was the sort of thing you might do when you got the livery of a lord or were awarded a degree. For Shakespeare, entering the service of his first patron, Lord Strange, might have been such a moment. If the

Grafton picture is indeed of him, it does no harm to suppose that, like any successful young Elizabethan man, he bought himself a nice doublet and had his picture painted to send back to the family: proof to proud parents, and to his wife and children, that he was doing well. And whilst all this is pure speculation, the portrait does help us to imagine him at this point in his life and to get rid of the received image of Shakespeare as a balding middle-aged man in a ruff – an establishment figure. Here is a young Elizabethan who could be the artist who would soon write the greatest cycle of plays since the medieval mysteries and the ancient Greek dramas – his early histories, all of which were written in his twenties. Shakespeare looked like this: a young blade, diffident, sensitive, intelligent, witty, ambitious; a provincial poet making his way in the world, a face glimpsed in the seething crowds around the yards and carriage gates of Bishopsgate and Shoreditch.

The Mystery of Shakespeare's Early Career

So let us suppose that some time in the winter of 1588–9, Shakespeare joins a company based in London. Three or four years later he emerges as a playwright with several hits to his name; by the end of 1592 he has written his first great character, the villainous Richard III, and his fame is assured. But here's the mystery: what did he do in between, and with whom did he work?

It is assumed that his earliest solo plays were written around 1588–90, but nothing is certain. Precious clues come from the title page of what may be his earliest play, the Roman tragedy *Titus Andronicus*. When this was published in 1594 its title page named three companies, including that of Lord Strange (who had become Earl of Derby the previous year), which had successively put on the play: 'The Earl of Derby, Earl of Pembroke, and Earl of Sussex their Servants'. If this order is right, it is possible to sketch a very tentative picture of his early career that goes something like this:

In September 1588 the Queen's Men lose both their star, Tarlton, and a key patron, Robert Dudley. The next year Shakespeare joins the company of Ferdinando, the new Lord Strange, a member of the great Lancashire family of the Stanleys. They probably play summers in Shoreditch and winters at city inns like the Cross Keys, where they are in November 1589. He spends nearly two years with Strange, and writes *Titus Andronicus* at this time. For Strange he also writes the two plays that begin his great series on English history: *The Contention of the Houses of York and Lancaster* and *Richard Duke of York* (which we know as *Henry VI* Parts 2 and 3). They are his first great successes. Then, in May 1591, Strange's company splits up. The original core group go to Henslowe's new Rose theatre south of the river, while the young Richard

Opposite: *An unknown Elizabethan aged twenty-four in 1588: the same age as Shakespeare in the year he perhaps came to London. It closely resembles the Folio engraving, so could this be a portrait of the artist as a young man?*

SVÆ 24
1588

Burbage, loyal to his father, remains at the Theatre in Shoreditch. Shakespeare stays with him with his scripts, which now include the *Henry VI* plays, *Titus* and *The Taming of the Shrew*. In late 1591 (probably at speed with a collaborator) he writes *Henry VI* Part 1 – the 'prequel' to *The Contention*, which is acted at the Rose by a company of players from both Strange's Men and the Admiral's Men, for whom Edward Alleyn, Marlowe's star actor, performed the main roles. At this time Shakespeare would have got to know Alleyn and Marlowe personally.

Then, in 1592, Pembroke's Men, very likely the missing link in Shakespeare's still mysterious early career, come into the picture. Shakespeare and Burbage probably act for a while with this company. The Pembroke family are the greatest patrons of poetry at this time – the earl's young wife Mary had a special interest in drama – and this is the beginning of the relationship with the family, which will last for the rest of Shakespeare's life.

A young writer fired by his early success, Shakespeare already has in mind a sequel to the three *Henry VI* plays, and *Richard III* may have started life for Strange (in it the poet flatters his patron by inflating the historical role of his ancestors, the Stanleys, at the battle of Bosworth). He perhaps finishes the play in mid- or late 1592 for Pembroke's Men (the play has a little puff for one of Pembroke's ancestors too). But the following spring a devastating outbreak of plague, in which more than 10,000 people died, hits London. The theatres are immediately closed for fear of contagion; in the summer Pembroke's Men find themselves out of work and the company folds. Just turned twenty-nine, Shakespeare is forced to seek a new patron and another source of income. In the winter of 1593–4, he and Burbage work for Sussex's Men. Finally in May 1594 they both join the newly formed Chamberlain's Men with old friends and colleagues from Strange's Men, and return to The Theatre in Shoreditch. From now on we are on firm ground. From confusion and speculation we can move to a clearer narrative of Shakespeare's career as a professional writer.

Insecurity and Loyalty

The hypothetical picture above gives a rough idea of the wheeler-dealing by which Shakespeare built up a career, finally committing himself at the age of thirty to the Chamberlain's Men with a group of actors and entrepreneurs whom he had known for a long time. In those early years there were a number of theatre owners, several noble patrons and lots of companies – as many as thirty are recorded from that time. But the circle of actors and writers in London can never have comprised more than a couple of hundred people. In this little world of shifting groupings Shakespeare worked for more than one entrepreneur and

his plays passed through the hands of more than one company. He swapped patrons and theatres, sometimes with rival companies playing the same building. Living at times hand to mouth, it was a precarious profession: companies folded, the plague struck, the city authorities clamped down, theatres were closed. A steady income was never guaranteed. You lived on your wits.

Shakespeare's early professional career, then, was like that of any writer in theatre or film today, working for a number of masters. But loyalty to the group was very important. And for some reason, perhaps simply because they liked and trusted each other, the Burbages were his preferred people, although no one yet knows how the relationship started.

The Early Plays: Rivers of Blood and Shaggy Dog Stories

The order in which the young Shakespeare wrote his first hits is largely speculation. As we have seen, the earliest tragedy was *Titus Andronicus*. The latest linguistic analysis suggests that this was a collaboration with another writer, George Peele, who wrote for the Queen's Men. It's a young man's play full of rhetoric and violence, the Elizabethan equivalent of a Quentin Tarantino movie. No doubt those in the cheaper seats loved all the blood and guts – but then they saw it in the streets outside every day. Heads are cut off and eyes gouged out in other Elizabethan plays, of course, but there is something peculiar about Shakespearean violence and aggression. Gentle Will he may have been to his friends, but a key part of his psychology is aggression and violence, as when Marcus discovers his mutilated daughter:

> Why dost thou not speak to me?
> Alas, a crimson river of warm blood,
> Like to a bubbling fountain stirred with wind,
> Doth rise and fall between thy rosed lips

Titus is so grotesque and horrible that earlier generations than our own found it hard to believe that it was really Shakespeare who wrote it. But this was the rhetoric of the time: a shadowing of speeches made on the scaffold before even more terrible violations of the human body were done for real as punishment and edification – another kind of public theatre. When Olivier played Titus in Poland in the late 1950s the play was seen as true to life by packed audiences, for whom nothing in it seemed improbable in the light of the unexampled cruelties of the mid-twentieth century. If anything, the ornate control of the verse keeps the lid on the horrors, as it does in the sonorous Latin of his model, the Roman Seneca.

Shakespeare also wrote lyrical romantic pieces at this period. Maybe *The Two Gentlemen of Verona* (or at least an earlier version of it) is another youthful play – perhaps even his first solo effort. The accomplished elegance of the verse shows he had developed his writing skills and suggests considerable experience as a jobbing man of the theatre. But the play is dramatically unambitious and he may not yet have learned how to use his actors. It does contain beautiful poetry, however, including the famous speech that capitivated Viola de Lesseps, Gwyneth Paltrow's character in the film *Shakespeare in Love*:

> What light is light if Silvia be not seen?
> What joy is joy, if Silvia be not by –
> Unless it be to think that she is by,
> And feed upon the shadow of perfection.
> Except I be with Silvia in the night
> There is no music in the nightingale

The prose of the comic Launce, on the other hand, sounds like something straight out of a Stratford guildhall show, written in the Elizabethan equivalent of a Birmingham accent: 'I think Crab, my dog, be the sourest-natured dog that lives. My mother weeping, my father wailing, my sister crying, our maid howling, our cat wringing her hands, and all our house in a great perplexity, yet did not this cruel hearted cur shed one tear. He is a stone, a very pebble-stone, and has no more pity in him than a dog ….' There follow twenty lines piling misconstruings on top of each other as Launce plays out for the audience what is literally a shaggy dog story: 'This hat is Nan our maid. I am the dog. No, the dog is himself, and I am the dog. O, the dog is me, and I am myself …. '

And so on, for as long as the performer could milk the audience. A speech like this is simply the fossilized record of a fluid text done 'extempore', as he would have said. The success of the scene depended on the improvising skills of the clown and his ability to play the crowd. The clowns were the stars of the first main phase of the professional theatre, before the great tragedians like Alleyn took over. The best of them was the Queen's Men's Tarlton, who died in September 1588, and was so funny that on one memorable occasion the queen had to ask him to leave the stage because she was laughing so much. Many of his gags became staples for the next generation; and one of them, as it happens, concerned a dog. Crab's scene-stealing non-speaking role was never repeated by Shakespeare: it is his only part for a dog. So was *Two Gentlemen* a version of a show originally written for the Queen's Men and Tarlton – or did Shakespeare simply take the gag from an old Tarlton show, recycling it for his own company

ABOVE: *A sketch of* Titus Andronicus *in performance, c. 1605? Originally done for Lord Strange, one scene perhaps alluded to a remarkable screen at Strange's Lathom House, now destroyed, which was painted with signs of the zodiac.*

after the clown's death? This seems more likely. Perhaps Shakespeare was harking back to a great comic act, rather as a modern West End show might bring, say, Morecambe and Wise back to life. But, wisely, it was not a trick he would play twice. Legends are best left alone.

A Master of Both Comedy and History

Although his early hits were history, not comedy, Shakespeare's essential bent is comic – he can't resist it, even in tragedy. His contemporaries thought him 'best for comedy'. Unsurprisingly, not all his jokes have stood the test of time. Some are topical, some are in-jokes, some depend on the sort of word play beloved of Elizabethans but that can strike us as rather laboured today, especially when he is sucking up to the literary pretensions of an aristocratic or legal audience. But what is so wonderful is that in our modern world so much of Shakespeare is still such great fun, even when he is in tragic mode. Indeed, it is perhaps his sense of comedy that makes his tragedies work so well on stage. These days we may not understand all his words, nor did they get everything at the Theatre or the

Globe, of course; but in the twenty-first century Shakespeare at his best is still the most fun we can have in a theatre.

Nevertheless it would be with histories, not with tragedies or comedies, that Shakespeare would overtake Marlowe and soon have his rival chasing him, imitating him. Eventually his brand of history would run the Queen's Men out of town and out of business. Especially in the aftermath of the Armada, there was a big nationwide audience, built up by the Queen's Men's ceaseless tours, for plays dramatizing the national story. This was where Shakespeare's interests lay.

His *Henry VI* plays began a brilliant sequence for which he quarried the Tudor chroniclers of the Wars of the Roses, Hall and Holinshed. Yet Shakespeare's obsession with history was surely driven not only by the box office but by his own psychology. He had been brought up with stories of old England and its kings, the medieval Catholic past, the splendour and cruelties of English history, and he loved them. But even when he was only in his mid-twenties, his plays could be distinguished from the Queen's Men's propaganda. He had an instinctive feel for the complexities of history, where right and wrong exist on both sides and where a multiple perspective can suggest the chaotic reality, the 'pressure of the time'.

His fascination with history would lead him to write, by 1593, the most ambitious theatrical entertainment written by a single artist since the ancient Greeks. The only parallel in English was the Mystery Cycle, whose conventions were now plundered by him for secular passion plays – plays in which Richard of York, scourged with a paper crown and chastising Queen Margaret as a 'tiger's heart in a woman's hide', would become a new Man of Sorrows. Shakespeare was in the process of a journey from Mystery through History to Tragedy.

Making It

But still there is no certain mention of him by name. In late 1590 there is an intriguing reference in print by Edmund Spenser, author of the *The Faerie Queene*. That December Spenser's *Teares of the Muses* appeared, with an address to Lady Alice Strange, a renowned literary patron and wife of Shakespeare's Ferdinando. In it Spenser praises 'our pleasant Willy' as a brilliant writer who, mysteriously, 'dead of late ... chooses to sit in an idle cell than so himself to mockery sell'. As Shakespeare was quite possibly in Strange's service at this moment, does this refer to him? And if so, what does 'dead of late' mean and what 'mockery' had he suffered? Given that Shakespeare was soon to receive a critical mauling at the hands of one of London's most famous pamphleteers, Robert Greene, it may be that in 1590 he had already excited the jealousy of his rivals.

The previous summer, the preface to Greene's *Menaphon* addressed 'to the gentlemen of both universities' by his journalist friend Thomas Nashe had sneered at the 'very mechanical mates ... [who] in servile imitation of vainglorious tragedians ... leave the trade of noverint [lawyer's clerk] whereto they were born and busy themselves with endeavours of art'. He talks of those who 'could scarcely latinise their neck verse' yet try to write 'English Seneca ... afford you whole Hamlets ... imitate the Kidde [in] home born mediocrity ...'. While ostensibly aimed at Kyd, the attack is in the plural – on more than one playwright who is imitating 'vainglorious tragedians'. And none was more up and coming than the man who, that year perhaps, had done that exercise in English Seneca, *Titus Andronicus.*

The next year, 1591, Spenser may mention Shakespeare again in a discussion of contemporary poets, this time wrapping him in a classical metaphor: 'last but not least Aetion ... a gentler shepherd may no where be found, whose Muse full of high thoughts invention doth like himself heroically sound'. That word 'gentle' stuck with him all the way through. And if this description is indeed of Shakespeare, Spenser's remarks are very important because they show he was no longer just a theatrical jobber but was recognized as a man with a gift. Everywhere now English poetry was felt to be on the rise, and for the movers and shakers, patrons like the Stranges and the Herberts and practitioners like Spenser, new and extraordinary talent was something they wanted to foster. Shakespeare was now a fully fledged poet.

On stage Shakespeare was soon outdoing Marlowe: even his early plays exhibited deeper moral concerns than Marlowe's. Their styles, of course, are very distinctive: Shakespeare had a more natural feel for ordinary people and their speech – an enviable common touch. And Shakespeare also had a feel for what his audiences liked. He knew a good story when he saw it; whereas Marlowe's choice of material, though always interesting, was not always entirely successful. When, for example, Marlowe tried to outdo Shakespeare with a history play, *Edward II*, he chose a reign oddly lacking in significance and a plot that cannot have endeared him to some in high places. Shakespeare, on the other hand, was always careful in his choice of plots: very few don't work. In fact the only one that doesn't, *Timon of Athens*, he sets aside unfinished. He was a derivative writer in the best sense, usually borrowing and adapting an existing plot and always going after the inherited, 'right' way of working it, with a great feel for the basics of storytelling. Also, although some of his contemporaries denied it, he paid close attention to structure. He must have known the debate in Philip Sidney's *Defence of Poesie* on how to construct a dramatic plot, with, for example, its dissection of Euripides's *Hecuba,* which Shakespeare may have studied at school.

Probably already picked out by Spenser, 'our Willy' was shaping up as a talented young artist with a winning manner. In contrast to Marlowe's arrogance, class envy and atheism, Shakespeare was 'smooth', 'honey tongued' and 'sweet'. From the start he knew what his patrons liked, and, as he said later through the mouthpiece of his Prospero, the aim of his project was above all 'to please'.

Foreign War

He was not a man to court controversy. The early 1590s were edgy times to be an artist: the theatre was increasingly viewed with suspicion by the city authorities; there were fanatics on all sides, and Elizabeth was as worried about Puritan extremists as she was about the Catholic underground. There were strange prophecies and unsettling news stories. On 19 July 1591, a crazed Puritan fanatic, William Hacket, who had proclaimed himself the Messiah from a cart in Cheapside, was hanged, drawn and quartered.

That year English armies were fighting in France and Ireland, and alongside the Protestants who were struggling to gain independence from their Spanish overlords in the Netherlands. Here and in Normandy the Spanish were close to establishing bases from which they could mount a far more effective invasion of England than they had in 1588. Rumours abounded of another Armada. At home, out of work war veterans, many maimed or crippled, were to be seen everywhere on the roads, even between Stratford and Warwick. Huge numbers of people were on poor relief. All this added to a growing public mood of disillusionment with the regime.

Meanwhile, Elizabeth's government was still prosecuting the war against internal and external enemies. That winter further English contingents were raised and sent to help their Dutch allies in the Low Countries. Elizabeth's state archive in the Public Record Office contains lists of payments to secret agents, along with the keys to their ciphers. Robin Poley, one of the most dangerous of them, turns up in Brussels, Antwerp and Flushing 'on her majesty's secret business'. Marlowe, too, was swimming in these dangerous waters at this time. For while his plays were packing in audiences at the Rose in London, in December, in his other role as a secret agent, he went to Flushing.

Looking out over the wide, sandy estuary of the Schelde, the fortified town of Flushing was a solid point amid miles of marshy shores and a hinterland plagued by malaria, which had killed far more English troops than had enemy action (among them the poet Philip Sidney, whose brother was now English governor in Flushing). It was the entry point for the English forces: munitions, supplies, profiteers and double agents all came through here. And that winter, already charged and acquitted in one murder case, Marlowe was

arrested on more dangerous charges: an informer with whom he had shared a room had reported that he had talked about going over to the Catholic side, and that he had been experimenting with counterfeiting money. The charges may seem unbelievable, and possibly were trumped up. But then Marlowe was a man who sailed close to the wind in more than just his penchant for tobacco and boys. Evidently someone thought the wind he was catching was the Counter Reformation blowing from Rome. After an interview with the governor he was sent back by sea to England, to face his spymaster Walsingham.

That same winter the storm clouds rumbling over the Netherlands were echoed in England. In Stratford national and international politics continued to make themselves felt. A massive swoop on Baddesley Clinton in October had narrowly failed to net all the main Jesuits with their local supporters. In late November 1591 the government announced new laws against Catholics, inflamed by the writings of hardliners such as Robert Persons, who hated the queen, and William Allen, whose printed diatribes called her a heretic, an antichrist and criminally insane. It was easy, of course, for men such as Allen, safe in exile, to use such inflammatory language. For those on the ground, however, it only worsened the intolerable situation in which the English Catholic community found itself. The Jesuit missionaries themselves now lived in permanent fear of the terrible fate that awaited them. The queen's agents in the shires stepped up the pressure on recusants; the safe houses were all under surveillance by informers; in a desperate letter the head of the Jesuits, Henry Garnet, wrote: 'There is nowhere left to hide.'

Early in 1592 the government began a new squeeze of the disaffected. Recusancy lists were drawn up in every town, and in March John Shakespeare was named in a list of Stratford citizens who had 'obstinately' refused to go to church for Easter communion, although his excuse – that he had absented himself because he feared being served with a writ for debt – was accepted. It was an old excuse: John clearly still had friends in the town. But the battle for the soul of old England was almost lost. It would be left to John's son to carry it down in a different guise to later generations.

THE BIG TIME

Back in London, safe in the thronging masses of the big city, William Shakespeare's work was now rapidly broadening out to include richly comic and romantic pieces, often about men and women who fall in love despite the pressures of society, family and convention. One early show, *The Taming of the Shrew*, represented his first foray into a favourite area, the battle of the sexes.

In this reworking of an older comedy, he questioned some of the patriarchal assumptions of Tudor society, but in the ending rather lamely (to our taste at least) acquiesced in the male view. But throughout the 1590s he would quarry these themes with increasing assurance and humour and write great women's parts that pricked the pretensions of men. The many women in his audience would surely have expected no less.

His early history plays reveal other characteristic preoccupations. He was obsessed with justice, aggression, the violence of the state, the battle of conscience and power – not to mention his fascination with role playing, with people who are other than they appear. All these were threads that would run through his plays until the end. And whether the drama was about love between men and women, or about the affairs of state, things were seen from a multiple perspective. He was always setting up opposed worlds, characterized by contrasting image systems. This kind of rhetorical exercise went back to the curriculum at school, but it became one of his entrenched writing habits. All writers, of course, have their tricks, structural and verbal, as he was later to remark ruefully:

> Why write I still all one, ever the same
> And keep invention in a noted weed
> That every word doth tell my name
> Showing their birth, and where they did proceed?

In April 1592 *Henry VI* Part 1, the prequel to his *Contention of the Houses of York and Lancaster* and *Richard Duke of York*, was acted at the Rose on Bankside. It continued through May and June with fifteen shows, and Henslowe's account book shows that 16,344 people paid to see it from the galleries alone – a figure that should be more than doubled to calculate the total box office. So he was pulling in between 2000 and 3000 a performance. Shakespeare had a big hit on his hands. At this very moment an English army was fighting in Normandy, on the old battlefields of the Hundred Years War, and there was huge public interest in the unfolding events. A play on the last great war fought by the English abroad could hardly have been better timed, and in August the pamphleteer Thomas Nashe wrote about the great popular success of the English hero Talbot in *Henry VI*:

> How it would have joyed brave Talbot (the terror of the French) to think that after he had lain two hundred years in his tomb, he should triumph again on the stage, and have his bones new embalmed with the tears of

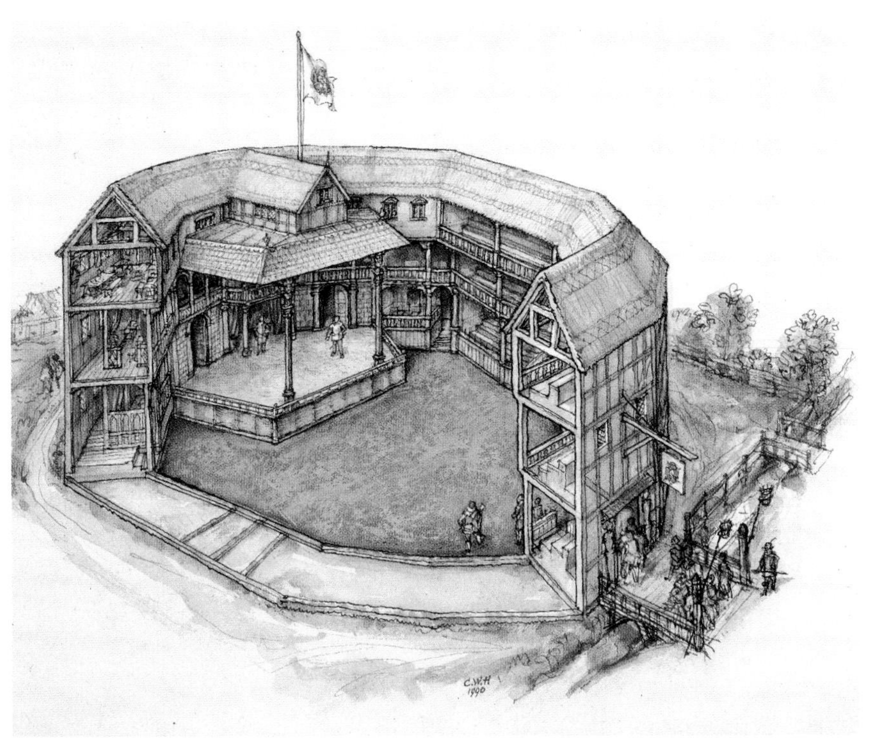

LEFT: *The Rose Theatre, imagined on the basis of the recent excavations.*
BELOW: *Shakespeare performed* Henry VI *at the Rose for Strange's company. Here Julian Glover plays Talbot in the scene that had the groundlings in tears in 1591.*

> ten thousand spectators at least ... (at several times) who in the tragedian that represents his person, imagine they behold him fresh bleeding.

It was what one might call Shakespeare's first rave review. History, comedy, English, Italian – he could do it all. And to some in the literary establishment that was cause enough to accuse him of being a conceited upstart, and even a plagiarist.

Success Breeds Envy

In late summer 1592, for the second time in six months, the commissioners in Stratford were adding Shakespeare's father's name to a list of 'obstinate recusants'. In London, we can imagine William working on *Richard III* in his room in Bishopsgate. Around that time the pamphleteer and Queen's Men writer Robert Greene, now dying, wrote an embittered open letter to three leading lights of the theatre, the university wits Marlowe, Nashe and Peele. At the centre of it was an extraordinary attack on young Shakespeare.

In words livid with resentment Greene started by disparaging actors, mean players with no loyalty who will sell writers down the river, 'puppets that spake from our mouths, those antics garnished in our colours'. Then he turned to the chief object of his fury in the most famous passage written about Shakespeare during his lifetime:

> There is an upstart crow, beautified with our feathers, that with *his tiger's heart wrapped in a player's hide* supposes he is as well able to bombast out a blank verse as the best of you, and being an absolute *Johannes Factotum* [Jack of all trades, universal genius, a Mr Do-it-all], is in his own conceit the only Shake-scene in a country.

That it is Shakespeare who is under attack is plain from the pun on his name and from the allusion to the scene in *Henry VI* Part 3 (italicized by Greene to make sure his readers got the point) where Richard of York taunts Queen Margaret as a 'tiger's heart wrapp'd in a woman's hide'. As far as Greene was concerned, Shakespeare was an upstart actor who had the effrontery to emulate authors who were his betters. Implied here too perhaps was the charge that he had been plagiarizing their scripts (which in this context would suggest the Queen's Men's plays – and it was true that a number of Shakespeare's plays had plots lifted from the Queen's Men's shows).

We know that Shakespeare was upset at Greene's attack on his talent and integrity. As Spenser had earlier suggested, it may even have made him want to hide away. But one thing was clear from such a high-profile attack. He had made it.

CHAPTER EIGHT

The Duty of Poets

WISDOM IS THE PRESERVER OF THINGS

Greene's pamphlet lambasting Shakespeare came on to the bookstalls in Paul's Yard in autumn 1592, soon after Greene's death. In December his printer, Henry Chettle, published a fulsome apology for the slanders, accompanied by an elegant compliment to Shakespeare's character. The inference is that Shakespeare now had influential friends who could demand a retraction. This, our first account of what the poet was actually like, is particularly interesting as it is absolutely contemporary, whereas the tributes in the Folio were written posthumously.

> About three months since died M. Robert Greene, leaving many papers in sundry booksellers' hands, among others his *Groatsworth of Wit*, in which a letter written to divers play-makers, is offensively by one or two of them taken ... With neither of them that take offence was I acquainted, and with one of them I care not if I never be [Marlowe?]: the other [Shakespeare], whom at that time I did not so much spare, as since I wish I had, for that as I have moderated the heat of living writers, and might have used my own discretion ... that I did not, I am as sorry, as if the original fault had been my fault, because myself have seen his demeanour no less civil than in the quality he professes [i.e. in his professional life] besides divers of worship [i.e. several high-ranking personages] have reported his uprightness of dealing, which argues his honesty, and his facetious [polished] grace in writing that approves his art ...

Chettle's carefully chosen words offer a fascinating insight into the young Shakespeare: upright in his dealings and honest, with a happy grace, in life as well as in art, prefiguring Jonson's tribute years later to Shakespeare's 'free and open nature'.

Another Attack?

But some of the mud stuck, if a commemorative volume for Greene, published in 1593, is anything to go by: it speaks of the men who 'eclipsed his fame and Purloined his plumes'. And the satirical barbs continued, if a curious passage in a play of that year, which pokes fun at someone from provincial Warwickshire, is about Shakespeare. And it comes in, of all plays, a merry version of the old tale of Guy of Warwick:

> SPARROW: I'faith Sir I was born in England at Stratford-upon-Avon in Warwickshire.
> RAINBORNE: Wer't born in England? What's thy name?
> SPARROW: Nay I have a fine finical name. I can tell ye, for my name is Sparrow; yet I am no house Sparrow, nor no hedge Sparrow, nor no peaking Sparrow, nor no sneaking Sparrow, but I am a high mounting lofty minded Sparrow, and that Parnell knows well enough, and a good many more of the pretty Wenches of our Parish i'faith.

'Sparrow' in Elizabethan English is a cant term for a lecher, a womanizer. Parnell is his Stratford wife, his 'sweet wench' whom he got with child before leaving Warwickshire. The key to the joke is the pronunciation of spear and sparrow, which sounded very similar in sixteenth-century English. 'Finical' was a pejorative word favoured by Greene's friend, the journalist Nashe, and means excessively fastidious – 'finicky' today. So, with his 'finical name', Sparrow the Warwickshire clown comes from Stratford-upon-Avon and describes himself as 'a bird of Venus and a Cock of the game', which sounds like a tilt at the author of the newly published *Venus and Adonis* (the sparrow is the bird of Venus). If this is getting at Shakespeare – and it is difficult to imagine otherwise – it is worth pointing out another odd detail: the Stratford Sparrow has abandoned his wife.

Plague and Patronage: Southampton and His Circle

On 2 February 1593 the public theatres in London were closed by the plague, and would stay shut until June 1594. By the summer Pembroke's Men had collapsed, forced 'to pawn their apparel and to stay at home'. While the

epidemic raged, Shakespeare was obliged to seek an income elsewhere. Although it was still possible to perform plays at court, in private noble houses and outside London, Shakespeare swiftly turned to other means of support for there were mouths to feed back in Stratford. He found a patron.

Patronage was the key for an ambitious poet: it supplied a source of income and social advancement. Chettle's apology had demonstrated that by the winter of 1592 Shakespeare already had friends among the well-to-do who would act for him to bring pressure against a publisher. Spenser's earlier remark – if it is about him – shows he had broken into literary circles. 'Our Willy' was now well known and moving among the great and the good. To have poets in your entourage, to sponsor poetry and to have poems dedicated to you was one way for a nobleman to become a Renaissance prince in late sixteenth-century London. Poetry, then, could be turned by its creator into gold.

Shakespeare's choice of patron was a pointed one. The Earl of Southampton was literary, beautiful, bisexual and from a Catholic dynasty, with estates in Hampshire at Titchfield and Beaulieu. By 1592 the young earl had replaced Philip Howard, the imprisoned Earl of Arundel, as the great hope of English Catholics. Southampton's father had been the most illustrious Catholic in England: a strong supporter of the Old Faith who had famously said that it was better to lose all he had than submit. He had died in mysterious circumstances soon after aiding the Jesuit Edmund Campion. Southampton's mother, a Montague, continued to maintain sanctuaries for priests at her house in Sussex and in London at Southampton House in Holborn, the centre of a highly cultured circle that patronized not only poets but also musicians such as the Catholic William Byrd. It was not surprising, then, that Southampton had been in the guardianship of Elizabeth's chief minister, Lord Burghley – effectively a hostage – from the age of nine to twelve.

There may even have been family connections between Southampton and the Warwickshire Shakespeares. Back in 1583, members of the Arden family had been found sheltering in Southampton's houses. The contacts that led to Shakespeare seeking Southampton's patronage would no doubt be revealing, but it is in the nature of the times that we are never likely to know about them: these were not the sort of things people talked about.

ABOVE: *The Earl of Southampton, Shakespeare's patron, c. 1594: 'the dear lover and cherisher as well of the lovers of poets as of the poets themselves,' wrote the journalist Thomas Nashe.*

So, not quite twenty, with a large disposable income to look forward to on his majority, Southampton would be quite a catch for a poet. And it was to him

that Shakespeare dedicated his first published poem, *Venus and Adonis*, which was registered six weeks or so into the plague outbreak in April 1593. Written perhaps during the previous year or two, it may have circulated first in manuscript; printing was not usually the first sight of a work of poetry.

Venus and Adonis

The publisher of *Venus and Adonis* was Richard Field, a Stratford contemporary a couple of years older than Shakespeare. It was nicely produced with ornamental motifs, and very carefully proofread, so Shakespeare must have stood in Field's shop in the Blackfriars and corrected the poem off the first printed sheets – taking care perhaps to iron out his idiosyncratic spellings. He called it the 'first heir of my invention', which may mean a work he had had in draft since Stratford, but more likely that this was his first poem in print. Quoting Ovid, he announced his intent in a motto:

> *Vilia meretur vulgus; mihi flavus Apollo*
> *Pocula Castalia plena ministret aqua*
>
> Let what is cheap excite the wonder of the common herd;
> For me may golden Apollo minister full cups from the spring of the Muses

His ambition was to be an English heir to Ovid, as critics of the day would soon point out. The poem was prefaced by a letter from Shakespeare to Southampton, 'the Right Honourable Henry Wriothesley Earl of Southampton and Baron of Titchfield'. It does not prove, however, that he was already a member of the earl's circle: poets did not always ask their dedicatees in advance to use their name, and not all were impressed or grateful. This dedication, one of only two surviving letters written by Shakespeare, exhibits the self-effacing class-consciousness that runs right through his career.

> Right Honourable,
> I know not how I shall offend in dedicating my unpolished lines to your lordship, nor how the world will censure me for choosing so strong a prop to support so weak a burden. Only, if your honour seem but pleased, I account myself highly praised, and vow to take advantage of all idle hours till I have honoured you with some graver labour. But if the first heir of my invention prove deformed, I shall be sorry it had so noble a godfather, and never after ear [plough] so

barren a land for fear it yield me still so bad a harvest. I leave it to your honourable survey, and your honour to your heart's content, which I may wish may always answer your own wish, and the world's hopeful expectation.
Your honour's in all duty,
William Shakespeare

To us the tone is a little smarmy, but excessive self-deprecation was fitting in his day for a lower middle-class writer seeking noble patronage. Whatever Southampton felt about it, the poem was a big hit. It went through ten printings up to 1617, most copies of which were read to destruction: very few examples

TO THE RIGHT HONORABLE
Henrie VVriotheſley, Earle of Southampton,
and Baron of Titchfield.

Ight Honourable, I know not how I ſhall offend in dedicating my vnpoliſht lines to your Lordſhip, nor how the worlde vvill cenſure mee for chooſing ſo ſtrong a proppe to ſupport ſo vveake a burthen, onelye if your Honour ſeeme but pleaſed, I account my ſelfe highly praiſed, and vowe to take aduantage of all idle houres, till I haue honoured you vvith ſome grauer labour. But if the firſt heire of my inuention proue deformed, I ſhall be ſorie it had ſo noble a god-father: and neuer after eare ſo barren a land, for feare it yeeld me ſtill ſo bad a harueſt, I leaue it to your Honourable ſuruey, and your Honor to your hearts content, vvhich I wiſh may alvvaies anſvvere your ovvne vviſh, and the vvorlds hopefull expectation.

Your Honors in all dutie,

William Shakeſpeare.

Left: *Shakespeare's letter to Southampton mixes courtly deference with the dialect word 'eare' – to plough – an Old English verb almost obsolete in the sixteenth century, but which might still have come easily to a countryman.*

survive. Among its first readers was a madman, William Reynolds, who fantasized that Queen Elizabeth loved him and that the poem was a coded 'secret hope of some great love in the queen towards me'. It would prove especially popular among students, who liked a polished bit of high-class erotica. 'I'll worship sweet Mr Shakespeare,' wrote one, 'and to honour him will lay with his *Venus and Adonis* under my pillow.' Like a lot of country boys, Shakespeare was good on sex.

Here is the goddess pulling her boy lover into her 'ivory pale', the white circle of her arms:

> I'll be a park, and thou shalt be my deer:
> Feed where thou wilt, on mountain or in dale;
> Graze on my lips, and if those hills be dry,
> Stray lower, where the pleasant fountains lie.
> Within this limit is relief enough,
> Sweet bottom grass, and high delightful plain,
> Round rising hillocks, brakes obscure and rough ...

The luscious topography of Venus's body is obvious: fountains, hillocks and dales; the grass in the bottom of a valley, of course, is the most succulent; the brakes (thickets) are her pubic hair. So the Bird of Venus and Cock of the Game sought to titillate students (and young lords like Southampton, who seems to have liked erotica). But in the charged political and religious atmosphere of the early 1590s, was this the kind of verse that a self-respecting poet should have been writing? There were some who thought not.

Erotics Versus the Pursuit of Virtue

In his *Defence of Poesie*, written in 1582, Philip Sidney had already linked the creative art of the poet with the pursuit of virtue: 'Since our erected wit maketh us to know what perfection is, and yet our infected will keepeth us from reaching unto it'. The idea behind this was religious. The modern reader, of course, would not see moral improvement – or, for that matter, political education – as the reason to read a poem. Today we would rather agree with Keats, that poetry is about feeling – the 'fine excess' of poetry that stretches minds and sensibility with an inventiveness outstripping our expectation. We look to a great poet to see more than an ordinary person. As Seamus Heaney puts it, 'This is how poems help us live ... They take and give our proper measure.'

But in the sixteenth century 'our proper measure' was hard to separate from the religious view of the world. And the religious view of the world was at the centre of the cultural crisis of the age. For that reason, in Shakespeare's early years in London there raged a great debate on the duty of poets.

As we have seen, Southampton's circle was tainted with the Old Religion. Southampton himself had been a prize in the struggle between the regime, the missionaries and the Catholic moderates. At this time Burghley had commanded him to marry his own granddaughter: Southampton had pleaded for time, conferred with a priest and eventually refused. It brought him a huge fine of £5000. Years later it was discovered by Elizabeth's inquisitor, Richard Topcliffe, that Southampton's confessor and spiritual adviser had been his cousin, the charismatic Jesuit priest Robert Southwell, who had at one time sheltered in the earl's mother's Holborn house. This discovery points to an intriguing connection at this formative moment in Shakespeare's career, for Southwell was distantly related to Shakespeare through the Ardens. But he was also a poet, and it was Southwell who produced the most urgent manifesto for poetry in the early 1590s.

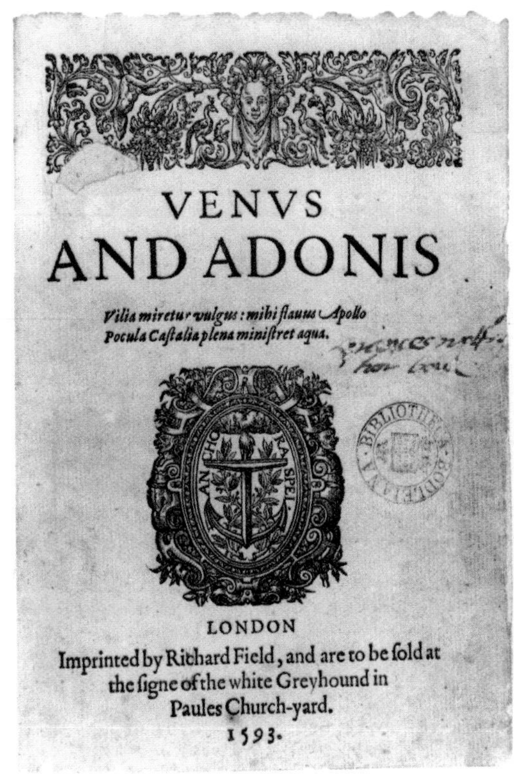
VENVS
AND ADONIS

Vilia miretur vulgus: mihi flauus Apollo
Pocula Castalia plena ministret aqua.

LONDON
Imprinted by Richard Field, and are to be sold at the signe of the white Greyhound in Paules Church-yard.
1593.

ABOVE: Venus and Adonis, *which many male readers thought a guide for the 'bold-faced suitor'. It soon had cult status among students: 'we shall have nothing but pure Shakespeare' said the Cambridge in-crowd.*

Shadow Lives: Robert Southwell

By the time *Venus and Adonis* was published Southwell was in prison awaiting his trial and execution. But his poems, pamphlets and political tracts were widely circulated among the intelligentsia in manuscript and even in printed form. They were read by everyone from the queen to Burghley, Bacon and their torturer Topcliffe.

Southwell had been in England since 1586, living underground, moving from place to place and trying to 'bring succour to the faithful'. Hot on his heels, Topcliffe had nearly got him in October 1591 when Southwell and eleven leading Jesuits had met at their safe house close to Stratford at Baddesley Clinton. The next year, staying in London at Southampton House, Elizabeth's Public Enemy Number One had walked the streets in broad daylight in a black velvet cloak, a saintly Scarlet Pimpernel. Southwell had Hampshire family connections, too, and his track as a hunted man naturally led to the Southamptons at Titchfield.

He was also a central figure in the political debate among Catholics over the question of their allegiance to the queen. It was Southwell who drafted an extraordinary response to the government's anti-Catholic measures of autumn 1591: *An Humble Supplication to Her Majesty*, addressed to the queen herself, insisted that it was possible to be both patriotic and a Catholic. Printed in early 1592 at a secret press, it was much read and often admired, although Queen Elizabeth is said to have replied that to do what Southwell asked, to allow Catholics freedom of worship, would be 'to lay my body at their feet'. It had been easy for those living in safety on the Continent, implacable enemies such as William Allen, to dismiss Elizabeth as an illegitimate heretic; those like Southwell, who were on the ground in England with their lives on the line, were more sensitive to the temper of the English, the perception of foreign threat and the widespread love of the queen. But by then the damage had been done for the English Catholic community.

ABOVE: *The only known image of Robert Southwell. The marks of privation are clearly visible in his face.* OPPOSITE: *Southwell's manifesto to his cousin 'Master WS': 'Poets, by abusing their talent, and making the follies, and feignings of love the customary subject of their base endeavours, have so discredited this faculty....'*

At the same time Southwell entered into the debate about poetry. Even if he had not been able to change the views of the political establishment, as a poet and writer he was able to influence its literary counterpart. He was also covetous of literary fame, fascinated by the role of poetry in changing hearts and minds. He saw a need for a spiritual poesy in an age of violent, bawdy entertainment in the world of the public theatres, the bear- and bull-baiting arenas and the stews (brothels), and of Renaissance game-playing in the world of the sonneteers.

Southwell wrote many poems, not all of them successful, but some startling in their fantastic and original imagery. Most famous was 'The Burning Babe', which Ben Jonson particularly admired, and which Shakespeare used in *Macbeth*. Printed in 1595, his poems went through thirteen editions in a generation and were counted among the most successful of the age – alongside Shakespeare's *Venus and Adonis*. Together they represent the twin poles of Elizabethan devotional poetry, the one to God, the other to Love.

'My Loving and Good Cousin': The Mystery of WS

Southwell was concerned about the role of the poet in what he saw as an Age of Tyrants, a time of persecution like that of the Christian martyrs in the later

Roman Empire. His ideas were put down in a remarkable letter that became an influential tract for the times and that has hitherto unexplored bearings on Shakespeare's biography. For Southwell seems to have urged the rising young talent of the day to write religious poetry.

TO MY WORTHY
GOOD COSEN
Maiſter W. S.

WORTHY COSEN,

POETS, by abuſing their talent, and making the follies, and faygnings of loue the cuſtomary ſubiect of their baſe endeauours, haue ſo diſcredited this facultie, that a Poet, a Louer, and a Lyar, are by many reckoned but three words of one ſignification. But the vanity of men cannot counterpoyſe the authority of God, who deliuering many parts of Scripture in verſe, and by his Apoſtle willing vs to exerciſe our deuotion in Hymnes and ſpirituall Sonnets, warranteth the Art to be good, and the vſe allowable. And therefore, not only among the Heathen, whoſe Gods were cheifely canonized by their Poets, and their Paynim Diuinity oracled in verſe: but euen in the Old and New Teſtament it hath beene vſed by men of greateſt piety, in matters of moſt deuotion. Chriſt himſelfe by making a Hymne, the concluſion of his laſt Supper, and the Prologue to the firſt Pageant of his Paſſion, gaue his Spouſe a methode to imitate, as in the Office of the Church it appeareth, and to all men a patterne to know

A 2 the

Composed perhaps just before his capture in July 1592, and circulated as a preface to a manuscript collection of his poems, the letter was addressed to his 'loving and good cousin' who, he said, had encouraged him to publish his poetry. His cousin, he asserted, was a far superior poet, but Southwell took him to task over the role of poets in such an age, insisting on their obligation to write spiritual work. In a dedicatory poem to the reader Southwell spelt out precisely what he had in mind: 'Still the finest wits are (di)stilling Venus' rose … playing with pagan toys …' He clearly admired his cousin's talent, though not his erotic themes. In the end, he concluded, 'it rests in your will …'.

Is this mere convention? Venus, after all, is at the heart of all love poetry. Or had Southwell read *Venus and Adonis* in Southampton's house? Several poets in the early 1590s were affected by Southwell's plea, most famously the Protestant Edmund Spenser. Thomas Lodge was another: it changed his life's direction. In the final lines of the letter Southwell smiles about his own 'ditties' compared with the much finer verse of his loving cousin:

> Blame me not (good Cosin) though I send you a blame-worthy present; in which the most that can commend it is the good will of the writer; neither arte nor invention giving it any credite. If in me this be a fault, you cannot be faultlesse that did importune me to commit it … In the meane time, with many good wishes, I send you these few ditties; adde you the tunes, and let the Meane, I pray you, be still a part in all your musicke.

Although in early editions the addressee is called 'my loving and good cousin',

in the one brought out in 1616 (coincidentally or not, just after Shakespeare's death) his initials are given. They are WS.

Spies and Informers

Venus and Adonis hit the bookstalls in the summer of 1593. That spring had been grim, with terrible weather, plague and growing unemployment all contributing to a general disillusionment with the government. Amid rumours of a new Spanish invasion, the prosecution of recusants had intensified. There were disquieting signs of xenophobia, especially against the supposed cosseting of 'Flemings and Strangers' resident in London; racism was always bubbling below the surface of Elizabeth's England. In May a nasty libel was nailed to the door of the Dutch church in London, lumping French and Dutch immigrants together with the Jews ('Like the Jews you eat us up as bread') and threatening them with death unless they 'fly, fly and never return'. Beefed up with allusions to Marlowe's plays, the libel was signed, a little too transparently, 'Tamburlaine'. But the power of the state would soon come crashing down on two of Shakespeare's main theatrical acquaintances and rivals.

Recently lawyers acting for the Archbishop of Canterbury, John Whitgift, had published *Conspiracy for a Pretended Reformation*, arguing that religious radicals were conspiring to overthrow Church and State. Orthodoxy was more and more the cry. In 1593 there was a spate of polemical books against Presbyterians and Puritans, and an official drive to root out dissent. Parliament passed a bill to deal with the 'wicked practices of seditious sectaries and disloyal persons'. As always, literature, publishing and the theatre were among the main targets.

The Dutch libel pointed the finger at Marlowe. In its wake the playwright Thomas Kyd's rooms were ransacked by the authorities. Their report states that 'vile hereticall Conceiptes denyinge the deity of Jhesus Christe our Saviour [were] fownd emongst the papers of thos Kydd prisoner'. After which another hand has scribbled in a different ink 'which he affirmethe that he had from Marlowe'.

Kyd denied any knowledge of the papers, which may have been planted, and attributed their presence to the fact that he and Marlowe had once shared rooms. He was interrogated, tortured, and died from his injuries the following year.

A few days after the 'discovery' of these papers Marlowe himself was arrested and examined by the Privy Council. A secret agent in government pay, he had already been arrested once that winter, on the Dutch island of Flushing, on the basis of an informer's report that he had been forging coins and had expressed an intention to go over to the Catholic side. True or not, there was also the question of his plays. Of his recent shows, *Edward II* was a portrait of a corrupt court, time-serving courtiers and a weak ruler; *The Massacre at Paris* was about one of the most controversial events in contemporary history, the pogroms conducted against the Protestant Huguenots. Allegory was a complicated matter taken very seriously by the government. A writer could be faced with the rack, and even execution, for a historical work perceived to have 'application to the times'. Marlowe was released, but only on a kind of bail: he had to present himself to the authorities daily.

MARLOWE'S MURDER

On 30 May Marlowe went to a meeting at Deptford. Here, within sight of the centre of Elizabethan power, the palace at Greenwich, was an area dominated by government and naval establishments, and many of the grand houses along the river frontage were connected with them. Disembarking at the Watergate – still there today, overgrown and sprouting weeds, washed by the greasy green swell – Marlowe would have walked down a narrow lane to a row of houses along the waterfront. Here a Mrs Bull kept her lodging place: not a tavern, as legend has it, but a government safe house run by a widow who had family connections with the queen's spymaster, Sir Francis Walsingham.

With Marlowe that day were three men, all government agents who operated on the dark side of Gloriana's body politic. Nicholas Skeres was a street thug and Ingram Frizer a blackmailer and petty shark, but the third man, Robin Poley, was a major player in the world of espionage, the secret theatre of the Elizabethan age. A former Catholic, he had been the *agent provocateur* in the most savage of all the Elizabethan government's stings, the Babington Plot. There were dark stories of male victims falling in love with him, anguished whispers of sodomy, of sex used in entrapment: 'My beloved Robin (as I hope you are),' wrote his biggest and saddest catch, Antony Babington himself, in a farewell letter: 'otherwise of all two footed beings the most wicked'. Marlowe's sort of man perhaps?

Why the meeting was held is not known, nor whether it was official. Maybe Marlowe meant to flee the country by ship from Deptford. Maybe he wanted Poley to intercede with the Privy Council to take the heat off him. Whatever the reason, the four men ate, walked in the garden and smoked, before tempers flared in the early evening and Marlowe was stabbed between the eyes by Frizer.

It sounds like a professional job: modern assassins are trained to go for the throat or to stab the eyes. But, not surprisingly, the coroner in a naval town decided it was misadventure – an argument 'over the reckoning' (the bill) as they claimed at the inquest. The killer was pardoned swiftly and quietly, just as Poley himself had been freed after the Babington Plot. A scribal copy of the

intelligence note on Marlowe's 'heretical Conceiptes' was carefully altered by a government official after the event, to tidy the case up. Bureaucracies in a police state are the same everywhere.

Some years later, in *As You Like It*, Shakespeare put a rather enigmatic comment on the killing into the mouth of the clown Touchstone, who compares himself to the 'most capricious poet, honest Ovid' who was exiled for his verses by the emperor Augustus: 'When a man's verses cannot be understood, nor a man's good wit seconded with the forward child understanding, it strikes a man more dead than a great reckoning in a little room.'

The grim pun on a famous Marlowe line, 'infinite riches in a little room', suggests who Shakespeare was thinking about. And with it a pointed hint at the real charge: was it also Marlowe's plays that had got him into trouble?

Marlowe had been Shakespeare's first great inspiration. They had come from the same social background and were the same age, but Marlowe went up the fast track via university. Success for him had been so swift, so easy and so big that he may have thought he could get away with anything. A man 'liable to sudden privy injuries', perhaps Marlowe had just got caught up in the paranoia of the time. For an artist on the public stage that was easy to do – unless, like Shakespeare, you kept things close to your chest.

Poetry in a Graver Vein

While the theatres remained closed, Shakespeare may have written *The Comedy of Errors*, a brilliant reworking of a piece by the Roman comic playwright Plautus, which Shakespeare had probably read in Latin at school. By now he was becoming an expert at his craft and the play is very cleverly plotted; it retained its popularity well into James I's reign. And where some of his early shows, such as *Love's Labour's Lost*, seem over-wordy to a modern audience, *The Comedy of Errors* still works a treat with its helter-skelter action based on the mistaken identity of two sets of twins (the father of twins himself, Shakespeare made twins the central characters in two of his plays, and pulled it off). Some of the key plot ideas are particularly interesting: shipwrecks, storms, personal loss, parents and children, the reuniting of a family; the potential of tragedy in comedy. These were themes to which he would return compulsively all his life.

He was also working on more non-dramatic poetry. In summer 1593 he had promised Southampton a 'graver work' than *Venus and Adonis*, and on 9 May the following year he duly registered for publication *The Rape of Lucrece*. The poem was a typical Renaissance humanist reinvention of a classical theme, with perhaps a strand of Christian allegory that we can no longer decipher. Certainly 'graver',

then – though surely not answering the criticisms levelled at secular poetry by Southwell. The letter of dedication to Southampton was still self-deprecating and class-conscious, but its phrasing was now more assured. It also stressed duty, suggesting that he was now in Southampton's service and receiving money.

Money clearly meant a lot to Shakespeare. His father had been broken financially and driven from office; the son would work hard to restore the family's fortunes. He might be paid no more than £10 by his patron for a poem; but, long-term, such a relationship might raise very much more. There is a later story that Southampton gave him £1000 for the purchase of a property: unlikely, perhaps, but still, a hint of the rewards that might lie ahead.

THE MAGNIFICENT ELEVEN: THE COMPANY IS FORMED

In the same month that *The Rape of Lucrece* was registered, Shakespeare, with Burbage, joined a new company formed by the Lord Chamberlain Hunsdon, the company with which he would work for the rest of his career. Along with Edward Alleyn's Admiral's Men, they would come to bestride the London theatre world like colossi. The Admiral's Men did Marlowe plays with Alleyn as the star at the Rose on Bankside; the Chamberlain's Men had Richard Burbage playing the leads in Shakespeare's shows at the Theatre in Shoreditch.

The roots of the company went back a long way. Some of the group had been with him in Pembroke's Men in 1592, some (Burbage, Kemp, Sly, Philips) with Strange's company in 1590; it is possible that Shakespeare had known John Hemmings in the Queen's Men back in 1587. Many of them had Warwickshire and Worcestershire connections. As we have seen, after the split of Strange's company in 1591, Shakespeare had most likely stayed with the Burbages (father James and son Richard, respectively leaseholder and leading actor) in Shoreditch. This was the crucial connection with what would become first the Chamberlain's Men and then the King's Men: the greatest acting company in the history of the theatre, which would build the Globe and perform the plays of Shakespeare, Ben Jonson, Beaumont and Fletcher, Massinger and Shirley until the closing of the theatres in 1642 at the start of the Civil War.

In June the theatres reopened and the new company ('my Lord Chamberlain's Men') played alongside the Admiral's Men for Henslowe at Newington Butts, a mile from London Bridge. The theatre was not a favourite of the actors, not just because of the long walk involved but on account of its insalubrious setting over a sewer opposite the Fishmongers' company almshouses.

In Henslowe's account book a line is drawn after 13 June; it marks a watershed in English drama. From that date all his performances were by the

RIGHT: *Shakespeare's patron Lord Hunsdon. A blunt-spoken, popular figure, Hunsdon created a new company out of the remains of Strange's Men after Lord Strange's death by poison in April 1594.*

Admiral's Men, probably at the Rose, and relations with the Chamberlain's Men ceased. Shakespeare, Richard Burbage and the rest of the company went on tour to hone their act after the long lay-off. They played Marlborough that autumn, then came back to London, where in early October their new patron, the bluff-spoken Lord Hunsdon, wrote to the Lord Mayor asking for a licence for his players to continue their occupation of the Cross Keys during the winter. Hunsdon's letter reveals the cajoling, threats and bribes required:

> Where my now company of players have been accustomed for the better exercise of their quality, and for the service of her Majesty if

The Workes of William Shakeſpeare,

containing all his Comedies, Hiſtories, and Tragedies: Truely ſet forth, according to their firſt *ORIGINALL.*

The Names of the Principall Actors in all theſe Playes.

Illiam Shakeſpeare.

Richard Burbadge.

John Hemmings.

Auguſtine Phillips.

William Kempt.

Thomas Poope.

George Bryan.

Henry Condell.

William Slye.

Richard Cowly.

John Lowine.

Samuell Croſſe.

Alexander Cooke.

Samuel Gilburne.

Robert Armin.

William Oſtler.

Nathan Field.

John Underwood.

Nicholas Tooley.

William Eccleſtone.

Joſeph Taylor.

Robert Benfield.

Robert Goughe.

Richard Robinſon.

Iohn Shancke.

Iohn Rice.

LEFT: *The list of actors in the 1623 Folio. The core group of the first eleven names goes back to Strange's company of 1589–90; some go back even earlier to the Queen's and Leicester's Men.*

need so require, to play this winter time within the City at the Cross Keys in Gracious [Gracechurch] Street. These are to require and pray your Lordship to permit and suffer them so to do … they have undertaken to me that, where heretofore they began not their plays till towards four o'clock, they will now begin at two, and have done between four and five, and will not use any Drums or trumpets at all for the calling of the people together, and shall be contributaries to the poor of the parish where they play according to their abilities.

This fascinating document suggests that the actors wanted a temporary winter move from Shoreditch to a converted inner yard or sizeable 'great chamber'. From that time, except for provincial tours in 1596 and 1597, the Chamberlain's Men would be based in London. On 15 March 1595 Richard Burbage appeared as joint payee with Will Kemp and William Shakespeare, 'servants to the Lord Chamberlain', for 'plays performed before Her Majesty' at court on 26 and 28 December. This is the first document that specifically associates Shakespeare with an acting company, and the first mention of his name with respect to a theatrical performance. It proves he was now a leading member of Hunsdon's company; he would stay with them, and the King's Men, which they later became, until he retired from the stage altogether.

'Most Excellent for Tragedy': The First Masterpieces

A stable and experienced company, assured political backing (for now at least) and a permanent theatre: it is all that any dramatist would desire today. It is no surprise that from this time Shakespeare spread his wings and his art widened and deepened. In London he staged shows at the Theatre, in the royal palaces and the lawyers' halls, and sometimes gave private performances at noble houses; he also played at town halls and guildhalls up and down the land. He was probably contracted to deliver two plays a year, giving the company formal consent that he could not publish them without the express consent of his 'fellows'.

Just turned thirty, Shakespeare was on a creative high. Over the next three years he wrote a string of brilliant plays, moving from being a straight entertainer to an explorer of deeper themes. He was now a thinking artist enriched by life, age, experience, politics and broader reading. In this second phase of his career we begin to see his seriousness, and his interest in the drama of personality which would culminate in *Hamlet*. Alongside these concerns he was continuing his project on English history, which he now took beyond the level of any of his contemporaries in three great history plays: *Richard II* and the two parts of *Henry IV*.

Richard II, with Burbage as the king, added a new dimension to his writing. Expressing himself in wonderful lyric poetry, Shakespeare was now presenting politics as a kind of morality play and the theatre as a source of moral power. Here we can see the beginnings of a cunning and conscious public artist. The deposition of Richard, a weak king, was a dangerous topic and had to be handled with very great tact: the first three printings of this, one of his most carefully written plays, do not include the deposition scene. It was a tale easily capable of being understood as political allegory, and it attracted great interest: Robert Cecil, Burghley's powerful younger son, was invited to a private show at

a London house in December 1595. Around the same time Shakespeare also remade an old Queen's Men show on King John, a very anti-Catholic play whose rhetoric he removed in a systematic and perhaps revealing way in order to open up his characteristic dual viewpoints and present on stage the clash of opposites.

But not all his tragedies were about history. *Romeo and Juliet* is a young man's play about love and death, adolescent angst and suicide. Shakespeare may have staged it in some form by late 1594 or early the following year; it was in print by 1597 and then revised by the author in collaboration with his performers at least until the publication of a second quarto in 1599. It was, and still is, a scintillating show full of energy and movement: masques, torch-bearers running on and off, and the ever-popular stage fights. The plot is driven by the fateful series of misunderstandings and coincidences that propel the drama to its tragic climax. The dominant feelings experienced by the audience are the oppressive heat of a Verona summer, the emotions being ratcheted up, the whizz-bang exhilaration of speed and clash, and, of course, the intensity of the lovers' passion. This sexually charged enactment of adolescence, which explains its emotional appeal to modern teenagers, was brilliantly conveyed in the recent film by Baz Luhrman. Has anyone other than Shakespeare ever dramatized so comprehensively the experience of adolescence?

Romeo and Juliet was a tremendous success, which had an instant effect on the imagination of audiences and the theatre world. Among the many literary references to it from the late 1590s, the critic Francis Meres declared that 'Shakespeare among the English is the most excellent … for Tragedy'.

Fairies and Mechanicals

Shakespeare was also, of course, a great comic writer. At the same time, in 1595 or 1596, *A Midsummer Night's Dream* was played, perhaps before the queen at court in Greenwich, for a wedding in the Stanley family. It was a new play with several sources, including the recent Guy of Warwick play in which Oberon, king of the fairies, wakens Guy with fairy music. *A Midsummer Night's Dream* is a characteristic and deceptively clever mix of light and almost dark, with typical reflections on the irrational power of Eros, Blind Cupid: a theme Shakespeare followed right to the end of his career. The play contains some wonderful courtly poetry mixed with hilarious low-life scenes involving a bunch of 'mechanicals': Shakespeare is always unerring in his observation of lower-class people, though the fun he pokes at them is never devoid of affection. But the comedy has a bitter-sweet edge, and the profundity is put in the hands not of the nobles, but of the weaver 'bully Bottom', the amoral fairies with their disdain for humans

('what fools these mortals be') and especially that creature of the old Warwickshire countryside, Puck, Robin Goodfellow.

> If we shadows have offended,
> Think but this – and all is mended –
> That you have but slumber'd here
> While these visions did appear.
> And this weak and idle theme,
> No more yielding but a dream …

This is the first of the author's many reflections about theatre as a metaphor for existence: the world as a stage. It is also the first of his questionings of the insufficiency of art itself. 'The best in this kind,' says Theseus of the acting profession, 'are but shadows.' And, in a curiously precise echo of Southwell,

> The lunatic, the lover and the poet
> Are of imagination all compact …

Shakespeare had struck gold. *Romeo and Juliet* and *A Midsummer Night's Dream* are about as exhilarating and magical as theatre can get. The two plays had an extraordinary effect on the theatre culture of the day, influencing each other, Shakespeare's later plays and the whole contemporary network of written language and speech. They showed the world what he could do. And, even more important, they showed Shakespeare himself what he could do.

Fools of Time: The Passion of Robert Southwell

Just as *A Midsummer Night's Dream* was being staged in the New Year of 1595, the final act of another drama was being played out – a drama of which Shakespeare could not have failed to be aware. In February, after two and a half years in jail, Southwell was tried before Lord Chief Justice Coke. The Jesuit was the epitome of reason, while the psychopathic state inquisitor Topcliffe raged. The verbatim record shadows Shakespeare's later explorations of power, conscience and cruelty:

> SOUTHWELL: I am decayed in memory with long and close imprisonment, and I have been tortured ten times. I had rather have endured ten executions. I speak not this for myself, but for others; that they may not be handled so inhumanly, to drive men to desperation, if it were possible.

TOPCLIFFE: If he were racked, let me die for it.
SOUTHWELL: No; but it was as evil a torture, of late device.
TOPCLIFFE: I did but set him against a wall.
SOUTHWELL: Thou art a bad man.
TOPCLIFFE: I would blow you all to dust if I could.
SOUTHWELL: What, all?
TOPCLIFFE: Ay, all.
SOUTHWELL: What, soul and body too?

Inevitably, though he continued to protest his loyalty to the queen, Southwell was sentenced to be hanged, drawn and quartered at Tyburn. Another kind of theatre in Elizabethan England, public executions were highly ritualized events intended to terrify and intimidate. After the dragging on a hurdle through the streets, the last-minute remonstrations, the calls for recantation and the declarations of faith and loyalty, came the dreadful sequence of torture and butchery, which began with the victim only partly hanged and therefore still alive. This is the kind of thing Shakespeare wrote about in *Julius Caesar*:

To cut the head off and then hack the limbs
Like wrath in death and envy afterwards ...
Let's kill him boldly, but not wrathfully;
Let's carve him as a dish fit for the gods,
Not hew him as a carcass fit for hounds:

Aggression was at the heart of Shakespeare's work, and at the heart of his time. Despite months of torture, armed with the techniques of meditation taught by his order, Southwell went through his terrifying ordeal with steely will: one of the 'fools of time' who 'die for goodness, who have liv'd for crime' as Shakespeare put it later in one of his sonnets.

The resonance of Southwell's tale reached to the very top. Mysteriously, his high-ranking Catholic friends – or Catholic sympathizers, such as Charles Blount, Lord Mountjoy – had a private audience with Elizabeth the night before his death, to convey to her Southwell's solemn oath that he intended no treason against her. After his execution they saw her again, to show her, of all things, 'a book Southwell wrote about the duty of poets' – the text of Southwell's plea to his cousin WS on the true role of poets. She, of course, was interested in poetry and books, wrote sonnets herself, and had translated Boethius and possibly even Seneca; she respected literary people. When she read it she is reported to have shown 'signs of grief'.

A Traitor to the Catholic Cause?

Shakespeare certainly read Southwell. In *Macbeth* he echoes the surreal imagery of Southwell's poem 'The Burning Babe' ('but newly born … a pretty babe all burning bright did in the air appear … such floods of tears did shed') when he writes:

> And pity like a naked new born babe
> Striding the blast, or heaven's cherubim horsed
> Upon the sightless couriers of the air,
> Shall blow the horrid deed in every eye
> That tears shall drown the wind.

But he had an open mind. He also read the work of the great Protestant preacher Henry Smith, published in 1593 by his friend Richard Field. Southwell and Smith make a fascinating pair of complementary literary influences: from opposing sides doctrinally, both write about power and conscience and both are literary models of great power. Southwell was influenced by English and Italian religious poetry; Smith by the Bible and Ovid. What Southwell showed was that the debate about the nature of the poet in the 1590s involved everyone, from all walks of life and across the whole spectrum of religious belief.

However, Southwell's plea to his fellow poets to write religious poetry seems to have been rejected by Shakespeare. The only possible exception is the dark and wonderful *Phoenix and Turtle*, which we now know was a memorial to a catholic widow, Anne Line, executed at Tyburn early in 1601. Later in his career he was criticized by Catholic underground writers in terms that suggest he was seen as betraying the cause. One tract off a Catholic secret press a few years later gives a list of Shakespeare plays and poems, and rejects his agenda with a specifically religious theory of tragedy:

> Of Troylus faith, and Cressid's falsitie,
> Of Rychard's strategems for the englishe crowne,
> Of Tarquins lust, and lucrece chastitie,
> Of these, of none of these my muse nowe treates

Living his double life between London and Stratford, he went his own way as a playwright for the public theatres, secular and humanistic. Of course, there were good pragmatic reasons to do so. But could he no longer believe in the religious universe espoused by men such as Southwell and his own father? John Donne, another former Catholic, would speak of a time when all coherence was gone. In the greatest phase of his art, Shakespeare would explore what that incoherence meant.

CHAPTER NINE

'A Hell of Time'

Hope in Adversity

By the summer of 1596 Shakespeare was already the greatest poet in the English language, and he would be still regarded as such today even if he had written nothing more after *Romeo and Juliet*. Well liked and discreet, he had the patronage of noblemen, and his language reveals an increasing familiarity with rich clothes, fine food and good taste. His shows had become regular post-Christmas entertainment for the queen. Apart, perhaps, from the long separations from Anne and the children, life was all it could be. But fate has a habit of striking when least expected.

The Death of Hamnet Shakespeare

Throughout all the time Shakespeare had been living in London it is assumed that his family were living in the Henley Street house in Stratford with his parents, his brothers and his surviving sister. According to a seventeenth-century diarist, he went home only once a year, presumably during the thirty days of Lent when the theatres were closed. It might seem as if he had in some sense abandoned his family, if not financially, then emotionally. But people have to adapt to their circumstances. London was where his employment lay – and therefore his income, which supported them. No doubt he wrote home, and both sides would have had to accommodate themselves to the situation as best they could. That summer, however, brought a double blow. On 22 July Shakespeare's patron, Lord Hunsdon, died. He was succeeded as chamberlain by Lord Cobham, who was not well disposed to the players. It was an ominous

moment professionally, for now the threat of closure hung over them. Much worse was to follow. The Stratford register of burials contains this simple entry: '1596 11 August Hamnet son of William Shakespeare'. The boy was eleven. We know that there was famine and plague in the Warwickshire countryside at that time, exacerbated by a run of wet summers and bad harvests, but the cause of Hamnet's death is unknown. Shakespeare's company was on tour in Kent in early August. Hamnet was very likely buried before his father got the bad news.

Shakespeare was thirty-two, no longer young by the standards of his time; and now his only son was gone. There can be no more shattering blow in life. Hamnet's death may also have been a turning point in the poet's art. Within the next year or two a change gradually came about not only in Shakespeare's themes but also in his way of writing, in his language and imagery. The great tragedies followed, plumbing 'the well of darkness'. This was not only a personal tragedy but a powerful intimation of mortality.

Often, when this kind of event occurs in the lives of very busy people, they go straight back to work to bury their sorrow in activity. Shakespeare continued to live in London, working in the theatre and separated from Anne and his daughters. They had no more children – at forty, she was perhaps now too old. But grief for lost children does not end – it widens and deepens over the years. Shakespeare's biographers have searched for possible clues in his work: a passage in *King John* about the boy and the empty room where his clothes still lie on the bed is often singled out, but it is impossible to say whether such writing is autobiographical. There is, however, as we shall see, compelling evidence to suggest his response to the death of his son in poems he wrote soon afterwards. These poems describe his love for a beautiful boy, and his passionate sexual affair with a married woman, both of which might be seen in some sense as responses to personal tragedy, especially perhaps in a middle-aged man.

But before we turn to those poems, some of the practical things he did in the next few months are also interesting in the aftermath of such a trauma. For example, he bought a large house in Stratford for his family, which he renovated. But the first thing he did, just ten weeks after Hamnet's death, is no less revealing. On the morning of 20 October 1596 Shakespeare went to the College of Arms in London to apply for a coat of arms and gentleman status for his father.

The Coat of Arms: 'Not Without Right'

The College of Arms is still there between St Paul's and the river, where it was rebuilt after the Great Fire of 1666. On the front window ledges stand painted wooden heraldic devices – griffons, unicorns and basilisks – the relics of bygone ceremonials. Portraits of former heralds stare down, including that of the irascible William Dethick who interviewed Shakespeare that day. Climbing the creaky wooden staircase, there is more than a faint whiff of Hogwarts, Griffendor and Ravenclaw. Up in the attic an artist paints devices on thick, crisp white sheets of vellum. This is the archive of the old English class system. Ask the Richmond Herald for the Shakespeare application and he will open a drawer to reveal, astonishingly, even the rough drafts with his predecessor's scribbles noting the main points of his conversation with the playwright that autumn. It is one of the most intimate moments of the biography.

Shakespeare's story is about history and literature, but also about class and social advancement: a family that in fifty years went from farmers to gentlemen. To acquire the status of gentleman involved looking back on the family's history and ahead to its future. For William, therefore, the meeting was particularly loaded with meaning because of the ups and downs of his father's career, the recent death of his son and his own considerable success in the theatre. (One of Dethick's colleagues, who resented the award of arms to Elizabethan parvenus, would later pointedly mark the sketch of their heraldic shield 'Shakespeare the player', focusing on the very insecurities that, as he reveals in his sonnets, Shakespeare felt all too deeply.)

Two different drafts survive of the application for 'tokens of honor and worthiness'. Dethick stated he had been 'credibly informed' that

> John Shakespeare of Stratford upon Avon in the Countty of Warwick whose parents and late antecessors were for their valiant and faithful service advanced and rewarded by the most Prudent Prince king henry the seventh of famous memory sythence which time they have continued at those parts in good reputation and credit. And the said John having married Mary daughter and one of the heirs of Robert Arden of Wilmcote in the said county gentleman, whereof for the encouragement of his posterity I have therefore assigned ... this shield or coat of arms.

In the second draft Dethick inserted the word 'grandfather' above the line about parents and antecessors, and 'for their valiant and faithful service' was changed to 'for his ...'. Did an older Shakespeare, apparently John's grandfather, fight at Bosworth in 1485?

A scribbled note at the bottom of the sheet tells us that twenty years earlier John had made a first application, which had gone no further; it was evidently

ABOVE: *The coat of arms designed by the College of Arms for John Shakespeare in 1596 for his 'posterity' – ten weeks after the death of his only grandson.*

around that time in 1576 when he had run into trouble. Also surviving is a damaged list of details about John, which was supplied to Dethick by the family. He had been

> A justice of the Peace and was Bayliffe (officer and cheffe of the towne) of Stratford uppo' Avon xv or xvi years past
> That he hath Landes and tenementes. Of good wealth and substance. 500li.
> That he married ....

So John was apparently now of 'good wealth' again (£500 no less); once more the connection with the Ardens was stressed, and the family were confirmed in the gentle status to which he had always aspired. The coat of arms, devised from the College's pattern books, was a spear; the motto, presumably chosen by William himself, was adapted from a popular emblem book, a weighty assertion intended to sum up the family and its principles: 'Not without right'.

It is hard not to find this a touching moment, especially if John had come up to London to accompany his son to the meeting. William had been an absent husband, father and son for ten years or more. But how poignant, this document drawn up to commemorate the 'name and good fame' of John's family, and to dignify his 'children and issue ... for the encouragement of their posterite'. For they had just buried William's only son, John's grandson, the last of the male children of the Snitterfield Shakespeares.

Career Crisis: 'The Players Are Piteously Persecuted'

Back at work there were other troubles on Shakespeare's mind. Pressure had grown on the players since Hunsdon's death: there were calls to ban plays and close the playhouses altogether. As Thomas Nashe remarked in a letter to a friend: 'Now the players are piteously persecuted by the Lord mayor and the aldermen, and however in their old Lord [Hunsdon]'s time they thought their state settled, it is now so uncertain they cannot build upon it.'

The Burbages' twenty-one-year lease on the Theatre in Shoreditch was coming up for renewal and the landlord, Giles Allen, a Puritan in sympathies, was making threatening noises: a big hike in rent and a short five-year lease, after which he wished to pull the building down. At the same time the experience of playing city venues like the Cross Keys had convinced Shakespeare and the Burbages that they needed a winter home. So they took a lease on a building inside the old monastic precinct of Blackfriars, a hall in which to build an indoor theatre, warm and comfortable, where they could ask higher prices and attract

a better clientele. But immediately they encountered strong resistance from well-to-do neighbours, who drew up a petition objecting to the building of 'a common playhouse ... which will grow to be a very great annoyance and trouble, not only to all the noblemen and gentlemen thereabout inhabiting, but also a general inconvenience to all the inhabitants of the same precinct, by reason of the gathering together of all manner of lewd and vagrant persons'. The Privy Council duly issued an order that 'forbade the use of the said house for plays'.

But the company were nothing if not resourceful. The clue to what they did next comes in a writ of attachment addressed to the sheriff of Surrey, returnable 29 November 1596: in it Shakespeare was summonsed to keep the peace – but in Surrey, south of the river. 'Be it known that William Wayte seeks sureties of the peace against William Shakespeare, Francis Langley, Dorothy Soer the wife of John Soer and Anne Lee, for fear of death and mutilation of limbs ....'

At first sight it may seem a shock to find 'gentle Shakespeare' threatened with arrest on charges of grievous bodily harm, but the wording was simply legal formula. The writ was in fact part of a bigger move against the theatre at that time by an important landowner in Southwark who was allied to the anti-players' faction in the city. And, crucially, it suggests that the company had moved to the south bank.

BELOW: *Sketch of the Swan in Paris Garden, where Shakespeare and his company played in the winter of 1596–7.*

Shakespeare's co-accused, Francis Langley, was the owner of the brand new Swan theatre in the manor of Paris Garden, 500 yards from Henslowe's Rose on Bankside. Langley owned the manor house there: a member of the Drapers' company and a typical Elizabethan entrepreneur, he had made his fortune as inspector for wool and cloth in London, extracting fees and fines from clothiers in a manner that had led to charges of violence and extortion. Now Langley was sitting pretty as a brothel keeper, rack landlord and fence for stolen goods, and had ploughed some of his ill-gotten gains into new investment possibilities in the theatre.

The instigator of the writ, William Wayte, was the stepson and front man of Langley's enemy William Gardiner, the sheriff of Surrey, a JP with jurisdiction over Paris Garden and Bankside. The wealthy, propertied Gardiner was a deeply unpleasant character, a crooked businessman who

got his way by menaces and blackmail. The writ came at a time of growing pressure by the civic authorities on the playhouses. Gardiner was perhaps operating on behalf of even bigger fish, and this may have been the first salvo in a bigger war. The pressures of running a theatre company were not confined to the perennial rollercoaster of the box office.

The Elizabethan Underworld: Southwark and Paris Garden

So in his time of crisis, in the autumn of 1596, it seems that Shakespeare had moved to Southwark. Tax records confirm that he was in Paris Garden for the next couple of years or so. All his co-defendants lived there too: Dorothy Soer had property leases in Paris Garden Lane, and in the late 1590s 'Soares rents' were well-known lodgings for actors. (He was still living close by three years later and in *Twelfth Night*, written in 1599, the sailor Antonio gives this recommendation: 'In the south suburbs at the Elephant is best to lodge.' The Elephant, a former stew house that had survived the periodic closures of the sex industry, lay on the river on the corner of Horseshoe Alley less than 100 yards from the Globe. Perhaps this was where Shakespeare was lodging, then, or at least where he took his meals and wrote – a case of Tudor product placement perhaps?)

Opposite: *St Mary Overy's dock, Southwark, 1881: at the entrance to Clink Street – on Shakespeare's walk to London Bridge.* Below: *A brothel on the south bank. The theatres existed cheek by jowl with the more venal entertainments of Southwark.*

It was not a place you would recommend a friend to stay in London, especially if they were going through a mid-life crisis, as Shakespeare was. A visitor strolling around Southwark in the late 1590s would have seen new buildings going up everywhere as houses were subdivided, gardens disappeared and hundreds of tenements were thrown up by speculators. It was such a rough neighbourhood that it was customary for landlords to put good behaviour clauses in their leases. The area's contempt for the civic authorities was notorious, as John Donne remarks in his first Elegy: 'we will scorn his policies … as the inhabitants of Thames' right side do London's Mayor'. Beyond the city limits, sixteenth-century Southwark was a place of densely packed houses and teeming alleys. Wealthy residents, such as Langley or his enemy Gardiner, still had space and privacy and could enjoy their gardens, but the poor huddled in squalid alleys, in single rooms and even stables. There were industries such as tanneries and glassworks; the streets were choked with rubbish and building materials, and the wharves with ferrymen and merchandise. And, as might be expected, it was a centre of crime.

RIGHT: *Southwark: 'a licensed stew' as one Puritan preacher called it. The centre of the Elizabethan entertainment industry, the area contained 300 inns and brothels – some mentioned in plays Shakespeare wrote when he lived here.*
BELOW RIGHT: *London Bridge. At the southern end (on the left) severed heads on poles greeted the traveller.*

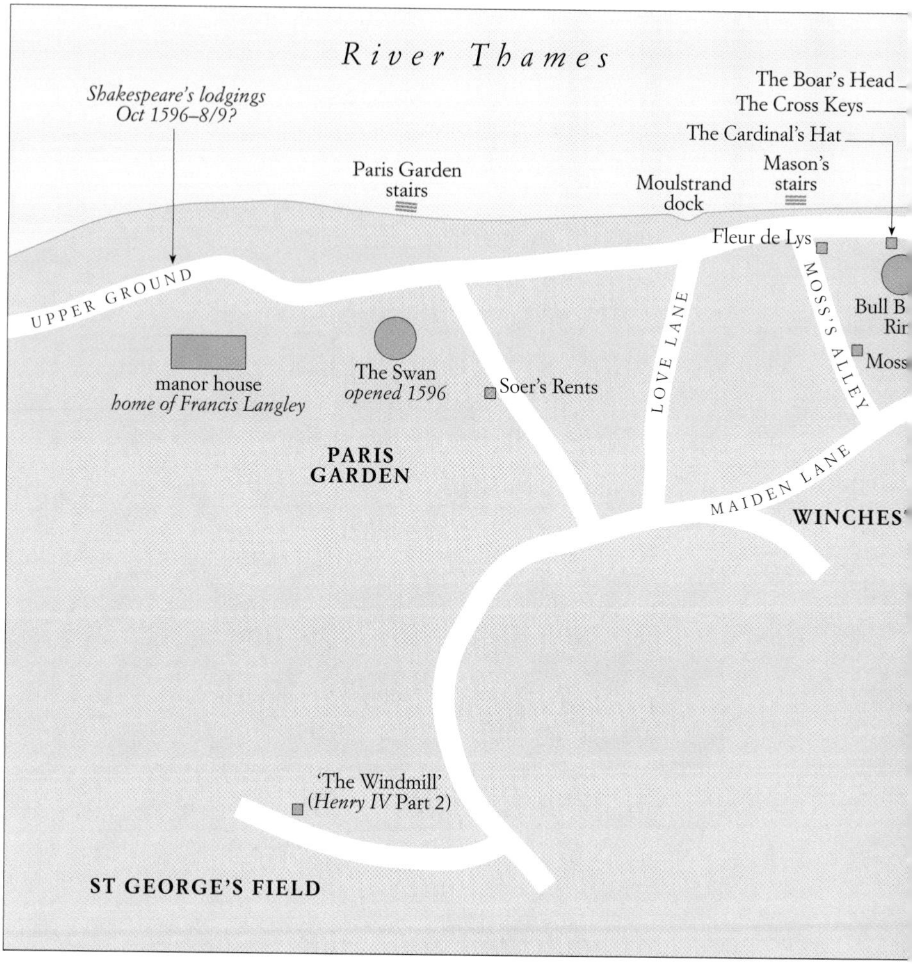

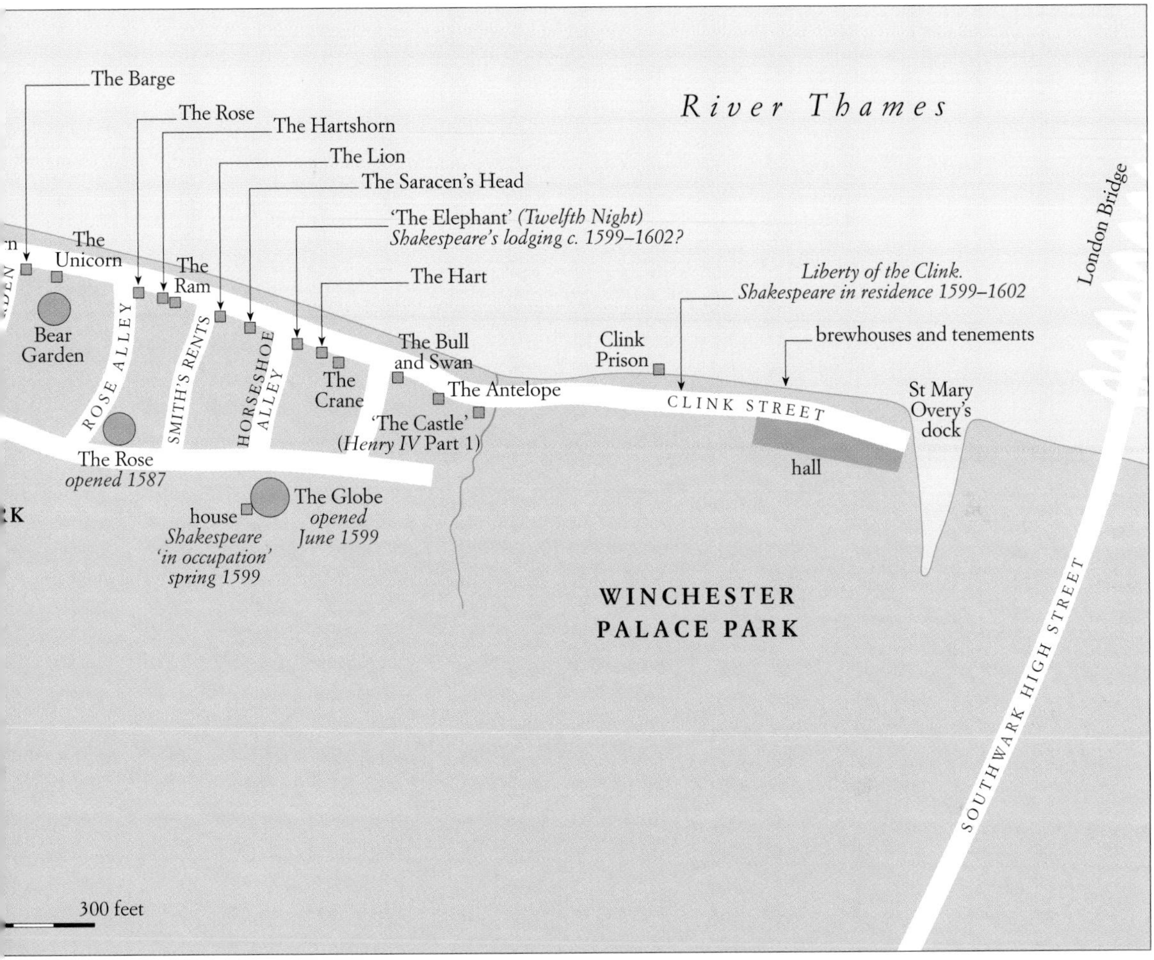

The Barge
The Rose
The Hartshorn
The Lion
The Saracen's Head
'The Elephant' *(Twelfth Night)*
Shakespeare's lodging c. 1599–1602?
The Hart
Liberty of the Clink.
Shakespeare in residence 1599–1602
brewhouses and tenements
River Thames
London Bridge
The Unicorn
The Ram
Bear Garden
ROSE ALLEY
SMITH'S RENTS
HORSESHOE ALLEY
The Crane
The Bull and Swan
The Antelope
Clink Prison
CLINK STREET
St Mary Overy's dock
'The Castle'
(Henry IV Part 1)
The Rose
opened 1587
hall
The Globe
opened
June 1599
house
Shakespeare
'in occupation'
spring 1599
WINCHESTER
PALACE PARK
SOUTHWARK HIGH STREET
300 feet

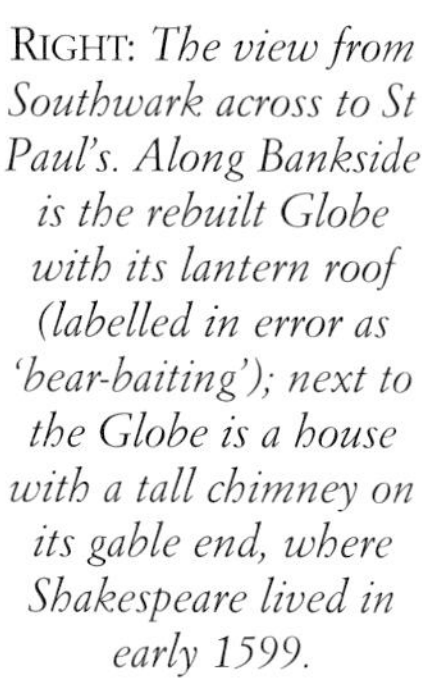

RIGHT: *The view from Southwark across to St Paul's. Along Bankside is the rebuilt Globe with its lantern roof (labelled in error as 'bear-baiting'); next to the Globe is a house with a tall chimney on its gable end, where Shakespeare lived in early 1599.*

The population boom in the late sixteenth century fuelled the entertainment industry in Southwark. A dense row of brick houses three or four storeys high ran along the river, and here the Rose had opened in 1587 and Langley's Swan in 1596; the Globe would follow in 1599. There were also 300 inns, brothels and alehouses in the area, offering skittles, bowling and gambling. Their owners could make a killing on them: one bowling alley in Paris Garden had its rent upped five times in as many years. Then there was the *frisson* of blood sports. Built back in the 1540s, the bear-baiting ring had gained instant popularity – to the disgust of moralists who complained that the poor 'every Sunday will spend one penny or two' betting. In the 1550s a custom-built bullring had followed. These spectacles appealed just as much to the rich, such as the inns of court lawyers. Bears like Sackerson (as Shakespeare's Falstaff mentions) were stars.

Alongside these public spectacles more private entertainment was on offer. Out of sight and mind of the ecclesiastical and city authorities, the insalubrious and at times waterlogged reaches of Bankside had been a red-light district since the fourteenth century. The journalist Thomas Nashe wrote a salacious poem about a visit to a brothel in a rambling tenement, where 'Venus' bouncing vestals' included the teenage Mistress Francis in her 'rattling silks'. It may not be a coincidence that Shakespeare's best tavern scenes, with Mistress Quickly and Doll Tearsheet, were written while he lived here.

So Bankside was where rich folk parted with their money; where players, prostitutes and pickpockets rubbed shoulders. No wonder, when Langley proposed his new theatre, that the Lord Mayor protested about playhouses themselves being magnets for disorder: 'ordinary places of meeting for all vagrant

ABOVE: *Sixteenth-century houses in Bermondsey Street, Southwark, which were still standing in 1893. In Shakespeare's day the street was the haunt of 'fences' who disposed of stolen goods.*

persons and masterless men that hang about the city, thieves, horsestealers, whoremongers, coseners, conycatching people, practisers of treason and other such like, where they consort and make their matches ...'. And somewhere in this nefarious world of tenements and actors' rentals at the Paris Garden end of Bankside was where Shakespeare had gone to ground at this time.

THE RIDDLE OF THE SONNETS

On 17 March 1597 there was some good news: the anti-theatre Lord Cobham died, and Lord Hunsdon's son took over as chamberlain; Shakespeare's company were reinstated as the Chamberlain's Men. With less than a month's notice, they got the call to do a show for the Garter Celebrations at Westminster on 23 April in front of the queen and the Knights of the Garter. Hastily Shakespeare began to put together an entertainment that would later become *The Merry Wives of Windsor*. But before that day came, his life was again to be shaken to the core.

And if his own private verses of this time are to be believed, all his views about himself were challenged in what Shakespeare says was for him 'a hell of time'.

It was perhaps around this time – spring 1597 – that Shakespeare was commissioned to write a series of seventeen poems to a young aristocrat. These sonnets, and those that followed, have become the most famous love poems in the English language. They contain acute meditations on love, death, sexual passion, procreation and the transfiguring power of time. But the most extraordinary thing about them is often overlooked. Most of them are to a young man.

At the heart of the sonnets is a love triangle involving the poet, the lovely boy and the poet's dark-skinned mistress. They describe his passionate love for the young nobleman, which was possibly non-sexual, even though Shakespeare was consumed with the boy's physical beauty; his powerful sexual passion for a married woman; and the increasingly frantic denouement as it becomes clear that the young man and the woman are also sleeping with each other. If the sonnets are about real life, they not only reflect on these relationships but possibly also offer a clue to Shakespeare's own emotional state after his son's death. But are they about real life? Were the boy and the Dark Lady living people, or literary inventions?

It is often said that we can't find out from his works what Shakespeare believed; and to a degree that assertion is true of his plays, which were crafted for their audience. But his poems are different because in most of them he was free to say what he wanted, and the indications are that he did so. A few scholars have dismissed the search for real people in the sonnets as fantasy. But there are strong reasons to think that Shakespeare used his poems as ways of getting things off his chest. In the case of the sonnets, the rawness and self-exposure evident in them, the explicitness about sex, is unbelievable as a mere literary game. Most readers would surely agree that they relate to real-life experience: if they are not autobiographical, it is hard to imagine what is. Shakespeare fell in love with these two people and was shaken by the affair.

But how can we be sure of their date? The sonnets were not published until 1609. Some of the poems about the boy and the woman, however, must have been written before 1598, because that year Francis Meres intriguingly mentions in his account of contemporary writers that Shakespeare's 'sugar'd sonnets' were circulating among his 'private' friends. By the following June the Lancashire poet John Weever had also read some of them in manuscript. Inevitably, some were soon pirated. In 1599 a small volume of poetry called *The Passionate Pilgrim* 'By W. Shakespeare' was published by William Jaggard. The title was an unscrupulous publisher's con: in fact very little in this mediocre book was by Shakespeare, but it did include three extracts from

Love's Labour's Lost – and two sonnets from the sequence about the boy and the poet's mistress.

Not surprisingly, Shakespeare was angry that the publisher, 'altogether unknown to him presumed to make so bold with his name'. The offence was perhaps twofold: that 'private', intimate verses had been printed which were not intended for publication; and that inferior stuff had been put out under his name. But the affair alerts us to the sensitive nature of the sonnets' content.

Initially Shakespeare seems to have thought about responding to the piracy: in 1599 he may have lodged 'a book of Sonnets' in the Stationers' Register, possibly as a holding operation, but then decided not to publish them after all. This furore clearly makes more sense if it took place close to the time of composition: the sonnets were new and faintly scandalous. And this in turn might suggest that a sizeable number of those poems dealing with the boy and the woman had been written by 1598–9 at the latest. As we shall see, the likeliest date is the spring and summer of 1597.

Verbal and thematic parallels with the plays also point to a date in the late 1590s. So too does the latest computerized linguistic analysis, which suggests that the sonnets are not, as has often been argued, the product of the early 1590s but were written by the mature Shakespeare – a man in his mid-thirties, ruefully jealous of his mistress having sex with her teenage lover, and seeing, as he looked in the mirror, a face soon to be 'lined with forty winters'. In more than one sonnet we see him as he saw himself: a man who, in Elizabethan terms, was no longer young, 'past my best'. So, although the poems are about the boy and the woman, they are also about him: his contemplations, as Yeats put it, are 'of time which has transfigured me'.

BELOW: *Title page of the 1609 sonnets. Most of the poems were written between the late 1590s and 1604.*
OPPOSITE: *William Herbert. No youthful image survives of the beautiful boy, who attracted devotees of both sexes, including his 'servant' Shakespeare.*

TO.THE.ONLIE.BEGETTER.OF.
THESE.INSVING.SONNETS.
Mr.W.H. ALL.HAPPINESSE.
AND.THAT.ETERNITIE.
PROMISED.
BY.
OVR.EVER-LIVING.POET.
WISHETH.
THE.WELL-WISHING.
ADVENTVRER.IN.
SETTING.
FORTH.

T. T.

Who Was the Boy?

The sonnets reveal that the boy was from a higher class than the poet (self-abnegation and a sense of social inferiority run through the poems). They indicate that he was young, beautiful and much loved, and that his name was probably William. A further clue to his name is offered by the enigmatic dedication of the 1609 published edition to 'Mr W.H.', who, says Shakespeare's publisher, Thomas Thorpe, was 'the onlie begetter' of the poems.

'Begetter' means 'parent' but also 'sole inspirer' or 'origin', and that is most likely what it means here. As so many of the sonnets to the young nobleman promise that he will live on in the poet's verses, common sense suggests that it was their inspirer and main subject who was the dedicatee.

Of the many candidates for the beautiful boy, only two have been taken seriously by modern scholars. The Earl of Southampton, the dedicatee of *Venus and Adonis* and *The Rape of Lucrece,* still has many supporters, but his name is not William; his initials are H.W., not W.H.; and there is no evidence for a relationship with Shakespeare later in his life. The new computerized linguistic tests for frequency of early and late words in Shakespeare's literary output place the first main group of sonnets to the boy (1–60) in the late 1590s, and Sonnets 61–103 probably belong around the same time. Sonnets 104–26 date from the late 1590s to 1604, as might be guessed from their apparent references to contemporary events. This dating is supported by internal hints that in his terms the poet was approaching middle age. All this suggests that the first poems in the cycle were new when they came to the attention of literary London in 1598, when they were privately circulated and pirated. If all this is accepted, one candidate for the beautiful boy stands out: William Herbert, born in 1580, who became Earl of Pembroke in 1601, and had first come to court in 1597, around the time of his seventeenth birthday on 8 April.

Herbert would later be a remarkable patron of drama and learning, a benefactor of the Bodleian Library in Oxford. The antiquarian John Aubrey called him 'the greatest Maecenas to learned Men of any Peer of his time or since'. Herbert was also renowned as a womanizer, but though 'immoderately given up to women', as the seventeenth-century historian the Earl of Clarendon wrote, 'he was not so much transported with beauty and outward allurements as with those advantages of the mind as are manifested in extraordinary wit and knowledge, and administered great pleasure in the conversation'.

That the seventeen-year-old William Herbert was the boy with whom Shakespeare fell in love is likely for many reasons. First, and most important, is his known closeness to the poet: Shakespeare and Richard Burbage had probably acted for Herbert's father's company back in the early nineties. It was to Herbert and his brother that Shakespeare's friends dedicated the Folio of his plays after the poet's death, speaking of the Herberts' 'many favours' to the plays and their author. Additional support comes from the dedication of the 1609

edition of the sonnets to 'Mr W.H.'. The publisher, Thorpe, made a special effort to cultivate William Herbert at this period, printing translations of St Augustine's *City of God* and Epictetus and Hall's *Discovery of the New World*, all with admiring dedications to Herbert. This in turn helps explain two mysterious details of the sonnets' dedication. The first is Thorpe's line describing himself as the 'well wishing adventurer in setting forth', making an analogy between printing and voyaging. If the dedicatee is Herbert, this would be a pointed flattery since only the previous month he had joined the council of the Virginia Company. Then there is the question of Thorpe's strange wording: why did he call him 'Mr' when Herbert in 1609 was an earl? Perhaps the title was meant to have a teasing evasiveness: if so, it looks as if this was picked up by Shakespeare's old friend Ben Jonson four years later in another dedication to Herbert: 'I cannot change your title, and have no need of a cipher.' Jonson would be in the know as far as the sonnets were concerned: and he seems to be suggesting that someone else had published a dedication that had changed Pembroke's title in order to hide something.

BELOW: *Mary Herbert, c. 1590. Patron, poet and editor, Mary was adored by poets for her generosity and her intellectual powers. Shakespeare used her manuscript play on Antony for his show on the same theme.*

Final supporting evidence comes from Herbert family interest in these poems. William himself wrote poetry, including some that refers to a dark mistress; other poems were semi-pornographic. Crucially, Pembroke's verse shows he had read Shakespeare's sonnets, of which there are many echoes, and in one he quotes 'Let me not to the marriage of true minds'. His cousin George Herbert, then a Cambridge undergraduate and an ardent Protestant, wrote to his mother in the winter of 1609, just after the sonnets came out, to say that he was aghast and recoiled from their obscenity. Also revealing are the sonnets of William's cousin Mary Wroth, who in 1612 had a passionate love affair with him that produced two children. Wroth avidly read Herbert's papers and composed a sonnet sequence to him in which the influence of Shakespeare's sonnets is pervasive. In one of these she refers to another poet, calling him an April morning. Given the peculiar importance of April in Shakespeare's sonnets to the boy, this, from William Herbert's own cousin and lover, is striking:

> Dear eyes, how well, indeed, you do adorn
> That blessed sphere which gazing souls hold dear,
> The loved place of sought for triumphs, near
> The court of glory, where love's force was born.
> How may they term you April's sweetest morn,

> When pleasing looks from those bright lights appear,
> A sun-shine day;

If, therefore, we accept William Herbert as 'Mr W.H.', the young man of the sonnets, it puts Shakespeare back in contact with the greatest literary family in England for whom he had worked in 1592. It might also supply a possible date for the first poems – April 1597. And, most importantly, this would put the start of Shakespeare's relationship with Herbert in a moment of intense crisis in his own life only months after the death of his own son.

'Thy Mother's Glass': Mary Herbert and the Wilton 'Academy'

Wilton House, the country home of the Herberts in Wiltshire, lay on one of the main routes to the southwest. It was rebuilt after a fire in the mid-seventeenth century, and only the centre part of the original Tudor structure remains; but the idyllic wooded setting along the river Wylye is the same. Such a heavenly ambience was matched by the charm and cultivation of the family. William's uncle, the poet Philip Sidney, had died heroically in the Dutch wars; Mary, his mother, was one of the most important figures in the patronage of sixteenth-century literature. As John Aubrey wrote, 'Wilton will appear to have been an Academy, as well as Palace, and was (as it were) the Apiarie, to which Men, that were excellent in Arms and Arts, did resort and were carress't.' And not just men. Women played a major role in the aristocratic patronage of letters in Tudor England, and it is no coincidence that three of the most interesting female poets of the time – Mary herself, Mary Wroth and Emilia Lanier – have connections with Wilton.

The authoress of poems and plays, Mary Herbert was also the patron of poets and actors, the dedicatee of some thirty books, and it was perhaps inevitable that a poet of Shakespeare's repute would attract her attention. In 1597 he was the leading lyric and dramatic poet of the day, author of the great theatrical successes of the moment: *Romeo and Juliet* and *Henry IV* Part 1. Perhaps Mary commissioned him to write the first poems in the sequence. At any rate, she seems to be referred to in the third sonnet:

> Thou art thy mother's glass, and she in thee
> Calls back the lovely April of her prime

From this it might be conjectured that Shakespeare was invited to Wilton by Mary Herbert to write poems urging her son to marry after, earlier in that

year, he had rejected the proposed marriage to a woman named Bridget de Vere.

'The Master-Mistress of My Passion'

Clarity over the dedicatee enables us to adduce some fascinating biographical details that offer a real insight into Shakespeare's inner life. All this hinges on the date of composition. It has long been noted that the first seventeen poems seem to form a group. If so, perhaps they were composed for Herbert's seventeenth birthday on 8 April 1597, a date whose significance as the first meeting is underlined in later sonnets.

From the beginning the poet addresses the boy with affection as his 'love'. The poems urge marriage on the young man, chiding him for self-love and self-absorption, warning him that beauty passes and time destroys. Whilst there is no need to think that all the sonnets were actually sent to the boy, the first seventeen surely were. At the beginning of the relationship, there is a formal distance:

> When I consider every thing that grows
> Holds in perfection but a little moment,
> That this huge stage presenteth nought but shows
> Wheron the stars in secret influence comment;
> When I perceive that men as plants increase,
> Cheered and check'd even by the self-same sky;
> Vaunt in their youthful sap, at height decrease,
> And wear their brave state out of memory;
> Then the conceit of this inconstant stay
> Sets you most rich in youth before my sight,
> Where wasteful time debateth with decay,
> To change your day of youth to sullied night;
>   And all in war with Time, for love of you,
>   As he takes from you, I engraft you new.

But after those first seventeen, the poems swiftly take on a passionate tone, as if to a lover:

> Shall I compare thee to a summer's day?
> Thou art more lovely and more temperate:
> Rough winds do shake the darling buds of May,
> And summer's lease hath all too short a date:

He refers to the androgynous beauty of the boy: his fair face, long hair and girlish looks (it should be added that Shakespeare was not the only poet to write of Herbert this way).

> A woman's face, with nature's own hand painted,
> Hast thou, the master-mistress of my passion;

Although Shakespeare wryly admits that, since nature made the boy male ('to prick him out' means both to mark down and to endow with a prick), 'thy love's use' (in the physical consummation of love) will be for the women in his life:

> But since she prick'd thee out for women's pleasure,
> Mine be thy love, and thy love's use their treasure.

Protection and Grief

It may be that in response to the passions unleashed here, the Herbert family temporarily broke off their relationship with Shakespeare. His references to shame and public censure suggest that his feelings for the boy had become embarrassingly public. But that this passionate friendship endured and developed into one that was close and affectionate is demonstrated by other poems in the collection spread over the next few years up to 1604. That it began with a great deal of projection is shown by Sonnet 53, a fascinating and revealing poem in which Shakespeare talks frankly about the multiple personas he has projected on to Herbert's androgynous figure. He compares the 'millions of strange shadows', images from poetry and drama – male and female – that he sees in Herbert's face and form. 'Describe Adonis, and the counterfeit/Is poorly imitated after you,' he writes, and then imagines the young man dressed in women's clothes (like a boy in the theatre) as Helen of Troy, 'and you in Grecian tires are painted new' (that is, in female headdress). He admits he is turned on by the thought of the boy dressed as a girl; but at the same time, with characteristic self-awareness, he admits that this passion is also, to a degree, projection.

However, many of the sonnets after the first seventeen are imbued with a surprisingly desperate sense of loss and death. Shakespeare speaks of the 'torture' of sleepless nights, a life where 'My grief lies onward and my joy behind'. This is a poet desperate with love or loss, as if something has snapped inside him:

> What potions have I drunk of siren tears
> Distilled from limbecks foul as hell within

He tells us he is 'With time's injurious hand crushed and o'erworn', and this is underlined by several allusions to his age. Strangely, though, looking at the face of the lovely boy, the poet refers to fatherhood as a source of anguished regret. Shakespeare, of course, was old enough to be the boy's father, but this does not explain his pointed description of himself as a 'decrepit father made lame by fortune's dearest spite'. He seems to be telling us that he has suffered a blow of the most intimate and hurtful kind that fortune could deal out *to a father.* And the blow is not to do with the boy:

> Ruin hath taught me thus to ruminate,
> That time will come and take my love away
> This thought is as a death.

Conscious that he has reached a mid-point in his life, Shakespeare speaks of his love with an intense passion loaded with a heavy, and terrible, sense of loss.

> For if you were by my unkindness shaken
> As I by yours, y'have passed a hell of time

Shakespeare's 'true sorrow' is usually explained as a response to his separation from the boy, but this cannot be the whole story. Whilst the early sonnets can be read as homosexual poems, in this light his affection and admiration for the boy take on a more complex and problematic colour. For his love is absolute, intense, overwhelming, in the way a father feels for a child. And the first sonnets, urging the boy to have a son, were, so it now appears, written only eight months after the death of his own son.

'He Was but One Hour Mine'

From the start the sonnets are death-obsessed, articulating an almost frantic defence of the need to procreate and have sons in one's own image. Several later sonnets to the boy are explicitly about weeping, sleeplessness and grief. It is really not doing Shakespeare justice if we do not take his words at face value. By the time of the multi-layered punning of the enigmatic Sonnet 33, these meanings and sub-texts are piled on top of each other with riveting assurance and agonized feeling:

> Full many a glorious morning have I seen
> Flatter the mountain tops with sovereign eye,
> Kissing with golden face the meadows green,
> Gilding pale streams with heavenly alchemy;

Anon permit the basest clouds to ride
With ugly rack on his celestial face,
And from the forlorn world his visage hide,
Stealing unseen to west with this disgrace:
Even so my sun one early morn did shine
With all triumphant splendour on my brow;
But out! alack! he was but one hour mine,
The region cloud hath mask'd him from me now.
  Yet him for this my love no whit disdaineth;
  Suns of the world may stain, when heaven's sun staineth.

The sonnet is based on a proverb, 'The morning sun never lasts the whole day', with hints at a turn of phrase still used in modern English – to be 'under a cloud'. The poem is not merely about physical separation but also about loss, both personal and metaphysical. 'Disgrace' in Elizabethan English meant disfigurement, loss of beauty or grace, as well as having the modern sense of disgrace. 'Staineth' suggests loss of colour and lustre, and even the idea of sustaining a moral blot, an eclipse; the Stainers' company dyed, or stained cloth; the verb 'to stain' also had transitive meanings – to take one colour away with another, but also to outshine or deprive lesser luminaries of their light. But here the image system takes on a religious connotation. 'Suns of the world' are also 'sons', mortals, humans; so 'heaven's sun' is the sun in the sky, but with the inevitable suggestion of heaven's *son*, Jesus; all of which floods the poem with vague but anguished suggestions of the incarnation and the crucifixion.

It is hard to imagine that poetry of this intensity is only about separation from the beautiful young nobleman, however much loved. Shakespeare here runs together loss of the young man, loss of his own sun/son and the loss of God's son. It would not have escaped an Elizabethan reader that the number of the sonnet, 33, was Jesus's age at the time of the crucifixion; and, coincidentally or not, it was also Shakespeare's age in 1597.

The sonnets have been the subject of many bizarre theories but it is surely inconceivable, if this sonnet was written in 1597, that it is not also about his son. This interpretation is reinforced by the image of the poet's sun/son shining 'in triumphant splendour' on his brow, for the brow was the place that, to an Elizabethan, showed the transparency of fatherhood. It was the seat of a father's pride in his issue and its legitimacy. If the dating is right, a modern psychologist would certainly be interested in Shakespeare's passionate, almost desperate, love for a seventeen-year-old in the year after his son's death. In today's terms, it was very adaptive, a kind of transference. It was a way of coping with crushing grief.

CHAPTER TEN

Shakespeare in Love?

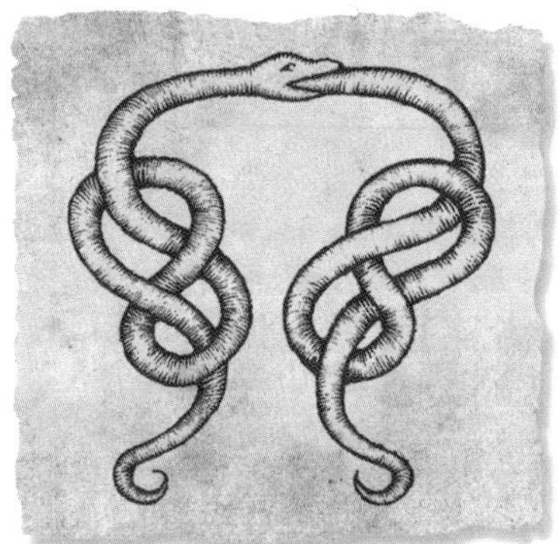

THE EFFECT OF LUST

On 28 July 1597, in the middle of all the traumas in the poet's private life, the London theatres were closed down by the authorities and remained dark until October. Pressure on the players had been exacerbated by a scandal over a seditious play, *The Isle of Dogs*, whose authors, including Ben Jonson, found themselves in jail, face to face with the psychopathic Topcliffe and the sinister Poley. Perhaps this is the time alluded to in Sonnet 66 when Shakespeare speaks of his art being 'tongue-tied by authority'. In August his company began a lengthy tour from Kent to Bristol, perhaps the context of the miserable journeys Shakespeare describes in the sonnets, lamenting his separation from the boy. At any rate, one might guess that it was at this time that he wrote a number of private poems, seeking temporary consolation for his various griefs.

People do strange things at such times: some live for the moment; for others, certainties are shaken; marriages can break up, and even religious people can feel that life is meaningless. The sonnets are in part self-analysis in response to just this kind of emotional upheaval. And now, married for nearly fifteen years and living apart from his forty-year-old wife, Shakespeare writes about a love affair with a married woman, which has left him wounded and exposed; all the more galling for a man who, as he has admitted, was so reticent about his inner life. And where his feelings for the boy

OPPOSITE: *Queen Elizabeth's courtly entertainments took place in a flirtatious fantasy world, obsessed by the cult of youth and accompanied by beautiful young male and female musicians.*

were of passionate love, although apparently not physically consummated, the affair with the woman was a sexual passion. It is time to look at the third character in the triangle of the sonnets: the enigmatic Dark Lady.

SEX AND THE CITY

It might be thought inevitable that a man who had lived apart from his wife for ten years would have affairs. The theatre is a sexy business with many pleasures and many temptations. Certainly the thought of those beautiful boy actors with their painted eyes, rustling in silk skirts, got Puritan preachers hot under the collar. The Elizabethans were very up-front about sex. For instance, when the astrologer and physician Simon Forman attended the State Opening of Parliament in 1597, and struck up a conversation with a gentlewoman serving at court, Joan Harrington, she went home and slept with him the same day. Women were part of the theatre audience: they too liked seeing boys as girls, and if they took a fancy to a leading actor, so be it. A law student's diary from 1602

BELOW: *Upper-class ladies gaming and drinking. 'These days women wander everywhere,' wrote John Case. 'They do business, they go to the theatre, they dine when it pleases them ... and they drink too.'*

repeats a story, possibly apocryphal, that Shakespeare bamboozled Burbage out of a well-to-do groupie who wanted to bed the star lead. John Aubrey, on the other hand, says Shakespeare would not be 'debauched' (that is, go to brothels); and that, when asked to do so, 'writ he was in pain' (that is, said he was ill). And perhaps a practised womanizer is unlikely to have displayed the anguished reaction to infidelity expressed in the sonnets. From which it might appear that Shakespeare was in love.

The Dark Lady

Many of the first 126 sonnets appear to be to the young man. But some of those poems reveal that the young man is sleeping with the poet's mistress. Then, starting with Sonnet 127, there is a sequence of poems to the woman herself. Their language is at times tender, at times misogynist and abusive. He complains that she has a 'steel-bosom', is disdainful, tyrannous and unkind; although, he admits:

> And yet, by heaven, I think my love as rare
> As any she belied with false compare

The details he gives about her are few. Unconventionally beautiful, she has black hair and eyes and is very dark-complexioned. She is married. She has had other lovers, including lords. She is well known ('the world knows') and there are some hints that she is of higher social standing than Shakespeare. Sonnet 150 mysteriously suggests that there was something about her condition or status that had engaged his sympathy, that her 'unworthiness aroused pity in me'. As for how the affair started, in Sonnet 134 he seems to say that he asked the young man 'surety like to write for me' – that is, to approach her as a proxy wooer, and that the woman had then pursued the young man, his friend, who 'came debtor for my sake'. For this Shakespeare blames himself: 'So him I lose through my unkind abuse'. In other words, he feels he has injured his friend by wrongfully using him as a go-between.

Shakespeare and the woman then begin a passionate sexual relationship. Her husband is evidently away, for on occasion the poet visits her at home, where he sees her playing the virginals. But he soon discovers that she is also sleeping with the young man. The poet says he loves her 'dearly', but bitterly regrets her power over him, which he sees as manipulative and controlling. He becomes a slave to her dominating personality, her beauty and her sexual power.

The so-called Dark Lady has proved a tempting pitfall to biographers,

and some would think it unwise to read the sonnets so literally. But again, if we take them as a mainly private record of real events and emotions, however much reshaped for publication, then Shakespeare's mistress must have been a real woman who moved in the societies of the theatre and the court, yet was in some way an outsider because of her colour and background. But who was she?

'Black Is Fair'

First, what does he mean by calling her black, a very complicated word in Elizabethan literature, where it can even be used as a euphemism for Catholic? Shakespeare explicitly says he is overturning literary convention ('I have seen roses damasked, red and white/But no such roses see I in her cheeks'). His mistress, he says, does not conform to the sonneteers' stereotype of a beautiful woman. In her face and her body ('her breasts are dun') she is 'coloured ill'. This emphasis is so pronounced throughout the poems that it is difficult simply to dismiss it, as some have done, as a literary conceit. It suggests that, whatever her background, the woman was what an Elizabethan would have called a Moor. And if she was a dark-skinned musician, known in theatrical and noble circles, then the strong likelihood is that she was of Levantine or Italian origin, and most likely Venetian – the Bassanos and the Ferraboscos, the main musical families in Elizabethan London, were both from Venice.

The date of Shakespeare's affair, as we have seen, is suggested by the appearance of two sonnets to the woman in the collection pirated in 1599; perhaps they were among the poems circulated among his 'private' friends the previous year. This again is supported by modern computer analysis of their vocabulary. Sonnets 127–54, the poems to the woman, include the very early marriage sonnet, 145; but their main period of composition is broadly in the late 1590s, with some revision through to 1603–4. Of course it is always possible that some were written earlier and have been reworked, but as it stands, the sequence comes from the late nineties. If the identification of the boy as William Herbert is correct, the affair most likely took place in the summer of 1597, when Shakespeare was thirty-three. This fits very well with verbal parallels with his plays of that time, and even perhaps with his allusion to his art being 'tongue-tied by authority', which suggests the period when the theatres were closed between July and October. This impression is reinforced by Shakespeare's references to his own age, which are underscored even more than in the sonnets to the boy. As he says to the woman, 'you know I am past my best' (a feeling perhaps accentuated, if the Folio portrait is at all accurate, by his premature balding: Elizabethan men were vain about their hair). So these are the poems

not of the man in his late twenties who knew Southampton, but of a man around Dante's age when he wrote the *Inferno*: *nel mezzo del camin di nostra vita* – in the middle of our life's road.

Sex, Guilt and Male Anxiety

The affair with the Dark Lady troubled Shakespeare deeply and he says he lost his reason: in the poems to her, the linking of sex and guilt is particularly pronounced. This seems to be as characteristic of his personality as his obsession with aggression and violence. To judge by the way he depicts men's and women's relationships in his plays, Shakespeare believed in the ideal of fidelity and a spiritual dimension to human love. Such ideas were widely canvassed and debated at the time, as in John Case's remarkable book on equality in Christian marriage. Shakespeare was a Bible-reading Christian, married at eighteen and possibly so far faithful – otherwise why should the affair have traumatized him so? His consuming sexual passion for a married woman fills him with guilt. He has broken his 'bed vows' to his wife Anne, as the other woman has to her husband. The sense of ageing with which the poems are shot through helps us understand their melancholy edge and self-flagellation. Shakespeare's sexual jealousy has a subtext of his own physical decline and anxiety about his sexual performance.

A sensitive, imaginative and supremely intelligent man, Shakespeare lived in a patriarchal society that shaped him and his attitudes. Drawn to both men and women, he seems to have believed in the possibility of true friendship and companionship between men and women, an equality articulated many times in his plays, as in Emilia's famous speech in *Othello*. In the greater intimacy of the sonnets, though, there are strong hints that he believes passionate friendship between men to be on a higher plane than their relationships with women. Shakespeare is drawn by the power of female sexuality, but at the same time threatened by it. And the disgust evident in his language has been seen by some critics – not all of them women – as misogynistic. This is perhaps where the scandal of the sonnets lay to an Elizabethan audience – not (as for early modern readers) in his love for the young man, but in the image of a powerful woman in sexual control.

From our perspective, the sonnets about the Dark Lady seem a classic male response to overwhelming grief: he throws himself into an all-consuming affair with a dangerous married woman, and in the poems this awakes all the old emotions and beliefs he was brought up with. Themes such as the corrupting power of lust on the soul, guilt and infidelity run through the later sonnets, which are all the more explicable if Shakespeare's upbringing was Catholic:

The expense of spirit in a waste of shame
Is lust in action; and till action, lust
Is perjur'd, murderous, bloody, full of blame,
Savage, extreme, rude, cruel, not to trust;
Enjoy'd no sooner, but despised straight;
Past reason hunted; and no sooner had,
Past reason hated, as a swallow'd bait,
On purpose laid to make the taker mad:
Mad in pursuit, and in possession so,
Had, having, and in quest to have, extreme;
A bliss in proof, – and prov'd, a very woe;
Before, a joy propos'd; behind, a dream:
  All this the world well knows; yet none knows well
  To shun the heaven that leads men to this hell.

These were the sentiments of much Elizabethan poetry, religious or otherwise. Thomas Watson, for instance, wrote of love as a 'bayt for soules'; for Robert Southwell 'Beauty is a bayt that, swallowed, choakes ... A light that eyes to murdring sightes provokes.'

It has been all too easy to see these sonnets as secular poems: in fact a strong religious sense pervades them, especially in those about lust and the soul, such as the almost medieval 146: 'Poor soul the centre of my sinful earth'. But perhaps they also contain an element of parody: employing religious imagery

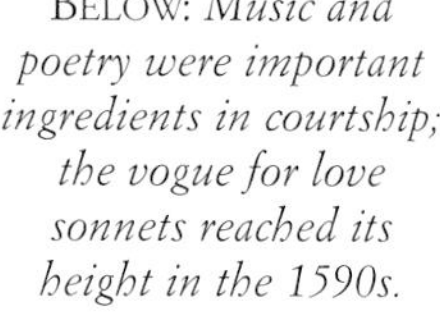

BELOW: *Music and poetry were important ingredients in courtship; the vogue for love sonnets reached its height in the 1590s.*

for an obsessive sexual relationship might have caused offence to some contemporary religious readers, but it is typical of Shakespeare's habit of situating himself between opposed thought worlds. In the end it is this that makes him such a modern mind, despite his roots in late medieval Christianity.

In several sonnets to the woman he puns on his own name and Herbert's. For example, in 135 he plays on a proverb ('Every woman will have her will'). Here Shakespeare's manuscript perhaps instructed the printer to emphasize his compulsively-obsessively clever punning on the word 'will' (meaning what is wanted; mental resolve; shall; his own name; the boy's name; and the male and female sex organs, as in 'willy' today). The spelling here is modernized, but the italics and capitalization may well be his:

> Whoever hath her wish, thou hast thy *Will*,
> And *Will* to boot, and *Will* in overplus.
> More than enough am I that vex thee still,
> To thy sweet will making addition thus.
> Wilt thou, whose will is large and spacious.
> Not once vouchsafe to hide my will in thine?
> Shall will in others seem right gracious,
> And in my will no fair acceptance shine?
> The sea, all water, yet receives rain still,
> And in abundance addeth to his store;
> So thou, being rich in *Will*, add to thy *Will*
> One will of mine to make thy large *Will* more.
>   Let no unkind no fair beseechers kill;
>   Think all but one, and me in that one *Will*.

There is nothing else quite like this in the poetry of Shakespeare's day: private, anguished, guilt-racked, obscene. Alongside his class anxiety are both spiritual anxiety and male anxiety about erections and 'willies'. His self-view – as a man in a male-dominated society – and even his sexual potency are dependent on, and yet threatened by, her female power; and he hates himself for it.

Shadow Texts: Whythorne's Love Affairs and Male Anxiety

These kinds of male anxieties are evident also in other writing of the time: particularly revealing in the context of the sonnets is the autobiography of the musician Thomas Whythorne. A private text not intended for publication, it contains many parallels, especially when describing the courtly world of musicians and

artists in which men of Shakespeare's background mixed with women of a higher class. Whythorne suggests we can see the sonnets, for all their literary artifice, as poems that began as private responses to a painful, confusing real-life situation.

The shy Whythorne was, like Shakespeare, a gentleman but not of high rank. This handsome, sensitive and talented musician, desperate in his affection at various times for a city widow, a courtly gentlewoman and a serving gentlewoman, reveals the heated atmosphere and erotic charge of the Elizabethan court and its artistic fringes. In Whythorne's world, men and women write sonnets to each other as gambits in love, just as Shakespeare's characters do. They read sonnets, send sonnets to each other and write them privately to get things off their chest.

Whythorne tells the tale of a married woman at court, of higher status, who falls in love with him. In a scene straight out of a Shakespeare play, she 'caused a chest of mine to be removed out of the chamber where I was accustomed to lie … and to be brought into a chamber so nigh her own chamber as she might have come from one to the other when she list without any suspicion. This chamber I was then placed in …. Then one day she took occasion to come alone into my chamber to see the marks of my sheets ….' (obviously, to see if he had a lover). But, says Whythorne, 'I was thoroughly determined that whatsoever came of it I would by God's grace never defile her wedlocked bed.' One remembers Shakespeare's remarks on breaking his own bed vows. Here and elsewhere Whythorne is writing of a real situation that asks us to see literature not just as artistic creation but as a response to real life.

His most graphic and interesting portrait is of the woman he loved most: a courtly woman who boasted of her power over men, how 'by a frown she could make them go pale, and by a smile feel joy again'. This is Whythorne speaking of his own 'Dark Woman':

> Having been sometime a courtier, and well experienced in the affairs of the world, with a great wit and a jolly, ready tongue to utter her fancy and mind, she took pleasure many times to talk and discourse of the things she had knowledge of by experience: as sometimes of religions, she would argue in matters of controversy in religion; sometimes of profane matters …. Sometimes she would touch upon the city, with the grades of the citizens, and not leave untouched the fineness of the delicate dames and the nice wives of the city. Sometimes she would talk of the Court, with the bravery and vanities thereof, and of the crouching and dissimulation, with the *bazzios de los manos* [hand kissing] that are there used by one courtier to another; and sometimes she would

> talk of the courting of ladies and gentlewomen by the gallants and cavaliers; and sometimes would talk pleasantly of the love that is made and used in all these places between men and women ...

This world of 'bravery and vanities', one imagines, was precisely the world of Shakespeare's proud mistress.

Shadow Lives: Emilia Lanier and the Woman's Case

So who was she? The subject of poems, a well-known musical gentlewoman, the mistress of nobles, she moved on the fringes of high society with her two Wills, the one a nobleman, the other a writer and actor. Distinguished by her dark skin, according to the poet she was, in some unexplained way, perceived by the world to be 'unworthy'. Despite many guesses, the identity of Shakespeare's lover remains a mystery. But if the sonnets are autobiographical and she was a real person, we probably do not have far to look to find her in the small world of theatrical and musical society in late 1590s' London.

Just such a woman moved in Shakespeare's circle at precisely that time. She first appears in the consultation books of Simon Forman in May 1597. A well-known 'astrological' physician, later mocked by Jonson in his play *The Alchemist*, Forman was highly sought after. Part doctor, part analyst and part soothsayer, his clientele was mainly lower-class but he also saw musicians, theatre people and aristocrats, and among his clients that year were the wives of Shakespeare's colleagues Richard Burbage, Augustine Philips and Richard Cowley, Shakespeare's printer Richard Field, Philip Henslowe, and even Shakespeare's future landlady Mrs Mountjoy. Forman's still largely unpublished notebooks give a wonderfully vivid portrait of the Elizabethan world: its ambition and class envy, its struggle for money and patronage, its medical knowledge and superstition, and the sexual habits of the time. The contents of the notebook that runs from May 1597 until the autumn of that year, probably the very period of the writing of the sonnets to the woman, are tantalizing.

On 17 May a courtly gentlewoman went to Forman's house in Philpot Lane near London Bridge. Her name was Emilia Lanier and she was seeking advice about her husband's prospects of advancement. Alfonso Lanier was from a French musical family, one of the queen's musicians; but at this moment he was about to leave his wife for several months, to accompany the Earl of Essex on his expedition to the Azores to attack the Spanish treasure fleet on its return from South America.

Her small talk was of preferment, class and sex. Like many of Forman's patients, Mrs Lanier wanted to know the future. Would her husband be

promoted? On the 25th she came again and revealed much more about herself. She told Forman she was twenty-four (actually she was twenty-eight). She was the daughter of Baptista Bassano from Bishopsgate – a member of the famous family of royal musicians, who had come from Venice in Henry VIII's day. Some years earlier she had been the mistress of the chamberlain, Lord Hunsdon, who until his death the previous summer had been the patron of Shakespeare's company. Hunsdon, she told Forman, 'had loved her well and kept her and did maintain her long'. However, in the manner of the upper classes, when she became pregnant by him, she was married 'for colour' [for appearance's sake] to Alfonso Lanier in October 1592. Whether she continued to be Hunsdon's mistress is not clear. Evidently young Emilia Bassano had been well known at court; now she lived with her husband, her four-year-old son Henry and her servants near the court in Longditch, Westminster. In a first hint of her lingering bitterness about her treatment by the patriarchal system that ruled the court, Forman notes 'it seemeth she had ill fortune in her youth'.

Right: *Courtly love in the upper classes. This needlework valance from c. 1575 evokes the refined world portrayed in plays such as* Love's Labour's Lost. *In Shakespeare's own private life, though, the sonnets suggest that the reality was altogether more raw, messy and painful.*

On 3 June Emilia returned with direct questions. Would her husband 'have the suit'? She was hoping for social advancement (it soon becomes clear that she loved the aristocracy and pursued it with disarming frankness). She revealed she was about twelve weeks pregnant and was worried by pains in her left side: she had previously had miscarriages, she said, 'many false conceptions'. Forman was intrigued by her. 'She is high minded' he jotted down in his notes. 'She hath some thing in the mind she would have done for her. She can hardly keep secret. She was very brave in youth ...' 'Brave', also used by Whythorne of his courtly women, meant splendid, showy, finely dressed. In other words she was a striking woman, like those depicted in paintings of Elizabeth's courtly festivities.

Mrs Lanier's court connections were wide: her kinsmen, the Bassanos and Ferraboscos, were the most important musical families there. Forman recorded that 'she hath been favoured much of her Majesty and of many noble men, and hath great gifts and been much made of. And a noble man that is dead hath loved

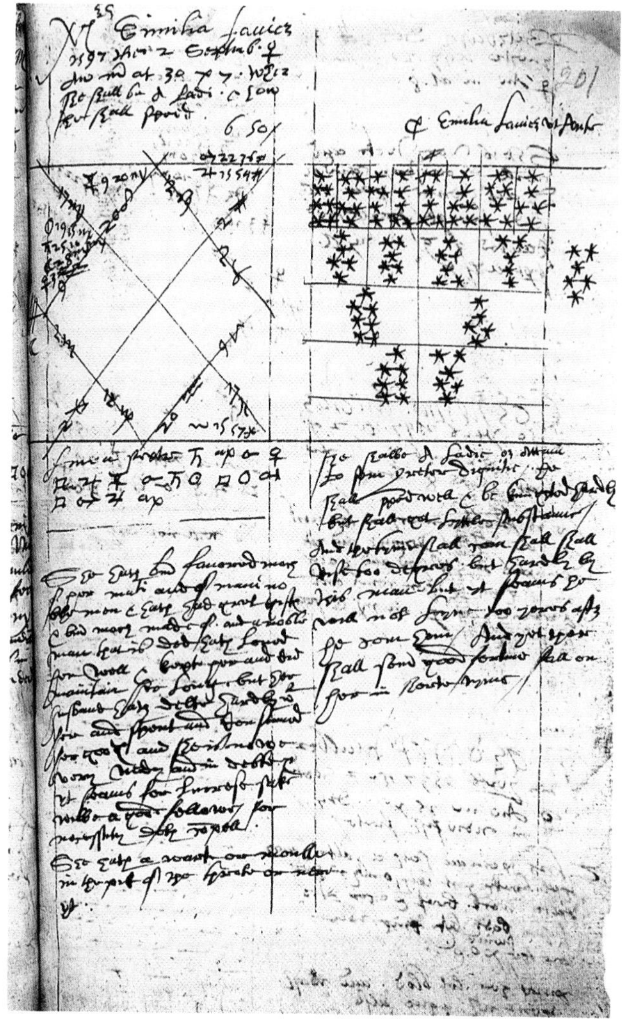

her well and kept her and did maintain her long.' To be 'favoured of many noble men' in that society meant she had taken them as lovers. Lord Hunsdon had been in his late sixties. For him a beautiful young mistress was a badge of power and masculinity – a trophy. At court, such women had semi-official status.

To be able to move in such a world Lanier must have been well educated and accomplished in poetry and music, as befitted a gentlewoman (she had probably been a ward in the household of Susan Bertie, Countess of Kent, a patroness of poetry, whom she later referred to as the 'mistress of my youth, the noble guide of my ungoverned days'). From her late teens, Lanier had been part of the cult of youth at Elizabeth's court, where the now ageing queen 'danced six or seven galliards a morning, besides music and singing' accompanied by talented young gentlewomen on the virginals. In this very sexualized atmosphere the beautiful young women of the court, like Lanier, cut quite a dash, as was described by Nashe in his famous pamphlet 'Christ's Tears over Jerusalem' of 1593:

ABOVE: *Emilia Lanier's horoscope, 11 September 1597, from Simon Forman's papers, a still unexploited source for Shakespeare's intimate circle. That summer Forman was having an affair with Elizabeth Cowley, wife of one of Shakespeare's company.*

> Gorgeous ladies of the Court … their eyes framed to move and bewitch [like] angels painted in church windows with glorious golden fronts beset with sunbeams … their breasts they embusk up on high, and their round roseate buds immodestly lay forth to show there is fruit to be hoped. They show the swellings of their mind in the swellings and plumpings out of their apparel ….

That's what it meant to be 'brave'. Many years later, living 'clos'd up in Sorowes Cell', Emilia would recall with exhilaration the thrilling power of her self-image in the days when 'great Elizaes favour blest my youth'.

On 16 June she returned once more to Forman. By now her husband may have been preparing for the voyage – Essex's fleet was due to depart on 10 July. Impecunious, desperately seeking advancement ('in hope to be knighted', she says), he had enrolled as one of Walter Ralegh's gentleman volunteers. Now she wanted to know 'whether her husband shall come to any preferment before he come again or no, and how he shall speed'. But she was not happy in her marriage. She told Forman she was receiving an annual pension of £40 from Hunsdon's estate and possessed many jewels that he had given her, and had another allowance left to her by her father, but Alfonso had frittered it away. 'Her husband has dealt hardly with her and spent and consumed her goods and she is now very needy and in debt.' Gender and class antagonisms and anxieties are bubbling under the surface here. Forman, fascinated, cast another horoscope and made more notes (which are not always easy to follow, but the gist is clear): 'She shall be a lady or attain to some great dignity. He shall speed well and be knighted hardly but get little substance. And the time shall come she shall rise two degrees. But hardly by this man. But it seems he will not live two years after he come home. And yet there shall some good fortune fall on her in short time.'

ABOVE: Playing the Virginals, *a textbook of 1611. Music, like poetry, was a desirable accomplishment for serving gentlewomen in the court, such as the young Emilia.*

Her pregnancy was now causing her much pain and she had morning sickness: 'the foetus kicks not', noted Forman after examining her. He gave her a purgative to procure a miscarriage, which took place a few days later. No wonder she was bitter. She had been at the very centre of things; but now her husband had left her in a parlous state and she had lost another baby. Perhaps this experience helps to account for the streak of anger and coldness in her, especially towards men.

Her next recorded visit to Philpot Street was ten weeks later, on 2 September. Her question was 'whether she shall be a lady, and how she shall speed'. Forman cast another chart. From her questions, and given the continued absence of her husband, one might wonder whether she had become involved with someone else. On the 11th she consulted Forman again, and this time, excited by her looks, her personality and her 'history', he tried to have sex with her (as he frequently did with female patients in exchange for waiving his fees). Emilia refused. Eventually she did sleep with him, but did not allow him to have intercourse, though Forman 'felt all parts of her body willingly and kissed her often'. At this point, in his only specific detail about her physical appearance,

Forman noted that (like Shakespeare's Imogen in *Cymbeline*) she had a mole below her throat.

Lanier's husband came back some time some time after the end of October. The fleet had encountered many problems and been nearly wrecked on the Goodwin Sands: one ship in particular, the *Andrew*, was in the news that month (and that autumn Shakespeare would mention it in his new script, *The Merchant of Venice*). But there was to be no promotion. Some time later Forman added to Alfonso's horoscope that 'he was not knighted, nor worthy thereof'. Under Emilia's he also said that 'she shall not, nor was not now worthy thereof'.

Shakespeare's Mistress?

It's a fascinating tale, especially revealing for the intimate insight it gives into social exchanges, sexual habits, and class and gender jealousies in Shakespeare's circle at this time. For, of course, given his patients, Forman's consulting room *was* part of Shakespeare's circle. And what of Lanier herself? Favoured by the queen, admired by many lords, the mistress of Hunsdon: was she part of Shakespeare's circle too?

When Forman's diary was examined in detail for the first time thirty years ago, it was indeed suggested that she was Shakespeare's mistress. The Dark Lady's attributes in the poems after all might have applied to more than one woman in 1590s' London, but surely not that many. The suggestion, however, was not well received by those scholars who were reluctant to allow real people into Shakespeare's private life, and who sought to separate the works from the author's life and times. Feminist critics also objected to Lanier appearing as an appendage, a sex object of the male poet. A generation later, the situation is very different. Lanier is accepted in her own right: her poetry is taught on university courses, published in modern editions and in anthologies of women's writing of the period. Now it is time to pose the question again. Shakespeare's London was, after all, a very small world.

Coming from a family of royal musicians Emilia Lanier, née Bassano, was no doubt musically accomplished herself; it was customary in such families to train daughters as well as sons. They were people of high standing in London's courtly and artistic society, including the theatre world. But most interesting are the Bassanos' origins, for they were Jews. At least two of her uncles also married Jewesses, and although they conformed as Catholics in Venice and as Protestants in London, they retained a consciousness of their Jewishness. (This would not have been a bar at court – the queen herself had a Jewish lady-in-waiting.) The Bassanos' forebears worked in silk: their coat of arms was a mulberry tree – *morus* in Latin, which also means 'Moor'. They must have been dark-skinned, for when two of Emilia's cousins appeared in a London court case they were described as 'black men', which is how one might expect Sephardi Jews from northern Italy to appear to Londoners. In Elizabethan eyes, then, Lanier, although outwardly conforming and baptizing her children into the Protestant Church, was doubly an outsider: of Jewish descent and with the looks of a 'Moor'.

Shakespeare must have known her, for she had been the mistress of his patron. Although Lord Hunsdon only became patron of his company in 1594, prior to that he had been responsible for court performances at which royal players and musicians would have been familiar figures. Shakespeare could hardly have been unaware of the mistress of such a powerful man. It is also now known that Lanier later knew Ben Jonson, who worked with her kinsmen on his masques. Even more intriguingly, her mother, Margaret Johnson, had a nephew named Robert, who would later become a royal lutenist and collaborate with Shakespeare, writing music for several plays, starting in 1609, the year of the publication of the sonnets.

So both before and after 1597, Mrs Lanier had close connections with Shakespeare's circle. Indeed, she looks and sounds startlingly like the woman in the sonnets. Here we enter the realm of diverting speculation rather than that of verifiable historical fact, but if she is that woman, then Shakespeare's remarks on her skin colour and unconventional beauty take on a peculiar significance, as do the poet's references to her 'unworthiness' on which he took pity, and to her unspecified foreignness. Even the dates fit: Lanier's husband was away from July until the end of October 1597, when it is possible that at least some of the sonnets to the woman were written. What makes her even more interesting is that she later became the first woman in England to publish a volume of poetry, which was registered in 1610 soon after Shakespeare's sonnets came into print. In its preface she lectures women who are not loyal to other women ('leave such folly', she says, 'to evill-disposed men'). And she bitterly castigates men for their inconstancy and their habitual and unthinking unkindness to women: 'Forgetting they were born of woman, nourished of women, and that if it were not by the means of women they would be quite extinguished out of the world, and a final end of them all, do like vipers deface the wombes wherein they were bred.' And here, from a long religious poem, is Lanier's proto-feminist manifesto on the rights of women:

> Then let us have our Libertie againe,
> And challendge to your selves no Sov'raigntie;

> You came not in the world without our paine,
> Make that a barre against your crueltie;
> Your fault being greater, why should you disdaine
> Our beeing your equals, free from tyranny.

The idea that Shakespeare's lover might have written such verses is almost too good to be true. The poems are indebted especially to Samuel Daniel, the Pembrokes' house poet, but she had possibly also read Shakespeare. Her remarks about blackness are particularly interesting, as, for instance, when she calls Cleopatra: 'as faire/As any Creature in Antonius' eyes/… as rich, as wise as rare/As any pen could write … Yet though a blacke Egyptian do'st appeare …'. This focus perhaps owes more to Samuel Daniel and Mary Herbert than to Shakespeare, but it is fascinating nonetheless since, like Shakespeare, she insists on Cleopatra's blackness. Curious, too, are her games with the word 'will':

> If twere his Will that Cup might passe away.
> Saying Not my will but thy will Lord be done …
> Loe here his Will, not thy Will Lord …

Conversion

One further clue is given by Emilia's poem. Its title is 'Hail God King of the Jews': it is a poem about religious conversion which tells the tale of the conversion of a 'Moor' – the assimilation of the daughter of a Venetian Jew into the English Protestant state. As her father and his brothers remained conscious of their Jewish roots, it is ironic that her move for social acceptance finally led her to write a Christian poem (whose aim was to gain the patronage of noble women, including Pembroke's mother). It suggests she has gone through a violent conversion: Christ's passion is at the hands of 'Jewish wolves', and since she is writing about her own conversion, the poem's title would have little point unless she were a Jew. This brings into the picture an area of hot debate in the 1590s: the question of Jewish women's conversion and their marriage to Christians. And if Emilia Bassano was indeed Shakespeare's mistress, it is interesting that in that same autumn of 1597 he should have written a play about Venetian Jews which includes a character by the name of Bassanio (pronounced as three syllables, not four). The curious emphasis of Sonnet 134 on transaction, payment and forfeit is also noteworthy. His lover is accused of using love like a moneylender, seducing the boy who had come 'surety-like … under a bond', as a 'debtor' for the sake of the poet who is 'mortgaged' to her will; he speaks of a

woman who is 'covetous' and a 'usurer'. In Elizabethan England, the words 'Jew' and 'usurer' were synonymous.

Throughout his career Shakespeare maintained a deep interest in Italian culture, and especially in Venice: he probably read an Italian source for *The Merchant* in the original; he had access to Lewis Lewkenor's book on Venice in manuscript, and would read his new book on the city a couple of years later. His Jews are Venetian, although the London Jewish colony, with which we would expect him to be more familiar, was Spanish and Portuguese. If Shakespeare had a mistress who was the daughter of a Venetian Jew, it would add a further fascinating detail to the crises in both his professional and personal lives in the year after his son's death.

The End of the Affair: 'My Honest Faith in Thee Is Lost'

As published twelve years later, in the order in which Shakespeare chose to arrange them, the sonnets tell the tale of a journey of the heart, a relationship with a beginning and an end. And in the end he leaves us with the image of himself demoralized by the affair with the Dark Woman, unable to stop wanting her but knowing it is ruining him. Obsessed with sex and bodily decay, accusing her of breaking her bed vow to her husband and her promise of love to him, in Sonnet 152 he declares 'my honest faith in thee is lost', as if honesty between two people married to others had been a possibility. In a telling and pathetic image, in Sonnet 143 he sees himself as a 'neglected child' running after his mother who has other things on her mind:

> Whilst I thy babe, chase thee afar behind.
> But if thou catch thy hope, turn back to me,
> And play the mother's part, kiss me, be kind:

But his tough-minded and worldly-wise mistress, one imagines, did not wish to be his mother. Like the musician Whythorne, the poet Shakespeare found himself out of his depth. The last few sonnets in the sequence are livid with the sense of the poet's 'nobler part', his soul, betrayed by his bodily desire. He seems to tell us that he has venereal disease and fears that sooner or later his young friend may catch it too. Love is a fever and his reason has left him:

> Past cure I am, now reason is past care,
> And frantic mad with ever more unrest …
> For I have sworn thee fair, and thought thee bright,
> Who art as black as hell, as dark as night.

However self-deluding, he wants his reader (or himself?) to believe that this is a tale of lost faith; that he believed she would be true, that they made promises to each other, and swore 'deep oaths'. What such promises meant between two married people is left unsaid. The last of the sonnets, 153 and 154, are two versions of the same poem, which perform a distancing trick after the anguished revelations of the previous poems. They are about the cooling of the heat of sexual passion; and now the previous hints at venereal disease are out in the open:

> ... a seething bath, which yet men prove
> Against strange maladies a sovereign cure.
> I, sick withal, the help of bath desir'd,
> And thither hied, a sad distemper'd guest

The model for this pair of poems is an epigram in the widely read *Greek Anthology*, probably from the 1603 edition, a copy of which was owned by Ben Jonson; perhaps Shakespeare knew it through him. This sonnet may, then, have been written after 1603, looking back on events as he shaped the collection into a literary form. The poem connects the cure for love with the seething baths for the relief of sexual diseases. Its 'strange maladies' may refer to syphilis, which was believed by the Elizabethans to be a foreign, 'French disease'. 'Love's fire heats water' in 154 suggests burning urine, a common symptom. As regards 'the help of bath' in 153, it is possible that the reader would hear this (and was meant to) as the town of Bath, where in his time hot mineral baths were taken for the relief of sexually transmitted diseases. Curiously enough, Shakespeare's company's tour that summer took them to Bath in late September.

For Shakespeare the affair had evidently been a deeply wounding experience – especially, for a man who was so guarded, because it laid him bare. And yet, as happens time and again with great artists, out of loss came art.

Christians, Aliens and Jews

Things alien fascinated Shakespeare. His plays abound with references to distant lands, foreign commodities, strange artefacts and exotic cultures. Falstaff imagines the sky raining potatoes, then an exotic new arrival from Peru via Virginia. On stage Shakespeare represents Moroccan and Russian ambassadors, and Caliban the Carib islander. He talks of the perfumes of Arabia, Lapland sorcerers and the veils of Indian women. Through these shards of alien worlds, he explored the distortions and caricatures that cultures create of each other. Repeatedly he represented cultures that define themselves as ideological

opposites engaged in a dynamic process of interaction: Rome and Egypt in *Antony and Cleopatra*; the indigenous islander and the colonist in *The Tempest*; the fissured Christian world of the eastern Mediterranean, of white and Moor in *Othello*. And one of his early explorations of the Other was *The Merchant of Venice*, on which he had been busy before the theatres reopened in late 1597.

The story of the bond of a pound of flesh was an old folk tale, but Shakespeare used an Italian story called *Il Pecorone*, published in 1558, for which no Elizabethan translation is known; so presumably he read it in Italian. He was also much indebted to Marlowe's powerful and grotesque *The Jew of Malta*, revived in 1594 during the trial of Ruy Lopez, a Portuguese Jewish physician convicted of attempting to poison the queen.

'There shall be no mercy for me in heaven,' Shylock's daughter Jessica says, 'because I am a Jew's daughter .... I shall be saved by my husband; he hath made me a Christian.' More than with most of the plays, interpretation of *The Merchant of Venice* has been in the eye of the beholder. By the late 1590s there was a small colony of Christianized Jews in London, with a few more in Bristol and Oxford. The Jews of London outwardly practised Christianity but privately held synagogue in their houses, and maintained their rituals, including circumcision. Stow, in his history of London, says that the community was centred on Houndsditch at the end of Bishopsgate, where Shakespeare and the Bassanos lived up to 1596, and that they were mostly pawnbrokers and sellers of old clothes. There were only a couple of hundred, but their small number bore no relation to the threatening aura that attached to them – the product of a long history of anti-Semitism in England going back to the blood libels of the Middle Ages.

Like all English people of his age, Shakespeare was brought up in an anti-Semitic culture and must have imbibed such tales as a child. His subsequent experience of Jews may have been somewhat different, but in the plays he sometimes reflects the prevailing view, using the word 'Jew' as an oath or in jokes that suggest the deprecating attitude to them that was part of normal Christian speech. The play puts Machiavellian and anti-Semitic politics in the mouths of some characters and elsewhere engages the audience's sympathies for Jews ('does not a Jew bleed?'). And although his new play was in no way designed to comment on the Jewish 'question', it still touches on critical issues such as conversion to Christianity. The result is, to us, an extremely uncomfortable mix of romance and racism, in which the quality of mercy is decidedly strained.

Like Marlowe's *The Jew of Malta*, it had wide relevance as part of the artist's response to the Elizabethan state's treatment of outsiders. But is it anti-Semitic? Some characters support the removal of strangers, but others reject it. Perhaps such theatrical conflict was what he was aiming for. But then again, this

was drama written for a popular audience, and Shakespeare typically harnessed the dramatic excitement of anti-alien feelings and therefore ran the risk of inflaming anti-alien and anti-Semitic sentiment.

For a modern audience this feeling is exacerbated by several failures in the play. In crucial areas it is surprisingly lacking in psychology, which is unusual in plays of this period. Jessica, the daughter of the Jew Shylock, exhibits no moral scruples as she helps to destroy her father and is one of the least delineated major characters in Shakespeare. Shylock's final exit is very hastily managed in Act IV, in a cheap plot device in which the tables are turned on him: the Jew can keep half his goods on condition that he converts. Having agreed, he exits with just three words: 'I am content.' The verdict arrived at by conniving lawyers is unpleasant, perhaps deliberately so, but it is unsatisfying to today's audiences. Finally, Shylock's conversion, the marriage of his daughter to a Christian and the giving of his property to her and her husband leave us – for all the fine speech about the quality of mercy – with the uncomfortable sense that the Jew himself has been very swiftly erased from the history of this particular fictional Venice.

ABOVE: *'Picture of a Jew' from a London book of 1562. 'I walk abroad o'nights/And kill sick people groaning under walls.' Marlowe's* Jew of Malta *(1589) dramatized the Tudor view of the Jew as murderer, poisoner, usurer and interloper.*

In the end, too many unresolved questions are left hanging in the air. Perhaps for personal reasons Shakespeare's eye was not quite on the ball – the play written very swiftly to fulfil his contract while working on a more important project, *Henry IV* Part 2? But still *The Merchant* leaves behind an uneasy edge, a sense of unresolved tension. Perhaps it embodies more of his personal experience than has been thought. In that light it might be worth looking at the merchant Antonio, a character which, it has been suggested, Shakespeare himself played, and the only one in his entire output who suffers from depression throughout. It doesn't happen often with him, but something is not quite right about *The Merchant of Venice.* Fairy tales can be more dangerous than they seem. Perhaps, with this one, being all things to all people was simply not possible.

CHAPTER ELEVEN

Shakespeare's Dream of England

HONOUR IS AIR

So the year after his son's death was one of extreme emotional ups and downs, and of tremendous creativity. In the autumn of 1597, having written *The Merchant of Venice*, Shakespeare was also finishing *Henry IV* Part 2, the core of his second great tetralogy on English history, a project very close to his heart. And where *The Merchant* was about the stranger, the second *Henry IV* play was about his vision of old England. That he could have written it through his 'hell of time' is a sure indicator of the solace he took in writing, and demonstrates again how creativity can come out of loss. In the *Henry IV* plays he created what is perhaps his greatest character, Sir John Falstaff. But Falstaff didn't start off as Falstaff, and the story is a fascinating insight into the way Shakespeare's life and his art were always feeding off each other.

THE OLDCASTLE SCANDAL

We need to backtrack for a moment. At Christmas 1596, Shakespeare's company were probably playing at the Swan in Paris Garden, and they also played two dates at court in late December. Among their shows that season was no doubt the first part of *Henry IV*, which he had written that year, and in which the character Falstaff makes his appearance – though called Sir John Oldcastle. Oldcastle had been a character in the original Queen's Men's play, now at least ten years old; but Shakespeare turned him into a lying braggart and a

hard-drinking habitué of brothels. The show was an instant success. But there was a problem. Oldcastle was a historical figure who had rebelled against Henry V and been executed: but in the new Protestant revision of English history, which had been set in stone by John Foxe's *Book of Martyrs*, Oldcastle was not a traitor but an early Protestant martyr. Unfortunately, the recently deceased Lord Hunsdon had been replaced as chamberlain by Lord Cobham, whose family, the Brookes, were descended from Oldcastle. In the winter of 1596 the Brooke family protested at Oldcastle being slandered as a fat old reprobate, and Shakespeare was forced to take the play off.

Was the insult deliberate? Or was it a simple boob on the part of the writer, taking over a name from his sources without thinking? Maybe. But it is hard to imagine that a working playwright in nineties' London, aware of the pitfalls of the censor, didn't known what he was doing by using a name so prominent in John Foxe's book. Cannily, Shakespeare simply changed Oldcastle's name to Falstaff. It was a good demonstration of the difficulties a playwright could run into, and probably reveals something of the poet's sympathies too – it is unlikely a Protestant writer would have used the name in the first place.

In early spring 1597 old James Burbage died. It had been a rough winter for him, aggravated perhaps by the mental distress he had suffered at the hands of the Blackfriars residents and the landlord of the Theatre. He left his long-running troubles with the Theatre and the Blackfriars to his sons Cuthbert and Richard. It was with good reason that, many years later, Cuthbert remarked that the ultimate success of the London theatres had 'been purchased by the infinite cost and pains of the family of Burbages'.

But they all stuck together. When, luckily, that spring Lord Cobham also died suddenly, the furore over Falstaff began to cool. The new chamberlain, Lord Hunsdon's son, brought Shakespeare's company back into favour. Next month the Chamberlain's Men performed at the Garter Celebrations what has long been assumed to be *The Merry Wives of Windsor*, a domestic comedy based on the fat knight (by now tactfully renamed).

A seventeenth-century story claims that Queen Elizabeth herself had requested 'one more play' about Falstaff, this time showing him in love; Shakespeare, it is said, dashed off the piece in two weeks. But new evidence suggests that *Merry Wives* cannot have been written until much later, after *Henry V* (1599), in which Falstaff dies. This clearly disappointed his many fans, including, it seems, the queen herself. It is now thought that the masque at the end of *Merry Wives* was the show performed to celebrate the election of new Knights of the Garter (including the new Lord Hunsdon) on 23 April 1597. It was only subsequently (at the queen's request?), with the typical

economy of a professional writer, that Shakespeare expanded it into a full-length play.

Not perhaps one of his most convincing works, *Merry Wives* bears the marks of a quick job: all prose, lots of wordplay, a throwaway plot. But it is a thoroughly professional job, and if it was really done to such a tight deadline, one can only take one's hat off to him. And was his use of the name Brooke for the cuckolded gull a deliberate two fingers to the late Lord Cobham and the Brooke family?

Falstaff: The Makings of an Elizabethan Hit

But from the first night of *Henry IV* Part 1 in the winter season of 1596 it must have been clear that in Falstaff Shakespeare had a great success on his hands. He probably wrote Part 2 in 1597. That autumn the Burbages' lease expired on the Theatre, the haggling went on, and they found themselves without a home. Back in Shoreditch they leased the Curtain for a season and it was here, in the lead-up to Christmas 1597, that they put on the further adventures of Falstaff, *Henry IV* Part 2, in which Shakespeare underlined his status as the most popular writer of the day.

Below: *As early as 1598 Falstaff's witticisms had entered the language. Seldom, if ever, in literary history can a fictional character have gained such instantaneous immortality.*

The character of Falstaff was the hit of the end of Elizabeth's reign. In a memorial poem in the First Folio of 1623, one of his friends describes the audience packing the galleries and the boxes to see him. Forget Ben Jonson and the others, they said, 'let but Falstaff come, Hal/Poins, the rest, you scarce shall have a room'. This is borne out by contemporary evidence. In February 1598 the Earl of Essex, a devoted theatregoer, added a gossipy postscript about a Cobham marriage in a letter to a friend: 'tell him for newes his sister is married to Sir John Falstaff'. The Countess of Southampton, writing to her son in Ireland about the birth of an illegitimate Cobham, is even more mischievous: 'all the news I can send you I think will make you merry is that Sir John Falstaff is by his Mrs Dame Pintpot made father of a goodly miller's thumb, a boy thats

all head and very little body, but this is a secret.' (Here's another Cobham joke – a cob is a small fish with a big head, also called a miller's thumb. Evidently, though Shakespeare had caused trouble, there were many who saw his side of the joke.) Within two or three years, tours had also made Falstaff a favourite in the provinces. In December 1600 Sir Charles Percy, a member of the great Northumberland family and a friend of the Earl of Essex, wrote from his home in Worcestershire saying that people in the metropolis 'will think me as dull as a Justice Shallow or Silence', knowing his correspondent would know just what he meant.

Falstaff's appeal is not difficult to see. There was an atmosphere of stasis and disillusionment at the end of the old queen's reign, and here was a show that hit the spot psychologically: corrupt politicians, bloodless princes and puritanical judges were contrasted with the full-blooded life of a true-hearted Englishman. It was an image of themselves that the audiences loved, whether high-born or low-born. There was much nostalgic harking back in Shakespeare's day, and in a time of anxiety and change the show magically conjured up old England. But it had a very hard edge of reality too, for it was anchored in real events of great contemporary relevance: civil war, rebellions on the Celtic fringe, and the suppression of a northern revolt, which would have recalled to many minds the Pilgrimage of Grace of 1536 and the Northern Rebellion of 1569. In the *Henry IV* plays the Percy family in particular are in the forefront, as they had been in 1569; and the northern rebels are lied to and betrayed by Machiavellian politicians, just as they had been by Henry VIII. Everyone in the audience knew this to be the reality of politics and 'honour', that 'mere scutcheon', as Falstaff calls it.

So what the government's 'readers' called 'application to the times' was more obvious to a contemporary audience than to us now. But the *Henry IV* plays work on many levels; they are also a haunting psychological story of fathers and sons, in Hollywood terms a maturation tale. Prince Hal's surrogate father, Falstaff, is the prince of misrule, a fat knight joking, drinking and whoring. Hal's real father, King Henry IV (whom Shakespeare himself perhaps played), is saturnine, weighed down by guilt about his usurpation of the throne and also by his sense of duty to God and his people. His son eventually grows up and rejects the underworld life inhabited by Falstaff and his friends, as is foretold in one of the greatest scenes in drama:

> FALSTAFF: … banish not him thy Harry's company: –
> banish plump Jack, and banish all the world.
> PRINCE HENRY: I do; I will.

But although Falstaff may be a braggart and a liar, he is life incarnate – as we see, for example, in the scene when, called to military service, he leaves the Boar's Head tavern in Eastcheap, always ready to blow his trumpet, even to his old companions:

> FALSTAFF: Pay the musicians, sirrah. Farewell, hostess; farewell Doll. You see, my good wenches, how men of merit are sought after: the undeserver may sleep, when the man of action is called on. Farewell, good wenches: if I be not sent away post, I will see you again ere I go.
> DOLL: I cannot speak; if my heart be not ready to burst – Well sweet Jack, have a care of yourself.
> FALSTAFF: Farewell, farewell. [*Falstaff exits*]
> HOSTESS: Well fare thee well. I have known thee these twenty-nine years, come peascod-time, but an honester and truer hearted man – Well, fare thee well.
> BARDOLPH [at the door]: Mistress Tearsheet!
> HOSTESS: What's the matter?
> BARDOLPH: Bid Mistress Tearsheet come to my master.
> HOSTESS: O, run Doll, run; run good Doll, come. She comes blubbered*. Yea, and will you come, Doll?
>
> *'Blubbered' means a tear-stained face

This is great writing of real people's speech: for example, the precision with which Mistress Quickly dates a decades-old meeting to the time when peas are podding (when the itinerant pea-pickers come to town, as Shakespeare would have remembered). We know Falstaff is a rogue, but Quickly's judgement is affectionate – 'an honester or truer hearted man' is the author's guide to how to see him – and it explains Hal's fascination with him. Falstaff is a great stuffed piece of life.

Shakespeare wrote greater plays and finer verse and prose, but he never surpassed the comedy of Falstaff's scenes in Cheapside and Gloucestershire. The passages involving Falstaff at the Boar's Head in Eastcheap, for instance, with Mistress Quickly and Doll Tearsheet, are marvellously observed counterpoints to the scenes of the great deeds of history, the actions of kings and armies. Then there is Falstaff's old friend Justice Shallow, a country JP who, Falstaff tells us, spent a lecherous youth in the brothels of Turnmill Street in Clerkenwell: a man who when 'he was naked looked for all the world like a forked radish, with a head fantastically carved upon it with a knife. A was so forlorn, that his dimensions to any thick sight were invisible, a was the very genius of famine, yet lecherous as a monkey and the whores called him mandrake…'

Shakespeare's knowledge of the brothels of Southwark and Clerkenwell is, to say the least, accurate in its local colour. It is amazing to think that the time when he was scripting Part 1 may have been the months immediately after his son's death, and that Part 2 was written during the following year.

The Author's Message to his Audience

The published text of *Henry IV* Part 2 also lets us eavesdrop on the brouhaha, which was evidently very considerable, over Shakespeare's traducing of the Cobham family's ancestor Sir John Oldcastle. In response, Shakespeare's enemies commissioned a play by Anthony Munday. Presented in autumn 1599 at the Rose, *The True and Honourable History of the Life of Sir John Oldcastle, the Good Lord Cobham* was designed to set the record straight. The preface showed that it was specifically intended to counter Shakespeare's portrayal:

> It is no pampered glutton we present,
> Nor aged counsellor to youthful sins;
> But one whose virtues shone above the rest,
> A valiant martyr and a virtuous peer.

The preface ended with a straight attack on Shakespeare's fraudulent portrayal of Oldcastle:

> Let fair truth be graced,
> Since forged invention former time defaced

This is remarkable evidence, not only of the author's propagandist aims but of the imaginative hold that Shakespeare's character had already exerted over contemporary audiences by 1599.

Shakespeare, however, had clearly felt the need to back-pedal. At the end of the printed text of *Henry IV* Part 2 is a page of additions, which suggests the way that he and his company attempted to defuse the controversy. In the first epilogue the author speaks straight to the audience, apparently commenting directly on the controversy:

> First my fear, then my curtsy, last my speech.
> My fear, is your displeasure; my curtsy, my duty; and my speech, to beg your pardons. If you look for a good speech now, you undo me, for what I have to say is of mine own making and what indeed I should say will, I doubt [fear], prove mine own marring. But to the purpose, and

> so to the venture. Be it known to you, as it is very well, I was lately here at the end of a displeasing play to pray your patience for it and promise you a better. I meant indeed to pay you with this; which if like an ill venture it come unluckily home, I break, and you, my gentle creditors, lose. Here I promised you I would be, and here I commit my body to your mercies. Bate me some [let me off], and I will pay you some, and as most debtors do, promise you infinitely: and so I kneel down before you, but indeed, to pray for the Queen.

Shakespeare does the same sort of thing at the end of *The Tempest* when the 'author' stands on the stage and speaks directly to the audience about their relationship. The audience, remember, knew him as both actor and author. He provided their entertainment, and the metaphor he used here for their relationship was commercial – an 'ill venture' was an unsuccessful trading enterprise. So the audience were the creditors of the playwright, and he was the debtor who always promised more, and kept in credit by delivering it.

But hidden in the clever showman's patter there was still an apology. Shakespeare said he had recently produced something 'displeasing' (in some eyes) that had lost him credit, and now he begged forgiveness. Perhaps these lines were actually delivered on stage by Shakespeare himself, who had played the part of Henry IV.

The second epilogue, spoken by a dancer, was even more to the point. It suggests that the saga rumbled on for months after Cobham's death and the removal of Oldcastle's name from the play (note also the showbiz promise of a sequel – *Henry V* is clearly already in the planning):

> One word more, I beseech you. If you be not too cloyed with fat meat, our humble author will continue the story, with Sir John in it, and make you merry with fair Katharine of France; where, for anything I know, Falstaff shall die of a sweat, unless already a be killed with your hard opinions; for Oldcastle died martyr, and this is not the man. My tongue is weary; when my legs are too, I will bid you good night.

Any resemblance to persons living or dead is purely coincidental!

Rebuilding the Family: Shakespeare Buys a House

In the months after his son's death, although he still continued to work in London, Shakespeare clearly felt the need for some practical and emotional input in Stratford. Early in 1597 he made the first move in his gradual accumu-

lation of property and land in the town and surrounding area. Like the coat of arms, it may have been something he had contemplated for a while, but perhaps Hamnet's death had focused his mind. Anne and the girls (Susanna was thirteen and Judith, the surviving twin, twelve) were perhaps still living in Henley Street with William's parents and two of his brothers, Richard, twenty-three, and Edmund, who had just turned seventeen. (William's sister Joan, now twenty-eight, was probably already married to the hatter William Hart; his brother Gilbert, now thirty, appears this year as a haberdasher in St Bride's in London.) It would have been a crowded household. On 4 May 1597, perhaps soon after the first sonnets were written to the 'lovely boy', William signed the papers to purchase his own house.

In Church Lane, on the corner opposite the old guild chapel, stood New Place, one of the biggest houses in Stratford. It could hardly have been closer to his old haunts: the schoolroom where he had spent so much of his young life was across the lane out of the side door. New Place had been built by Hugh Clopton, the medieval benefactor of the town, who was also responsible for the 'great and sumptuose bridge' over the river, and the guild chapel with its lavish cycle of paintings; a shining example of the old-style civic-minded Christian countryman. The present vendors were the Underhills, who had fallen on hard times. An important Catholic family recently hammered by the recusancy laws, they had been caught up with the Ardens in the Somerville Plot back in 1583. So the house had had more than one significant previous owner. And now, despite their fall in fortunes in the late 1570s, it was the Shakespeares' turn.

What William got was a late fifteenth-century half-timbered town house with five bays and a frontage of 60 feet. A front gate led into a courtyard, then a rear block and a barn. As an Elizabethan estate agent might have put it, the property benefited from a well and ten fireplaces, and, most important, a garden 180 feet long with other land beyond available by separate negotiation. So like a successful showbusiness writer today, he bought a large house with a private garden. The place had not been lived in for a while and was semi-derelict. It needed major renovation and the record of the corporation's purchase of surplus stone from him in 1597–8 suggests that this work took a year or so and that he may not have moved the family in for quite some time. In fact, his cousin Thomas Greene was still living in it as late as 1609, so Shakespeare may have rented part of it out to his relations. The deed of purchase says it cost £60, but the true purchase price was evidently concealed in the sale documents. In fact the house had gone for £140 in 1563 when Clopton's descendants sold it, and £110 in 1567 when the Underhills bought it. It is very likely, then, that the face price was only half what was actually paid.

Opposite: *New Place, Stratford, which Shakespeare purchased in 1597 and where he later died. 'A pretty house of brick and timber', the previous owners, the Underhills, were recusants who had been caught up in the Somerville Plot.*

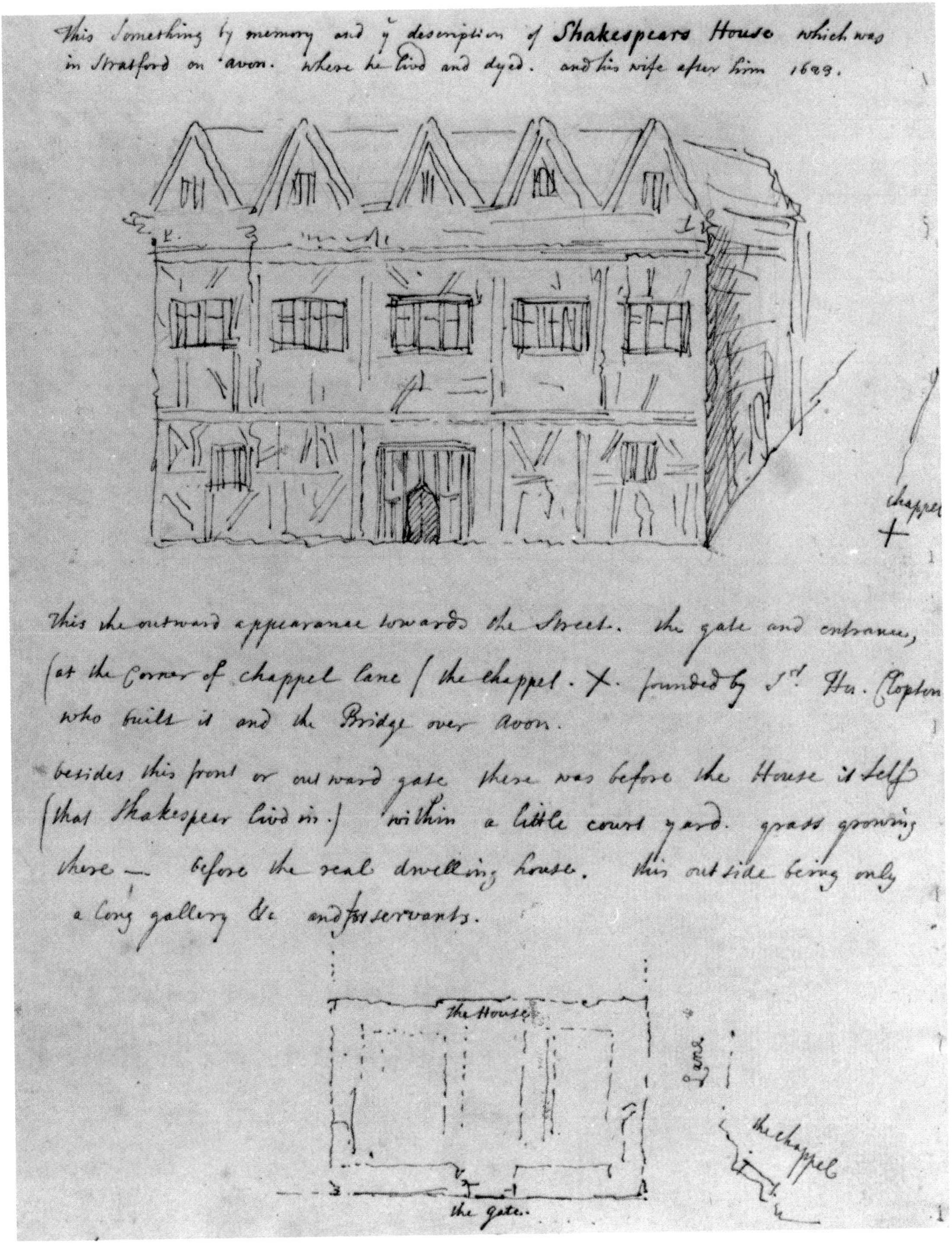

This Something by memory and y^e description of Shakespears House which was in Stratford on Avon. where he livd and dyed. and his wife after him 1623.

chappel
+

This the outward appearance towards the Street. the gate and entrance, (at the Corner of chappel lane / the chappel. X. founded by S^r. Hu. Clopton who built it and the Bridge over Avon.

besides this front or out ward gate there was before the House it self (that Shakespeer livd in.) within a little court yard. grass growing there — before the real dwelling house. this out side being only a long gallery &c and for servants.

the House

Lane

the chappel

the gate.

Whatever the price, he could afford it. He was probably on a contract to write two plays a year for at least £20 and maybe earned twice that with his other script chores. He also made money as an actor, as a shareholder and from private commissions. So he probably took home at least £60 a year, maybe more with work on the side. These are not huge sums: he is often portrayed as money-grabbing, but this is overstated. His property and land amounted to nothing like the holdings of some of his fellow actors; men such as Henslowe and Alleyn spent money like water; Condell owned inns and tenements in the Strand. But after ten years in showbiz he had made some money and had financial security. More important in his own eyes, perhaps, was that after all his father's disasters, he had rebuilt the family's fortunes.

Elizabethan Best-sellers: The 1590s' Top Ten

In London that winter the success of Falstaff saw Shakespeare creep into the lower reaches of the literary best-sellers. Plays at that time were not regarded as literature and no publisher expected to make much money on a play quarto. For Shakespeare, it was writing plays, acting and doing writing jobs on the side, together perhaps with money-lending, that made his money – not publishing. But in 1598 he had a modest breakthrough, in print as well as on stage. His recent hits *Romeo and Juliet, A Midsummer Night's Dream* and the Falstaff plays had cemented his status as the leading dramatist of Elizabethan London, and his name now began to appear on play quartos in order to sell them. In 1598 *Love's Labour's Lost* was published, 'corrected' by the author; it was the first play to be published with his name on the cover. The quarto of *Romeo and Juliet* says the show was 'often (with great applause) played publicly', and a second quarto soon afterwards would breathlessly advertise a better text, 'newly corrected augmented and amended'. At this point other dramatists began to echo his plays (especially *Romeo and Juliet*) and contemporary writers paid tribute more frequently to his stage work rather than to his printed poems.

A
PLEASANT
Conceited Comedie
CALLED,
Loues labors lost.
As it vvas presented before her Highnes
this last Christmas.
Newly corrected and augmented
By W. Shakespere.

Imprinted at London by W.W.
for Cutbert Burby.
1598.

Below: *Title page of* Love's Labour's Lost, *the 1598 revision of a play probably written in the early 1590s for Lord Strange and his circle of literary friends.*

The numbers of play quartos sold were not great. *Henry IV* Part 1 (seven printings) was his best, followed by *Richard III* and *Richard II* at five

each. These were outstripped by *Mucedorus*, of all plays (a comedy of 1598 once attributed to Shakespeare; nine printings), and, less unexpectedly, by Marlowe's *Dr Faustus* and Kyd's *Spanish Tragedy*. A print run of a couple of thousand would be good going. So not much money was to be made from quartos: *Venus and Adonis* outsold Shakespeare's best-selling play by four editions. A top ten best-seller list for the period shows us that the favourite reading of most Elizabethans seemed to be a mixture of scripture and self-help spiritual manuals.

The Elizabethan book-buying public was God-fearing and Protestant. And some of these books enjoyed big sales, even by today's standards. A single print run of the Psalms or the Book of Common Prayer might be 2000 or 3000; the former went through 124 editions in twenty-five years. The theatre audience was a different matter, with a dozen venues and four main theatres; London tickets sold in one venue could top 10,000 a week. For a playwright, quartos of plays meant only a few pounds on the side. Shakespeare was working in a different marketplace with a different audience.

Hard Times in Stratford

Back home in 1598, a severe food crisis had developed. Stratford had been devastated in the mid-1590s by two fires, which Puritan preachers connected with the slow pace of change to God's true law in this still ungodly town. The town's economic problems had been aggravated by bad harvests, much rain and unseasonal temperatures with late snow. The burial register shows that the death rate was up; many people succumbed to diseases associated with malnutrition. There were complaints about those who hoarded 'like wolves', looking after themselves while the town's 700 paupers waited for the corporation dole. A 'note of corne and malte' that February listed the holdings of the better off who were storing more malt than was necessary for personal need. William Shakespeare, still of Henley Street, was named among them, but it was a common tale at that time. That autumn the disasters in Stratford led the town to petition the Privy Council for relief from the latest subsidy voted by Parliament, and an old family friend of the Shakespeares, Richard Quiney, came to London.

He stayed at the Bell near St Paul's, from where he wrote a letter to his 'Loving good friend and countryman Mr. Wm Shackespere', asking for help with a loan of £30 – not for the corporation's expenses, but for his own debts: 'You shall friend me much in helping me out of all the debts I owe in London, I thank God, and much quiet my mind, which would not be indebted.' Quiney's letter, good evidence for the language used between friends from the same town, appears to be about a private loan on which Quiney offered sureties and interest.

Shakespeare agreed to help, for on 4 November, Quiney wrote to a Stratford friend, 'that our countryman Mr. Wm. Shak. Would procure us money', even though the conditions of the loan had not been agreed. Shakespeare was obviously seen as one of the wealthier townsmen of Stratford, and, like his father, was happy to lend money as part of his business.

The sequel to Quiney's visit was happy. The queen agreed to relieve 'this town twice afflicted and almost wasted by fire' and the government reimbursed Quiney for his expenses on his London trip. The Quineys and the Shakespeares stayed close: Richard's son Thomas would marry William's daughter Judith – although the union was not, as it turned out, a fortunate one.

Such visits remind us that through friends, or by the local carriers, the Greenaways, William would have sent letters home – instructions for the builders at New Place, for example, on the purchase of stone, or to his lawyer regarding court cases. He would have received letters, too, from his daughter Susanna, for instance, who was literate, and from his wife, Anne, if she could write – she would have perhaps dictated to Susanna if not. Country gifts, too, were customary: Warwickshire cheeses, a new linen shirt, new gloves, useful things for the city. And, along with the news of the troubles of the town, there would have come more intimate pieces of gossip. Their next-door neighbour and friend, the draper George Badger, was fined £5 after many warnings 'for his wilful refusing to come to the hall'. Badger was a staunch Catholic who paid his fines and went to prison for recusancy, and was eventually deprived of his alderman's gown as John Shakespeare had been. There had been a great fuss in town that September when Badger had been elected bailiff, 'thought by the greatest number of aldermen to be the meetest man'; his refusal to attend cost him another £100.

And there was no doubt smaller gossip too: Anne's looking after the affairs of her father's old shepherd Thomas Whittington, who was now retired and living with the Paces in Shottery; John Smith's fine for sowing woad (for dyeing) in the chapel orchard; players' companies still coming through. The stuff of small-town life. Who's in, who's out. As well as writing and playing, this too was still Shakespeare's life, the strong pull of his 'countrymen', his background, which would eventually draw him back home.

CHAPTER TWELVE

Ambition: The Globe

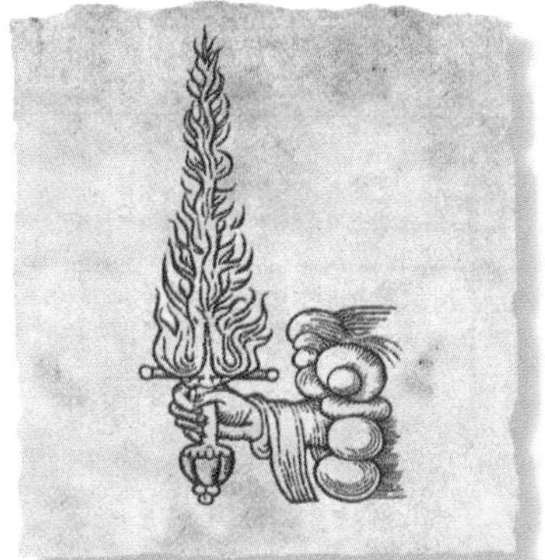

I Am the Author of My Daring

In 1599 Shakespeare was at the mid-point of his career. Already recognized by his peers as the best at both comedy and tragedy, now, in his mid-thirties, he entered an incredibly fertile, creative phase. This was no doubt partly due to changes in his personal life about which we cannot know: age, experience, new influences and, as we have seen, loss, which has been a catalyst in the lives of many great poets. But these changes also came about because of professional pressures – in particular Shakespeare's response to a new wave of mostly younger dramatists who challenged his supremacy just at the point when he had achieved mastery of his drama of personality. But whilst getting bums on seats was still a prime motivation, another challenge now seemed to be assuming greater importance: an artistic and psychological ambition. He was now on the artist's journey into the interior.

The first fruit was a quartet of great plays. *Henry V, As You Like It, Julius Caesar* and *Hamlet* were all being written or drafted that year. Shakespeare would prove himself a master of all forms – history, comedy, satire and tragedy – and it was in this next year or two that he turned to tragedy. Between 1598 and 1601 his art took a leap forward as his verse became much more accomplished; there was a toughening of the language, a new freedom of metaphor and allusion, and a freer handling of the rhythm of the verse line. In this change he was pushed by his rivals, just as Marlowe had earlier driven him. A string of new faces – Marston, Jonson, Chapman and later Middleton – were all experimenting with genres and styles.

Important too at this time were changes in the companies and playhouses. From this time, and for much of the next decade, his rivals were not only the companies he had always competed with but the new boys' companies that used indoor theatres, artificial light and elaborate stage effects. To sophisticated audiences the newly reopened theatre of the Paul's Boys by the Cathedral, and the indoor Blackfriars, were more appealing than the rowdy popular theatre – the 'common stages', as the shows of Shakespeare and his colleagues were called – up in the suburbs in Shoreditch.

In all this creative ferment, one particular relationship deserves to be singled out. It made its mark in many ways, on and off stage, but in one area of influence it was particularly fascinating. Did Shakespeare come into direct contact with the greatest drama of the ancient world, Greek tragedy, both through Latin versions and through stage productions in London? If so, the catalyst was a cantankerous, turbulent black dog of a man called Ben Jonson.

The Great Leap Forward: Enter Ben Jonson

In the autumn of 1598 the bricklayer, classicist and playwright Ben Jonson killed an actor called Gabriel Spencer with a rapier in a duel in Shoreditch Fields. (They were both irascible sorts: only a few months previously Spencer himself had killed a man in his lodging house in Holywell Street.) At his trial Jonson was found guilty of 'felonious and wilful killing'; he saved his skin only by reciting what were known as 'neck verses' (Psalm 51) in Latin and pleading benefit of clergy, which by long tradition enabled a convicted criminal to pass as a clergyman and so obtain a discharge from the civil courts. Latin was Ben's thing: it saved him, and it made him.

Now branded with the 'Tyburn T' on his thumb, Jonson touted round for work. Down on his luck, and never an easy man to work with (he notoriously bit the hand that fed him), he sent a script to the Chamberlain's Men. Shakespeare, according to a late but plausible story, saw his talent and gave him a chance. So during the winter of 1598–9 Jonson worked for Shakespeare's company and got to know him. His first play, *Every Man in His Humour*, was staged that autumn at the Curtain in Shoreditch. Shakespeare may even have had a hand in retouching the script for the stage.

It was said later that, although Shakespeare had been generous to him, Jonson 'had not returned the same gentleness'. Jonson was passionate to a fault about the moral and didactic role of theatre, and about the craft required to write for it. Fiercely sure of his literary judgements, although he owed his break to Shakespeare, he thought his colleague's shows broke all the classical rules of action, place and time: they were not made with appropriate craftsmanship.

Left: *Ben Jonson, who sniped at Shakespeare's 'Tales, Tempests and other such Drolleries' but 'loved him this side idolatry, as much as any'.*

Still a paid-up member of the bricklayers' guild, he saw poetry in the same light: after building it up from the sound foundation of a prose draft, he then worked it into verse carefully loaded with Latinisms. In print he even supplied his plays with footnotes to make sure the reader got all his clever references. So when Jonson said later of Shakespeare that he never blotted a line, he meant it to be taken as admiration, but also as criticism.

Jonson's influence was not only theatrical. As with all creative relationships in the arts, he seems to have spurred on Shakespeare's ideas and his reading. After 1598 Shakespeare's use of classical sources changed and broadened; he had a very strong ego and almost always took up artistic challenges. Their relationship would last until Shakespeare's death, but it was notoriously prickly. Jonson wrote later that he had loved him 'this side idolatry' and generously

compared him with the ancients. But even in his first play he made snide remarks at Shakespeare's pretensions to gentility, mocking his newly acquired coat of arms. In a later preface to *Every Man in His Humour*, he derided those authors who

> with three rusty swords,
> And help of some few foot-and-half foot words,
> Fight over York and Lancaster's long jars.

and offered instead, with a swipe at Shakespeare's *Henry V*, a new kind of play

> Where neither Chorus wafts you o'er the seas;
> Nor creaking throne comes down, the boys to please;

Although from the same social class as Shakespeare, Jonson saw himself as a scholar, a Latinist. He had a remarkable library of Greek and Latin classics, and was consulted by scholars of the day. That was his province and he saw the magpie Shakespeare, with his grammar school Greek and Latin, as a lesser light. Shakespeare could take offence at slights on his character, but seems to have taken Jonson's rumblings in good part. A famous joke at his own expense bears a ring of truth. At the baptism of Jonson's son, Shakespeare stood godfather. Asked what he would give the boy as a present, he suggested some silver alloy (latten) christening spoons: 'I'll get him some latten spoons. Then Ben can translate them for me.'

Jonson commonly lent books to his friends and surely did so to Shakespeare. For *Julius Caesar,* written this year, Shakespeare almost certainly used Euripides's *Iphigenia in Aulis*; and while he may have known Erasmus's Latin translation at school, the fact that he was writing the play when working with Jonson suggests that he might have borrowed a copy from him. Equally exciting is the possibility that at this time he read Aeschylus, the most 'mighty line' of the ancients and the nearest to the Elizabethans in poetic style. This could have been through a Latin printed version owned by Jonson, but it is also possible that in 1599 Shakespeare could have seen an adaptation of Aeschlyus's greatest tragedy on the London stage. This was the moment when he started to write the first of his great tragedies, *Hamlet.*

That year at the Rose on Bankside the Admiral's Men put on two plays telling the tale of the murder of Agamemnon on his return from Troy, and the revenge and madness of his son Orestes. The texts were probably by Thomas Dekker and Henry Chettle, working on a script left to the company by Jonson and tinkered with by George Chapman, who had recently published the first part of his famous translation of Homer's *Iliad.* In the close-knit world of literary London the Greek classics were in the air, the 'must-reads' on everyone's list. Dekker, for one, excitedly boasted of his knowledge of 'the real thing'. The Rose plays were called *Agamemnon* and *Orestes' Furies* – titles that match those in the most accessible Latin version of Aeschylus's *Oresteia.*

Shakespeare's Euripidean parallels have long been noticed. Dryden was the first to see his debt to *Iphigenia* in *Julius Caesar.* For two centuries now scholars have also noticed close parallels between *Hamlet* and the *Oresteia.* These were once attributed to 'archetypal patterns'; but Shakespeare was a conscious artist who rifled many sources for his inspiration and plots, and it is much more likely that he simply borrowed from one of the greatest of all works of literature. In *Hamlet* the graveyard scene and the closet scene, neither of which has a parallel in the source texts, seem directly inspired by the Orestes story. It is hard not to think that Shakespeare had actually seen it on stage, or read the parallel scenes in Aeschylus's *Libation Bearers* (Henri Estienne's edition had a very user-friendly crib whose Latin was well within Shakespeare's compass).

Equally suggestive is the role of Hamlet's faithful friend Horatio, crucial in building the audience's sympathy for Hamlet but again absent in the play's sources. Horatio effectively plays the role of Pylades, the faithful friend who supports the wavering revenger Orestes in both Aeschylus and Euripides (the latter Jonson we know had in his library). Dekker and Chettle's plays have not survived, but even a rough literal translation of the 1550 Latin version of Euripides's *Orestes* gives an inkling of what the audience heard at the Rose in 1599:

> Oh good Pylades
> Nothing is better than a loyal friend
> Not gold, nor kingdoms sure can weigh against
> A noble heart, a true and generous friend.
> Through every danger you have been my guide
> And now again do spur my fit revenge
> And still are by my side. But yet give pause;
> To speak your virtues more would be offence
> And I will cease before I praise too much.

This surely reveals the source of one section of the play that Shakespeare was writing in 1599–1600: this is Hamlet speaking to Horatio. The same goes for the scene in the bedchamber with his mother Gertrude, over which hangs the

shadow of sex and death; but despite Gertrude's remarks, it is modelled not, as Freudians have said, on the tale of Oedipus, but on that of Orestes.

In short, Shakespeare, like a top scriptwriter today, was a professional through and through. He had perhaps read Latin versions from Jonson's library, and more than likely sat in the audience at the Rose and saw Dekker and Chettle's shows. The impact, even in Chettle's journeyman versifying, is likely to have been as powerful as it always is when the greatest works of literature are encountered. In the Greek drama, fate and human destiny allow no room for Christian providence and the audience is left with the remorseless power of the gods. Our failure to understand the true nature of the gods – all too human as it is – is no excuse, any more than it will be in *King Lear*. As the unforgiving Dionysus tells humankind in the *Bacchae*, 'You understood too late'.

This is an area of Shakespeare's creative process of which next to nothing is known, but it is perhaps no accident that his friends praised him as fit to stand beside the ancient tragedians. These recent discoveries perhaps help to explain how Shakespeare came to write full-blown tragedy in the Greek spirit. For this was precisely the territory into which his ambition would now lead him.

Yesterday Shoreditch, Tomorrow the Globe

He would make that journey with, for the first time in three years, stability in his professional career: as a shareholder in a new playhouse owned by the company. In the winter of 1598–9 Shakespeare and his colleagues decided to make a permanent move south of the river. By Christmas, the long-running feud over the company's lease in Shoreditch had reached an acrimonious impasse. Their landlord, Giles Allen, was now demanding not only his plot of land but the fabric of the theatre that stood on it. John Hemmings' friend and neighbour, the merchant Nicholas Brend, had just inherited a plot of land 100 yards from the Rose in Maiden Lane on Bankside. They secured an option on a lease, and decided to take advantage of the Christmas holiday. On the night of 28 December, with snow falling and the Thames freezing over, the Burbages, together with the most experienced theatrical carpenter in London, the contractor for the Rose, Peter Street, plus a dozen workmen and a few armed heavies, marched up to Shoreditch and set about dismantling the Theatre. (This, in fact, was as per their lease, which had permitted old James Burbage to 'take down the buildings he might erect'.) Over the next few days they carted the pieces through the city and across the frozen river to the new site where, over the next six months, the Theatre would be rebuilt as the Globe.

Early in 1599 the Warwickshire mafia organized a business plan for the

new theatre. The rebuilding would be an expensive undertaking and they were still leasing the Curtain for their daily shows, so backers were needed. They approached two Aldermanbury contacts, the merchant William Leveson and Thomas Savage, a goldsmith neighbour of Hemmings and Condell (in one of whose houses Hemmings lived). The Savage connection may have dated back all the way to Strange's company, for Savage was a Lancashire man from Rufford, the Hesketh's' home village, and his wife was a Hesketh. Then a share issue was made, half to the Burbages, the other half going as one-tenth each to Shakespeare, Hemmings, Condell, Sly and Philips. On 21 February a thirty-one-year lease was signed and construction began.

The site consisted of seven gardens abutting the Bishop of Winchester's park, bounded by the old park ditch which was now used for sewerage and drainage. On it stood a house and a row of decaying tenements with fifteen residents. The site was liable to flood at the time of the spring tides because the Thames had no embankment, so the theatre had to be constructed on a 130-foot-long wharf of timber piles partly driven into the sewer ditch, which was bridged for audience access. No wonder Jonson called the Globe 'flanked with a ditch and forced out of a marsh'.

The site was recently located at the junction of today's Park Street under Southwark Bridge Road. A small excavation was able to determine the exact shape and size of the theatre, which was polygonal (possibly with twenty-four sides), 100 feet across, with a stage almost 50 feet wide, a pit and three galleries. Capacity was an amazing 3300 people – virtually double that of its modern successor on Bankside. Over the stage was a gabled lantern and the motto *Totus mundus agit histrionem*, which, loosely translated, means 'All the world's a stage'. A house was constructed next door; a recently discovered post-mortem document of Brend senior, dated 17 July that year, refers to the 'newly built house with a garden in the occupation of William Shakespeare and others'.

It had many advantages over Shoreditch: the site was also out of the jurisdiction of the city, but it could be reached in a few minutes by river taxi from Blackfriars and the inns of court; it was close to the bear pit and the bull baiting; the brothels and inns of Southwark were also nearby, crowded around St Saviour's at the end of London Bridge. Recently, archaeologists have added grim immediacy to our picture of the area and its varied entertainment industries: the latest excavations around Bear Garden Lane have unearthed the skulls of mastiffs smashed by the chained bears; the bones of old blind bears torn to bits by the dogs; and a thick layer of hazelnuts, the equivalent of popcorn for an Elizabethan matinee crowd.

In the first half of 1599, while the Globe was under construction, they were still using the Curtain in Shoreditch. *Henry V* was first played here – this, then, was Shakespeare's 'wooden O'. At this time the company lost an important member, their clown Kemp. A stand-up comic, a virtuoso song and dance man and an unpredictable and uproarious ad libber, Kemp had been the darling of the groundlings. But Shakespeare and the rest of the company were moving towards higher-class shows with a more refined and fixed text, and it may be that 'artistic disagreements' were the cause of Kemp's departure. All we know is that he left before the Globe opened, with words of bitterness and recrimination.

ABOVE: *The clown Will Kemp: a 'shag-haired' instrumentalist and dancer who could 'make a scurvy face and draw his mouth awry'. Shakespeare split with Kemp in 1599, perhaps because Kemp wouldn't stick to the script.*

By the end of the year, down on his luck, he decided to raise money by dancing his famous jig all the way to Norwich. Kemp had been a draw in towns right across England, and his sacking made news. He later complained of 'lyes' told of him by 'an impudent generation of ballad makers and their coherents', among whom may have been perhaps some of his erstwhile colleagues, if the epilogue to the tale of his jig is anything to go by: 'My notable Shakerags ... for that I know you to be a sort of witles beetle-heads, that can understand nothing, but what is knockt in to your scalpes ... I knowe the best of ye by the lyes ye writ of me.' Was it Shakespeare who had sacked him? Whatever happened, such a crowd-puller was not easily replaced. Shakespeare's two new plays for the season of 1599 had no part for a clown. The show must go on.

A Killing in Southwark

The first night at the Globe seems to have been set for a date in June, and that month Henslowe's takings next door at the Rose dipped alarmingly. As the weather got hotter, there was tension in the streets. On 6 June, while the painters were putting the finishing touches to the Globe, a vicious fight took place between two of Henslowe's playwrights, John Day and Henry Porter. A collaborator of Chettle's, Day was a 'rogue and base fellow' in some eyes. Porter had been a leading writer for the Admiral's Men for the previous two years or so; an early collaborator with Jonson on *Hot Anger Soon Cold* and author of vigorous English social dramas, such as *The Angry Woman of Abingdon*. He had real promise: the previous year the critic Francis Meres had placed him alongside Shakespeare in a group of the best contemporary comedy writers.

That day, according to the coroner's jury, 'moved by the instigation of the Devil, and of malice aforethought', the raging Day stabbed Porter in the left side

'with a certain sword, in English, a rapier'. Porter died the next morning – another talent of the age gone. Day got off with manslaughter and capitalized on it over the next few months with topical shows such as *The Blind Beggar of Bethnal Green* in which the duellist Captain Westford, who had been in Spain, was said to be 'well practised in the desperate fight of a single rapier'. Perhaps Day had been more skilled in such fighting than the unfortunate Porter. But clearly in Southwark all human life was there, and it was swiftly turned into art.

New Theatre, Old Rivalries

Recent evidence suggests that the Globe theatre opened on 12 June with *Julius Caesar*, after careful calculations by an astrologer to hit on the most auspicious opening day and hour. On the old calendar that day was the summer solstice, the shortest night, and it coincided with a new moon (which the almanacs judged 'best to open a new house'). A more practical consideration was that a high tide would spare the posh people in the audience from getting their clothes dirty on a long walk across smelly mudflats.

Grander and more elaborately decorated than the Theatre, the Globe was soon a magnet for Londoners and foreign visitors. *Julius Caesar*, for example, was seen on 21 September 'very ably acted by a company of about fifteen' by a Swiss traveller, Thomas Platter of Basle. It was Shakespeare's twenty-first play and marked ten years at the top. A grim political piece, it touched on major talking points of the day: how to tell a tyrant from a just ruler? How and when to justify assassination? Somewhat unremitting in its lack of comic relief, it was lit up by brilliant scenes between Brutus and Cassius that used, but surpassed, Euripides's parallel scenes in his *Iphigenia*. Gallingly for the self-proclaimed classicist Jonson, it was everything he aspired to write.

The Globe's opening refuelled old showbusiness rivalries. The Chamberlain's Men led with their strongest shows; six months later, faced with a declining share of box-office receipts, Henslowe and Alleyn cut their losses, left the Rose and moved north to the new Fortune, near Cripplegate where they would rebuild their audience and mount a new challenge. But with more theatres and bigger audiences, a younger generation of playwrights was now vying for prominence, and the pace of artistic ambition began to quicken in London's theatre world.

Throughout this time Ben Jonson had been working for Shakespeare's company, but he had his own ideas about what poetry should do. Comedy, he thought, should be 'neere the times', and in the autumn he made his bid for leadership of the avant-garde in London's theatre world. At the same time a young Middle Temple lawyer, John Marston, writing for a boys' company, the Children of St Paul's, came out with a darkly comic satire called *The Malcontent*.

Right: *London's reconstructed Globe on Bankside gives a wonderful impression of the physicality of Elizabethan playhouses, with the stage roof 'fretted with golden fire'.* Opposite: *'I am not what I am': Viola in* Twelfth Night *at the modern Globe. The use of male actors to play women's parts in recent productions has illuminated the rich possibilities of sexual ambiguity in Shakespeare's text.*

Chapman, the translator of Homer, was competing too, and soon the rules of the game were shifting away from Shakespeare's history- and comedy-dominated drama of personality to social satire and rhetorically florid, classically influenced tragedy of state. No doubt this was to do partly with artists' responses to their own society and partly with changing tastes and fashions, but this working out of rivalries within the new wave gives a terrific insight into Shakespeare as a writer responding to trends. For under commercial pressure, with a big investment at stake, his company were soon wheeler-dealing, head-hunting and even pirating other companies' scripts. In this atmosphere, late in 1599, the War of the Poets began.

The Boys' Companies and the War of the Poets

In the early 1600s the new craze for boys' companies in indoor theatres caused even Shakespeare and his colleagues to glance nervously over their shoulders. With Jonson and Chapman as their poets, a remarkable troupe of boy players acted with a charm and grace that seems to have made them more attractive than their adult rivals. They also offered vocal and instrumental music, for which they were specially trained. And sex appeal too: the playwright Thomas Middleton advised the London gallant 'to call in at the Blackfriars, where he should see a nest of boys able to ravish a man'. Puritan sermonizers, needless to say, were shocked. But there was good acting to be seen, too: Ben Jonson himself praised the power of little Salathiel Pavy, only thirteen when he died, who for three years had been 'the stage's jewel'. A foreign visitor from Germany in 1602 spoke of a pre-show of music from an organ, lute, mandolins, flutes and violins, and of a boy who sang so delightfully that the nuns in Milan could not excel him: 'we have not heard his equal in all our travels'.

'What, are they *children*?' Hamlet asks with a twinkle. In reply Shakespeare made Rosencrantz drily dismiss the 'eyrie of children, little eyases, that cry out on the top of question and are most tyrannically clapped for't'. But he was worried: 'These are now the fashion, and so berattle the common stages – so they call them.' (The 'common stages', of course, meant Shakespeare and his company.) At the centre of it all was the furrow-browed Jonson. The butt of much barbed satire, he never forgot the violence of the quarrel in which he and John Marston came to blows.

The matter dated back to September 1599, when the twenty-three-year-old Marston, then still a lawyer at the Middle Temple, was making his name as a combative satirist and pamphleteer. It began with a mocking representation of Jonson on stage. But Jonson too liked a

fight – after all, he had killed a colleague in one. His new play *Every Man Out of His Humour* opened at the Globe at about the same time; in it he attacked the kind of romantic comedy at which Shakespeare excelled, and announced his own theory of art and satire.

What Shakespeare felt about this is not known, but young Marston, who greatly admired him, went after Jonson, mocking his slowness and his pretensions to learning with a clever lawyer's wit. Over that autumn and winter Marston's *Histriomastix* ('The Actor-chewer') was performed by Children of St Paul's at the Cathedral theatre. In it, Marston dismissed Jonson as a 'heavy translatting-scholler' who looked down on the common sort, sucked up to the judiciary and charged a hefty £10 a play. Some writers might have thought that there's no such thing as bad publicity. But Jonson had a thin skin and he wrote a bitter retort: it was all 'black vomit', 'excrement', 'base filth motivated by malice', and the actors who performed the plays of his whippers were a bunch of 'servile apes'.

So this was the new climate: metropolitan wit, with lashings of exuberant, over-wordy satire. It was not Shakespeare's preferred arena, but he felt he should respond to this shift in taste and may have begun his own foray into satire, *Troilus and Cressida*, around this time. But first, between January and late March 1600, he put on *As You Like It* at the Globe. It was taken from a French romance set in the Forest of Ardennes, which becomes the magical Arden of his childhood, complete with the old resident hermit of legend: the leafy place of exile where they lived 'like the old Robin Hood of England … in the golden world'. The company had a new clown now, the singer Armin, a goldsmith's apprentice who played a Jonsonian Touchstone. As a nod to the new wave, Shakespeare inserted the melancholic satirist Jacques (which literally means 'privy'), but Jacques's gripes are left behind by brighter, lighter spirits – especially, as so often in his comedies, by the women, who have all the best lines.

According to a later acting tradition, Shakespeare played the aged Adam, but he perhaps doubled as the Warwickshire yokel William. He was by now well known to his audiences as both author and actor, so everyone would have appreciated the joke.

> TOUCHSTONE: How old are you friend?
> WILLIAM: Five and twenty, sir.
> TOUCHSTONE: A ripe age. Is thy name William?
> WILLIAM: William, sir.
> TOUCHSTONE: A fair name. Was't born i'the forest here?
> WILLIAM: Ay, Sir, I thank God.

TOUCHSTONE: Thank God – a good answer. Art rich?
WILLIAM: Faith sir, so-so.
TOUCHSTONE: Art thou wise?
WILLIAM: Ay Sir I have a pretty wit.
TOUCHSTONE: Art thou learned?
WILLIAM: No sir

Touchstone then shows off William's lack of learning with a quick flash of Latin pedantry: '... ipse is he. Now you are not ipse, for I am he.... Therefore tremble, and depart.' Shakespeare was no longer afraid of being mocked for his 'small Latin'.

And the 'war' went on. Marston was next, with *Jack Drum's Entertainment* in the spring of 1601. Jonson had now left Shakespeare's company to put on *Cynthia's Revels* with the Children of the Chapel at Blackfriars. Shakespeare's next show, *Twelfth Night or What You Will*, with Armin as the clown Feste, was played at the Globe in early 1601. It was Shakespeare's Ovidian riposte to Jonson's criticism of romantic comedy in *Every Man Out of His Humour.* This was romantic comedy combined with social satire and touched by a bitter-sweet melancholy: a tale of lost twins, mistaken identity, gender bending and cross-dressing (an area that Shakespeare always found a very satisfying and intriguing source of comedy) with the battle of the sexes thrown in for good measure.

As its first audiences recognized, the model was the Latin comedy of Plautus; but Shakespeare's play was in a different league of sophistication. It also contains a series of great songs. *Twelfth Night* represents the peak of Shakespeare's festive comedy but with an edge, especially in the merciless (and, to us, unsettlingly cruel) deconstruction of Olivia's Puritan steward, Malvolio. This is part of a minor but persistent theme in the play, with its jibes at extreme Puritans and Brownists, an early sect of radical nonconformists. Puritans and curates were clearly not his – or his audiences' – favourite people.

The aftermath of the War of the Poets would rumble on for the next two or three years. It was during this time, when the vogue for satirical drama was at its height, that the Chamberlain's Men became alarmed enough to purloin one of their rivals' scripts. The company were short of this sort of stuff – it did not, after all, play to Shakespeare's strengths, and Jonson had gone to a rival outfit – so they resorted to bare-faced literary piracy. The Children's company had cheekily performed the Chamberlain's Men play *The First Part of Jeronimo*; so they retaliated by procuring Marston's *Malcontent*, a very topical show in its tilts at court immorality and intrigue, the prevailing atmosphere of the end of Elizabeth's reign. The Chamberlain's Men answered the charge of theft by

claiming that the book of the play had been mysteriously lost and then found. Intellectual property rights were hard to assert in Shakespeare's theatre world. As we would say, that's showbiz.

Ireland: A Real War

But back in 1600, hanging over the quarrels on stage was an altogether bigger dissension. The critical political situation was worsened by several tensions in the body politic, primarily the continuing uncertainty about the succession and the colonial war in Ireland. In the charismatic figure of the Earl of Essex – the English Achilles, as the poet Samuel Daniel had called him – both these strands came together. And they came at the end of a decade of discourse about Ireland from writers as varied as Edmund Spenser (author of *The Faerie Queene*, who lived there and wrote a tract called 'The Present State of Ireland') and John Donne (who in his Elegy no. 20 wrote of 'Sick Ireland, with a strange war possessed'). Playwrights, too, were now using history to touch on the Irish question: for instance, George Peele in his *Edward I*, and a lost play about Henry I performed by the Admiral's Men in 1598, both looked at the beginnings of English empire in Ireland. In his history cycle, especially *Henry IV* Part 1, Shakespeare also tackled past English wars with Celtic neighbours. Elizabethan audiences were attuned to such nuances and could make the topical connection.

In August 1598, at the battle of the Yellow Ford, the Irish nationalist Earl of Tyrone had defeated the English forces and captured their key fort in Ulster. In autumn the rebellion had spread to the province of Munster, with talk of 'shaking off all English government', Ireland's 'Norman yoke'. In response, Elizabeth had appointed a new military commander and dispatched him with reinforcements, and in January 1599 had filled the vacant post of vice-regent with her favourite, Essex. It was in Essex's vice-regency that Shakespeare's play on a foreign war, *Henry V*, had been staged at the Curtain and the Globe. In it the chorus likened the 1415

campaign in France to that of 'the General of our gracious Empress', Essex, in Ireland. Something in this didn't please, for the next year the play was published with all of the choruses cut. In his critique of militarism in *Henry V*, put into the mouths of the common soldiers, some have seen Shakespeare's misgivings about Essex, his awareness of growing public alarm at the war in Ireland, and a disillusioned ambivalence about the reasons behind, and the consequences of, English empire building. 'What if the war be unjust?' ask the famine-stricken soldiers before Agincourt. The soldiers in 1415 had been treated as badly as Elizabeth's Irish army conscripts had been for the last twenty years, and now maimed Irish veterans were to be seen everywhere on the roads of England.

Essex failed: the unauthorized pact he made with Tyrone caused fury in London, where Elizabeth saw such mediation as an insult to her honour and authority. At the end of September 1599, Essex returned from Ireland. At ten in the morning he burst unannounced, 'full of dirt and mire', into the queen's room at Nonesuch Palace, where he found her 'newly up' in a state of undress, 'hare about her Face'. His political judgement and his personal conduct now combined to damn him. Placed under house arrest and denied access to the queen, he was tried by his peers and stripped of his titles and office, although cleared of treason. But his dramatic and irretrievable loss of favour pushed the increasingly desperate Essex to make a rash bid for the crown, hoping to exploit the worries over the succession. And in February 1601 the poets found themselves living out in real life Jonson's maxim that theatre should be 'neere, and familiarly allied to the time'.

THE ESSEX REBELLION AND THE DEPOSITION PLAY

Essex's rebellion of February 1601 was preceded by an amazing incident that, if nothing else, reveals the power that was believed to reside in the theatre. On the 5th the conspirators had a meeting with members of Shakespeare's company and persuaded them to put on *Richard II*, which featured the deposition of the monarch, the following Saturday afternoon. These were very dangerous waters: the play was sufficiently sensitive to have had the deposition scene cut in no fewer than three printed quartos. The theme had been particularly controversial since the publication in 1599 of a book by Sir John Hayward that told the same story. It had been dedicated to Essex with a very pointed phrase: 'great thou are in hope, greater in expectation of a future time'.

Hayward seems to have intended no treason, but he nearly died for it. Just how seriously such things might be interpreted is shown by an abstract in the state papers from the government's investigation of the book. Like a CIA 'reader' in the Cold War, the examiner concludes that Hayward had:

OPPOSITE: *The Earl of Essex in 1596. A theatregoer and long-time Shakespeare fan, he was 'wondrous pleased' with the 'conceit' of Shakespeare's play on Richard II – and nearly brought the company into serious trouble as a result.*

> selected a story 200 years old and published it, intending the application of it to this time, the plot being that of a king who is taxed for misgovernment, and his council for corrupt and covetous dealings for private ends; the King is censured for conferring benefits on hated favourites, the nobles become discontented, and the commons groan under continual taxation, whereupon the Kings is deposed, and in the end murdered.

As always in authoritarian states of any colour, the past can serve to discredit the present. The mere narrative or re-enactment of history could be seen as subversive. Elizabeth was furious: believing Hayward's offence to have been deliberate, she demanded he be tortured on the rack.

The case had wider repercussions, too. In June 1599 the register of the Company of Stationers carried a note 'That no English histories be printed except they be allowed by some of her Majesty's privy Council' and that 'no plays be printed except they be allowed by such as have authority'. Any book of this nature was to be brought under the control of the archbishops of Canterbury and London and, ominously, 'such books as can be found or are already taken let them be presently brought to the Bishop of London to be burnt'. Censorship and book burning were all part of the Elizabethan state.

In this light it seems hard to avoid the conclusion that Shakespeare and his company were sympathetic to Essex, who we know had long loved the play's 'conceit'. At any rate, *Richard II* went ahead at the Globe on the afternoon of Saturday the 7th, with the deposition scene: Burbage presumably played Richard. The next day Essex and a group of armed followers tried to get the city to rise up, but to no avail. Essex was captured and his supporters, including the Earl of Southampton, were arrested.

Shakespeare's company were inevitably commanded to explain themselves. They sent one of their number, Augustine Philips, to speak on their behalf. The Public Record Office preserves the intelligence reports on Essex, interrogations of conspirators and verbatim transcripts of the trial. Among those papers is a fascinating document written on 18 February 1601, the day before the trial opened. Examined 'upon his oath' by Lord Chief Justice Popham and two other chief justices, his words recorded by the stenographer, Philips did his best:

> He sayeth that on Friday last, or Thursday, Sir Charles Percy, Sir Jocelyn Percy and the Lord Montegle with some three more spake to some of the players in the presence of this examinant to have the play of the deposing and killing of King Richard the Second to be

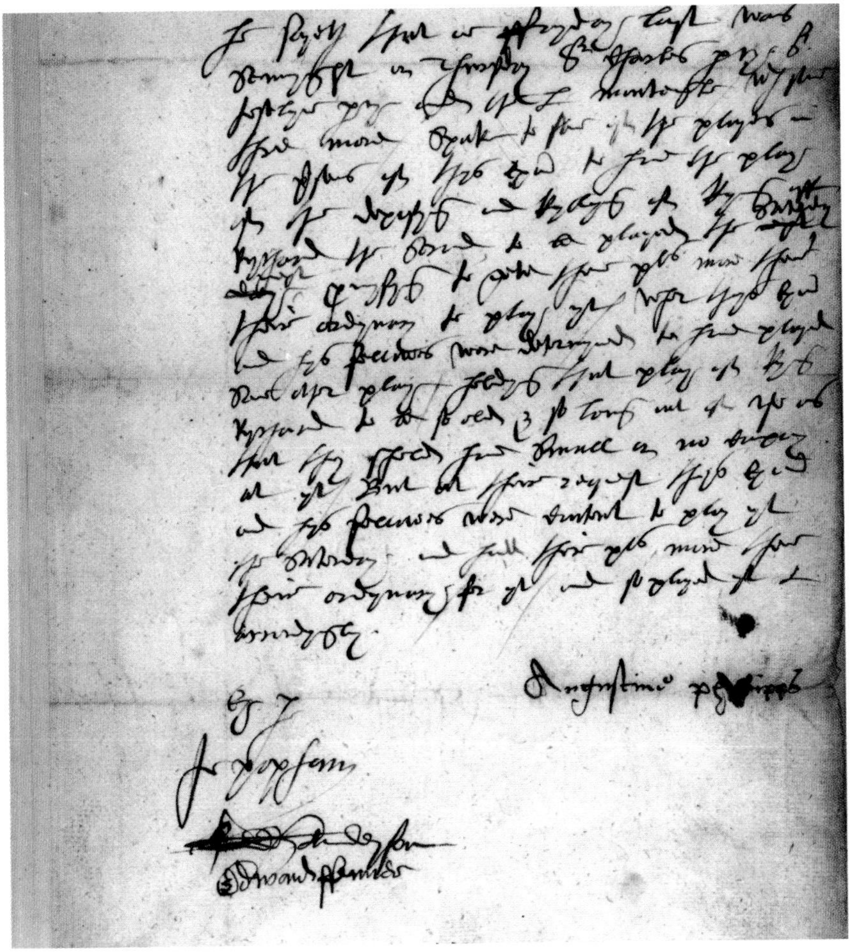

LEFT: *The record of Philips's interrogation. The precedent of the deposition of Richard II caused Elizabeth's government, and the queen herself, peculiarly intense anxiety.*

> played the Saturday next, promising to give them forty shillings more than their ordinary to play it. Where this examinant and his friends were determined to have played some other play holding that play of King Richard to be so old and so long out of use as that they should have small or no company [audience] at it. But at their request this examinant and his friends were content to play it the Saturday and had their 40 shillings more than the ordinary for it and so played it accordingly.

The sheet is signed by Philips and his examiners. Probably Shakespeare and the rest of the company had instructed him to stick to the money story; as always with interrogators, one should offer only what is asked for.

RIGHT: *Southampton in the Tower, 1604: older and sadder than the golden boy of ten years before – and perhaps a little wiser?*

The trial was over quickly, Essex and Southampton sentenced to death. On 24 February, the night before Essex's execution, Shakespeare's company were summoned to perform before the queen. Was that deliberate on her part? Southampton's sentence was commuted to imprisonment in the Tower, where he was memorialized, lank-haired and sheepish, in a wonderful painted portrait with a black cat. He had been lucky.

'I Am Richard II'

There is a fascinating tailpiece to this story, which links Elizabeth, Essex and Shakespeare's *Richard II*. That same year, on 4 August, the old antiquarian William Lambarde came to the queen's private chamber in east Greenwich to present her with his 'pandecta of all her rolls, bundles, membranes and parcels', a collection of historical documents retrieved from the Tower. What follows is Lambarde's account of their conversation:

> Her Majesty fell upon the reign of King Richard II. Saying 'I am Richard II. Know ye not that?'

LAMBARDE: Such a wicked imagination was determined and attempted by a most unkind Gent, the most adorned creature that ever your Majesty made.
HER MAJESTY: He that will forget God, will also forget his benefactors; this tragedy was played forty times in open streets and houses.

The exchange leaves one with sympathy for the queen, old and isolated, weighed down now by the burden of office, though still with her finger on the pulse of things: she knew how many times the show had been staged. Later in the conversation, still bothered by it, she came back to the theme: 'then returning to Richard II. She demanded, 'Whether I had seen any true picture, or lively representation of his countenance and person?' As she perused the archive, Elizabeth's last words were these: 'In those days force and arms did prevail, but now the wit of the fox is every where on foot, so as hardly a faithful or virtuous man may be found.'

THE WAR OF THE POETS: LAST PHASE

The late spring or summer of 1601 saw the final phase of the War of the Poets play itself out in the edgy artistic climate after the demise of Essex. Marston had replied to Shakespeare's *Twelfth Night or What You Will* with his own *What You Will*, again for the Paul's Children. Then Jonson put on his *Poetaster* with the Children of the Chapel at the Blackfriars. *Poetaster* is about ancient Romans, but it implicitly, and unwisely, contrasted Augustus's wise rule, the age of poets such as Virgil, Horace and Ovid (all of whom are characters in the play), with an English state dominated by malice, intrigue and envy, in which the talented outsider is done down by envy. In his prologue Jonson, as always, can't let go of his moralizing (or his wounded self-regard):

know, tis a dangerous age,
Wherein who writes had need present his scenes
Forty-fold proof against the conjuring means
Of base detractors and illiterate apes

All of which, no doubt, was lapped up by the intelligentsia: the students and inns of court lawyers who crowded the galleries for the latest instalment of clever literary references, in-jokes and satirical defamations. Jonson was now a spectator sport all of his own, and the wits queued to see his 'unwieldy galleon' outsailed by the breezy sails of his detractors, lighter in the water and quicker on the turn. Topicality was the rage.

But this was never Shakespeare's forte (or his interest – it would probably have seemed a waste to him to devote a whole play to such controversies). For a reply his company employed the talented freelancer Thomas Dekker, who that autumn got back at Jonson with *Satiromastix* ('The Chewer-up of the Satirists'), which was first played by the Chamberlain's Men at the Globe. But by now Shakespeare himself was sufficiently interested in the controversy to be drawn into writing a lengthy satirical classical play: *Troilus and Cressida.*

The new play seems to have been taken as another tilt at Jonson – some saw a burlesque of Jonson in the figure of Ajax. Shakespeare was now moving into Jonson's territory, ancient Greece. *Troilus and Cressida* was a satire that attacked everything: a play with no moral centre, in which all are as crooked as each other. It is a long play and very learned – Chapman's weighty Homer was obviously part of his reading. But the play's registration was delayed and then subject to getting 'sufficient authority', which hints at licensing difficulties. It was eventually published as 'played by Chamberlain's Men at the Globe', but then reprinted with those words removed and a new preface claiming, strangely, that there had been no stage performances. This suggests that, like *Sejanus*, the play had fallen foul of the authorities. Contemporary satirists had often made play with Essex as the English Achilles, and the statesman William Cecil (Lord Burghley) and his son Robert as the greybeards in the Greek camp. If the play was taken in that way by the authorities – had Shakespeare perhaps been 'intending the application of it to this time'? – it is not surprising it was swiftly taken off.

By then Shakespeare had *Hamlet* on at the Globe with the added passage about the great brouhaha over the children's companies, the 'little eyases', wryly remarking that 'the boys carry it off, even Hercules and his load' (the image of Hercules carrying the globe was on the flag that flew above their own theatre). This effectively marked the end of the War of the Poets, if not of the creative disagreements and abrasive friendship of Shakespeare and Jonson. They resumed relations in 1609–10: Jonson still making jibes at Shakespeare, Shakespeare putting little in-jokes into his plays that only Jonson would have recognized.

Hamlet: The Invention of the Human

So changes in taste, writing and themes came about as a response partly to contemporary politics, partly to new challenges and styles, and partly to the sheer fizz of theatrical rivalry at a time when there were many good writers – some of them really good – and when the younger generation was bidding to outdo the old. Shakespeare, however, always kept ahead of his rivals; he was always somehow new and fresh. And now, typically, he pulled another rabbit out of the hat, by recasting the old revenge tragedy of the late 1580s in a new and thrilling guise.

THE

Tragicall Hiſtorie of

HAMLET,

Prince of Denmarke.

By William Shakeſpeare.

Newly imprinted and enlarged to almoſt as much againe as it was, according to the true and perfect Coppie.

AT LONDON,

Printed by I. R. for N. L. and are to be ſold at his ſhoppe vnder Saint Dunſtons Church in

ABOVE: *The 1605 printing of* Hamlet *advertised bonus scenes. 'The younger sort takes much delight in Venus and Adonis,' wrote one contemporary, 'but Hamlet pleases the wiser sort.'*

Hamlet was probably first staged in 1600, and the confusingly different texts – representing his first version, his revision and his abridgement of the revision, with references to the War of the Poets – were written between 1599 and 1601. As with most of his best plays he didn't invent the main plot but took it from an old play, perhaps by Thomas Kyd, and on one level writing the show now was simply a clever commercial move, as revenge tragedy was enjoying a major revival. Perhaps, as with his reworking of the Queen's Men's plays, he was deliberately remaking a popular old play with one eye on the box office, just as Hollywood today will remake a hit of ten or fifteen years before. And when he shifted the goalposts everyone else responded, in much the same way that a successful Hollywood remake will push other studios into action in the same genre. Marston immediately wrote *Antonio's Revenge*; and late in 1601 Ben Jonson was paid by Henslowe's company to update Kyd's *Spanish Tragedy*, one of the greatest hits of the previous fifteen years.

Hamlet has got the lot: plot, action and speed; love, intrigue and murder. Shakespeare could have *longueurs* in his plays, but the most theatrical, like *Romeo and Juliet* and *Hamlet*, have a fantastic energy and speed of plot that lead the audience irresistibly on. The tale is a simple one. Old Hamlet, king of Denmark, is mysteriously dead; his suave brother succeeds and marries his widow, young Hamlet's mother. The time is out of joint: in the court there is debauchery and cynicism, in the world threats of war and revolution, in the heavens omens of destruction. In a scene of thrilling power and drama, old Hamlet's ghost – who figured in the original play – tells his son that he has been murdered by his brother and that Hamlet must take revenge. From then on the show goes like a rocket to its final tragic but heroic end, especially in the revised version in which Shakespeare knocked out a few scenes and a couple of lesser soliloquies to keep things racing. (In its uncut length, at four and a half hours it was far too long for an Elizabethan audience used to 'two hours traffic of the stage' at the Globe.)

In *Hamlet*, Shakespeare famously uses the soliloquy – the lone hero on stage talking to the audience – to get to his inner thoughts. And Hamlet's language uncannily represents a mind in action: anxious, excited, ruminating, always on the move. This psychology, this portrayal of inwardness, was one of the concerns of late Elizabethan culture. In this, Shakespeare was influenced by the contemporary debate over the 'humours'; but where in Jonson's hands such ideas could become rather static and preachy, Shakespeare brilliantly worked them into the action.

Hamlet is perhaps the most commented-upon work of art in existence. In its delineation of personality and its portrayal of inwardness modern critics have seen nothing less than 'the invention of the human'. But on one level *Hamlet* is just a rattling good story. As in several other shows, Shakespeare uses the device of the play within the play – here both as a metaphor and with electrifying effect in the plot. There is, too, an eclectic plundering of religious themes of the age: Hamlet, for example, is a student at Wittenberg University, Luther's alma mater, and Calvinist allusions have been detected in the play. But how quickly and easily Shakespeare slips into Catholic ideas of purgatory: a warning to those who pursue his inner beliefs from his public art. Yet after the final curtain the ghost remains in the mind: remembrance; the world of the spirits. Whilst losing none of its theatricality, the revenge play has now cleverly shaded into a requiem for a lost spirit world. The pre-Reformation past is beginning to recede, and now Shakespeare can dramatize it, exorcizing the ghosts.

They loved it: not only the groundlings but the university wits too. English actors were soon taking the show abroad to Danzig, Warsaw and many other places, and a German version of the play survives which was produced in his own lifetime. In 1607 it was even played on a ship off the shore of Africa to an audience that included local dignitaries (see page 299).

Death and Remembrance

But in Shakespeare's personal life that autumn there was sorrow. On 8 September 1601, just before *Troilus and Cressida* was staged and perhaps just before the adapted *Hamlet* came back at the Globe, John Shakespeare was buried in Stratford. A father's death is important in a man's life. It is inconceivable that William did not go back to Stratford – if not for the funeral, then surely to comfort his mother. It is, of course, dangerous to read autobiography into the plays. Hamlet's father's ghost was, after all, in the original play in the late 1580s. But the ghost's fire-and-brimstone description of purgatory makes us pause for a moment, given the timing of the play in the autumn of his father's death.

The testament found in the eaves of the Henley Street house contained a solemn request to his family, and most of all to his eldest son, to perform the correct Catholic rites – to say masses and to pray for him in purgatory. But had William himself left all that behind? Was he now a patriotic, sceptical

Englishman in the new Protestant age? One might guess that for him it was no longer a matter of consolation in religion. His mind was too open, his habit of empathy too deep-rooted, to side with one view any more. By now he understood the nature of the world and the human condition. In John Donne's telling phrase, the coherence was gone, and in his next dramas, whether consciously or not, he would explore what that meant.

So that autumn, as *Troilus and Cressida* enjoyed its brief and inglorious run, Shakespeare buried his father in the churchyard by the river. The town to which he had returned was a different place from the one he had known in childhood. Since the 1580s, Stratford's old generation had been sidelined. Old friends were still there, still conscientious objectors: the Sadlers, the Badgers, the Wheelers. But new people were in charge now, aligned to the Protestant state and its local magnates, such as the Grevilles. In his father's day the corporation had paid many acting companies to provide entertainment for the town in the guildhall. Soon they would be paid to go away. It was a sign of the times.

What an irony it was, then, that Shakespeare had bought the second biggest house in town with money made from the stage. Stratford was now in the throes of economic depression, exacerbated by the fires of 1594 and 1595 and the downturn in the economy of the country as a whole in the late nineties. The harsh winter of 1601 that hit gate receipts at the Globe affected the countryside far worse. A third of the population of Stratford were officially registered as paupers.

The mood in the town was shifting, too, in the face of growing Protestantization: there were snooping beadles, bothersome constables, creeping Sabbatarianism. Alderman Richard Quiney, a stalwart defender of his townspeople's rights, was killed in a night brawl with men of the local lord, Fulke Greville. The view from the window of New Place was changing; in the streets there were whispers that the social fabric was disintegrating, rulership failing and nature punishing mankind. Puritan preachers especially were not slow to point these things out. For them, the problem was that the town was still not godly enough.

Looking at the events of that year, Shakespeare could have been excused for thinking, as his John of Gaunt had said, that his native land was 'leased out like to a pelting farm'. But for his descendants he was determined to carve out his little patch of the sceptred isle. In May 1602 he paid £320 to the Combe family for 107 acres divided into about a dozen strips in the common field. And on 28 September that year he purchased a little cottage in Chapel Lane on a lease from the manor of Rowington, the village from which his paternal grandfather had probably come. Now, at the height of his career, and about to return to the bright lights of London to create his finest work, the fruition of his own personal artistic vision, Shakespeare was nevertheless investing in his roots.

S. Paules Church
The water house
The Gally fuste
THAMESES
The Bear Gardne
The Globe

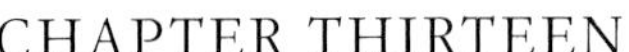

CHAPTER THIRTEEN

The Theatre of the World

BECAUSE I SEE THE HUMAN CONDITION

In 1602 Shakespeare was at the peak of his career, the foremost dramatist of late Tudor London. And now for the first time we have detailed first-hand knowledge of his private life. Indeed, our sources enable us to go right into his street, through the front door of the house in which he lived – and even to hear his voice. In this year, when it is now agreed that *Othello* was written, he was living once again north of the river, in a house on the corner of Silver Street and Monkwell – known to locals, with a delightful synchronicity for today's *Harry Potter* fans, as Muggle Street.

Shakespeare's neighbourhood lay just inside the city wall in its northwest corner, where crumbling bastions towered over a warren of tenements and livery halls, looking out over sewage-filled ditches to the northern suburbs. This may have been an area his father knew: the Glovers had a small hall close by at the western end of Beech Lane. Shakespeare now lodged with a French Huguenot family, Christopher and Mary Mountjoy. Their house was destroyed in the Great Fire of 1666, its successor in the Blitz, and the site itself vanished during post-war development under the central reservation of the carriageway at London Wall. Yet this is one of the most vividly documented corners of the old city, with wonderful detail in Tudor street maps, parish books, local court records, the archives of the guild companies and even plans of individual tenements.

OPPOSITE: *London c. 1605 with the Globe in the foreground and the magnificent St Paul's across the river.*

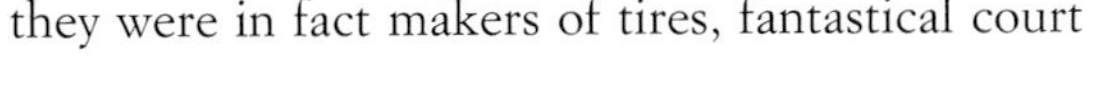

The Mountjoys are often described as wigmakers but they were in fact makers of tires, fantastical court

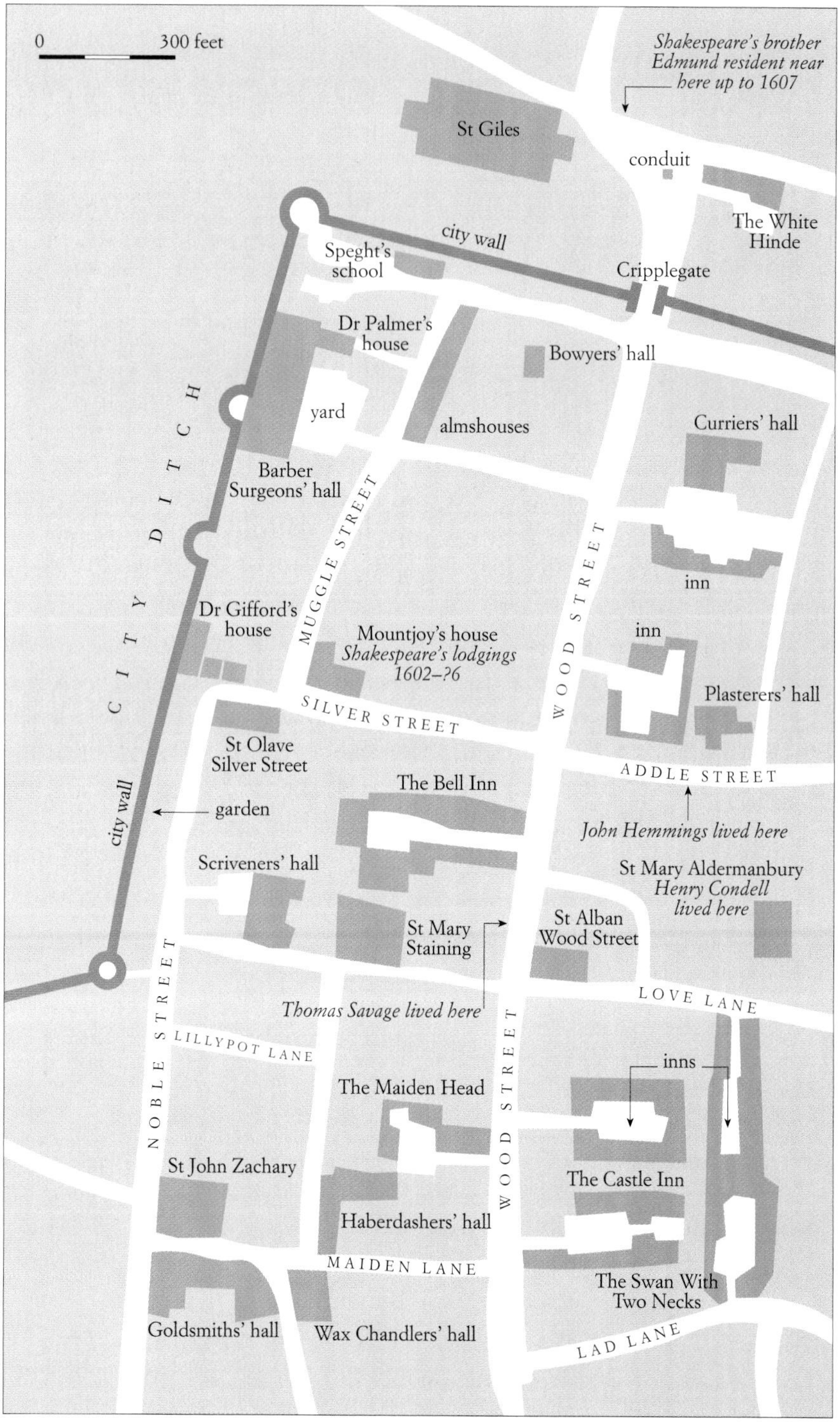

RIGHT: *Shakespeare's neighbourhood from 1602 to c. 1606. Silver Street was the home of gold- and silversmiths, and several theatre colleagues lived close by.* OPPOSITE: *Shakespeare lodged with the Mountjoys, who made tires by royal appointment: the kind of rich headdresses worn by Queen Elizabeth.*

headdresses of gold and silver thread woven with pearls and jewels, the kind of thing worn only by royalty and aristocrats. One of Queen Elizabeth's tires was described as 'a jewel, being a ship of Mother-of-Pearl garnished with rubies and pearls'. Among the Mountjoys' clients while Shakespeare was living with them was James I's wife, Queen Anne. Shakespeare refers to such creations in several plays: Falstaff, for example, speaks of 'a ship tire, the tire valiant, or any tire of Venetian admittance' – the art came originally from Venice. So Mountjoy was an artist and craftsman of substance, tire-maker to the court and to well-to-do families who came in from the provinces for their fittings.

As its name suggests, Silver Street was known for its goldsmiths and silversmiths. The Mountjoys' was one of the 'divers fine houses' described by Stow in his 1598 survey, and it is shown in the Agas map – conventionally drawn – with two big gables. Like its neighbours, it must have been of three and a half storeys with jettied upper floors. It is pleasant to imagine Shakespeare living in one of the upper front rooms that looked across to St Olave's Church, and over undulating rooftops to the massive bulk of Old St Paul's half a mile away. The Property Commission maps drawn up after the Great Fire show it L-shaped, with a 63-foot frontage and the same depth down Muggle Street. The ground floor would have had a shop and a workshop glittering with silk, Venice gold and silver thread and jewels, its benches covered with 'cloth of gold' and 'tissue' – gold woven on a light silk base. Although the women servants did the sewing, the male apprentices milled the gold thread and assembled the tires. These were high-quality craftspeople, working on one of the most esteemed of the upper-class decorative arts in turn-of-the-century London.

The Mountjoys' connections were with court, country and the theatre world. Christopher's friends included the families of Hemmings and Condell. And they were a family with tales enough to provide the plot for a domestic drama all on their own. Christopher was a difficult sort; Mrs Mountjoy had affairs. In 1597 she went to the astrologer and physician Simon Forman privately, thinking she was pregnant (by her lover Thomas Wood who lived nearby in Swan Alley?). It is intriguing to think she could have rubbed shoulders in the waiting room with the likes of Winifrid Burbage, Emilia Lanier and Philip Henslowe. The parish register for that year records the death of an infant as 'Mrs Mountjoy's child'. And before too long, the family's ups and downs drew in their famous lodger.

A year or two after he came to live in their house, Shakespeare found himself playing a part in one of his own plots. Mountjoy's apprentices lived in the house, and one of them, Stephen Belott, was a nice boy with good prospects. Mrs Mountjoy seems to have taken a shine to him and was keen to arrange a match with her daughter, but Belott was slow on the uptake and she asked Shakespeare to be a go-between (a common practice, incidentally, in Tudor marriage negotiations). Whether or not it was 'honey-tongued' Shakespeare who did the trick, the couple did indeed marry, in St Olave's on 19 November 1604. Belott set up in business on his own, but quarrelled with his father-in-law over the promised dowry. The case ended up in court and has left us 26 documents that name Shakespeare, one of them with his signature, along with the depositions of household members, apprentices and servants. Among them was Joan Jonson, who told how Mrs Mountjoy 'the defendant did send and persuade one Mr Shakespeare that laye in the house to persuade the plaintiff to marriage'. When it comes to his turn, we hear Shakespeare speaking in his own voice.

He says Belott was a 'very honest and good fellow' who 'did well and honestly behave himself and was a very good and industrious servant in the said service, though he did not in [Shakespeare's] hearing avouch that he had got any great profit and commodity by the service'. The poet remembered that Mr Mountjoy 'did bear and show great goodwill and affection' and had often spoken well of his apprentice 'and did make a motion unto the complainant of marriage with Mary, and Mrs Mountjoy did solicit and entreat the said deponent [Shakespeare] to move and persuade Belott to effect the said marriage'. Shakespeare was perhaps close to Mrs Mountjoy, though to suggest he might have been responsible for her pregnancy in 1597 is perhaps to over-stretch the evidence. Shakespeare says he did speak to the couple, and 'made sure by him they gave their consent and agreed to marry'; unfortunately, however, he did not remember the terms of the marriage portion beyond a cash sum and a load of household movables and tools. In the end, since no one could agree on that crucial point, in a Solomonic judgement the court referred the case to the arbitration of the elders of the Huguenot church. They decided that both sides were a bad lot (*tous pere e gendre desbauchez*) and awarded Belott £6 13s 4d. Mountjoy never paid up.

For a professional anatomizer of human foibles and follies, perhaps it all raised a smile. Another idea jotted down in his notebook. But such a tale only highlights the rich web of contacts offered by his daily life in that tiny area jammed in between the city wall and the goldsmiths' quarter. Around St Olave's there were interesting neighbours. The musician Henry Sandon was a fellow

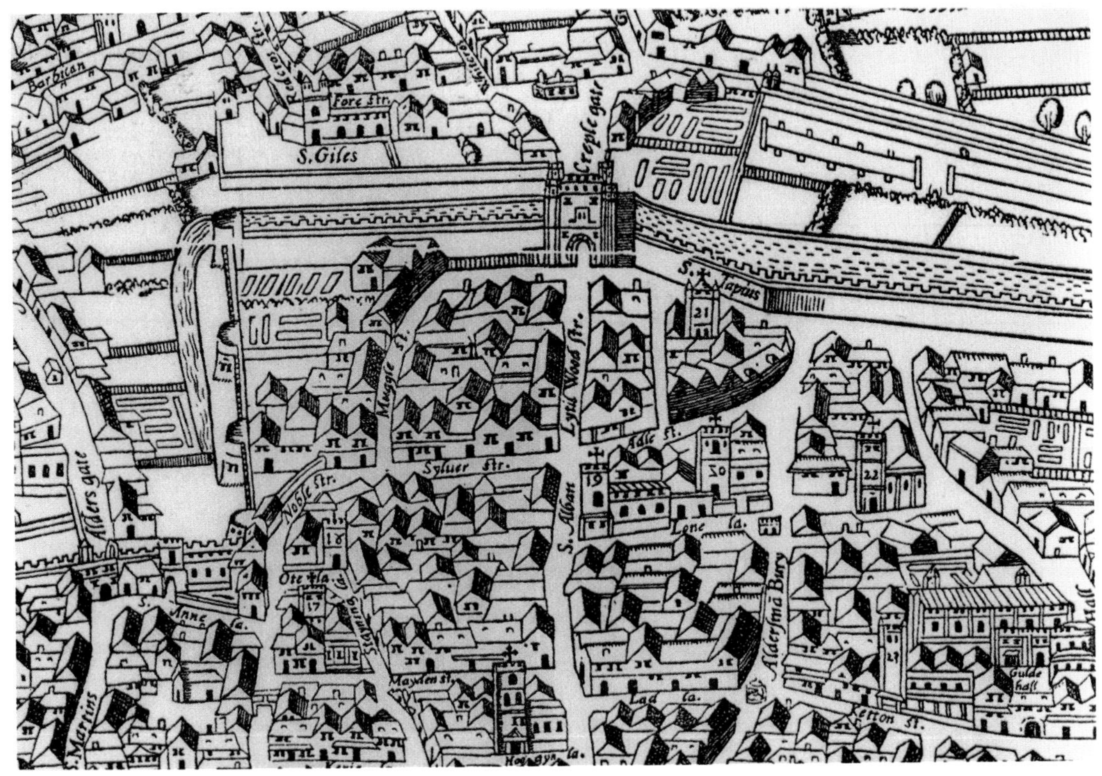

ABOVE: *The Agas map of c. 1558 shows Shakespeare's house with a double gable on the corner of 'Muggle St' and 'Sylver St': the corner of the city wall not yet filled up by the infill developments of the 1580s and 90s.*

parishioner, as was the painter William Linby. John Hemmings lived a few yards away in Addle Street in a property owned by Thomas Savage, the goldsmith who had funded the Globe deal. In the neighbourhood were several scriveners, useful for getting clean copies of plays fast. A few yards away Nicholas Hilliard lodged in Gutter Lane, in a tenement sometimes so cold in winter that he couldn't paint his minutely observed miniatures.

Tenements and Inns

But Shakespeare also rubbed shoulders with the poor. If he went down Muggle Street, he was in a fascinating little neighbourhood tucked into the very corner of the old city wall. Fifty yards or so up the street on the left was a gateway that led up a little lane to the hall of the Barber Surgeons, the doctor-physicians of the time. Here, four times a year, they held public lectures with autopsies on convicted felons. At least two doctors were near neighbours: Dr Gifford lived only a few yards away in Silver Street, Dr Palmer on the north side of the hall. On the other side of Muggle Street, butting on to the back of Shakespeare's house, were twelve almshouses for 'aged and poor' people, their faggots and

bags of charcoal stacked outside for the cold weather. And a few yards beyond them was a group of buildings owned by the Clothworkers: recent infill in the property boom of the last twenty-five years. Thanks to the guild's site maps, we can effectively walk inside them.

If you stood at the end of the street with the city wall facing you, on your left was a narrow gate by a brick wall: head down the entry towards the corner tower and you would come out into a yard facing a three-storey tenement block that backed on to Dr Palmer's house. This was a warren of little rooms occupied by single men – some of the vast number of domestic servants in the city. Among them was an Irishman, Patrick 'Murfee'. Past them was Mr Beastie's house and garden, under the city wall. To the right, across the yard, was the old medieval chapel and hermitage of St James, now known as Lambe's chapel; and jammed up against it was Mr Speght's grammar school, a three-storey house with a hall and parlour, a little kitchen and an outside latrine. Among Speght's boys was John Chappell, who at this time became a member of the Chapel Children playing at Blackfriars. The sound of the school bell would have been just audible from the Mountjoys' house.

So those were the neighbours Shakespeare rubbed shoulders with in the street or the taverns – or at Dr Palmer's, if the venereal troubles described in the last sonnets were real ones. If he needed an alehouse that served food, there were several local 'ordinaries': the Mitre in Wood Street and the Dolphin in Milk Street were the best known, but there was a small inn in Silver Street itself, later known as the Coopers Arms. Such places usually had a kitchen with an oven and a taproom, and a range of small chambers and outbuildings of two or three storeys round a yard: good places to write, as food and drink could be served privately if desired, and candles were free. Lying just inside the wall at Cripplegate, on the main route out to the north, were several great carriers' inns for long-distance travellers. North of the Mountjoys' house, for example, by St Giles, was the White Hinde, used by Durham and Yorkshire carriers. The Maiden Head, the Worcester carriers' base, was maybe the one used by Shakespeare, Condell and Hemmings – Midlanders all. The largest were the Swan with Two Necks, and the Castle, a fifteenth-century establishment with an inner yard 40 yards across. Bigger than theatres and, like them, galleried on all sides, the carriers' inns occupied the entire space between Lad Lane, Wood Street and Aldermanbury. From here, trains of pack animals left bearing the produce and luxuries of London and of a wider world.

This, then, was Shakespeare's neighbourhood when he wrote his greatest plays. Travellers and loaded pack animals were constantly crowding into the inns in the warren of narrow alleys round about, so it must have been full of

OPPOSITE: *Sixteenth-century housing at Cloth Fair, Smithfield, demolished in 1900. This gives some idea of what the corner of Silver Street would have looked like. The Mountjoys' house was probably of three storeys with an attic.*

MIDDLE
STREET E C

noise, colour and vitality. Nothing yet regularized and therefore nothing monotonous, this was the life of a great pre-modern city that we can no longer see in the developed world. All these coaching inns had been demolished by the late nineteenth century, although until not so long ago you could still have seen the badge of a swan with entwined necks carved in the rubbed stone lintel of an old carriage gate, just round the corner from Shakespeare's old haunts.

OTHELLO: BLACK IS FAIR

So it was probably in the Silver Street house, or at the tables of the 'ordinaries' where he ate in the evenings, that he wrote *Othello*, which out of the darkness and inwardness of *Hamlet*, emerges with a painful clarity and emotional intent. The story, set in sixteenth-century Venice, overtly falls in with the exotic history plays which started with Marlowe's *Tamburlaine*. Its background is the clash of Christian and Muslim. For the Elizabethan audience its immediate historical context was the greatest political theatre of the day: the Mediterranean in the time of Philip II. But that's only the backdrop to a story of racism and jealousy of a white man towards a black man, and of how love is destroyed by jealousy. Othello is the noble older warrior married to the beautiful white woman Desdemona. Iago is the man who destroys him, who hates Othello's marriage with a white woman and who lays a 'train' to trap him whilst affecting to love him.

Venice, as we have already seen, was a place of special interest to Shakespeare: meeting place of east and west, home to his Jew and now his Moor. There was no single model for *Othello* – Shakespeare took the basic story from Cinthio's popular *Hundred Stories*, one of his staple source books. But other reading shaped its imaginative world and the fabulously rich hinterland that he creates for his characters. Among the new books he had just read were Leo the African's *Geographical History of Africa*, published in November 1600, and Lewis Lewkenor's book on the Constitution of Venice (Lewkenor and Shakespeare could have met at Wilton in December 1603 in the company of the Venetian ambassador). Philemon Holland's 1601 translation of Pliny's *History of the World* was another source. A Coventry schoolmaster, Holland was dubbed the 'translator general of the age' for his great renderings of Pliny, Livy and Plutarch. Shakespeare loved his work, and for *Othello* he quarried it for its fabulous exotica: medicinal gum of Arabian trees, mines of sulphur, chrysolite and mandragora all come from the rich prose of Holland, whose description of the Pontic Black Sea 'which evermore floweth and runneth out into Propontis ... and never retireth back ... sometimes frozen and all an yce' Shakespeare deftly shapes into a magnificent cadence reminiscent of Marlowe:

Like to the Pontic sea
Whose icy current and compulsive course
Ne'er keeps retiring ebb but keeps due on
To the Propontic and the Hellespont

'NEGARS AND BLACKAMOORES' IN ELIZABETHAN LONDON

But real-life encounters go into such plays too. *Othello* was not the only drama about Moors in the last years of Elizabeth. The fascination with the exotic 'other' was shared by the groundlings and the court – where soon, in a 'masque of Blackness', the Queen and her ladies would wear black make-up to appear as 'Ethiopes'. A play about racism towards black people, then, was touching on a current preoccupation on the streets of London. So what was Shakespeare's experience of black people? As we have seen, there is a tantalizing possibility that his mistress had been a dark-skinned woman of Venetian Sephardi Jewish origin; but he must also have met 'moors' of North African, and even West African, origin.

He may have met black women as prostitutes, especially in nearby Turnmill Street in Clerkenwell, where the famous Lucy Negro, a former dancer in the Queen's service, ran an establishment patronized by noblemen and lawyers; Lucy was famous enough to be paid mock homage in the inns of court revels at Grays Inn. Shakespeare's acquaintance, the poet John Weever, also sang the praises of a woman whose face was 'pure black as Ebonie, jet blacke'.

There were probably several thousand black people in London, forming a significant minority of the population. They were employed in particular as servants, but also as musicians, dancers and entertainers. In the months before Shakespeare wrote the play their presence had become a major issue since their numbers, recently increased by many slaves freed from captured Spanish ships, had caused them to be designated a nuisance. In 1601, the year Shakespeare was thinking about *Othello* and reading Leo the African, the Cecil papers (still held at Hatfield House) disclose the kind of government policies we have already seen in relation to gypsies and itinerants: 'the queen is discontented at the great numbers of "negars and blackamoores" which are crept into the realm since the troubles between her Highness and the King of Spain, and are fostered here to the annoyance of her own people'. A plan was mooted to transport them out of the country. In July 1602 Cecil was dealing along these lines with merchants, one of whom wrote: 'I have persuaded the merchants trading to Barbary, not without some difficulty, to yield to the charges of [pay for] the Moors lately redeemed out of servitude by her Majesty's ships, so far as it may concern their lodging and victuals, till some shipping may be ready to carry them into Barbary.'

BELOW: *Young black servants in the 1630s, the kind of people revealed in the 1590s' registers in Aldgate.*

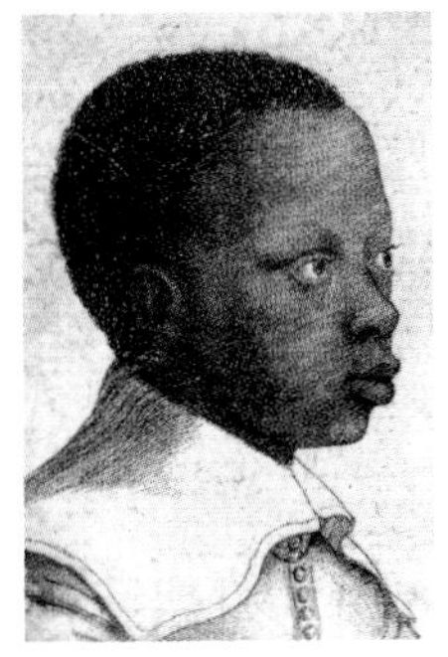

No more than now should we take a government's pronouncements on such matters at face value. But it is an interesting question how they thought this might be done, for by now many black people, baptized Christians, were living as citizens in London, Bristol and other cities. For example, in the records of the small parish of St Botolph's outside Aldgate, among French and Dutch immigrants and one East Indian (from today's Bengal) we find twenty-five black people living in Shakespeare's lifetime. They were mainly servants, but one man lodged at the White Bell next to the Bell Foundry in Whitechapel Road and perhaps worked there (was he a West African skilled in bronze casting?). Some are given high-status Christian funerals by their employers, with bearers and black cloth. Among the names are these:

> Christopher Capperbert [Cape Verde], a blackemoore
> Suzanna Pearis a blackamoore tenant to John Despinois
> Symon Valencia a blackamoore
> Cassangoe A blacke A moore tenant to Mrs Barbor
> Easfanyyo a neagar servant to Mr Thomas Barbor a merchaunt
> Robert a negar
> A Negar whose name was suposed to be Frauncis. He was servant to Mr Peter Miller a beare brewer dwelling at the sign of the hartes horne in the libertie of Eastsmithfield

Among later names we find 'Anne Bause a Black-more wife to Anthonie bause trompetter'; 'John Come Quicke, a Blacke-Moore, servant to Thomas Love a captaine'; and, saddest in this list, 'a blackamoore woman that died in the street, named Marie'.

Forgotten lives and forgotten histories. Sometimes these stories cross over with other sources: a woman, for example, who was concerned about the health of her black servant's little daughter took her to Simon Forman. In his notebook Forman diagnosed the little girl as 'cold of heart': evidently she was suffering from profound depression. Human stories, as always, tell a different tale from official papers. But this too was the reality of Shakespeare's London, and it can hardly have escaped him.

So black people may well have been part of his daily life around St Helen's Bishopsgate or Silver Street, and his knowledge of them could have deepened over the twelve years or so since he had written the part of the conventional stage villain Aaron the Moor in his early play *Titus Andronicus*. But had he come to know any black people intimately? It is possible, as we have seen, that he had

Left: *A noble Moor: the Moroccan ambassador painted in England in the winter of 1600–1. Shakespeare's company played before him at court that Christmas.*

had a black mistress. But that he could have met at least one noble high-ranking Moor is well documented.

In 1600 an embassy from Morocco came to London and stayed half a year. The Moors' temporary neighbours were fascinated by their daily routine of prayers and, then as now, foreign cooking and eating customs occasioned much comment, not all of it particularly open-minded. The publisher of Leo the African's *History* dedicated the book to the ambassador, who during his stay sat for an Elizabethan portrait painter. The work, which still survives, is inscribed: 'Abdul Guahid the ambassador of Barbary, 1600, aged 42' and presents a powerful image of a noble Moor. As it happens, the Chamberlain's Men played for the ambassador during Christmas 1600, so Shakespeare would have seen Abdul Guahid, and may even have met him.

The noble Moor, and indeed the child with a frozen heart, could both have been part of his experience. Such hints, brief as they are, suggest a surprisingly rich hidden narrative for black people in Elizabethan England and help us see in a different light those government calls for repatriation. Clearly Shakespeare knew a lot more about black people and racism than modern critics have cared to admit, and than we give him credit for. And attracted by the tale in Cinthio's *Hundred Stories*, he decided to write a play on the subject.

A Lynching Offence

Shakespeare's commitment to *Othello* is shown by its wonderful quality, and by the care with which he subsequently revised it after the promulgation of the Act to reform abuses of players in 1606. Its enduring power is shown by its effect wherever it has been performed since. In his day it was played at court, and on tour in the provinces: John Rice's Desdemona in Oxford in 1609 moved the audience to tears. Later audiences, however, didn't always like what they saw. A seventeenth-century English critic sneeringly saw the moral of the play as 'a caution to Maidens of quality without their parents consent to run away with Blackamoors'. In the early nineteenth century US President John Quincy Adams famously felt that 'the fondling of Desdemona with Othello onstage is disgusting' and took the great moral lesson of the play to be 'that black and white blood cannot be intermingled in marriage without a gross outrage upon the laws of Nature'. Audiences in the pre-Civil War South also found the play 'Unfit to be permitted in any southern state, revolting, an outrage, the duty of every white man to resent; if Shakespeare the writer of the play were caught in any southern state, he ought to be lynched for having written it.' Even in 1950s' Britain, audiences were shocked that Paul Robeson should kiss Peggy Ashcroft on stage. In the liberal first decade of the twenty-first century the issues it raises are still everywhere, as was shown by a powerful recent TV film transposing Othello's role to that of London's first black commissioner of police. In 1602 Shakespeare was holding up a mirror to human nature. And in it, once again, he shows us 'the stranger's case'.

'This Most Balmy Time': The Death of Elizabeth and the Accession of James

By 1602 journalists, pamphleteers, gossip columnists and astrologers were all hanging on Elizabeth's failing health. It was still forbidden to speculate in public about the succession. But everyone knew it would soon be the end of an age, and the older generation hoped for a change for the better. Astrologers and horoscope-makers were increasingly tempted to make prophecies: there were fears, hopes and, in some quarters, dire forebodings. The mood was captured in many poems of the day. There was much talk of James VI of Scotland becoming king: indeed, over the border they had been waiting for this moment. From Scotland came all the right noises. But still Elizabeth refused to commit herself.

Shakespeare's company's last performance for the queen was at Richmond Palace on 2 February 1603. On the 19th the theatres were closed in anticipation of her death, which occurred at the palace on the 24th. There was no tribute to her from Shakespeare. Is this significant? At least two fellow writers noted his silence: one, indeed, bluntly begged him to put pen to paper, but he did not. Shakespeare does appear, however, to comment on the event in a sonnet to his friend, the young man. Theirs was still, apparently, a close friendship – a long loving friendship now – which had endured separation for a time. For several years it had been intense, passionate – a tearful homoerotic intimacy. But things were calmer now, and the poem he now wrote linked the personal and the political – the inner and the outer worlds. Elizabeth, often identified with the chaste goddess of the moon, Diana or Cynthia, had finally endured her eclipse, but the aftermath had confounded all the prophets of doom. Internal references suggest that this may be Shakespeare's response to Elizabeth's death:

Left: *End of an era: Elizabeth's funeral procession painted by the historian William Camden. Many were glad to see her go, but a nostalgic cult of Gloriana would soon develop.*

Not mine own fears, nor the prophetic soul
Of the wide world dreaming on things to come,
Can yet the lease of my true love control,
Suppos'd as forfeit to a confin'd doom.
The mortal moon hath her eclipse endur'd,
And the sad augurs mock their own presage:
Incertainties now crown themselves assur'd,
And peace proclaims olives of endless age.
Now with the drops of this most balmy time
My love looks fresh, and Death to me subscribes,
Since spite of him I'll live in this poor rhyme,
While he insults o'er dull and speechless tribes.
    And thou in this shalt find thy monument,
    When tyrants' crests and tombs of brass are spent.

After forty-five years of religious and political conflicts and economic troubles, Elizabeth's death carried with it a weight that is hard for us to imagine now. Hopes of peace in 'this most balmy time' reflect the first months of 1603, when the surprisingly smooth transition to James's rule took place. What might take the modern reader aback is the pointed reference to 'tyrants' at the end of a sonnet which may be about the death of the old queen.

The King's Men

Meanwhile, the wheels of patronage were turning fast. The Chamberlain's Men were the premier acting company, with influential friends – the Pembrokes in particular seem to have been anxious to take the lead in driving James's early cultural agendas. Almost immediately, on 19 May, Shakespeare, Burbage, Philips and the rest were given letters of patent to be the king's acting company, in the kind of language of which Polonius would have heartily approved:

> freely to use and exercise the Art and faculty of playing Comedies, Tragedies, Histories, interludes, Morals, pastorals, Stage plays and such others like they have already studied … for the recreation of our loving Subjects as for our Solace and pleasure when we shall think good to see them … as well within their usual house called the Globe, as also within any town halls or moot halls or other convenient places within the liberties and freedom of any other City, university town, or borough whatsoever ….

LEFT: *There is no genuine contemporary portrait of the poet but this has better claims than most. Out of the stiff livery of the Folio picture, this is a believable denizen of the Mermaid (though the earring sadly may be a later addition).*
BELOW: *Richard Burbage: recent restoration suggests he had a drinker's nose.*

So they were now royal servants, the King's Men, their future assured – a balmy time indeed. In those early days of James's reign, many believed or hoped that religious change and renewal were imminent. The new king was a Protestant, but he had Catholic forebears and a Catholic wife. A true philosopher king, he hated religious extremism on both sides, and there were rumours that he would return England to Catholicism, or at least grant freedom of worship. On the other side, a group of Puritan clergy presented James with a petition on his way to London, hoping he would oversee further reform of the Church. Within the Church itself the climate encouraged many sermonizers not to rock the boat but to maintain the status quo. In court this cracking open of a closed shell saw those outcast or ignored by Elizabeth – people like Southampton, Shakespeare's first patron – rise again, looking for new opportunities.

In this mood many English poets saluted James with congratulatory poems, but again, not Shakespeare. After *Venus and Adonis* and *The Rape of Lucrece*, he, unlike his peers, had not composed eulogies or funeral elegies for the great and good (with the exception of the strange and wonderful *Phoenix and Turtle* of 1601), and he did not break that habit now. But many poets felt that the event marked the beginning of a new cultural climate, one in which religious verse would be highly praised. A number even switched from secular to sacred or philosophical poetry, and there was a veritable outpouring of religious verse in the period 1603–5. James himself had a track record as a patron of poetry. At his accession he republished his book *Basilikon doron*, which had first appeared in 1599, with instructions to his young son Prince Henry on poetry, specifically the poetry of virtue. Such moves announced James to the London literati as a man of high philosophical and poetic ambition.

ABOVE: *James I: superstitious and lazy, with a 'fearful nature' damaged by a violent and threatening childhood. But James was also canny, intelligent and a natural compromiser, which in 1603 was no bad thing.*

PLAGUE IN SILVER STREET

The king made his leisurely way down from Scotland during April and May 1603, staying at noble houses en route. But as he reached London, news came of a terrible outbreak of plague, the severest for ten years. That spring the theatres were closed. Across the city the parish books filled with page after page of burials as the death toll mounted to 1000 a week. In Shakespeare's tiny parish the first deaths came in June, rising to a climax in the hot weather of August. The royal musician Henry Sandon was buried on the 1st, along with his daughter Susan, the painter William Linby and his wife Margaret, the goldsmith Thomas Ellis and a dozen servants who lodged and worked in this corner of the city. Many children died, too. There were eighty-five deaths in August and September alone, in a parish of only 100 or so taxable houses. It was the devastation of Shakespeare's community. The minute books of the Barber Surgeons describe the cancellation of feasts, the money given 'for reliefe of the most miserable poor and needie persons that it shall please almighty god to visit'.

In such a climate it is dangerous and pointless to stay in town if you have the money and a place to go. Shakespeare and the company moved out to stay

by the river at Mortlake, where Philips had recently bought a house. This was to be their base for the next few months. James had been forced to delay his ceremonial reception in London while plague still raged. That autumn he made a stately progress through Hampshire, Berkshire and Oxfordshire, ending up in October with the Pembrokes at Wilton, where he remained until early December. There the King's Men, too, seem to have stayed for some time, earning a large fee of £30 for entertainments which included a play that was probably *As You Like It,* enacted before James on 2 December. Among the guests was Nicolo Molin, the Venetian ambassador.

So, as might be guessed from those sonnets written in 1603, Shakespeare still had close contacts with the Pembroke family. Wilton was in effect the alternative court during the plague months, and a glittering circle was there that winter. Mary Herbert herself was still going strong: the famous patroness of poets, editor of her brother's *Arcadia* and author of a play that Shakespeare would in due course use in manuscript for his own *Antony and Cleopatra.* The King's Men's prolonged stay at Wilton included a show to the town (a recent discovery in Trowbridge Record Office reveals that the burgesses paid £6 5s to the company). This detail does much to cement the picture of a continuing relationship between Shakespeare and Pembroke. The earl and his brother were great theatregoers and masquers, and loved to dress up and participate in courtly tilts and shows. The King's Men would fit in a masque for the marriage of Pembroke's brother the following year, between performances of *Measure for Measure* and *The Comedy of Errors.*

In London, plague deaths declined with the onset of colder weather. At the almshouses in Muggle Street the inmates sat round their wood fires and charcoal stoves and tried to stay warm. The city was silenced by a blanket of snow. On Christmas Day ambassador Molin made his way back from Wilton and wrote home: 'I got to London on Friday evening. No one ever mentions the plague, no more than if it had never been. The city is so full of people that it is hard to believe that about sixty thousand deaths have taken place.'

But with the Globe still closed, the company stayed out of town and relied for the time being on the patronage of the court. James's first winter in England was spent at Hampton Court, where the provision of entertainment was shared by the King's Men and two other leading companies. Upwards of thirty plays were made ready for the royal choice, including *A Midsummer Night's Dream* and other staples, such as *The Fair Maid of Bristol.* Although chief writer for the company, and perhaps also what we would call a director, Shakespeare was still acting, too: solid, middle-of-the-road parts, such as John of Gaunt, Henry IV and the Ghost in *Hamlet.* And this winter he also played in *Sejanus,* by his rival

Ben Jonson. It was a flop, and there is a certain pleasure in realizing that Shakespeare must have known what it was like to be in one!

'What We See Do Lie': How Shakespeare Felt?

Around this time Shakespeare wrote a small cluster of sonnets that, though framed with his customary reserve, seem to offer fascinating circumstantial details of his life, and even hints about his personal feelings. Following the sonnet about Elizabeth's death, these refer pointedly to politics – reinforcing the idea that in his private poems he was not writing mere artistic exercises, Petrarchan or otherwise, but putting down what he really felt. In the 154 sonnets there are in fact very few mere exercises (even the last two, versions of the epigram from the *Greek Anthology*, are chosen for their relevance to the tale). Most of them, on the contrary, are serious in a way that suggests he was mainly writing for himself, to get things off his chest, and, though some of them circulated among his friends, it is by no means certain that he showed every one to other people. In these sonnets from the momentous year of 1603–4 he surely says exactly what he wants to say.

Two in particular focus on the ceremonies for James's entry into London, and it is very interesting to see why this should be. Now a King's Man, Shakespeare was not merely an actor but a royal courtier, a Gentleman Groom of the Most Honourable Privy Chamber. And for the royal entry Shakespeare, Burbage and their colleagues were each issued with a length of scarlet woollen cloth, carefully listed in the account book of the royal wardrobe. In this class-conscious society the sumptuary laws were very strict about which cloth could be used by which social rank, and wool was definitely for commoners. Along with stablemen, gunners, cooks and even royal bakers, three acting companies are listed: Alleyn's Admiral's Men, Beeston's Queen's Men, and the King's Men with Shakespeare at the top of the list. To each went 'scarlet red cloth: 4 and half yards'. This has always been understood simply as a gift, but the yardage was the amount needed for a gentleman groom's livery jacket and breeches. As we know that the actors played roles in the procession (Edward Alleyn, for example, made a speech to the king as the Genius of London), it is most probable that Shakespeare and his colleagues also had a ceremonial function in their fine scarlet, perhaps with a speech to declaim at one of the great ornamental gates erected on the procession route.

Thomas Dekker, who scripted the pageant that accompanied James's grand entrance, described the crowds: 'a sea of people so the street could not be seen: women and children crowding every casement'. The Venetian ambassador, Nicolo Molin, recorded his impressions in a letter home:

> At eleven yesterday morning the king left the Tower. He was preceded by the magistrates of the City, the court officials, the clergy, Bishops and archbishops, Earls marquises Barons and Knights, superbly apparelled and clad in silk of gold with pearl embroideries; a right royal show! The prince was on horseback, ten paces ahead of the king, who rode under *a canopy borne over his head by twenty-four gentlemen, splendidly dressed, eight of whom took it, turn and turnabout* [author's italics]. The Queen followed with her maids of honour, and seventy ladies mounted splendidly dressed. In this order the procession moved from the Tower to Westminster, a distance of three miles all through the City.

Even a well-travelled diplomat like Molin was swept up in the mood of optimism that heady day. Among those riding behind the King were Shakespeare's old patrons, the Earl of Pembroke and, newly released from the Tower, a relieved and chastened Earl of Southampton. But in his two sonnets reflecting on the occasion Shakespeare, at this moment forty years old and worldly wise, was strangely cool, notably so in a specific reference in Sonnet 125 to the role of royal servants holding the canopy in the procession:

> Were 't aught to me I bore the canopy,
> With my extern the outward honouring,
> Or laid great bases for eternity
> Which prove more short than waste or ruining?
> Have I not seen dwellers on form and favour
> Lose all, and more, by paying too much rent ....

Which is to say, it's all spin – it's all show. The line about carrying the canopy does not necessarily mean that the King's Men were among the gentlemen bearers, but the use of the procession as a metaphor seems plain. The 'great bases' are perhaps the huge wooden arches with their brightly painted plaster figures, garish temporary stage sets for the royal show. These constructions with their obelisks ('pyramids' to contemporaries) had the crowds gawping. But in Sonnet 123 Shakespeare is again ambivalent:

> Thy pyramids built up with newer might
> To me are nothing novel, nothing strange,
> They are but dressings of a former sight.
> Our dates are brief, and therefore we admire
> What thou dost foist upon us that is old;

HIC VIR
HIC EST
IACOBO
REGI
MAGN
HENRIC
VII
ABNEP
Tu Regere Imperio populos Iacobe memento &c.
1 2 3 4 5
Stephen Harison.
Excude:

And rather make them born to our desire
Than think that we before have heard them told.
Thy registers and thee I both defy,
Not wondering at the present nor the past,
For thy records and what we see doth lie,
Made more or less by thy continual haste.
    This I do vow, and this shall ever be,
    I will be true, despite thy scythe and thee.

The use of 'foist' tells its own story (and he would soon mock the novelty of 'pyramids' again in an extended joke in *Antony and Cleopatra*). 'What we see doth lie', then, means not only the illusion of the world but the outward show of power. Measured and allusive, both these sonnets are shot through with an inwardness worthy of Hamlet, but also with a disdain for public honour, for the pretensions of the rich and for the elaborate show of state. At the end of Sonnet 125, connecting the outer world of politics with the inner world of conscience, Shakespeare draws a powerful and startling metaphor from contemporary politics:

Hence, thou suborn'd informer! a true soul,
When most impeach'd, stands least in thy control.

Ever sceptical of power and mistrustful of those who use it, our Mr Shakespeare. And if we had any doubt what he is thinking about in this cluster of poems, in the contemporary Sonnet 124 – a brilliant poem that melds the personal and the political, and in which the word 'love' almost seems to stand for 'faith' – he announces to our surprise what sounds like a personal credo. This is about as far as he ever shows his hand. Whether he is protesting too much, given his liveried role at the heart of the ceremonial, is for the reader to judge:

If my dear love were but the child of state,
It might for Fortune's bastard be unfather'd,
As subject to Time's love, or to Time's hate,
Weeds among weeds, or flowers with flowers gather'd.
No, it was builded far from accident;
It suffers not in smiling pomp, nor falls
Under the blow of thralled discontent,
Whereto th'inviting time our fashion calls:
It fears not policy, that heretic,
Which works on leases of short-number'd hours,

OPPOSITE: *This arch to celebrate James's entry into London was sponsored by the city's Italian citizens. Seventy feet high, in painted wood, it was one of the 'great bases' with their 'pyramids' or obelisks described in the sonnets.*

But all alone stands hugely politic,
That it nor grows with heat nor drowns with showers.
  To this I witness call the fools of time,
  Which die for goodness, who have liv'd for crime.

In the last couplet 'witness' is generally taken as referring to religious martyrs (as the scholar John Foxe had pointed out, 'martyr' is from the Greek word for 'witness'), and this meaning is also supported by his use of 'heretic' to describe 'policy', that is, government. But this poem is not meant to be closely pinned down. It is an enigmatic, dense meditation on politics and individual conscience, the 'child of state' and the martyrs, criminals who died for goodness; vague and unspecific, it nevertheless evokes a world in which values are topsy-turvy, in which people of different religious faiths die horribly for their beliefs. These, for an old Elizabethan poet, were the terrible real-life pressures on love and conscience. And if this is not delusory, don't these sonnets show us the same personality we have seen earlier? He is guarded and sceptical of power; a man who believes that conscience is an individual matter; who is diffident and self-deprecating (was that a class thing?) and yet is confident in his own great powers; a writer and observer who stands apart from the pageant and outward gloss of political power and stands 'hugely politic', sure that his verse will outlive this show. And with all this, is there not also a faint suggestion of contempt (or even malice?) for those who enjoy it so ostentatiously?

A Royal Servant

So, as always, Shakespeare leaves us with ambiguities. Public and private, conscience and power: antitheses that are at the very core of the sonnets – and, indeed, of the great tragedies. And, as always, there is the multiple viewpoint, even (or especially) when looking at himself. He had achieved high status, he was a royal servant wearing the king's livery, he was a gentleman with a coat of arms. He had coveted this, and he surely celebrated it, even though he wrote such words in private.

The appointment as a King's Man and as a Gentleman Groom of the Most Honourable Privy Chamber marked the achievement of those social ambitions he had left Stratford to fulfil; ambitions stemming from his father, who had first applied for a coat of arms before the collapse of his business in 1576. Shakespeare had craved acceptance and status, and now he had it: the coat of arms, the royal livery, Clopton's house. There were those who were pleased for him, who felt that his kind, though not high-born, were of an instinctive, natural gentility that marked them out. But, needless to say in such a class-conscious

ABOVE: *The Somerset House peace conference, August 1604. Behind the painter we must imagine Shakespeare and Burbage in their scarlet wool livery jackets as Gentlemen of the Privy Chamber, 'poor but free', as Shakespeare wrote, somewhat dramatically.*

city, there were also those who mocked. Ben Jonson's 'gentle Shakespeare' was always a double-edged compliment, part felt, part needling. Others, though, were more direct: in the College of Arms a rival colleague of the herald Dethick marked the poet down in a list of those unworthy to be gentlemen, among the self-made, upwardly mobile 'new people' of James's London. A mere 'player'. And in a play of this time, an ambitious young gentleman, Francis Beaumont, threw a wounding sneer at him, using John Shakespeare's former trade to mock the pretensions of his courtier son. In a speech condemning social climbing in the new courtly world of James he refers to excessive bowing and scraping: all those bending legs, 'some of which once so poor they were sockless ... and one pair, that were heir apparent to a Glover, these legs hope shortly to be honorable'.

Given the acute sensitivity to class inferiority that runs undisguised through the sonnets, this was maybe not shrugged off quite as easily as water from a duck's back. But, resplendent in scarlet, the King's Men now found themselves with roles to play in the ceremonies, as well as in the entertainments that studded James's first exciting months in London.

An unmartial prince, who hated war, James made an ambitious start, hopeful that after years of international tensions in Europe he could initiate a 'peace process' that might procure a lasting settlement. In the early summer of 1604 the Spanish were invited to send an embassy to London, and the royal accounts show that Shakespeare and the King's Men were in attendance on the Spanish ambassador from 9 to 27 August at the end of the peace treaty negotiations at Somerset House. This time they were not to be actors, but to play courtiers: to wait on the visitors and stand around looking good in their scarlet cloaks and

breeches. Plenty of bowing and scraping for Shakespeare and Burbage, then, and a lot of hanging about. Chafing to be back on stage, perhaps: it is easy to imagine that this time of enforced lay-off might have prompted the odd verse expressing disenchantment with pomp.

WRITING FOR JAMES

Among Catholics there were at first high hopes for the new reign: James was canny, clever, could hold his own in university debate; and he made all the right moves, among them freeing Southampton. Many people, including Catholics who had been frozen out in the stifling favouritism of Elizabeth's later years, now re-emerged into public life. Fascinating new light on James and Anne of Denmark's private views has recently emerged from the record of their conversation 'in the privacy of their bedchamber'. He was Protestant (but with a Catholic mother, of course), she Catholic, which he had no problems with, so long as she was discreet. James loved plays, loved the King's Men (and young men, of course, too!). And from now on the court calendars recorded regular performances by the King's Men. James's ambitions in the diplomatic field meant a constant crowd of ambassadors at court and the demand for shows shot up: sometimes fourteen, fifteen or even twenty in one Christmas season.

BELOW: *A masque costume by Inigo Jones. Ben Jonson made a mint out of such transient fantasies, while admitting they were merely conspicuous consumption and 'wasted wit'.*

One of the hazards of the job – as with the entertainments presented to Theseus in *A Midsummer Night's Dream* by the Master of the Revels, Philostrate – was that a play the King's Men had ready might not be 'preferred'. Sometimes the court went for something popular but less demanding, especially masques, which on occasion the King's Men performed, although the courtiers themselves loved to dress up and act in them. These elaborate poetic allegories with music and stage effects, scripted by top writers like Jonson and designed by the most talented artists and craftsmen, such as the architect Inigo Jones, were not, however, always edifying occasions. One entertainment for the King of Denmark in 1606 included a masque of noble ladies who became so inebriated that the 'Queen of Sheba' fell into the king's lap; the royal visitor himself had to be carried to bed drunk, 'not a little defiled with the presents of the Queen, which had been bestowed upon his garments; such as wine, cream jelly and cakes'. For a King's Man such things, it would appear, went with the job.

IN FULL POWERS

Shakespeare the writer – as opposed to the courtier-player – was now in a phenomenally creative period, driven by the possibilities of the new age; by fears

and hopes; by artistic maturity – the ability to write what he wanted; and by his relationship with his audience and the skill and experience of his company. In short he was, in Pablo Neruda's felicitous phrase, in full powers.

Where did Shakespeare do his writing? Alone with an oil lamp in an upstairs room in Silver Street? Or in a crowded 'ordinary' nearby – the Mitre, say, in Bread Street, where two pence bought a table and food, and candles were free? Or perhaps at a favourite small local tavern, in a back room through the main taproom and beyond the kitchen? Recently he has been portrayed as a frequenter of brothels, who wrote about the seedy world of Turnmill Street from first-hand experience. But the seventeenth-century diarist John Aubrey records a story to the contrary: that 'he was not a company seeker'. That he was a drinker is more likely, especially after what he describes as his 'hell of time' in the late 1590s. Ale was an important part of the diet in his day, even for children; he had vintners as friends; and, as now, his was a very stressful profession and its members were no doubt high in the league table of drinkers (Ben Jonson wrote whole poems about his favourite inns). Again, we don't know, but he writes drink scenes with unerring realism, and, as we shall see, there is a story that it was drink that got him in the end.

And what of his writing habits and discipline? With morning rehearsals and afternoon shows at the Globe, when did he write? At night? Or did he get up at six and do three hours before breakfast? This again we shall never know; but, remarkably, we do have an example of his writing in progress.

These pages, apparently in his own hand, form part of the manuscript of *Sir Thomas More*, a play about the scholar and former Lord Chancellor executed by Henry VIII and later sanctified by the Catholic Church. There is still some dispute over this, and it is not clear why Shakespeare should have done something for another company at this point in his career. But collaboration in his theatrical world was frequent and casual, and the writing of the *More* scenes, the imagery, the grammar and spelling, are all characteristically his. Handwriting experts also confirm that the hand matches the few known specimens of Shakespeare's signature. If so, it is interesting that he should have been approached about a play on More just after Elizabeth's death: this would have been a problematic subject while she was alive. More was revered among Catholics for refusing to acknowledge Henry VIII as head of the Church in England, and the first draft (even though it omitted this crucial motivation) had been cut short by the censor in the early 1590s with a string of interventions that still mark the manuscript, including a curt 'Leave this in at your peril!'

The manuscript is the work of five writers: a typical collaboration of the period. Three pages only are in Shakespeare's hand; a fourth page by him was

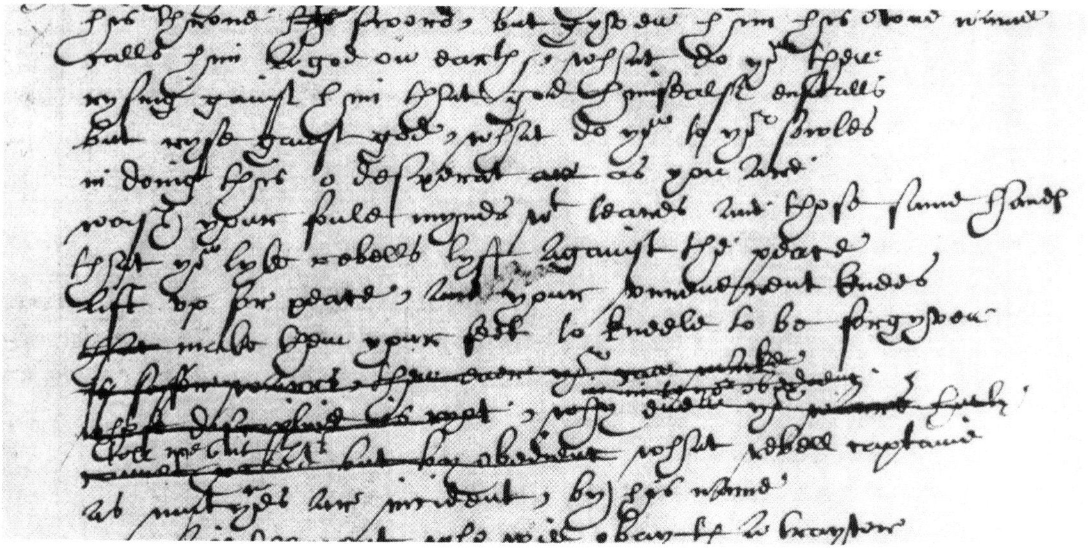

ABOVE: *Shakespeare's hand in the More manuscript: (in the fourth/fifth lines, 'what do you to yr soules/in doing this'). Among his idiosyncratic spellings, 'scilens' for 'silence' is found only in his writings.*

written out by a professional scrivener. What is fascinating is that in this draft we can see his corrections, his second thoughts, a hint of the way he worked, enabling us to understand better the famous remark by his colleagues that 'his mind and hand went together, and what he thought he uttered with that easiness that we have scarce received from him a blot in his papers'. It may be only a draft, but it is impressive stuff: a classic Shakespearean analysis of order. In this scene More faces the mob on the so-called 'Ill May Day' of 1511, when London was convulsed by an anti-immigrant riot: the kind of thing still grimly familiar in our own time, it was a little local attempt at ethnic cleansing. More confronts the crowd with an appeal to reason, to God and to their common humanity. In what follows the punctuation is Shakespeare's (three commas only), except for a question mark added to help the sense. Apart from a slip in line six, Shakespeare's only change of thought was to put 'with' instead of 'and' in line two.

> imagine that you see the wretched strangers
> their babies at their backs, with their poor luggage
> plodding to th' ports and coasts for transportation
> and that you sit as kings in your desires
> authority quite silenced by your brawl
> and you in ruff of your opinions clothed
> what have you got? I'll tell you, you had taught
> how insolence and strong hand should prevail
> how order should be quelled, and by this pattern

> not one of you should live an aged man
> for other ruffians as their fancies wrought
> with self same hand self reasons and self right
> would shark on you and men like ravenous fishes
> would feed on one another

It is a classic Renaissance image; a classic case, too, of Shakespearean empathy; the 'stranger's case', the idea of putting ourselves in the shoes of the persecuted, feeling for the suffering of the downtrodden victims of prejudice and violence – and the further idea of seeing beyond the immediate hot prejudice of rival groups and imagining ourselves as strangers in a world where such things are the norm. It is a lesson we have still not learned 400 years on; in our news bulletins we have all seen the wretched strangers with babies at their backs in Bosnia or Rwanda. In the end More asks the mob to consider where would they go if they were in the strangers' shoes, what they would do if *they* were thrown out of England.

> Why you must needs be strangers. Would you be pleased
> To find a nation of such barbarous temper
> That breaking in hideous violence
> Would not afford you an abode on earth,
> Whet their detested knives against your throats,
> Spurn you like dogs, and like as if that God
> Owed not nor made not you …
> … What would you think
> To be thus used? This is the strangers case,
> And this your mountainish inhumanity

Never Blotted a Line?

Sir Thomas More remained a draft – the play was never staged. A quick rewriting job for someone else: a favour, perhaps, during the period when the theatres were closed by the plague? But for a draft it is awesomely coherent. All writers are different, of course, and technology, then as now, influences the means of production (for one thing, paper was expensive). But with the stress in sixteenth-century education on memory training and oration, perhaps pre-modern habits of organizing thoughts and constructing speeches were more disciplined than ours.

Hemmings and Condell say Shakespeare never blotted a line, to which Jonson responded that he wished Shakespeare had blotted a few more, criticizing him for not crafting more carefully. However, Jonson also says that

Shakespeare was a poet 'not born but made', that he was a craftsman who would 'strike the second heat/upon the Muse's anvil, turn the same/(And himself with it) that he thinks to frame'.

So he didn't often blot, but he also struck the second heat. Perhaps in the end these two ideas are not contradictory: from the manuscript of *More* it is clear that the act of writing itself served to prompt thoughts and changes (in one passage he replaces unconvincing 'watery pumpkins' with 'sorry parsnips'!). These are the nuts and bolts of the creative process: he puts it on paper, crosses out and improves. But the draft is still well ordered, the sequence of thought and image worked out. Perhaps, as befits one working in an oral medium, he shaped the structures of verse speeches in his mind even when there was no paper in front of him, as he walked about the city. And one assumes his habits of thought were more disciplined than, say, those of Proust, who rewrote even his proofs. There is, after all, a world of difference between a ten-volume novel drawing on memory, in which the very act of proofreading elicited still more remembrance, and the construction of a tightly knit verse play of maximum three hours' length for a demanding mass audience of whom a lot was expected in terms of understanding and concentration. Even if, as Shakespeare puts it in the epilogue to *The Tempest*, the chief goal of his 'project' was simply 'to please'.

But it was never so simple, one imagines, for the mature Shakespeare, to settle just for pleasing. None of the plays of this period is a throwaway as, say, *The Merry Wives of Windsor* was. *Measure for Measure*, his first play for James, is a characteristic meditation on morality, sex and lust, with a pronounced Catholic colour. Even his least successful show from this time, *All's Well That Ends Well* – a strange satire of human manners, as if in response to Jonson's manifesto for comedy – has its moments. All the plays of 1604–6 grapple with serious moral themes; but the best are the greatest of all works of drama.

A Private Christian

Questions of morality, then, were clearly at the front of Shakespeare's mind at this time. But as for where his religious faith was, this is impossible to answer with any certainty. The plays don't betoken a religious trajectory: some have a broadly religious resolution, of course, and in this phase religious imagery is thicker on the ground – not only did he recall old things such as prayers, rituals and texts, but his current reading included Catholic material. Recently it has been strongly argued that the mature Shakespeare was a crypto-Catholic – some have even painted him in his youth as well nigh a trainee Jesuit. But this seems overstated. The reality is likely to be less dramatic, and more consonant with the history of so many English people of his time. By 1603–4, after all, Shakespeare could be

criticized by a Catholic writer ('I C') in a text published by a secret Catholic press, for being a secular poet, not Christian or edifying enough. Is there a suggestion here too that he was a former Catholic who had betrayed the cause?

Shakespeare was born of a Catholic family, but perhaps lost his parents' religion as an adult, although what he imbibed with his mother's milk and through his Warwickshire roots stayed with him in his heart, as those things shaped by childhood almost always tend to. The thin evidence for his private life in London suggests that he was not a regular churchgoer, and perhaps even avoided going to church; unlike Hemmings and Condell, he never belonged to a London parish; and he lived for some time with Huguenots, who attended the French church and were not obliged to obey the Church of England rules on Sabbath-breaking. Most curious is the fact that, although his name appears in a tax demand dated 6 October 1600 as a resident of the Liberty of the Clink, and he may well have lived there from 1599 to 1602, he has not been found in any of the annual lists of residents of the local parish, St Saviour's, compiled by the church officers who collected tokens purchased by churchgoers for compulsory Protestant Easter communion. This is intriguing, and perhaps significant. Did he tell the churchwardens that he had taken Easter communion in Stratford? Such hints might tend to suggest that the absence of personal revelation in his works, which has so exercised his modern readers, and fuelled the fantasies of the conspiracy theorists, is no accident but a deliberate act of self-concealment on his part. This would make complete sense in someone of his background, whose family religion was defined by the law as treason, and whose father was pursued by the government's bounty hunters and thought police. In this world of 'suborned informers,' as he put it, the stoic poet stood aloof.

What we know of his inner life looks the same. He listened to Protestant sermons, and he also knew about the 'touch of the holy bread' and the 'evening mass'. He read both Henry Smith and Robert Southwell, and probably took both with a pinch of salt. Along with Ovid and Plutarch, the Bible was still his book. Now he probably owned the Protestant Geneva version; but there are echoes in his plays of Tyndale, the old Bishops' Bible (used at church and school when he was young) and the Catholic Rheims version. In short, as one would expect, he was a Christian, but his mind was wide and his scepticism of any system of power was pronounced. Conscience was a personal matter. If he retained in his heart a sympathy for the Old Faith of his parents, he kept his cards close to his chest. That this was his character he tells us in Sonnet 48: 'How careful was I when I took my way', that is, when he started out on his journey. 'Each trifle under truest bars to thrust .... From hands of falsehood, in sure wards of trust .... Within the gentle closure of my breast.' But whatever

else, his habits of thought do not look like those of a Protestant – still less a Puritan. ('If I thought *that,* I'd beat him like a dog!')

The Repertoire

With the plague contained, if not entirely over, the theatres reopened in 1605 and Shakespeare found himself back in the old routine: acting at the Globe in the afternoons, rehearsing new plays and revivals in the mornings. They probably rehearsed the first scenes on Monday morning, the next 'act' on Tuesday, and so on through the week – the custom in repertory in England up to the 1920s. Their role as the King's Men put more pressure on this already tight schedule. With a new court establishing new canons of taste, but also curious to see old plays, revivals were in demand: *Merry Wives* and *The Comedy of Errors* were put on before Christmas 1604, for example, and *Love's Labour's Lost* and *The Merchant of Venice* (a favourite of James's) early in 1605.

It would be fascinating today to see the shows that the King's Men played alongside *Lear* and *Macbeth* when Shakespeare was at his peak as the company's writer-in-chief. We would surely see his own plays more in context, and maybe also understand his audience better. Non-Shakespeare shows at the Globe between 1604 and 1606 included *A Larum for London,* a grim anti-Spanish diatribe about the siege of Antwerp; a social comedy, *The London Prodigal*; the controversial *Gowry*, about the Gowrie conspiracy; a very popular older show, *The Merry Devil of Edmonton*; and *The Fair Maid of Bristol*, one of the best-loved romances of the time; and, to ring the changes, *The Miseries of Enforced Marriage*, which offered social realism with domestic violence and murder. It is always instructive to remember that the great Burbage had to learn these kinds of parts as well as Lear and Antony. And although Shakespeare's plays were surely the main draws, the rest of the repertoire offers a revealing insight into the company's judgement of their audience, and into the artistic compromises that they had to make to ring the changes. Some shows, like Middleton's *Revenger's Tragedy* are lurid, fast-moving *théâtre noir* with sparkling, hard-edged poetry; but others, like Rich's *Devil's Charter*, were second-rate stuff; and at least one, *Thomas Lord Cromwell*, was a third-rate work by third-rate jobbers.

The nature of the repertoire suggests how competitive the professional theatre must have been. A dozen or more London playhouses, four of them huge places that could each hold between 2000 and 3000 people, and three of them within sight of each other on Bankside, all vied for trade. And that is not to take into account bull- and bear-baiting and the other attractions of the south bank. On top of this the King's Men were playing at court, sometimes in the

evening, and doing special runs for big court occasions. They kept on touring, too – in October 1605 going all the way down to Devon, for example. With an active repertoire of twenty or thirty shows – of which they might be called on to perform a dozen or more over Christmas for the King – this constitutes a workload that could only be achieved by a company strong on flexibility and multi-skilling and with formidable *esprit de corps*.

So time for new writing – and reading – had to be found when and where it could. Nor can there have been many opportunities to nip off home for a few days. It is easy to believe John Aubrey when he says that Shakespeare only went 'home to his own country' once a year. Anne brought up the children on her own.

THINKING OF LEAR

On 29 October 1605, if you had strolled down from Silver Street to the conduit at St Michael le Querne, you would have seen Cheapside thronged with people. Every casement and balcony on the five- and six-storey shops and merchants' houses was bursting with spectators, for this was the day of the Lord Mayor's pageant. The theme this year was of the moment: 'The triumphes of re-united Britania'.

In a series of tableaux in the streets, with kingdoms personified and Neptune on a lion, the entertainment told the mythic history of ancient Britain with its capital, New Troy, by the Thames, 'which was once one sole monarchy, but now divided into three several estates with hurt and inconvenience ensuing'.

It was a political parable for the time. Ideas about the unification of Britain and of Britishness – and, conversely, of the threat of division of the kingdom – were in the air. In Parliament King James had outlined his views on the advisability of making one 'Great Britain', and a stream of pamphlets and historical treatises had followed. So artists, poets and playwrights were naturally also thinking about these themes. And that autumn Shakespeare himself was working on a play about the dismemberment of Britain and the collapse of rulership.

The initial optimism at James's accession had not endured. Catholic hopes of religious reform, now seen to have been misplaced, were supplanted by hopes that the unjust ruler might be overthrown.

BELOW: *The 1608* Lear *title page. Based on a traditional folk tale with a Cinderella-like beginning, the play resonated the profound anxieties in the body politic in 1605–6.*

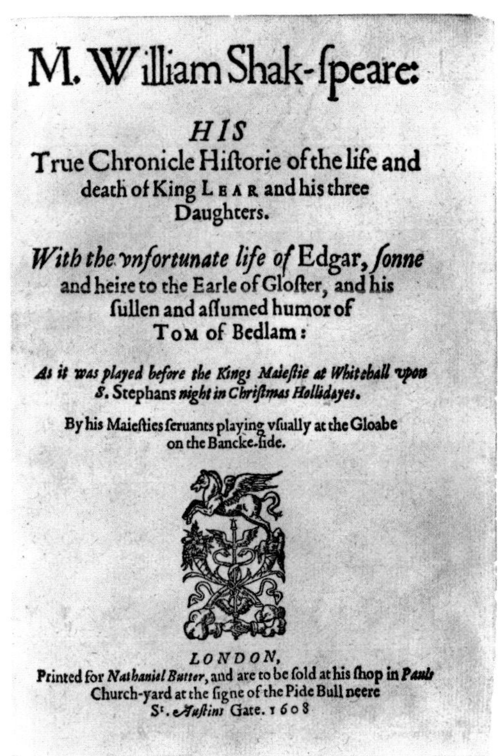

M. William Shak-ſpeare:

HIS

True Chronicle Hiſtorie of the life and death of King LEAR and his three Daughters.

With the vnfortunate life of Edgar, *ſonne* and heire to the Earle of Gloſter, and his ſullen and aſſumed humor of TOM of Bedlam:

As it was played before the Kings Maieſtie at Whitehall vpon S. Stephans *night in Chriſtmas Hollidayes.*

By his Maieſties ſeruants playing vſually at the Gloabe on the Bancke-ſide.

LONDON,

Printed for *Nathaniel Butter*, and are to be ſold at his ſhop in *Pauls* Church-yard at the ſigne of the Pide Bull neere S^t. *Auſtins* Gate. 1608

The almanacs for 1605 prophesied dramatic change, eclipses 'presaging greevous and wretched accidents'. And that sense of spiritual crisis permeated Shakespeare's writing too that autumn. The 'late eclipses of the sun and moon' to which he refers took place in September and October, and chimed with the 'Wonderful Predictions' which prophesied that 'piety and charity shall wax colde, truth and justice shal be oppressed … and nothing shall be expected but the spoyle and ruine of the common society'.

It nearly happened. That November saw the great crisis of the reign, the Gunpowder Plot, when the whole body politic was almost upturned. So Shakespeare's latest play was written during a time of sensational and fateful events, and it brings the trajectory of his career to an amazing climax. The play was *King Lear*.

The story begins with the time-honoured love test. The old king foolishly asks his daughters how much they love him: the two wicked sisters are good at deceit and first flatter, then ruin, him. The youngest, Cordelia, loves him but refuses to enter into such a charade. From there Shakespeare remorselessly takes us into horrors, almost cruelly insisting that we watch them. Lear's world falls apart; the kingdom is dismembered; order is turned upside down; children destroy their parents. In the end the wicked die, but only after the characters we care about most die too. Lear's beloved Cordelia is killed, and the old king dies of a broken heart. Clutching at straws, it might be said that love conquers, even in death, but the play is exacting, harrowing and staggering in its range.

The tale itself was a very old one, appearing in the work of the twelfth-century romancer Geoffrey of Monmouth, and more recently in Sidney's *Arcadia*. But most important to Shakespeare as a source was an old play based on the Lear story. Only published in late 1605, the play – no tragedy but with jigging rhymes and a happy ending – had been in the repertoire of the Queen's Men way back in the 1580s. So Shakespeare had known it twenty years earlier; maybe he had even acted in it. And it was a tale that had nagged at him all through his career.

So one day in the autumn of 1605, let us imagine, Shakespeare wandered down Cheapside, past St Paul's churchyard, and browsed in John Wright's shop at Christ Church door by Newgate Market. There, in a freshly inked pile of quartos on the flap board of the shop, lay this old favourite, now available for the first time in print: 'The True Chronicle History of King Leir and his three daughters … As it hath been divers and sundry times lately acted'. Given his long fascination with the tale, Shakespeare could not have resisted it. Of the new Lear play he wrote based on it, two versions have come down to us. One is Shakespeare's first draft, printed by Nathaniel Butter in 1608 'for his shop at the

Sign of the Pied Bull in Pauls churchyard'. Butter was not a good printer and it's a bad text, but he seems to have had an unusually difficult manuscript to work from, as if for once the author's rethinks and changes had blotted more than a line or two. A second version, printed in the 1623 Folio by his colleagues, seems to represent the author's considered revisions after the experience of watching it on stage. So he committed much thought to the play; and it shows. In the eighteenth century it was deemed so horrible that it was regarded as unplayable; prevailing taste demanded a happy ending. In modern times it is often called the greatest of all dramas.

The text of *Lear* contains tiny hints that seem to find echoes in the Silver Street neighbourhood. For example, on 1 December the christening took place in St Olave's Church of a baby girl, the daughter of his neighbour, the well-to-do embroiderer William Taylor. She was baptized Cordelia: the first appearance of the name in this form. Did Shakespeare, one wonders, stand godfather to her?

Near neighbours, too, were the doctors Palmer and Gifford. Both *Lear* and *Macbeth*, the other play written in 1605–6, include doctors among their characters. Interesting, then, is Lear's grim reference to dissecting Regan to find out why she is so cruel: 'Let them anatomize Regan; see what breeds about her heart. Is there any cause in nature that makes this hardness? what is it breeds around her heart?' Might this have been suggested by the public dissections carried out 50 yards away from Shakespeare's house by his surgeon neighbours?

Shadow Texts: Samuel Harsnett and the Devils of Denham

So, like any professional writer, Shakespeare was a sponge: stories of the street, things he saw, people he met, news of the day, sermons and tracts, all went into the mix. But he was a voracious reader, too, and books played their part. On his desk that autumn, for example, was John Florio's translation of Montaigne, which he often used. This time his attention focused on the essay 'On the Affections of Fathers to Their Children'. He looked back, as he often did, at Erasmus, whose *Praise of Folly* he mined for the Fool's deconstructions of power. He also dipped into Sidney's *Arcadia* for his version of the Lear story. But one book he read at that time over-reached them all psychologically, and offers a striking insight into how he thought about a source and appropriated its ideas for his art. It concerned the bizarre case of the Jesuits and the Devils of Denham.

The book had been printed in the last month of Elizabeth's reign by an acquaintance of his, James Roberts, whose printing house lay over the wall beyond Cripplegate in the Barbican. It was a Protestant polemic sponsored at the highest level of government: 'A Declaration of Egregious Popish Impostures, to with-draw the harts of her Majesties Subjects from their

allegeance, and from the truth of the Christian Religion professed in England, under the pretence of casting out Devils'.

This nasty piece of anti-Catholicism contains a sensational account of a series of exorcisms performed by Jesuit priests many years before at a house in Denham in Buckinghamshire. It includes a documentary appendix of verbatim confessions and interrogations of those exorcized, many of them poor people: serving women like Sara Williams and her sister Fidd. The author, Samuel Harsnett, was a Privy Councillor and chaplain to the Bishop of London: a learned and cultivated man of taste and imagination, but with that streak of cruelty often found among people in power at those times when the theologian and the executioner go hand in hand. His book was intended as part of a national campaign against belief in the spirit world, possession and exorcism – one of the atavistic holds the Catholic priesthood was felt still to possess over its naive and old-fashioned adherents in the countryside. But it also raised much wider questions about the nature of power and authority, the existence of spirits and miracles. So the story was of peculiar significance to those in power. And it was of additional interest to Shakespeare since the text mentions the executions of people he knew – his kinsmen Edward Arden and John Somerville, and his teacher's brother Thomas Cottam.

One of the exorcizing priests, Robert Debdale of Shottery, must, in fact, have been known to him personally. Years before, Debdale had gone to Rome with Shakespeare's schoolmaster Simon Hunt. He had returned with Campion and died on the scaffold in 1586. During his time underground, Debdale had been chaplain of a Catholic recusant family in Denham, the Peckhams. (Tucked away in a leafy suburb by the river Colne, their house is still there, though recently restored as a golf clubhouse – any remaining ghosts have surely departed now.)

The exorcisms had been performed in 1586, in the frightening build up to the Babington Plot. Using the interrogations of the participants with the eye of a dramatist, Harsnett tears the actions and beliefs of the Jesuit exorcists to pieces. Conjuring up spirits, like praying for the dead and 'incantation', was a papist charade. As far as he and his sponsors were concerned, the age of ghosts and devils was over.

For Shakespeare (as for the modern reader) it seems to have been a disturbing text, only lightened by Harsnett's breezy showman's patter. The testimonies are gruelling, and the cumulative effect is both compelling and revolting; after a while the reader's mind reels at the smell of the potions used as emetics, the needles in legs, the acrid incense and the gruesome relics. Although the concepts behind the cult of exorcism were not so alien to a seventeenth-century

person as they are to us, the words and images convey a sense of stumbling into another world. Troops of devils come forward one after another – Pippin (who makes his victims 'to lie in fields and gape at the Moone'), Hilco, Smolkin, Lustie huffe-cap, Hiaclato ('the monarch of the world … whose only followers were two men and an urchin boy') and the extraordinary gang of devils who torment poor Sara Williams: 'Maho, Killico Hob and these four, Frateretto, Fliberdigibbet, Hoberdidance, Tocobatto, were devils of the round or Morrice whom Sara in her fits tuned together in measure and sweet cadence' ('lest you should conceive that the devils had no musicke in hell', adds Harsnett, helpfully).

Here, in short, was a documentary record of what it is like to be mad: a graphic depiction of physical and mental torment and a conjuring of the archaic imaginal world that the ideologues of the Protestant Reformation sought to do away with. To a professional writer interested in the pathology of possession it was a gift. The tale is a series of short dramas, and Harsnett tells it with stage directions, using all the theatrical metaphors from comedy and tragedy to the farcical and the grotesque. Here literally, was the incoherence of which John Donne would write. And Shakespeare's use of the text suggests that he did not just skim it, as he sometimes did. He read it with deepening fascination, perhaps noting down phrases and ideas in his commonplace book; digesting it before he wrote his play. In the storm scene in *Lear*, for example, he uses the names of the devils who appeared to the serving woman Sara Williams; except that this is a world, he will show us, where there are no devils. Inhumanity is the real evil, and he is going to show us what happens when human beings 'shark on each other'.

Many of the words and phrases he borrows from Harsnett he had never used before – 'playing bo-peep', for instance. Outlandish ones especially caught his eye: 'auricular', 'apish', 'gaster', 'asquint' and 'pendulous' are just a few. His borrowings, though, concentrate on Harsnett's vicious lexicon of pain: images of the human body beaten, pierced, flayed, gashed, scalded, tortured, pierced and finally broken on the rack. In the exorcisms, for example, one particular action is repeated as each of the victims is bound tightly in a chair, sick on magic potions, choking on incense, grim relics stuffed in their mouths. Anne Smith tells how three times 'they did bind her so fast ... in a chair as they almost lamed her arms and so bruised all parts of her body with holding tying and turmoiling of her'. Another old lady is 'an old body unapt and unwieldy, as an old dog to a dance … to teach an old corkie woman to writhe and tumbel'. And just as the devils come back in the gobbledegook of Poor Tom in the storm in *Lear*, so does this image. Shakespeare uses the word 'corky' for the first and only time in his plays in the horrific scene when Gloucester is tied to a chair and blinded:

GONERIL: Pluck out his eyes ....
CORNWALL: Bind fast his corky arms ... Bind him I say.
REGAN: Hard, hard! O filthy traitor! ...
CORNWALL: To this chair bind him ....

Harsnett's book, of course, must have been all the more affecting to Shakespeare given his Catholic upbringing. It was a kind of sadistic blockbuster, surreal, savage, literary, full of black humour, and it stuck with him. There are strong echoes of its language in three of his late plays, and also in his revision of *Othello*. So the book penetrated Shakespeare's imagination deeply, its contents transmuted into the much bigger canvas he was creating, with its iterative imagery of human suffering. Nor was it just a question of borrowing words, names and images. For out of it seems to have emerged the central metaphor of the play: the storm as a kind of exorcism (indeed, the play as a kind of exorcism?). In mulling over Harsnett, then, he seems to have found a key to transform the old story, and the old source play, into metaphor: creating the terrible apocalyptic surge to which the play rises in the middle, when the bonds are loosed and the storm of man-made evil and cruelty engulfs humankind so that human life becomes as cheap as that of beasts in the face of pitiless gods: 'As flies to wanton boys ... they kill us for their sport.'

WHAT IS LIFE?

We are left with the same question as at the end of Euripides's greatest tragedies: if that is all life is, what is life? *Lear* was, in a sense, Shakespeare's answer to Harsnett. Or at least to the culture, the mind-set and the structures of power that produced it, and to the events it describes. Wherein lies authority? Can the principle of nature be elicited and defined by reason? Is humanity on its own? Is authority an attribute of the divine, its exercise – as James himself declared – an aspect of the supernatural? Are there still miracles and prophecies? Or is the age of miracles dead?

The language in which he does this was the culmination of the style he had developed since *Hamlet*. A fantastically rich vocabulary drew on everything from popular song and madmen's jingles to Latinisms, French words and his own coinages. But the crucial emotional tone of the play comes from good old English words – often monosyllables. 'See' and 'feel', for example, are at the heart of the play ('I see it feelingly,' says Lear towards the end.) 'Kin' and 'kind' form another favourite semantic cluster, which opens up rich possibilities of meaning: spreading from its basic linguistic root, which defines a relationship between human beings, to become an expression of the most important

necessary human quality of those relationships, kindness. Such words he worries like a dog (as in *Hamlet*: 'a little more than kin, and less than kind'). And in *Lear* always it is these monosyllables that carry meaning most feelingly:

> Thou knowst the first time that we smell the air
> We wawl and cry …
> Then kill, kill, kill, kill, kill, kill! …
> Howl, howl, howl, howl! O, you are men of stones! …
> For as I am a man I think this lady to be my child ….
> And so I am, I am ….

It is tempting, too, to look back to the plain language he heard in the streets of Stratford: the words his mother and father spoke, and those of the peasants in the fields. To simple country people words are like physical objects: things to touch and see. Indeed, in their simplicity there is almost a moral value, and in Shakespeare the strongest emotions are expressed not in Latin or French words, or in scholastic phrases – resonant though they sometimes are in the mouths of kings or upper-class Roman heroes – but in those old English monosyllables: kith, kin, kind, hate, kill, live, die, good, love ….

And so in *Lear*, with such a range of language, he takes us into the world of horrors and the dispossessed. Here are the kind of people we have met in the town books of Warwickshire in the 1580s, the blind 'idiot' child, the Bedlam beggars, the people he rubbed shoulders with in the plague-ridden streets by his London lodgings. These are the people the king has not cared for as he should:

> Poor naked wretches, wheresoe'er you are,
> That bide the pelting of this pitiless storm,
> How shall your houseless heads and unfed sides,
> Your loop'd and window'd raggedness, defend you
> From seasons such as these? O, I have ta'en
> Too little care of this! Take physic, pomp,
> Expose thyself to feel what wretches feel,
> That thou mayst shake the superflux to them,
> And show the heavens more just.

Plainly this has not just been written to please the nobs, to get bums on seats, or as a quick rewrite of an old play to discharge a contract. It is as demanding as popular entertainment can get – a testimony to the intelligence of his audience, to their capacity for language and to their range of response. Shakespeare turns

a sectarian rant into a tale of people trapped by the evil of the times, an evil that is man-made. In the end, in Lear's speech to Cordelia he seems to remember Robert Southwell's meditation on prison, liberty and the divine mysteries from the *Epistle of Comfort*, with its image of birds in a cage:

> LEAR: Come, let's away to prison;
> We two alone will sing like birds i' the cage.
> When thou dost ask me blessing, I'll kneel down,
> And ask of thee forgiveness; so we'll live,
> And pray, and sing, and tell old tales, and laugh
> At gilded butterflies, and hear poor rogues
> Talk of court news, and we'll talk with them too,
> Who loses, and who wins; who's in, who's out;
> And take upon's the mystery of things,
> As if we were God's spies; and we'll wear out,
> In a wall'd prison, packs and sects of great ones
> That ebb and flow by the moon.
> EDMUND: Take them away.
> LEAR: Upon such sacrifices, my Cordelia,
> The gods themselves throw incense. Have I caught thee?
> He that parts us shall bring a brand from heaven,
> And fire us hence like foxes. Wipe thine eyes;
> The good years shall devour them, flesh and fell,
> Ere they shall make us weep: we'll see 'em starve first.
> Come.

Under what circumstances a person writes verse like this we can only guess. Even in its moments of tenderness, the amplitude of the language in *King Lear* is violently, outrageously indecorous. Did he really come up with this sort of thing in the back room of a crowded 'ordinary'? Does this not feel more like solitary, midnight writing?

Nor does a dramatist write like this without the actors to perform it: the text always has to be tailored to the company. After the demise of Kemp, there are no parts for clowns in *Henry V* and *Julius Caesar*. Female characters grow in stature after the arrival of John Rice and William Ostler. And here is the old team, together for so long, mature, able to do anything – and evidently with total faith in their writer: Burbage as Lear, Hemmings with his fussy old courtier parts as Gloucester, Armin as the Fool singing his weird rhymes, jingles and songs.

Shakespeare was a great comedy writer: he had a natural feel for it (did that come from his 'merry-cheeked' father?) and for the poignant way the comic intermingles with the tragic, to say nothing of his natural comic verve. But he also knew that destruction is the nature of the angel of history. Old worlds are destroyed, new ones come into being; our dearest things are lost, but the wounds heal in time. Some of them.

THE POINT OF TRAGEDY

Aristotle, in his famous definition of Greek tragedy in the *Poetics,* says that tragic drama is an imitation of life: 'an imitation of an action which is serious and complete, and which has a kind of magnitude. Its language is well seasoned, with each of the kinds of seasoning used separately in its different parts. It is dramatic, not narrative form. And through pity and fear it accomplishes a purgation of the emotions.' It was a definition of a Greek art form, of course, not an English one; but in his greatest plays, such as *Lear*, Shakespeare does this. He shows us the worst and offers us, through tragic catharsis, a retrospect of life and a foretaste of death, heartening us through our survival to take an ethical stance and to 'bear us like the time'. As we have discovered from his family background, his childhood and schooldays, he learned to see from both sides in a time when coherence had gone and chaos had come. And he makes his greatest drama about that, almost deliberately piling on the suffering for the audience. And yet, as is the nature of tragic drama, the play's nihilism is softened by the ultimate destruction of the wicked, and by some strange consoling force of what can only be called providence.

But is it a Christian providence, or is it more like the Greeks would have understood it? The play has been variously labelled Christian, pre-Christian and even post-Christian. And although the story is safely located in British myth and pagan prehistory, there is an element of truth in all three. *Lear* is Christian in the sense that this is art created for a Christian audience, art whose author has quarried religious imagery, words and stories. This is as one might expect from a lifetime Bible reader like Shakespeare (the Book of Job, for example, is another obvious influence hovering in the play's background). But what kind of Christianity? The play is not Protestant, of course, but it is not Catholic either, although there is evidence that Catholics saw it as a commentary on their times.

But *Lear* cannot be forced into such particular distinctions. A sprawling, indecorous, prophetic miracle play with religious and political subject matter, it harks back to the mystery plays Shakespeare saw on carts in Coventry as a kid, to the old Queen's Men's play with its happy ending. At times realistic, satirical, obscene and scatological, with its snatches of songs, mad rhymes, devils' names, jigs and street slang, this is a tale situated in a landscape of violence and

alienation. It is easy to see why it so appealed to twentieth-century writers, such as Samuel Beckett. And whether we read it as pre- or post-Christian, it spoke about the spiritual condition of Shakespeare's England.

One last point remains, and it is about the author's intentions. This is a play for the king by the King's Men: a play that passed the red pen of the Master of the Revels (although some differences between the two versions of *Lear* are now thought to be due to censorship). It is a play about a king and the disastrous division of his kingdom. There were things put in it to flatter and interest the royal patron. But at the same time, in its subtext the drift of the play is oppositional, and it is hard to believe that this was not intentional.

Four hundred years on, perhaps we delude ourselves in thinking that we can really get close to Shakespeare as he composes a work such as this. But maybe we can get an inkling of the way his mind was working when we remember his obsession with the Lear tale going back to the old Queen's Men's play. It was a story he had first alluded to years before, in *The Two Gentlemen of Verona*; a tale that flickers through his career (it crops up again in *The Merchant of Venice* and *Richard II*); and he would revise it later, rewriting Lear's most famous scene for even more power and nuance, a sure sign that the play really mattered to him.

Ben Jonson attacked him for having no moral stance, as did Samuel Johnson two centuries later. In the twenty-first century we know that he is always true to life. *Lear* gives the lie to the idea that Shakespeare's art is not in some sense oppositional. He is not didactic, like Sidney or Jonson. He doesn't tell you what he thinks, or what you should think, and he never preaches. Rather he sets up oppositions, multiple viewpoints, and then holds his mirror up to nature. So in *Lear*, in his topicality, in his use of such loaded and contemporary sources, maybe we can get a glimpse of a Jacobean public artist working at the very highest level. And here we can sense, too, underneath his customary reserve, Shakespeare's deadly seriousness as an artist: what one modern critic has called 'his cool and cunning authority in the face of his times'.

His company performed *Lear* before the King and court at Whitehall on St Stephen's Day 1606, the year after the Gunpowder Plot and on one of the few old saints' days still observed in the Anglican Church. This gives us a measure of how far he felt he could go with his patrons, and how far his patrons felt they could go with him. Seen in that light, the show that night at Whitehall is as emblematic a moment in the history of Western culture as Michelangelo's last working day, breaking the Rondanini pietà, in the spring of Shakespeare's birth, or Descartes' dream of the union of all science in a wall stove in Ulm three years after Shakespeare's death. It is a bridge between the old and the new, between the no longer and the not yet.

CHAPTER FOURTEEN

Gunpowder, Treason and Plot

FEAR AND TERROR

The astrological almanacs had prophesied terrible things for 1605, focusing with uncanny precision on the autumn. The forty-year prognostication of 1567 foresaw disasters following eclipses predicted for September and October: 'Charity shall wax colde, truth and justice shal be oppressed'. Shakespeare's writing of *King Lear* during the autumn of 1605 dramatizes this mood, and while the play was still on his desk came the defining event of James's reign, the moment that changed everything: the Gunpowder Plot.

THE POWDER PLOT

On 5 November the government made the sensational discovery of a Catholic attempt to blow up the king and all his Parliament. The principal conspirators – Catesby, Tresham, Winter – all had Stratford connections; indeed, the Catesbys were distantly related to Shakespeare through his mother. The plot was Warwickshire- and Worcestershire-based, and their safe house, the home of the Grant family, lay a mile outside Stratford at Clopton House near Snitterfield. The head of the Jesuits in England, Henry Garnet, had stayed there a little earlier while on pilgrimage to St Winifrid of Holywell. The next day he had moved on to Huddington in Worcestershire, the home of the Winters. Here, then, was a web of intrigue with deep roots in the poet's part of the world.

Right: *The execution of the Gunpowder Plotters, 1 February 1606: the gruesome process of judicial punishment in Shakespeare's England. Many of the plotters would have been known to the poet.*

After the arrest of their hit man, Guy Fawkes, the masterminds were hunted down through rain-sodden country lanes, past Stratford into Worcestershire. Panic-stricken, the Grants, John Shakespeare's old business partners, sent a messenger to the Badgers in Henley Street with 'a cloakbag full of copes, vestments, crosses, and other relics.' The Grants' house was raided and razed to the ground – today the only sign of it is a line of grassy humps by the present farm. At Huddington they took their last supper, and in the middle of the night held mass, ashen-faced, before the final headlong flight. In their haste their powder was ruined as they crossed the flooded river Stour. Tresham and Catesby were eventually trapped at Henlip Hall in Staffordshire, and, like Macbeth, Catesby died fighting. The house is still there, in a wooded hollow – an old people's home today, but with shot holes still visible on the façade. They are weathered and fading now, disappearing into the grain of the old stone, just as the violent passions that ignited this tragic history are themselves beginning at last to recede.

The End of History?

In one stroke the balmy time of Sonnet 107 was no more. The plotters had hoped to recover the past, to restore the Old Faith; in fact, they had shattered

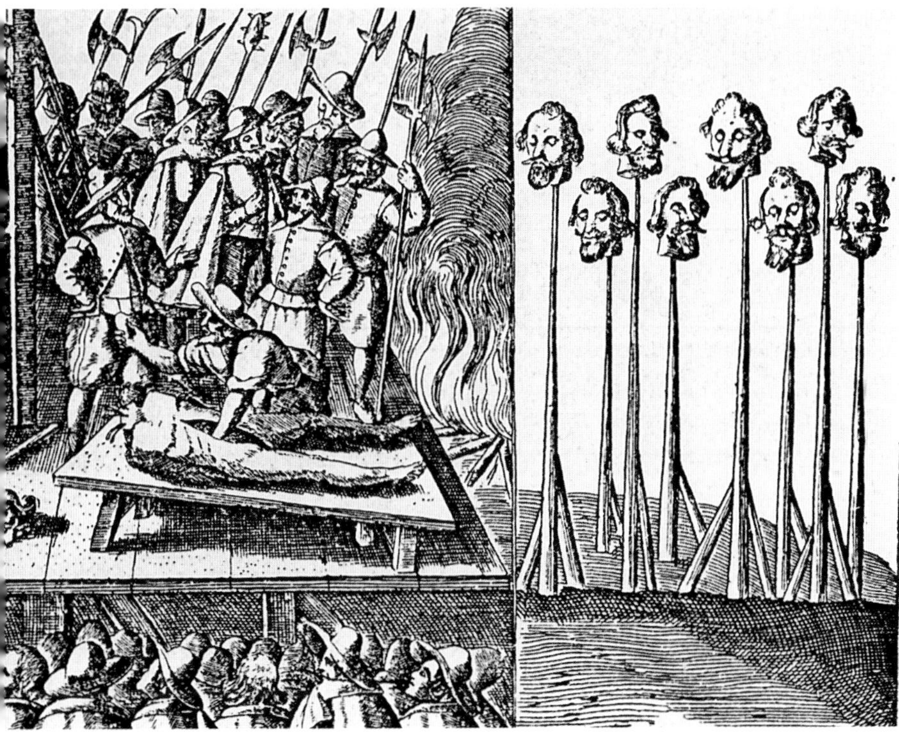

all hope of a return to older days. James announced he had had a premonition of the plot. On 9 November, before Parliament, the king gave his scriptural interpretation, which next day was underlined in a sermon at St Paul's. His was a straight theological argument. The plot was the devil's work. God had saved him. And in foreseeing it, the king had underlined his status as the Lord's Anointed – he had been saved by his prophetic soul. (The document still hangs in the Noes voting lobby, and even today Yeomen of the Guard still ritually inspect the cellars before every State Opening of Parliament.)

The next year the government mobilized opinion. The show trials of the conspirators in January and March drove home the official version: the assassination plot had been the work of a group of fanatics spurred on by the Jesuits. James intended this interpretation to become central to England's sense of identity, emphasizing the kingdom's place in God's providence. National identity was perceived to be at stake now and a liturgical celebration was provided to commemorate it. Powder Day would imprint its significance on the national psyche: a watershed in the Reformation from which there would now be no going back. In terms of Reformation politics it marked the end of history – or, at least, the old version of it. Powder Day – transformed into Bonfire Night –

is still celebrated by the British. And even today some of the old bonfire societies burn effigies not just of Fawkes but also of Catesby and the pope. As we approach the 400th anniversary, each November in Lewes, Rye and other towns in the south of England, the parades, banners, bonfires and burning effigies remind us that the dust has not yet quite settled on the religious struggles of the sixteenth century.

Witches and Plots: The Theatre Cashes in

It is probable, though not certain, that Shakespeare finished *King Lear* during the aftermath of the plot in the winter of 1605–6. The trials were avidly followed by the public, and, as it would in similar circumstances today, the entertainment industry hurried to respond. There are several Gunpowder Plot plays, including Dekker's *The Whore of Babylon*, Marston's *Sophonisba* and Barnabe Barnes's *The Devil's Charter*. All of them are packed with anti-papist rhetoric, as were poems such as Dekker's *Double P*, the anonymous *Devil of the Vault* and *The Jesuit's Miracles*. Dekker's play is overt: his Whore sends Jesuit assassins, Protean jugglers, from Rome to kill Elizabeth:

> He's brown, he's grey, he's black, he's white
> He's anything! A Jesuite!

In Barnes's play, which was composed for Shakespeare's company, Pope Alexander VI makes a contract with the devil to destroy all powers opposed to his rule in Rome. In this Punch and Judy show for grown-ups, Barnes brings the devil himself on stage to confront the pope after necromancy, exorcisms and elaborate stage business with 'exhalations of lightning and sulphurous smoke'.

Grab them in the first minute! On one level this was just to give the audience what they wanted. In its aggression, social realism and sexual politics Elizabethan theatre always reflected the anxieties and tastes of the day, just as the extreme passions and violence of popular drama do on present-day television. But on another level the language of these plays, which include Shakespeare's Powder play, *Macbeth*, bristles with the ideological controversies of the period.

Written through the summer of 1606, with final tinkerings in late autumn, *Macbeth* rides the hysteria, just as *Measure for Measure* had ridden the euphoria surrounding the arrival of the scholar king who would usher in a new religious age. But as always Shakespeare is more ambiguous and oblique than his fellow dramatists.

Macbeth has tremendous pace and attack. The three witches and their terrible brew, the storm, the omens, the murder, the throat-grabbing panic and suppressed hysteria of the aftermath – all the work of a master working in swift, bold strokes. And again it is a play for James. Scottish themes were already in vogue in the London theatre, and *Macbeth* plays on specific royal interests. Witchcraft was one: James had even written a book on the subject. Scottish royal pedigree was another: the king believed that he was descended from Banquo, and Shakespeare makes much of this in the witches' prophecy (his specialist reading here included the Latin texts of two modern Scottish histories by Leslie and Buchanan). So there was plenty to make the king sit up and watch – and even to flatter him. As for the general mood of terror and threat, this is less specific. Unlike Barnes and Dekker, Shakespeare does not write anti-Catholicism into the play, although he drags in the trial of the Jesuit Henry Garnet in the gatekeeper's famous speech on 'equivocation' in Act II, Scene I. This amazing and daring piece of theatre breaks into the excruciating tension after Macbeth's murder of King Duncan with a drunken stream of consciousness based on one of the oldest of English children's jokes ('Knock, knock, who's there?'). But here it is miraclemongers and dead terrorists at the door:

24 *NEWES FROM SCOTLAND*

that hee did woorke it by the Diuell, without whom it could neuer haue beene so sufficientlye effected: and thervpon, the name of the said Doctor *Fien* (who was but a very yong man) began to grow so common among the people of Scotland, that he was secretlye nominated for a notable Cuniurer.

Above: *King James was deeply interested in evil spirits and witchcraft and believed in the power of the devil. In Scotland he personally interrogated witches before having them burned at the stake.*

> *Enter a porter. Knocking within.*
>
> PORTER: Here's a knocking indeed! If a man were porter of hell-gate he should have old turning the key. [*Knocking*] Knock, knock, knock. Who's there, I'th' name of Beelzebub? Here's a farmer that hanged himself on th'expectation of plenty: come in time; have napkins enough about you; here you'll sweat for 't. [*Knocking*] Knock, knock! Who's there, in' th'other devil's name? Faith, here's an equivocator, that could swear in both the scales against either scale; who committed treason enough for God's sake, yet could not equivocate to heaven: O, come in, equivocator. [*Knocking*] Knock, knock, knock! Who's there? Faith, here's an English tailor come hither, for stealing out of a French hose: come in, tailor, here you may roast your goose ....

ABOVE: *Macbeth and Banquo meet the three weird sisters, from Raphael Holinshed's 1577* History of Scotland, *a key source for Shakespeare's play.*

The porter is the guardian of hell's gate from the medieval mystery plays Shakespeare had seen as a child. The main references are to the now condemned and executed Garnet (whose alias was Farmer). The mysterious English tailor is an absolutely contemporary image from late November or early December, only a month or so before *Macbeth* was first performed. In London a tailor had been arrested for claiming a miracle had taken place by means of a straw dipped in Garnet's blood (napkins dipped in his blood were already coveted by the faithful). The reference to equivocation concerns the Jesuit practice of avoiding lying but being economical with the truth so as not to incriminate oneself under interrogation. Garnet had refused to reveal what he knew of the Gunpowder Plot, in order to protect what he had heard in the privacy of the confessional.

The transcripts of Garnet's interrogations survive in the public records. The shadow text behind the porter scene is a series of dramatic exchanges, a theatrical dialogue then well known in London:

> 'Were you not asked by Catesby for some great attempt, either by gunpowder or otherwise, for the Catholic cause .... How say you, Mr Garnet, did Mr Tresham equivocate or no?'
> 'I know not.'

> [And then, written in his own shaking hand]: 'I have remembered something which because they were long before my knowledge of the powder plot, I had forgotten ....'

So it was Garnet who had not been able to equivocate himself to heaven. The 'Scottish play' is still an object of superstition among actors, a reputation no doubt born in part out of the grim subject matter. It is also one of the shortest of the plays: the additions for later performances were not by Shakespeare, and it may be that what we have is a cut-down version of his original script, with added songs. This perhaps helps explain why, great as some of the writing is, the play, lacking parallel plots, is thin compared with others of this period.

Whatever Shakespeare's private sympathies, it is hard to imagine the person who wrote this being committed to Garnet's side. The fact was that both Bloody Mary and Protestant Elizabeth had unleashed terrible cruelties on to the people of England because of matters of conscience. We have no reason to think that, like most patriotic English people, Shakespeare did not believe the plot to be horrendous in its magnitude. But as he says in Sonnet 124, he was standing above it now, 'hugely politic'; he was living in a Huguenot household, only rarely, perhaps, attending Protestant church, and he certainly never held any office in his local London parishes. He was staying out of it. Perhaps living between two places made that easy to do.

OLD LOYALTIES IN WARWICKSHIRE

In a small town like Stratford, though, it was less and less easy to stay out of it. The Powder Plot ended a period of several years during which anti-Catholic persecution had lightened. Until then, church papists could satisfy their consciences and still avoid fines by attending ordinary services, only drawing the line at holy communion. In Elizabeth's early years, as a foreign visitor noted, there had been virtual 'freedom of worship' in the privacy of one's own home, and the queen had wisely refused to allow her subjects to be forced to take communion as a test of loyalty, keeping closed the 'window into people's souls'. This status quo had continued in the early years of James. But after the plot, the government clamped down on church papists. An Act of Parliament was now passed mentioning particularly those 'who adhere in their hearts to the popish religion' but 'do nevertheless the better to hide their false hearts repair sometimes to the church to escape the penalty of the law'. Everyone now had to receive holy communion at least once a year, or pay a huge £20 fine in the first year, £40 in the second and £60 in each succeeding year. Local constables had to give the justices of the peace the names of all papists absent from communion.

Easter was the most important Church festival, when it would have been unthinkable for a Catholic to take Protestant communion. And it is in this light that we must view the remarkable list of twenty-one persons brought before Stratford's church court in May 1606 for not receiving communion on Easter Day, 20 April. For among them, now aged twenty-three, was the poet's daughter Susanna.

In the charged aftermath of the Gunpowder Plot, Susanna didn't attend Easter service in Stratford church, and refused even to respond to her first summons. Significantly, among the other recusants on the list were old neighbours, such as the Wheelers, the Reynoldses and the Cawdreys, all former aldermen and high bailiffs, and all avowed Catholics. Here too were family friends, such as Hamnet and Judith Sadler, the godparents of Shakespeare's twins. They were old people now, and clearly still committed to the Old Religion. Speaking for himself and his wife, and faced now with being compelled to take Protestant communion, Hamnet petitions time 'to cleanse his conscience' – confirming that they had abstained on principle. Only discovered in 1964, this list is an important testimony to the family's long-term affection for the Old Faith.

The Timon Mystery

Back in the capital the Powder plays were packing them in. The London stage was at its peak of production, and Shakespeare's company faced a constant demand for new plays. But a good one took several months to write, and it was necessary to plan programmes maybe half a year ahead. In 1606, while writing *Macbeth*, Shakespeare was also re-reading Plutarch with a view to a show based on the story of Antony and Cleopatra. Like many great writers, he had more than one project in mind at any one time, and Plutarch's *Lives* would give him two of his next three. Interestingly enough, the story for the other play he wrote at this moment, *Timon of Athens*, is also in Plutarch, as a digression within the life of Antony. So it sounds very much as if he wrote these plays from late 1606 into 1607: *Antony and Cleopatra* was in performance by early 1607. A collaboration with Middleton, *Timon* was inserted into the Folio edition of Shakespeare's works only at the last minute, and the text we have looks unfinished. There is no evidence that the play was ever performed, so it may offer an intriguing glimpse into a full-scale Shakespearean work in progress.

Timon is not tragedy – it's satire. It's the tale of a man who had it all: a Jacobean 'Bonfire of the Vanities' in which greed is good. The focus is not so much on money itself and its corrupting power, but on the colluding attributes of greed and guile – the mainspring of many Jacobean city comedies, but not of Shakespeare's shows. It doesn't quite come off. By his standards, the writing is

at times forced, uneven and repetitive, while the characters are masque-like, lacking the rich mental hinterland that he gives, say, Shallow and Silence. The fool is his dullest and most unfunny. And the tone does not suggest a soul standing back, 'hugely politic'. The violence of the language, the anger and aggression suit the plot, but an author still needs to be capable of feeling it in order to analyse it: and clearly Shakespeare was. Genteel critics of an older era than our own thought he must have had a nervous breakdown to have written such bitter stuff, but anger, aggression and malice are always latent in his make-up, and throughout his career he worked them out in his art.

Why was *Timon* never finished? Unusually, Shakespeare had chosen a plot with fantastic emblematic power but insufficient movement, which is perhaps why he felt it didn't work. But maybe the real reason for leaving it uncompleted was psychological rather than dramatic. Satire was not Shakespeare's natural bent, and he himself was not a misanthrope. So far was he from hating mankind that for once his ability to imagine the other, his chameleon-like empathy, what Keats called his 'negative capability', got in the way. His heart was simply not in it.

Collaboration: Shakespeare as Script Editor?

The ceaseless pressure to produce new writing meant that new talent always had to be brought on. Co-authorship was common, and sometimes freelancers were hired. Among them was Thomas Middleton. Born in 1580, the son of a wealthy London bricklayer and a moderate Puritan, he had been a student at Oxford in the late 1590s but left without a degree, desiring, like any number of ambitious and attractive young men, 'to be with the players daily'.

Apprenticeship covered a multitude of sins, and Middleton's career shows how a young writer worked his way up. In his first collaborations, with Dekker, he wrote for the Admiral's Men and the Children of St Paul's; then, in 1605, he worked on scripts for the King's Men, and his hand has been recognized in *Macbeth*, possibly as reviser, and extensively in *Timon of Athens*. In his role as writer-in-chief, overseer and shareholder, Shakespeare was responsible for bringing on new writers such as Middleton. It would be especially so from mid-1606, when he was suddenly faced with the major task of revising his old shows in response to new censorship legislation.

The working relationship with Middleton gives us an insight into Shakespeare's role now as the company's chief writer-in-residence. About thirty new shows were written for the Globe repertoire between 1599 and 1606 and, as we have seen, this included many by other playwrights: Jonson, Dekker, Wilkins and Middleton with his scorching *Revenger's Tragedy*. Others were

anonymous. But among the plays performed then by the King's Men are some that, intriguingly, were printed at that time with Shakespeare's byline: *The London Prodigal* of 1605 and *A Yorkshire Tragedy* of 1608. The popular tragi-comedy *The Merry Devil of Edmonton* was later also credited to him.

A Yorkshire Tragedy, a dramatic murder story based on actual contemporary events, is less than a third the length of a big tragedy and was staged as one of four short pieces. Its main protagonists, the Calverleys, were recusants living near Wakefield. The father murders his young son and attempts to murder his wife and their other child. Despite the quarto of 1608 being published as by Shakespeare, there is no doubt that Middleton wrote most, if not all, of it, just as he wrote all of *The Puritan*, published 'by WS' in 1607. But there are also traces of two other hands. One was possibly that of George Wilkins, who at that time wrote a show for the King's Men entitled *The Miseries of Enforced Marriage*, which dealt with the background to the Calverleys' story. Wilkins collaborated with Shakespeare on *Pericles* very soon afterwards. But the other hand, which retouched only a page or two, could just be Shakespeare's. It can be detected in the harrowing scene of the little boy's murder, a script fit to grace the most violent episode of *EastEnders* today. Since the play is unaware of the outcome of the affair, it was almost certainly put together in a few weeks to take advantage of what we might call a tabloid sensation.

This example tells us something about collaboration, too. Another aspect of Shakespeare's role as writer-in-chief was to 'augment', 'correct' and 'oversee' other scripts. A third of all shows in this period were joint efforts, and with Henslowe the proportion creeps up to a half. It is quite possible, for instance, that the collaboration of Wilkins and Shakespeare on *Pericles* involved a script submitted to the company which Shakespeare read and was interested enough to take over, retouching Acts I and II and completely rewriting the last three.

In the past this kind of thing has been hard for us to accept – in matters of 'genius' we all like to believe in sole authorship. Working in tandem with less talented jobbers doesn't fit with our idealization of Shakespeare as the lone creator. But anyone involved today in scriptwriting for movies, comedy or television knows what it is like to work in a high-pressure entertainment business. Often 'authorship' doesn't exist. It may take several writers to get a film on; a senior house writer may simply retouch someone else's work, and the executive producer may take credit for something that he or she had little or nothing to do with. Alternatively, the senior writer may supply the original concept and pass it over to another hand for development, but still take a fee and a credit. This is especially likely when writers reach middle age. What is interesting in Shakespeare's career is that it happens relatively early, at the age of forty-two.

Of the dozen plays he wrote after *King Lear*, half were collaborations. Was this company policy? Was he running out of steam? Was something amiss (for example, had he been ill)? Or had he realized he ought to find the time to enjoy the fruits of his labours? To these questions we will return.

Puritans and Players: More Battles

Meanwhile, the fall-out from the Powder Plot went across the board. There had long been pressure against the theatre from Puritans; from Paul's Cross sermons were regularly preached on the immorality of the players, who were condemned as 'schoolmasters of vice and provocations to corruption'. In May 1606 an Act of Parliament to 'Restrain the Abuses of Players' became law. Designed to curb profanity in the theatre, it imposed a fine of £10 for every transgression. Profanity – irreverent and blasphemous language – isn't defined in the Act. It was left to the eye (or ear) of the beholder and hence cunningly demanded self-censorship. In the case of royal servants regularly playing at court, discretion was all the more necessary.

What Shakespeare and his colleagues feared is revealed by a comparison of the Quarto of *Othello*, which is thought to be a pre-1606 text, and the revised Folio text, published after his death. The first version contains more than fifty oaths and profanities, especially in the racist misogynist rants of Iago; the Folio text has none. The oaths are mainly old English ones using the name of God, such as 'Zouns' (God's wounds) and 'Sblood' (God's blood), although the fact that 'Tush' is dropped from the play's opening line suggests the company were jumpy about what might be thought profane – as well they might be at £10 a throw.

So, soon after May 1606, *Othello* and other plays were systematically trawled to remove oaths. The necessary rewrites involved changes of sense, metre, syntax and rhythm, which could hardly have been left to the actors or the prompt boy, and helps to explain why Shakespeare might have farmed out some work that year. Sometimes lines are rewritten, or new ones substituted. Shakespeare used the opportunity to tinker with *Othello*, making significant cuts and adding 150 lines, including a powerful new speech for Emilia at the end of Act IV which asserts the rights of women against the unkindness of men:

> Let husbands know
> Their wives have sense like them: they see, and smell,
> And have their palates both for sweet and sour,
> As husbands have. What is it that they do
> When they change us for others? Is it sport?
> I think it is: and doth affection breed it?

I think it doth: is't frailty that thus errs?
It is so too. And have not we affections,
Desires for sport, and frailty, as men have?
Then let them use us well: else let them know
The ills we do, their ills instruct us to.

Some changes, on the other hand, are tiny details, such as Othello's interjection (italicized here), which breaks Desdemona's original single line in the terrible exchange before she is murdered.

DESDEMONA: Kill me tomorrow; let me live tonight!
OTHELLO: Nay, an you strive, –
DESDEMONA: But half an hour!
OTHELLO: *Being done, there is no pause.*
DESDEMONA: But while I say one prayer!
OTHELLO: It is too late.

Here we see the sharpest brain in the theatre scrutinizing a script and tweaking it to get even more power out of the text in performance: a sure sign that this was a work to which he felt particularly committed.

The End of the Line for Tragedy?

The shows put on at court by the King's Men at Christmas 1606 included *King Lear* and probably *Macbeth*. By early 1607 *Antony and Cleopatra*, which contains some of Shakespeare's most gorgeous and assured poetry, was also in the repertoire. A dynamic, complex, four-hour marathon, it marks a major shift in tone.

Antony and Cleopatra is about a famous passion, the theme of many contemporary poems and plays, including works by Mary Herbert and Samuel Daniel. But in Shakespeare's hands the tale is also about a turning point in history – the fall of the Roman republic and the rise of the empire. It dramatizes two opposed world views, those of Rome and Egypt, which he conjures with image systems of a cynical politic Rome and a reckless perfumed Egypt crushed by the remorseless power of events. So it shares with many other plays a sense of the loss of an old world and the beginning of a new one. And where *Timon* is a failure, this is the work of a master absolutely on top of his game: as Coleridge put it, the work of a 'giant power'.

At the same time it marks a shift away from the painful inner struggles of *Othello*, *King Lear* and *Macbeth*. This play is about human actions on the stage of history. And, of course, whereas Shakespeare was able to invent freely in

Hamlet, *Othello* and *King Lear*, here he has to stay close to the story. So the shift is partly in subject matter, but perhaps partly also a conscious choice by the artist. Shakespeare was not some natural untutored genius. Since his talent blossomed in the mid-1590s, with *Romeo and Juliet* and *A Midsummer Night's Dream*, he had always been a conscious artist. Cunning and guarded, he knew what he was doing and where he was going. The world view sustained through *Hamlet*, *Measure for Measure*, *King Lear* and *Macbeth* had been founded on the thought world he had grown up with: the Christian imaginal universe, its value system and its idea of nature. The absence of this theme from *Antony and Cleopatra* suggests that for him, at least in tragedy, it was exhausted. He was satisfied as an artist: in *King Lear* especially he had said what he wanted to say.

Shakespeare clearly felt free now to look at a classical story and do it straight; *Antony and Cleopatra* gives the impression of being a technical *tour de force*, which he may have enjoyed doing for its own sake (sometimes he recycles the prose in North's translation of Plutarch with only the necessary changes to turn it into verse). So on this occasion he may have delivered his contracted piece without having sweated blood emotionally. But it still exhibits that quality seen throughout his writing career: the constant capacity for self-renewal. Even in a failure like *Timon of Athens*, Shakespeare never does anything without magic and surprise. In *Antony and Cleopatra* the master of his craft makes his own accommodation to Jacobean tastes. And in few, if any, of his plays do we get a greater sense of the presence of the angel of history.

The return to Plutarch raises another interesting question. His *Lives of the Noble Greeks and Romans* are models for life: Shakespeare was drawn to them throughout his career. Wonderful texts for a professional writer, they had great appeal to the older generation of Renaissance humanists. Plutarch is a pagan priest and moralist; fair, calm, reasonable and humane. As their author intended, it is impossible to read such lives and not see the curve of your own.

Back in Stratford: A World Elsewhere

The bitter winters of the early years of the seventeenth century left their trace in Shakespeare's work at this time: the image of 'wind fanned snow' crops up more than once. While the King's Men were busy at court over Christmas and the New Year of 1606–7, Warwickshire was in the grip of the 'Great Frost'. On rutted, frozen roads travel proved very difficult. The dramatist John Marston describes noble ladies in their carriages struggling across the countryside, their hair shining with 'glittering icicles all crystalline … periwigged with snow, russet mantles fringed with ice stiff on the back …'. And all the while Shakespeare was increasing his holdings in the Stratford area.

In those days investing in land was the best way to build up a nest egg. The previous summer he had invested £440 – a very large sum indeed – on a stake in the revenues from the tithes in the common fields at Welcombe just outside the town. His gradual accumulation of land – including an extension of the garden at New Place – must have focused his mind more and more on home.

He was certainly back in Stratford in June 1607, when his daughter Susanna married Dr John Hall. Hall was not a local man and, interestingly enough, he was a moderate Puritan; but Shakespeare evidently trusted him and came to lean on him – they went to London together on Stratford business in the last year of the poet's life. A casebook of Hall's survives – a mine of information, still largely unexploited, about the family connections. In it he treats Catholics and Protestants impartially – even 'Romish priests'; so he was the opposite of a fanatic, as one might expect in a doctor. So maybe, as in so many families in England, the theme of reconciliation was underlined at home. Times change; the beliefs, customs and ideals that made William, that he had imbibed with his mother's milk, were no doubt still there, part of the family myth. But England was now a Protestant country, and there was to be no going back to his father's England.

Perhaps Shakespeare was now spending more time away from the theatre. In this later period of his career, he seems to have undertaken a number of private commissions. For the Earl of Rutland, one of Essex's friends and a devoted theatregoer, he devised a shield with a motto and wrote accompanying verses for a royal knightly pageant. Such emblems, which form the chapter headings of this book, were much cultivated in Renaissance culture: the more riddling they were the better. They had long fascinated Shakespeare and he uses them in several of his plays. At this pageant it was the emblems of the Pembroke brothers that attracted most attention: William Herbert's showed a gleaming white pearl, with a motto from Ovid – 'My strength comes only through integrity'. Given Shakespeare's intimacy with Herbert, is it possible that he composed this too?

Rural Revolt: The Old Countryside in Flames

But while the better-off were partying, the countryside was beginning to burn. A string of bad harvests had brought the rural poor in the Midlands to their knees; rain-sodden 1607 was already shaping up to be grim, and the following year would be worse still. There had been sporadic violence in Midlands towns against recent enclosures as avaricious landlords bought up freehold strips in the common fields, rearranged them into blocks and enclosed them – all for private profit, in particular sheep farming. In the first week of June 1607, while preparations were under way for Susanna's marriage in Stratford, riots flared up

across Warwickshire and Northamptonshire as several thousand peasants demonstrated against the enclosers. In north Warwickshire 3000 rebels gathered at Hill Morton to protest against 'the incroaching tyrants who grind the faces of the poor'. The smell of burning was in the air.

Shakespeare, of course, was a landowner now; a poacher turned gamekeeper. Although his interests were in maintaining the common field strips, and not in digging them up, he would have a stake in both sides when the enclosing mania reached Welcombe, as it did in 1615. But he was not oblivious to the risings of 1607, as we know from an intriguing source that he read for his next play.

That summer he was reading Plutarch again and writing his second late Roman play, *Coriolanus*. Like *Antony and Cleopatra*, it follows North's Plutarch very closely. Both Antony and Coriolanus were cited by sixteenth-century moralists as notable examples of pagan Romans who lacked patience – the one committing suicide, the other rebelling against his country. Both stories turn on powerful women, too – Antony's on his black lover and her passionate life; Coriolanus's on his faithful wife and dominant mother. Out of the latter tale Shakespeare constructed a brilliant, hard-edged political thriller, again leaving aside the multi-layered Christian preoccupations of his tragedies for a classical narrative of personal political destiny, laced with a strong dose of homoerotic bonding. The play again represents a drawing back from the intensity of the earlier tragedies, but there is no denying the fierce artistic input, and it has found many advocates in modern times. Bertolt Brecht's brilliant analysis of the opening scene's class divisions – obvious for the political-theatrical agenda of the East German Berliner Ensemble in the early 1950s – underlines the key element of class struggle that was present in the Jacobean original.

The Diggers' Manifesto

So the wedding celebrations took place against a background of social revolt, and hard on their heels came grim news. The day after the marriage, over the county border at the village of Newton in Northamptonshire, a crowd of between 2000 and 3000 peasants had been attacked by a private army of local landowners and justices of the peace. The rebels were easily dispersed, leaving fifty or so dead. Their leaders were hauled off to Northampton, where they were summarily condemned to death, then hanged, drawn and quartered on a scaffold in the centre of the town. It was the same punishment that had been meted out to Campion and Southwell, but now there was a different enemy.

The so-called Diggers of Warwickshire had drawn up a manifesto to put their case to the local authorities, the JPs and freeholders, and Shakespeare managed to obtain a copy. Like the peasants in the great revolt of 1381, the Diggers

still have faith in the king and his goodwill; they still want a king. Shakespeare would have agreed with that. And they go on to use the metaphor of the body politic: 'Loving friends and subjects under one renowned prince, for whom we pray long to continue in his royal estate … his most true hearted Commonalty …. We as members of the whole, do feel the smart of these encroaching tyrants, which would grind our flesh upon the whetstone of poverty …'. This same metaphor, with its arms and members, Shakespeare would use, memorably, in the opening scene of *Coriolanus*. As they marched, the Diggers had sung a song brimming with workers' patriotism: 'From Hampton-field in haste/we rest as poor delvers and day labourers/for the good of the Commonwealth till death ….' And death it was to be. Across the Midlands, many were shocked by the brutality of the retribution. On 21 June a sermon was preached in Northampton by Robert Wilkinson, who again used the Diggers' image of the body politic to preach against all violence, including that perpetrated by rulers 'who reformed wickedness with a greater wickedness'.

So history's battles were moving on, from religion to the rights of the common people; but there were still those confrontations of individual conscience and power, and of rights and duties, that had always so engaged Shakespeare. One would guess that, like any middle-class property owner, he looked on such events with mixed feelings. Sympathy for the downtrodden, the stranger's case, is clearly present in his psychological make-up, but so too is an abhorrence of lack of order and a mistrust of the uncontrolled mob, which came naturally to any Elizabethan. But politics were becoming more and more complicated: the voice of the rural poor, suppressed in Elizabeth's day, was clamouring to be heard. Civil war was on the horizon. And in *Coriolanus*, taking a lead from the real-life struggles around him, Shakespeare coolly juxtaposed it with the brutal self-interest of the patrician military class.

With *Coriolanus* and *Antony and Cleopatra*, Shakespeare had found his distance; as an artist he had satisfied himself, and he now left these themes behind. In the last phase of his career he would be trying for a very different kind of play. The scholars of Elizabeth's Protestant Reformation had believed it was possible to get back to a pristine Church of England purged of the influence of Rome. The Diggers hoped to retrieve an older England, purged of Norman law and even of the French language. But once a thing is gone, it is irretrievable. What has gone is not a veneer, but the thing itself, the system of belief that gives meaning to everything, including language itself. That is why, after the revolution, a new language must come too. And in his next plays Shakespeare seems to be looking for a new language for a new time.

CHAPTER FIFTEEN

Lost Worlds, New Worlds

NATURE IS WONDERFUL IN HER WORKS

We don't know what Shakespeare was doing on the early morning of 5 September 1607. Perhaps he was lying in bed in an Oxford inn – that week the King's Men were on tour, and we know they played Oxford on the 7th. But as he said in *Coriolanus*, there is a world elsewhere.

Far away that morning – 'jump upon that hour', as he would have put it – imagine a very different scene. A swollen estuary fringed with tropical forest opens out into a wide bay where a ship with furled sails lies at anchor. On deck a crowd has gathered under an awning; among them an English naval officer and several Africans in blue cotton robes, with heavy gold anklets and ritual face scars. The sun is not yet scorching, though there are soon damp patches on the visitors' shirts as sweat runs down under their doublets. The call of colobus monkeys echoes across the water. Two men come on to the quarter deck, halberds in hand:

> BERNARDO: Who's there?
> FRANCISCO: Nay, answer me: stand and unfold yourself.
> BERNARDO: Long live the king!
> FRANCISCO: Bernardo?
> BERNARDO: He.
> FRANCISCO: You come most carefully upon your hour.
> BERNARDO: 'Tis now struck twelve; get thee to bed, Francisco.
> FRANCISCO: For this relief much thanks: 'tis bitter cold,
> And I am sick at heart.

A few minutes later, as the sun rises higher above the forest and screeching grey parrots swoop downriver, the hero appears:

> HAMLET: Angels and ministers of grace defend us!

It's an extraordinary idea – a fantasy worthy of a post-modern film-maker. But the story is true.

On 5 September 1607 *Hamlet* was performed on board the *Dragon*, anchored off the coast of Sierra Leone in West Africa. Among the audience were African dignitaries following a running paraphrase in Portuguese. The players did *Richard II*, too, further down the coast, before sailing on to India; unfortunately, there is no record of these Jacobean precursors of the 'Shakespeare Wallah' performing before the Great Moghul on his marble throne.

Last Phases: Burn-out or Retirement?

In his less exotic world on Bankside, since the building of the Globe, Shakespeare had enjoyed a period of wonderful creativity, through *Twelfth Night*, *Hamlet*, *Measure for Measure*, *Othello*, *Lear*, *Macbeth*, *Antony and Cleopatra* and *Coriolanus*. Between 1599 and 1606 he had written at least fourteen plays, among them some of the greatest works of literature. He was a man confident in his powers, responsive to the time and the art. He could write for the groundlings at the Globe and yet also find the right tone for the inns of court, for provincial town councils and for aristocratic houses, not to mention his royal patron.

But then comes a slowdown. As far as we know, Shakespeare was writing for another seven years after the summer of 1607. But in that time he wrote only three plays on his own, and four more with collaborators. The inference is that he ceased to do his two contracted pieces a year, and perhaps that he was beginning to phase himself out of writing for the stage altogether. Had he perhaps lost the fierce creative energy that had driven him to such spectacular results in the late 1590s and early 1600s? It is not that he was old: he was only forty-three in 1607, and still under fifty when he did his last work. Was he burnt out? Was this a long-planned retirement? Had Anne finally put her foot down? Or did he simply not want to work so hard? Realistically, this last is as good a guess as any.

Two of the late plays, *The Winter's Tale* and *The Tempest*, are among his masterpieces. A new kind of drama blending comedy, romance and tragedy, and featuring music very prominently, they represent no diminution of his talent. Nor do they look as if they were written simply to fulfil a contract, as some of his lesser plays do. Their language is the extension and culmination

of what is, by now, his very personal style (on which he had mocked himself ruefully in Sonnet 76 – why does *everything* I write always sound like *me*?). In addition, their themes of forgiveness, reconciliation and redemption touch on some of his most characteristic concerns, which hark right back to early works, such as *The Comedy of Errors*. In short, the plays still look like writing to satisfy an inner need.

LONDON: THE DEATH OF BROTHER EDMUND

Performing those plays continued as ever, despite the by now all too familiar severity of the winter. Christmas 1607 was bitter, with heavy snowfalls, and the Thames froze over. The agile turned arabesques on skates of bone and wood, while out-of-work boatmen crowded round the braziers at the hot chestnut stalls below Overy Stairs. The King's Men performed at court on 26, 27 and 28 December, and, despite the cold, probably played the Globe on the afternoon of the 31st. That morning, however, some of them had attended the funeral in Southwark of Shakespeare's younger brother, Edmund.

Of the poet's siblings, Joan had stayed in Stratford, married a local hatter and lived modestly all her life in the familiar surroundings of Henley Street.

BELOW: *A frost fair on the frozen Thames. The 1607 freeze provoked a holiday mood: one woman had sex on the ice 'so she could say she had got a child on old Father Thames!'*

Gilbert was now forty-one: a haberdasher, he divided his life between London and Stratford, just like William. Of Richard, who would have been thirty-two at this time, there is little trace. But Edmund, the youngest, had followed William to London and on to the stage as an actor. In 1607 he was living close to Silver Street in the Cripplegate area, where that summer he had buried an illegitimate infant son, Edward. He was only twenty-seven when he died. The register at St Saviour's notes a payment of 20 shillings for the funeral, with 'the ringing of the great bell': clearly an expensive ceremony when one could purchase a basic funeral for 2 shillings. Someone cared, and it was probably Edmund's rich and famous eldest brother.

Pericles: Old Fable into New Genre

After the service, on his way out of the church, Shakespeare would have passed the tomb of the fifteenth-century poet John Gower. In the literary world of Jacobean London Gower was old hat, but Shakespeare clearly had a soft spot for his poetry. Perhaps it was the kind of thing he had loved from his childhood. At any rate, the next extraordinary shift in Shakespeare's artistic career was to take Gower's old tale of Prince Pericles of Tyre and turn it into a new kind of play, influenced by the current fashion for masques but harking back to the romantic fables of fifteenth-century Catholic England.

Pericles is a romantic fairy tale, a morality play in which good triumphs mysteriously over evil, in which husbands are reunited with their lost wives and parents with their lost children; it depicts a world in which gods still appear and the miraculous can still happen. This antique air is deliberately accentuated by bringing old John Gower on stage as the narrator, speaking comically old-fashioned choruses in an affectionate parody of himself, which helps lend the whole tale the wide-eyed air of a childhood fable.

By May 1608 Shakespeare had written and staged *Pericles*, which introduces us to the magnificent verse and magical phrasing of his late period:

> A terrible childbed hast thou had, my dear;
> No light, no fire: the unfriendly elements
> Forgot thee utterly; nor have I time
> To give thee hallow'd to thy grave, but straight
> Must cast thee, scarcely coffin'd, in the ooze;
> Where, for a monument upon thy bones,
> And aye-remaining lamps, the belching whale
> And humming water must o'erwhelm thy corpse,
> Lying with simple shells.

The imagery behind this is Christian, although it comes from a pagan source. It announces the great theme of the last plays: redemption through the divine, and through nature and children. That February his first grandchild, Susanna's daughter Elizabeth, was born. Was the proud grandfather in Stratford on the 21st for the christening? In any event, daughters and babies would loom large in his last plays.

ABOVE: *The 1608 novel of* Pericles *showing the narrator Gower and perhaps implying that this is a picture of the stage show. Could it be Shakespeare himself?*

Not surprisingly, *Pericles* has been seen by some as tinged with Catholic imagery. In fact, Shakespeare was ever the sponge, soaking up tales, metaphors and thought worlds and blending and interweaving them to create something of his own. The play appealed to Catholics, to be sure, but also to James's court. Shakespeare still had a foot in both worlds psychologically: at the end the virgin goddess Diana of Ephesus appears on stage in a manner recalling the humanist allegories of the Virgin Mary but perhaps owing as much to the plot resolutions of Euripides, which Shakespeare certainly read in Latin:

> My temple stands in Ephesus: hie thee thither,
> And do upon mine altar sacrifice ....
> Awake and tell thy dream.

There are, however, problems with *Pericles*. The play was omitted from the collected works by Hemmings and Condell, which is surely telling us something. The first two Acts don't look like Shakespeare at all. Some have argued that he is writing a deliberately inept pastiche, but this seems hard to credit. The first part in fact was written by a Catholic hack, George Wilkins, who kept a tavern in Turnmill Street, the notorious brothel area in Clerkenwell by today's Farringdon Station. Wilkins had already written *The Miseries of Enforced Marriage* for Shakespeare's company, so he was in their pool of jobbers. An unsavoury character, separated from his long-suffering wife Margaret, he was involved in many court cases as a result of his violent and abusive behaviour to women. He knew the Mountjoys in Silver Street, and evidently knew Shakespeare himself; much has been made of this recently, suggesting that 'gentle Shakespeare' was a womanizing misogynist and habitué of brothels. Yet it seems hard to believe that the creator of Beatrice, Rosalind and Hermione was

a misogynist, even though he had been brought up in the male-dominated world of Tudor England and often sought patriarchal solutions in his plays. His ideal concept of love is held to the end, even though the ideal nuclear family has a poor record of success in his plays and is tortured almost to death on stage in *The Winter's Tale*.

Shakespeare was older now, of course, and marked by life. His last romances are characterized by redemptive mothers and daughters, but he adopts a puritanical view of the sexuality of his young heroines. The brothel scene in *Pericles* and its brutal male language are indeed horribly misogynistic, but surely this is intentional, to make his audiences feel disgust and identify with the purity of his heroine Marina. And in any case, it is by no means certain that Shakespeare formally collaborated with Wilkins, let alone had a close relationship with him. The last three Acts certainly contain some of his most affecting writing, and the scene in which the prince finally recognizes his lost daughter is one of the great moments in drama.

Pericles was a hit. A novel was even written as a spin-off, just as might happen today. To a world gradually being drained of a sense of the supernatural the play brought back a sense of enchantment, and its first audiences surely responded to that. Its imagery seeped into their psyche, stirring up half-forgotten tales, rituals, beliefs and feelings. Ever the prickly classicist Ben Jonson called *Pericles* a 'mouldy old tale', sneering at all these late romances as 'Tales, Tempests and other such Drolleries'. But then he was no doubt jealous: he didn't have Shakespeare's near-perfect talent for picking the right plot.

The Sonnets Published: 'Wretched Infidel Stuff'

Just a few months later, in August 1608, the theatres closed again because of a new outbreak of plague. They would not reopen until late 1609 or even early 1610, imposing a very long break in Shakespeare's professional career, which may have come at a significant time in his life. It was as good a reason as any to get out of town, and there is some evidence that Shakespeare left London soon afterwards. On 17 August 1608 he had a legal case coming to court in Stratford, which he may have attended in person. Then, in early September, his mother, now possibly in her seventies, died and was buried at Holy Trinity. The family's last link with the age of the Catholic Queen Mary had gone. On the 23rd, his sister Joan's son, Michael Hart, was christened, and on 16 October Shakespeare stood godfather to William Walker, the son of an old friend of his father who had become town bailiff the previous year. Godparenting was regarded as an important commitment, and Shakespeare would certainly have been present at the baptism.

But even though the theatres were shut and Shakespeare was perhaps now spending more time in the country, work from his hand was still forthcoming. On 20 May 1609 a new book was advertised in the Stationers' Register, to be published later that year. It was called *Shake-speares Sonnets*, to which the publisher, Thorpe, added on the title page 'Never before Imprinted', as if to suggest a frisson of notoriety. Inside, in often graphic detail, was the tale of the poet's beautiful boy and the Dark Lady. Despite many later critics' prudish hopes that the sonnets were pirated, the current consensus is that they were taken from Shakespeare's own manuscript and were published with his authorization. His friend Thomas Heywood says plainly that he published them in his own name, and Ben Jonson's friend Drummond later heard the same. This seems conclusive, even though Shakespeare seems not to have been around to supervise the proofreading.

So what had led him to publish these very personal and revealing poems more than ten years after most of them were written? It was surely not just to make a little money on the side, even though his main income, from the stage, had temporarily dried up. Although 'never before imprinted', some of the poems had long circulated among his 'private friends', who had admired at least the 'sugar'd' ones. And friends with true literary judgement must have seen that the poems, even the dark ones about lust, were great, and must have told him so. He knew himself how good they were (he knew that, he tells us, when he wrote them); and no doubt he had tinkered with them over the years, as he did with all his work, ordering them, shaping them into a more formed and 'literary' collection, playing teasingly with the autobiographical tale they seem to reveal. He knew he ought to publish them. The problem, of course, was the content.

Shakespeare, then, was responsible for the selection, punctuation, italicization, and, crucially, the order of the 154 sonnets, of which the last two are versions of the same one; 153 is the number of prayers in the Catholic rosary, and, although any relationship is distant (if anything, these are really a secular parody of the sacred), some numberings do shadow the old prayers he must have known as a child. The sonnets probably span a lengthy period and it is not possible to say how far they were revised as his plays were. Of the first 120 or so, many seem to have been written to the beautiful boy over several years; some, as we have seen, depict a love triangle, apparently with the boy and the poet's mistress;

Below: *'My God,' wrote seventeen-year-old George Herbert, an early reader of Shakespeare's poems, 'Doth Poetry Wear Venus livery? Only serve her turn? Why are not Sonnets made of thee?'*

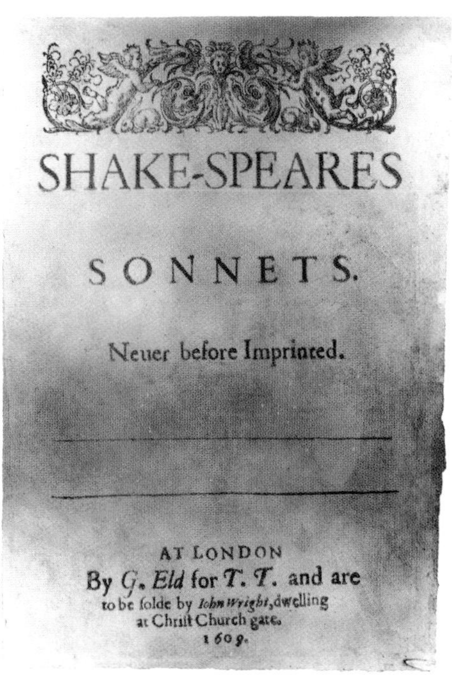
SHAKE-SPEARES

SONNETS.

Neuer before Imprinted.

AT LONDON
By G. Eld for T. T. and are
to be solde by *Iohn Wright*, dwelling
at Christ Church gate.
1609.

several are about the individual and politics; and the last group, the most unsparing in their depiction of physical passion, are to the Dark Lady (although there is no evidence of them ever being given to her – few women, one imagines, would have been pleased to receive such bitter verses). Placing them in a sequence that appears to constitute a single tale, he makes the sonnets end regretfully in the defeated poet-lover seeking love's remedial bath. He even slips in his marriage sonnet, 145, out of the way near the end. Whether the collection includes other poems to his wife, or to anyone else, has never been discerned. But the order is evidently his: who else would have given 'Full many a glorious morning', with its allusion to the death of Jesus, the number 33? Who else would have inserted his youthful sonnet to Anne between the strongly religious 144 and 146, with their visions of heaven and hell?

So how were the sonnets received by the reading public? The poems to the boy are unlikely to have seemed as scandalous then as they did to nineteenth-century readers, who wished he had never written them. The idea that they were pirated came from Victorian editors unwilling to take their ostensibly homosexual love at its face value. After all, in an age that criminalized homosexual acts – in the days of Wilde and Bosie – the 'gentle bard' would have been sentenced to hard labour. The real contemporary scandal, so modern scholars think, was the graphic portrayal of the sexual power of an independent and even predatory woman. Raw, self-lacerating, subverting the Petrarchan sonnet tradition by talking overtly about lust, erections and genitalia: even today, verse of such coarse sexuality from a leading poet might not go down well with the reviewers in some of the quality broadsheets. And, of course, the mainstream choice, and that of his anthologizers, is still 'Shall I compare thee to a summer's day' rather than 'Lust in action'.

The sonnets may not have sold too well. Shakespeare perhaps overestimated the open-mindedness of even his most discerning readers in 1609. 'Wretched infidel stuff,' scribbled one exasperated early reader. William Herbert's cousin George was dismayed by their mixture of religious imagery and explicit sexual content. And within a year, strangely enough, Emilia Lanier registered her own religious poems, which would be prefaced with a cry from the heart about men's abuse of women.

Prince Henry: A New Court Culture

Meanwhile, the world of the arts and patronage in London was changing fast. A new wave of style and taste was bringing about changes in the theatre as visible as the shift from the improvising clowns to the tragedians back in the 1590s. King James's fifteen-year-old son Prince Henry now announced his arrival on

ABOVE: *Imitating the chosen warrior of Arthurian legend, Prince Henry seizes Opportunity by the forelock, c. 1610.*

the public stage with his own court – a new arbiter of taste, who in his short life would pioneer what was almost England's lost Renaissance.

Under Elizabeth the country had been somewhat archaic in its culture, with a deeply nostalgic strain. Now the prince and his entrourage encouraged an influx of new ideas in art, music and literature. Henry was a great patron and collector, and Florentine artists, Dutch portrait painters and Italian architects were invited to London. English collectors began to visit Italy to collect classical sculpture;

copies were commissioned of the Uffizi series of panels that depicted famous figures in modern literature and the arts. At the centre was Henry's court, modelling itself on the great European Renaissance courts of the sixteenth century.

Henry was fascinated by the tradition of festivals at the Florentine Medici court, in which elaborate masques were seen as essential adjuncts of princely magnificence. Huge resources were now put into such spectacles to dramatize the ideals of the New Age 'so that the World might know, what a brave prince they were like to enjoy'. These shows needed authors of real erudition, and Ben Jonson, who was already a writer of royal masques, now rose to prominence, with the architect Inigo Jones responsible for set and costume design. In summer 1609 a series of lavish entertainments was staged for the investiture of Henry as Prince of Wales, and it seems that Shakespeare's *Cymbeline* was specifically written for this occasion. Long and intricate, it is a play of its time with its allusions to royal myths, its masque-like devices and its courtly nonsense. Its plot twists are so silly that Shakespeare has to send himself up to get away with them – though no doubt that made his royal and noble patrons laugh too. But all the same, the play carried a serious point. It is about British myths and Virgilian prophecies: Cymbeline lived at the time of Christ; and the plot is resolved by a landing at Milford Haven, mirroring Henry Tudor's arrival by ship at the same auspicious place before his defeat of Richard III at Bosworth, which inaugurated the Tudor dynasty. So a Roman version of the Tudor advent myth makes a bizarre foretelling of James's united Christian Britannia.

'Sacred Things Must Needs Be Wrapped in Fable and Enigma'

But the different uses to which Shakespeare's drama could be put are dramatically revealed in a case that ended up in the Court of Star Chamber. While *Cymbeline* was getting laughs in Whitehall, up in the wilds of Yorkshire a local acting company founded by Sir Richard Cholmeley was playing to very different audiences. Formed around a local family of artisans, the Simpsons of North Egmont, near Whitby, this was a travelling company of thirteen men and two boys who worked in the north for the last fifteen years of Shakespeare's life. They found an audience in most towns in the shire and played at a dozen or so great houses every year, acting one or more plays and staying a night or two in each place. But they were a Catholic company.

Towards Christmas 1609 these strolling players performed at Sir John and Dame Julian Yorke's house at Gowthwaite in Nidderdale, where government informers reported a scandal. That night a comic 'interlude' had taken place: during a disputation between a 'popish priest' and an English minister the

Left: *Wonderful costumes like this were created for masques in which nobles like the Herberts performed. 'Such things are but toys,' wrote Francis Bacon, though he too was prepared to spend a fortune – £2000 on a single show – to impress the king.*

Protestant had been humiliated and hauled off stage by the devil, leaving an angel holding the hand of the priest. The play, it was asserted, had been wildly applauded – the audience had 'mocked and derided' the state religion. As a result the Lord Chief Justice declared the Yorkes guilty of defamatory libel and fined the couple the enormous sum of £1000 each, Sir John's brothers £350 apiece, and the small audience of local friends collectively £300. The extraordinary thing about this story is that the interludes on the Cholmley players' tour were merely satirical burlesques in between the main entertainment, which consisted of full-length plays: *King Lear* and *Pericles*.

The investigators interviewed the actors, among them the labourer William Harrison, who said that in their stagings of Shakespeare they had 'acted from printed books and nothing was added'. So these were what the censor called the 'allowed texts', the printed Quartos of the plays published over 1608–9. The playing of *Pericles* before Catholic audiences is especially interesting because it also appears soon afterwards in a booklist at the English Jesuit College at St Omer in France, where such plays were performed by the students in full costume with scenery. It sounds as if *Pericles* was seen as some kind of mystery play or saints' play in which Shakespeare explored the themes of patience and redemption. How far people saw Christian allegory in it is another matter, but, coupled with the overt themes of purity and corruption, the epiphany of the virgin goddess Diana of Ephesus is particularly striking. The German Protestant Martin Luther had condemned 'those who would turn Diana into the Virgin Mary', whereas Christian humanists had argued that Jupiter, Apollo, Diana, Christ and Mary were but names for the many powers of the 'one god and one goddess'. 'Sacred things must needs be wrapped in fable and enigma,' wrote one sixteenth-century humanist. 'But for you, since Jupiter, the best and greatest god, is propitious to you, when I say Jupiter, understand me to mean Christ and the true God.'

In this light the apparition of Jupiter in *Cymbeline* and of Diana in *Pericles*, or the thunder of Apollo's oracle in *The Winter's Tale*, take on a tantalizing ambiguity, the meanings of which we can no longer pin down. Shakespeare's last plays are a radical remix of ideas in which almost anything goes: tragedy and comedy, high life and low life, rhetoric and street language, the sacred and the profane, ritual and riot. And in this new world of words, he is trying to work in ideas about religion in the broadest sense. Or perhaps we should say the concepts *behind* religion – love, redemption, the soul. By now we are a long way from the mystery plays: but at times in the dramaturgy, the symbolism and even the language of his late plays, we feel as if we have come full circle. God could no longer be named on stage, so use the gods. And again, these do not look like the habits of mind of a Protestant.

Coincidence or not, it was now that the historian John Speed revived his attack on Shakespeare for the Oldcastle slanders, linking him with the Jesuit Robert Persons as 'the papist and his poet'. Although this comment was made specifically in reference to that controversy, it may carry a wider implication. Were there still people who felt that Shakespeare had not abandoned the spirit world of his ancestors, the old English world of pre-Reformation Christianity? Indeed, as late at the Civil War, a generation on, radical pamphleteers would lump his plays in with the sort of 'prelatical trash' read by seminarians and royalist crypto-Catholics. Apollo or no Apollo, they knew a hawk from a handsaw.

Writing for Blackfriars: The Move to an Indoor Theatre

When the theatres finally reopened the King's Men found themselves with not only the Globe but a new indoor theatre too, which offered Shakespeare major new artistic challenges. The Burbages, it will be remembered, had first obtained the lease on the Blackfriars in 1596, hoping to pioneer a comfortable, warm, indoor theatre with artificial lighting, only to fail to get planning permission and be forced to sublet. Bad winters (and most of them were) hit takings at the draughty Globe very badly; as Jonson said in *Poetaster*: 'this winter has made us all poorer than so many starved snakes; nobody comes at us'. Then after several frustrating years, in August 1608 they had recovered the Blackfriars. The winter of 1609–10, with the plague at last at bay, was therefore their first opportunity to use the venue, and they formed a new group of shareholders, who included Shakespeare, Hemmings, Condell and Sly.

The theatre stood in a fashionable district on the opposite side of the Thames a couple of hundred yards from St Paul's, and since the streets round about were stone-laid, it was accessible to playgoers even in the worst weather. The neighbours were a cut above those in Southwark. The Royal Wardrobe was next door, the Master of the Revels near by. The Cobhams and the Hunsdons, court officials and the royal treasurer, were among the important figures who had houses and gardens in or near the old monastic buildings.

The Blackfriars monastery, which had been dissolved by Henry VIII, occupied a plot 125 yards square with a large garden, all now divided up and leased out by property developers. On the west wall the Apothecaries' hall butted on to Water Lane; to the east, on St Andrew's Hill, was the Royal Wardrobe; to the north lay Shoemakers' Row and Carter Lane, the latter with its famous coaching inns, the Mermaid and the Bell, where the poet's Stratford friends stayed. To the south a series of lanes led down a hundred yards to the river and the water taxis at Blackfriars stairs.

The theatre had been constructed in the old frater of the monastic

buildings. It was quite a small space, only 46 feet wide by 66 long; but the very high ceiling accommodated two galleries for spectators, and it was lit by big candelabra hanging over the stage. The setting was intimate in size and acoustics, and beautiful lighting effects were possible. A contemporary poem remarks on the frisson of the 'torchy Friars' – heady entertainment for Temple lawyers before a meal of caviar, oysters and artichokes, and then a boat over to the more visceral entertainments of Bankside.

The intention was to use the Blackfriars as the company's winter home and the Globe in the summer. The new theatre would prove a great investment: although it had fewer seats, it attracted a posh audience and was twice as profitable to shareholders as the Globe. A city financier claimed in 1612 that the King's Men 'got, and yet doth, more in one winter in the said great hall by a thousand pounds than they were used to get on the Bankside'.

This was probably true, and was certainly resented. Constantly over the next twenty or thirty years 'persons of honor and quality' among the neighbours petitioned to close it on the grounds of rowdiness, fire risk and obstruction. At showtime, they complained, the streets around Ludgate were so clogged with theatregoers and 'heckney-coaches' that 'inhabitants cannot come to their houses, nor bring in their necessary provisions of beer, wood, coal or hay, nor the tradesmen or shopkeepers utter their wares, nor the passenger go to the common water stairs without danger of their lives and limbs'. These inconveniences were said to last 'every day in the winter time from one or two of the clock till six at night'. But Shakespeare and friends now had 'persons of honor and quality' to support them, too, and the Blackfriars stayed open. It would see the last great phase of the poet's career, when his final masterpieces were written with the indoor theatre in mind, with the magical effects in music, lighting and staging that it offered.

Second Thoughts: Rewriting Lear

The Blackfriars demanded a different approach to dramaturgy, staging and scripting. A fresh look at the whole repertoire was called for: plays that had long been shown in the huge and rowdy open-air theatres needed editing, cutting and restaging. All this reminds us that Shakespeare's texts were not fixed but developed over time, and probably had done so since the start. *Love's Labour's Lost*, for example, had been published 'newly corrected and augmented' back in the 1590s. No fewer than sixteen of his plays are known only through the Folio text published after his death, so their textual history is a blank. The rest all show signs of revision. Some are very short and may have been cut, like *Macbeth*. Others reveal careful reworking, which may have been done with the Blackfriars in mind.

It would appear that *King Lear* was rewritten for the indoor stage in the winter of 1609–10, although there is still some argument about this. A minority think the revision took place after Shakespeare's death; others have suggested that some changes were made to appease the censor. Censorship certainly played its part, but some of the differences between the 1608 and 1623 versions are hard to account for in any other way than as authorial. For example, Shakespeare cut the mock trial of Regan and Goneril: a good scene, but one that he perhaps felt held up the action. He also cut the magical awakening of Lear by music: beautiful, but verging too close to romance, maybe, in such a stark play. He reshaped some of the roles, especially Edgar and Albany – obviously he had watched the show with an audience many times and knew which bits worked best, just as a modern director and author will do today. But most interesting of all is his revision of the last scene.

This is what was published in the 1608 Quarto. The passage begins with Lear holding the body of his daughter Cordelia. It is not quite clear whether the first line refers to her, and it is open to interpretation in performance:

LEAR: And my poor fool is hanged. No, no life.
Why should a dog, a horse, a rat have life,
And thou no breath at all? O, thou wilt come no more.
Never, never, never. Pray you, undo
This button. Thank you, sir. O, O ,O, O!
EDGAR: He faints. My lord, my lord.
LEAR: Break, heart, I prithee break. [*Dies*]

In the later Folio text, Shakespeare has rewritten the passage in this way:

LEAR: And my poor fool is hanged. No, no, no life.
Why should a dog, a horse, a rat have life,
And thou no breath at all? Thou'lt come no more.
Never, never, never, never, never.
Pray you, undo this button. Thank you, sir.
Do you see this? Look on her, look, her lips,
Look there, look there. [*He dies*]
EDGAR: He faints. My lord, my lord.
KENT: Break, heart, I prithee break.

Here's a fascinating opportunity to watch Shakespeare putting a red pen through his own work after experiencing how it affects the audience. There are

several things to note about his changes, not least the rejigging to give the extraordinary single-line iambic pentameter with 'never' repeated five times. The 'break my heart' line of Lear is now given to Kent. But especially significant is the difference in the way he treats Lear's death. The Quarto simply gives us Lear's desperate desire to cease to be since Cordelia is dead. The Folio substitutes an ambiguity: it is impossible to determine from the text whether Lear dies from a broken heart through grief, or from a flood of joy at thinking his child is still alive. In performance the actor and director can go either way, or leave the audience unsure. Shakespeare pinpoints the focus of the action by shifting the stage direction to make him die on 'look there'.

The simplest addition comes a few lines later, in the final speech. In the first, Quarto version the speech is given to the Earl of Albany; now it is given to Edgar, the young son of old Gloucester. Albany is the senior character now that Lear is dead; he is left in power. But Edgar is the one who has gone through the sufferings of the play; the Christian knight, as it were, who has been hunted down and reduced to a 'naked unaccommodated man', he has seen the horrors and survived. The audience's emotional identification is with him.

> EDGAR: The weight of this sad time we must obey:
> Speak what we feel, not what we ought to say.
> The oldest hath borne most: we that are young
> Shall never see so much, nor live so long.

Edgar's words might stand for the experience of all those who had gone through the fires of the Reformation and Counter-Reformation, but also, on a bigger plane, of all those who have suffered at any time at the hands of tyranny and cruelty. This is why the play – deemed in the eighteenth and nineteenth centuries unperformable unless adulterated – has spoken perhaps most powerfully to the generations who have lived through the horrors of the twentieth century.

Musical Collaboration: Robert Johnson

The Blackfriars made Shakespeare rethink his art in other ways, too. Particularly interesting is the changed role of music in his last plays. There are hints of this in the first version of *King Lear*, and in *Antony and Cleopatra* in the heavenly music heard by Antony. But now the tastes of the Blackfriars audience would be more fully catered to. These tastes had long been established by the children's companies, whose shows included an hour's music before the play, during which boys 'sang so delightfully cum voce tremula to the accompaniment of a bass-viol, so lovely that it could not be equalled'. This kind of thing had been one of the

big draws at the Blackfriars in the recent past, before the King's Men took it over. Shakespeare was quick to take the idea and run with it, in particular using music offstage as an accompaniment to the action. In late 1609 he teamed up with a twenty-six-year-old court lutenist called Robert Johnson, related, as virtually all court and theatre musicians were, to the great Italian musical families the Ferraboscos and Bassanos. His kinswoman Margaret Johnson, who had married one of the Bassano brothers, was the mother of Emilia Lanier. Johnson belongs to a group of English composers that emerged around 1609 and developed a more declamatory style of song for the stage, a style essentially dramatic and strikingly different from the 'ayres' of John Dowland and his contemporaries. Working for the special conditions of court masques and public plays, especially in the indoor theatre at the Blackfriars, they emphasized speech rhythms and inflections, chordal harmonies and psychology: with Johnson the song takes on the atmosphere of its dramatic context. He is reported to have said that it was his intention to 'marry the words and Notes wel together'. To achieve this aim he evidently worked alongside his authors, and the result is a series of theatre songs closely tied to the action. Some, such as the haunting 'Full fathom five' from *The Tempest* and the sinister 'Howl, howl' from Webster's *The Duchess of Malfi*, have beautiful settings. Johnson's music has now been identified in *The Winter's Tale*, *The Tempest* and *Cymbeline*; among other commissions he composed the music for Shakespeare's collaborations with John Fletcher in *Cardenio*, *Henry VIII* and *The Two Noble Kinsmen*.

Ben Jonson Returns

It was during this excitingly creative time that Ben Jonson came back to the company. Some of his best shows, among them *Volpone* and *The Alchemist*, were written for the King's Men at the Blackfriars; and the company's Christmas repertoires at court over the next few years usually included Jonson's plays. Jonson was a big fish now that he and Inigo Jones had cornered the masque market, and, having acquired the status and credit he desired, he would make a long career of it.

So Shakespeare had the pleasure of working with his old rival again, even if he no longer trod the boards speaking Jonson's lines. Their relationship had clearly lost none of its edge – with Jonson nothing was ever forgotten. In his printed prefaces he rehearses his old grouses; he perhaps lampoons Shakespeare as Lovewhit in *Volpone*; and he still lets it be known that he thinks Shakespeare's recent work (*Pericles* in particular) is not what a serious dramatist should be up to. Shakespeare in turn would drop in-jokes into his plays for Jonson's benefit, and would later plot *The Tempest* in exact conformity with the classical unities

of time and place (the action takes place in a single location over a mere three hours), as if just to show his old friend that he too could follow the rule book if he really had to. Their relationship, however, was characterized by affection as well as rivalry, as is evident from Jonson's posthumous tribute in the Folio, in which he spoke what he knew in his heart. 'I loved him this side idolatry,' he says; but admits that Shakespeare had surpassed even the ancients, Sophocles and Euripides:

> Soul of the age!
> The applause, delight, the wonder of our stage ...
>
> ... And all the muses still were in their prime
> When like Apollo he came forth to warm
> Our ears, or like a Mercury to charm!

'Great Creating Nature'

The poet's late output points up the contrast between court and country. This comes out most strongly in *The Winter's Tale*, which he probably wrote in the winter and spring of 1609–10 to be performed at the Globe in the summer season starting in May. Writers of the time equated 'winter's tales' with old wives' tales – scarcely believable romantic fables. In a wonderfully karmic twist, for this show Shakespeare adapted a pulp novel, *Pandosto*, by his old rival Robert Greene, who had sneered at him as a 'Shake-scene' and a 'tiger's heart' nearly twenty years before. The play marks an imaginative return to rural roots with clowns, sheep fairs, pickpockets and old shepherds; and it takes some sarcastic swipes at courtly affectations, 'courtly smell, and ... courtly contempt'. The country scenes feel as if they were inspired in part by Stratford, right down to the specialist vocabulary from the wool trade.

The Winter's Tale mixes incredible resourcefulness of language with the simplest of structures. The plot represents everything Ben Jonson was denigrating in his jibe about Shakespeare's 'Tales, Tempests and other such Drolleries'. In a precipitously tragic first two Acts, King Leontes destroys his family through jealousy; his only son dies, his baby daughter is cast into the wilds, and he believes his wife has died of grief. Sixteen years later redemption comes when, as Apollo's oracle required, 'that which is lost [is] found'. The subject is time's destructive and redeeming powers, a theme also central to the sonnets.

There is a fascinating stylistic split in *The Winter's Tale*. The first two Acts are full of the most angry, aggressive language expressing sexual jealousy,

with repellent imagery of the stews (Leontes' wife, he says, has been 'sluic'd'). Great writers at the end of their lives often play freely with language, and Shakespeare's is now at its most demanding and rewarding. Here Leontes believes his wife is pregnant by his best friend:

> Too hot, too hot!
> To mingle friendship far is mingling bloods.
> I have *tremor cordis* on me, – my heart dances;
> But not for joy, – not joy ....

There follows a succession of rippling speeches that, within the constraints of ten-beat lines, magically conjure the free association of a paranoid mind obsessed by sexual jealousy:

> Inch-thick, knee-deep, o'er head and ears a fork'd one! –
> Go, play, boy, play: – thy mother plays, and I
> Play too; but so disgrac'd a part, whose issue
> Will hiss me to my grave: contempt and clamour
> Will be my knell. – Go, play, boy, play. – There have been,
> Or I am much deceiv'd, cuckolds ere now;
> And many a man there is, even at this present,
> Now while I speak this, holds his wife by the arm,
> That little thinks she has been sluic'd in his absence,
> And his pond fish'd by his next neighbour, by
> Sir Smile, his neighbour ....

The punctuation gets freer and freer, suggesting a mind falling over itself with horrible imaginings.

> Most dear'st! my collop! – Can thy dam? – may't be?
> Affection! thy intention stabs the centre:
> Thou dost make possible things not so held,
> Communicat'st with dreams; – how can this be? –
> With what's unreal thou co-active art,
> And fellow'st nothing: Then 'tis very credent
> Thou may'st co-join with something; and thou dost, –
> And that beyond commission; and I find it, –
> And that to the infection of my brains
> And hardening of my brows.

As with *King Lear*, we wonder how he wrote this – the rhythms, the associative chains, the violent metaphors, the mix of controlled Latinisms ('credent', 'co-active') with earthy vernacular ('collop', 'dam'). Was it alone late at night? With drink?

It contrasts strongly with the rest of the play, which concerns Leontes' redemption by his daughter, Perdita, who represents the healing power of romantic sexual love. With her language Shakespeare brings into play all his old lyric skills and, of course, takes from his beloved Ovid. He draws on the tale of Persephone and Pluto's chariot (though Shakespeare uses the Roman equivalents Proserpina and Dis), the classical myth of spring coming to the earth with which the young Perdita identifies. Despite the rather puritanical attitude to the sexuality of young women, typical of him at this stage, Perdita has an instinctive feeling for pure sexual joy and a oneness with 'great creating nature':

> PERDITA: O Proserpina,
> For the flowers now, that, frighted, thou lett'st fall
> From Dis's waggon! – daffodils,
> That come before the swallow dares, and take
> The winds of March with beauty; violets dim,
> But sweeter than the lids of Juno's eyes
> Or Cytherea's breath; pale primroses,
> That die unmarried ere they can behold
> Bright Phoebus in his strength, – a malady
> Most incident to maids; bold oxlips, and
> The crown-imperial; lilies of all kinds,
> The flower-de-luce being one! – O, these I lack,
> To make you garlands of; and, my sweet friend,
> To strew him o'er and o'er!
> FLORIZEL: What, like a corpse?
> PERDITA: No; like a bank for love to lie and play on ....

This is all drawing on the mainstream of classical poetry and the Neo-Platonic themes that run through Renaissance art.

A third stylistic contrast is the rogue Autolycus, 'son of Mercury', pick-pocket, tinker, and balladeer; mercurial, earthy, a man who cares nothing for the soul, preferring gambling and whores ('die and drab') and who says so in vigorous prose:

> My traffic is sheets; when the kite builds, look to lesser linen. My father named me Autolycus; who being, as I am, littered under Mercury,

> was likewise a snapper-up of unconsidered trifles. With die and drab I purchased this caparison; and my revenue is the silly-cheat: gallows and knock are too powerful on the highway; beating and hanging are terrors to me; for the life to come, I sleep out the thought of it ....

The countryman of Launce and 'Henry Carre with his pedlar's pack' in the Warwick town book, Autolycus is a man who knows 'court contempt'. He sings country songs about daffodils and larks, and gives sales pitches in Elizabethan rap ('come to the pedlar, money's a meddler'). A man who would cheerfully rob you and 'do you in', he is imaginatively the necessary snake in Perdita's garden:

> Pins and poking-sticks of steel,
> What maids lack from head to heel.

Tonally, the jagged syntax of 'Inch-thick', the Ovidian lyricism of 'O Proserpina' and Autolycus's bawdy swagger show Shakespeare at his widest-ranging. This is total mastery. Nobody had taken the English language further, and nobody has done so since. And he performs his old tricks, too, above all in the daring scene where Leontes, still stricken by grief and guilt sixteen years on from the family catastrophe, recovers his wife and child in that strange, affecting, yet not entirely happy ending, when the 'statue' of his wife (whom he thinks dead) comes alive like an alabaster effigy on a Jacobean monument suddenly rising from the tomb.

The statue story hints at Italian art and the sculpture galleries created by collectors such as the Earl of Arundel – all very current in 1610 with the Italian connections of Prince Henry's court. But a fascinating analogue for this scene has recently been discovered in a play published in 1605, in which, curiously enough, one of the romantic leads is an Earl of Pembroke. In *The Trial of Chivalry*, two close male friends fight over a lady, after which each thinks the other to be dead. Here, too, a statue is supposed to have been made of the dead lover ('A cunning carver cut out thy shape in white alabaster') so that prayers may be offered daily at its feet. In the climax the lover pretends to be the statue and is reunited with his lady: the one clear contemporary instance of a statue that comes alive on stage, and one that Shakespeare might well have seen.

Love and Resurrection

And last of all there is the psychology of it: what are we to make of the death of the young son and the rediscovery of the wife and daughter after so many years? The tale is in his source, but we may still wonder why Shakespeare chose this

particular story, and why he chose to tell it in the way he did. And in the statue scene, what is he thinking of? For a seventeenth-century viewer it had a clear religious undertow with an unmistakably Catholic resonance. Leontes is led by Paulina through a sculpture galley into what suddenly becomes a chapel. Given the touchy nature of proceedings for a Jacobean audience, Shakespeare carefully has Paulina insist that she is not assisted by 'wicked powers', that what will happen is 'holy', and that her actions are 'lawful'.

> It is requir'd
> You do awake your faith. Then all stand still;
> Or those that think it is unlawful business
> I am about, let them depart ....
> Music, awake her: strike! –
> 'Tis time; descend; be stone no more;
> approach;
> Strike all that look upon with marvel. Come;
> I'll fill your grave up: stir; nay, come away:
> Bequeath to death your numbness, for from him
> Dear life redeems you ....

The language, it need hardly be stressed, is religious. This is precisely the kind of 'prelatical trash' that Protestant radicals of the Civil War generation saw in Shakespeare. The scene brings together all the great themes of his late plays: reconciliation; recognition; redemption through children, through 'great creating nature', and through 'the gods'. He is reaching beyond realism, indeed beyond the insufficiencies of art itself, for things that were once the preserve of religion – ideas of love and resurrection.

But is the subtext actually religious? Or is Shakespeare, with his chameleon-like empathy, still doing what he does best – quarrying any thought or image system that serves his purpose and piecing together his borrowings to produce high-churchy art for a court (with a Catholic queen) that liked that kind of tone? The psychology is in the end impossible to pin down, and an analyst would have a field day trying to untangle it. On one level it is a rattling good yarn that 'should be hooted at like an old tale' – lost babies, storms, a bear, comedy, songs – which ends happily ever after, give or take a few deaths and a weight of loss and guilt that cannot quite be lifted. On another level, as modern audiences have rediscovered, its final image of a wounded family reunited after so many years makes it one of his most powerful and moving plays.

CHAPTER SIXTEEN
Tempests Are Kind

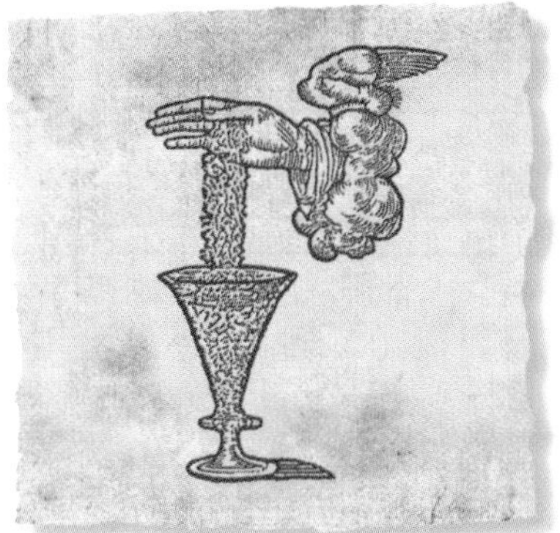

SATIS (ENOUGH)

The autumn of 1610 was rainy, and, as usual, the Oxford road would have been thick with mud. On 22 November Sir Dudley Digges MP, brother of Shakespeare's friend Leonard, the poet and translator, rode to Warwickshire to visit friends. Here was a man for the new age. Founder of the first national lottery, and a passionate patron of exploration, he had raised money to fund Henry Hudson's voyage to discover the Northwest Passage; with William Herbert and the Globe trustee William Leveson he was a member of the Council of the Virginia Company; he had even tried to drum up interest in an expedition to the North Pole. But now Digges was on his way to Aldington, just outside Stratford, to stay with his stepfather, Thomas Russell, a close and trusted friend of Shakespeare's, who would be the executor of the poet's will. So it was a good occasion for a meeting of old friends. And that November, as the fire burned low at Aldington, Digges told an extraordinary tale of shipwreck and survival, a tale to set the imagination afire. Shakespeare would turn it into his last masterpiece.

'SUPERIOR NOVELTIES' IN A FAST-CHANGING WORLD

By the time *The Winter's Tale* was staged in the summer season of 1610 at the Globe, Shakespeare was forty-six and had ceased to act. Christmas that year saw the usual exhausting run of fifteen plays at court. Still a shareholder in the company, Shakespeare was now writing very little, except revisions, although perhaps playing a role as executive producer, script supervisor and editor for the young playwrights Francis Beaumont and John Fletcher, who were taking over as principal writers.

Times had changed. The world of the poet's childhood in the late 1560s and early 1570s was a memory. Despite being, in our terms, only in early middle age, he was an old Elizabethan now. And how fast the world was changing. To the survivors of his parents' generation, the days of Queen Mary must have felt like another age. There was now a younger generation who saw England's Catholic past as not their own, but as that of another country. For them these were times not for looking back, but for looking forward to expanding horizons; it was an age of exploration in the macrocosm and the microcosm. The royal physician William Harvey, now working at St Bartholomew's Hospital by Smithfield, would soon propound his theory of the circulation of the blood. Henry Wotton's dispatch of March 1610 to King James from Italy told of the great astronomical discoveries that Galileo had made with the newly invented telescope. Everywhere was full of the news of these 'superior novelties'.

It has long been part of the myth of Shakespeare's biography that he made his farewell in *The Tempest*: it represents the journey home, the comforting idea that after all the storms he returns to his garden and has a last few happy years in retirement, the great soul at peace. Yet we have no evidence for his state of mind at this moment, and strictly speaking *The Tempest* was not his last play, for three collaborations followed. Nonetheless, it was his last work as sole author; and it seems to have been written at the time when evidence from a London court case establishes his address as Stratford-upon-Avon. And for a writer as intelligent, and as conscious of the illusion of theatre, as he was, it is hardly possible that an autobiographical edge to the plot was not in his mind. If *The Tempest* didn't exist, we would have had to invent it.

Deposed Dukes

A tale of shipwreck, sea changes and metamorphoses, *The Tempest* is a fable of redemption through children. It is also the tale of a Renaissance magus, Duke Prospero of Milan, who, having found more consolation in his library, neglected his duties and was overthrown by his enemies and exiled on a magical island. The plot stands out as one of the few that Shakespeare made up rather than borrowed. But several texts went into it, and they give us a fascinating glimpse into the bold and playful sweep of his imagination at the end of his career.

For example, in an anthology of modern Italian poets by Toscano, a book known in Jacobean England, he seems to have come across poems about, and by, a real-life Duke Prospero of Milan. A man 'possessed of great knowledge, the most versed in the universal understanding of history', this Prospero 'had a most noble and most extensive library where could be found books in all the

sciences'. The lines about the duke 'on whose dynasty the goddess Fortuna once smiled', but who was now deposed, closely shadow Shakespeare's tale:

> Now the wheel of Fortune has turned
> Oh hateful villainy! Their power into the abyss.
> But you Prospero, of that noble line of Dukes, the Muses
> Serve, the most noble of all occupations
> So despite the constant turning and changing of
> Impious Fortuna, she could not deprive you of your dignity.

Perhaps the story lodged in his magpie memory: 'My library was dukedom large enough ... volumes I prize above my Dukedom,' says Shakespeare's Prospero as he tells the story of his exile from Milan.

The plot of the play is simple. Duke Prospero lives on the island of his exile with his teenage daughter. Through his books he possesses magical and occult powers and can control the nature-spirit of the island, Ariel, and its brutish inhabitant, Caliban. When the play opens, the enemies who long ago deposed him have sailed away to a distant wedding and on their return voyage are wrecked on the island in a magically conjured tempest. (The storm as an emblem of Fortuna was a staple Renaissance theme, from Giorgione's great painting to engravings by Hollar and the emblem books that Shakespeare read and used, for example, in *Pericles*.)

Thus far, it could almost have been a revenge play. Prospero is a control freak, with lots of bottled-up aggression, and wants to take revenge on his enemies. But then he forgives them, and reconciliation takes place through the marriage of his daughter to the son of his enemy. That accomplished, the magician throws away his supernatural gifts as 'plotter' and stage manager, a magus of words and magic.

Like the other late plays, the tale also touches on contemporary concerns. The story of a deposed duke was current news in the summer of 1611 when the play was first shown: the overthrow of the scholarly Rudolph of Prague had aroused great interest in London. But in the writing, one text seems to have been especially important – not narrowly as a source, but as a wide inspiration – and it was another favourite from his schooldays.

Shadow Texts: Virgil

The Tempest is usually seen as related to the New World, especially in modern anti-colonial interpretations. But it is really a Mediterranean play. Its shadow text is Virgil's *Aeneid*, as Shakespeare tells us very clearly in Act II. The nobles who deposed Prospero are on their way back from Tunis to Naples – the same route Aeneas takes after his fateful encounter with Dido of Carthage. This we learn from a mysterious and seemingly irrelevant exchange between the perplexed survivors of the shipwreck:

> ADRIAN: Tunis was never graced before with such a paragon to their queen.
> GONZALO: Not since widow Dido's time.
> ANTONIO: Widow? a pox o' that! How came that widow in? Widow Dido!
> SEBASTIAN: What if he had said, widower Aeneas too? good lord, how you take it!
> ADRIAN: Widow Dido, said you? you make me study of that: She was of Carthage, not of Tunis.
> GONZALO: This Tunis, sir, was Carthage.
> ADRIAN: Carthage?
> GONZALO: I assure you, Carthage.

In the mouth of Gonzalo, the honest old counsellor, Shakespeare is letting us know that our guide is Virgil. In the *Aeneid* his hero landed on an island where rites of purification take place and he is released from the burden of guilt for his past deeds. And Shakespeare's play essentially follows Virgil in its pivotal scenes: the wreck, the ordeal of Ferdinand, the vision of the gods, the purgation and the marriage. The wrongdoers will achieve understanding and be purified, hatred will be overcome and reconciliation will take place. Shakespeare's audience, especially at the Blackfriars, would have got the point straightaway, for they were more versed in Latin literature than we are today.

'A Dreadfull Storm and Hedeous'

So *The Tempest* is a quintessential Renaissance transformation of a great classical theme. But although the setting is in the Mediterranean, Shakespeare, magpie-like as always, uses contemporary anthropological literature on the New World (such as Montaigne's essay on cannibals) to open up a secondary discourse about colonialism and imperialism. He was interested, too, in the idea of Prospero as a magus, an occult scientist like John Dee, Elizabeth's astrologer. All of which shows how dazzlingly and how playfully he could take the stories and intellectual currents of the day and turn them into popular entertainment. (The colonial debate in *The Tempest* continues to set up resonances, from Aimé Césaire in the Caribbean to Nelson Mandela and his fellow ANC prisoners on Robben Island – Caliban's 'This island's mine, by Sycorax my mother' is underlined in their precious copy, which eluded their jailers.)

ABOVE: *'All is but Fortune': Hollar's sketch of* The Tempest *as an allegory of Fortune – a great Renaissance theme. Tempests loom large in Shakespeare's late plays. 'Whom the poets call Fortune we know to be God,' wrote one sixteenth-century humanist.*

The question of New World voyages in *The Tempest* brings us back to Dudley Digges and his circle. Since the early 1590s, through his London contacts Shakespeare had known men such as John Florio, the translator of Montaigne; he had met foreign scholars and intellectuals, and had been in contact with explorers and magi at court. There is a long-standing myth, though direct evidence is lacking, that he belonged to a literary and scientific group that the antiquarian John Aubrey called 'the Club at the Mermayd in Fryday Street'. The Mermaid, close to the Blackfriars theatre, certainly was a literary meeting place. According to the great walker Thomas Coryate (who wrote to them from Aleppo in 1614 and from India in 1616), the 'company of right worshipful Sirenaicall Gentlemen' met on the first Friday of every month. Playwrights were among them, as Francis Beaumont confirms in verses to Ben Jonson in 1613:

> What things have we seen,
> Done at the Mermaid! heard words that have been
> So nimble, and so full of subtle flame

Shakespeare may not strike us as a clubby sort of person, but he knew many of the group very well, and in 1613 the Mermaid's owner witnessed a lease for him.

These connections are still little explored, but they open up fascinating possibilities. People like Digges, Coryate, Jonson, John Donne, Inigo Jones, the antiquarian Robert Cotton (who lent Ben Jonson books from his great library), the translator Holland, the publisher Edward Blount and the Levant Company's Richard Martin made up a formidable bunch of literary, artistic, scientific and mercantile figures encompassing all shades of opinion and belief. The story of one of the sources for the shipwreck in *The Tempest* is a fascinating example of the way the poet used contacts such as these for his plots.

On 2 June 1610 a ship named the *Sea Adventure*, backed by a consortium that included the Digges brothers, sailed for America. On the 24th the vessel was wrecked in a great storm off the Bermudas. The survivors returned home in September with tales of terrifying experiences and strange visions; that autumn their account was written up and circulated privately among the shareholders. It is an attractive speculation that Shakespeare might have obtained the manuscript of the story from Dudley Digges, stepson of his Stratford friend Thomas Russell. It was perhaps at Russell's house near Stratford that November that he held in his hands the account of William Strachy, dated 15 July 1610: 'A dreadfull storm and hedeous began to blow, which swelling and roaring as it were by fits, at length did beat all light from heaven: which like a hell of darkness turned black upon us, so much the more fuller of horror ... and over mastered the senses of all ...' After four days of terror they observed 'An apparition of a little round light, like a faint Starre trembling and streaming along with a sparkling blaze, half the height upon the mainmast and shooting sometimes from shroud to shroud ....'

The apparition the sailors had seen was, of course, the natural phenomenon known as St Elmo's Fire. Strachy's eyewitness account gave Shakespeare the detail he was looking for: the electric in-the-mouth fear as the ship splits; the uncertainty of perception in a world where nothing is quite what it seems. And so, armed with this tale, plus Virgil, Ovid and other old favourites such as Montaigne, he wrote *The Tempest* that winter, turning the spirits and voices imagined by Stratchy's sailors into Ariel, an airy progeny of Jonson's masques, and the frightened natives of the 'vex'd Bermudas' into Caliban (an anagram of cannibal), a child of Montaigne but also a Native American of a kind one could have met on the streets of London at that time.

'Let Your Indulgence Set Me Free'

At the end of the play, when the old enemies are reconciled and their children betrothed, Prospero makes a wonderful speech, which draws heavily on the passage in Ovid in which Medea mixes the dreadful potion to poison her children but which Shakespeare turns into a fabulous image of unearthly magic:

> Ye elves of hills, brooks, standing lakes and groves,
> And ye that on the sands with printless foot
> Do chase the ebbing Neptune, and do fly him
> When he comes back; you demi-puppets that
> By moonshine do the green sour ringlets make
> Whereof the ewe not bites; and you whose pastime
> Is to make midnight mushrooms, that rejoice
> To hear the solemn curfew; by whose aid, –
> Weak masters though ye be, – I have bedimm'd
> The noontide sun, call'd forth the mutinous winds,
> And 'twixt the green sea and the azured vault
> Set roaring war: to the dread rattling thunder
> Have I given fire, and rifted Jove's stout oak
> With his own bolt; the strong-based promontory
> Have I made shake: and by the spurs pluck'd up
> The pine and cedar: graves, at my command,
> Have waked their sleepers, oped, and let 'em forth
> By my so potent art. But this rough magic
> I here abjure: and, when I have required
> Some heavenly music, – which even now I do, –
> To work mine end upon their senses, that
> This airy charm is for, I'll break my staff,
> Bury it certain fathoms in the earth,
> And deeper than did ever plummet sound
> I'll drown my book.

Since the eighteenth century this speech has been seen as Shakespeare's farewell. The Prospero magic of course has precise affinities with the author and director who orchestrates the plot, plays with his characters to produce the desired effect, and then quits the stage. From a dramatist so conscious of theatrical illusion it is hard not to see this in some sense as a valediction (and was this why his colleagues pointedly opened his posthumous collected works with this play?). This conclusion gains conviction with Prospero's epilogue to his audience, which again lifts the veil on the illusion of acting. But here there is a twist: the flow of power is reversed. The spell is mutual, and it is the audience's belief that gives life to the illusion:

> Now my charms are all o'erthrown,
> And what strength I have's mine own, –
> Which is most faint: now 'tis true,
> I must be here confined by you,
> Or sent to Naples. Let me not,
> Since I have my dukedom got,
> And pardon'd the deceiver, dwell
> In this bare island by your spell;
> But release me from my bands
> With the help of your good hands.
> Gentle breath of yours my sails
> Must fill, or else my project fails,
> Which was to please. Now I want
> Spirits to enforce, art to enchant;
> And my ending is despair
> Unless I be relieved by prayer,
> Which pierces so, that it assaults
> Mercy itself, and frees all faults.
> As you from crimes would pardon'd be,
> Let your indulgence set me free.

He waits for applause, then exits. How typical of Shakespeare, the brilliant plotter of *Romeo and Juliet*; the illusionist of *A Midsummer Night's Dream*; the cajoling 'debtor' of *Henry IV* Part 2; the stage exorcist of *King Lear*. A professional man of the theatre, he knows exactly how to work us. This is the last of his many comments on the relationship between author/actor and audience. The actor puts the audience under a spell; but it is the audience's joining with the players that creates the atmosphere of enchantment in which the

actors do their work. If they do not, then his 'project' will fail – 'Which was, to please'.

TIME'S SCYTHE

In February 1612 Shakespeare's brother Gilbert, the nearest to him in age, died in Stratford. He was forty-five. Private mourning in Warwickshire was soon to be echoed by grief on a nationwide scale. That autumn a sea of optimism surrounded King James's two oldest children. In October Prince Henry held grand revels at court. He had already attracted high hopes as the focus of widespread expectation that a united Britain might overcome the religious conflicts of the older generation. This new arbiter of taste and patron of the arts had youth, beauty, talent and an ambition to play a part on the European stage. At the same time it was announced that Henry's sister Elizabeth would be marrying Frederick of Habsburg, the Elector Palatine. But on 6 November, after a short illness, Prince Henry, the Renaissance prince who had promised a new golden age, died.

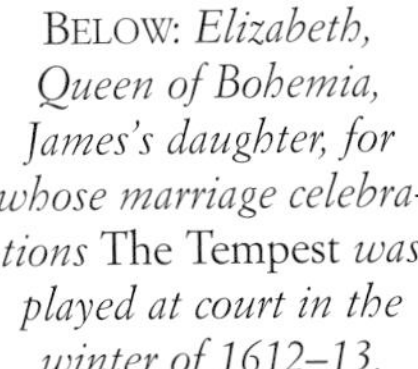

BELOW: *Elizabeth, Queen of Bohemia, James's daughter, for whose marriage celebrations* The Tempest *was played at court in the winter of 1612–13.*

His death had a profound effect: as with Diana, Princess of Wales, there was a magnificent funeral with extravagant expressions of public grief. After some deliberation the court decided to go ahead with Princess Elizabeth's wedding, and Shakespeare's company were hired to put on no fewer than fourteen plays the following February before a galaxy of foreign dignitaries in the Banqueting House in Whitehall.

Among old favourites and fashionable new pieces was the mysterious *Cardenio*, the one certain Shakespeare play that has not survived. It appears to be his first collaboration with the rising young star of the King's Men, John Fletcher. Written the previous year, *Cardenio* was played at court in February 1613 and again in June before the Duke of Savoy's ambassador in Greenwich; in the 1650s it was registered for publication in the names of both authors.

The play was evidently based on a story in Shelton's translation of *Don Quixote*, published in 1612. It is easy to see why Cervantes' post-medieval satire of the knightly quest should have attracted the creator of the old knight Falstaff for whom, famously, honour was but a word: 'Air, a mere scutcheon'.

All that survives now is a 1727 adaptation, which in places seems to contain fossils of Jacobean verse, some very muscular and idiosyncratic:

> I do not see the Fervour in the Maid.
> Which Youth and Love should kindle. She consents,
> As 'twere to feed without an Appetite:
> Tells me she is content; and plays the coy one,
> Like Those that subtly make their Words their Ward,
> Keeping Address at Distance. This Affection
> Is such a feign'd One, as will break untouch'd;
> Dye frosty, e'er it can be thaw'd; while mine,
> Like to a Clime beneath Hyperion's Eye,
> Burns with one constant Heat

If Shakespeare does not lie behind that, it is hard to think who else might – certainly not Fletcher. That a genuine manuscript was available to the eighteenth-century adaptor is proved by the survival of some of Robert Johnson's music with lyrics based on Shelton.

The play contains characteristic Shakespeare gags, such as when the villainous Don Henriquez pursues Leonora into a nunnery by pretending to be a corpse in a coffin (just as in *Cymbeline* Iachimo is smuggled into Imogen's chamber in a chest). This is not in the Cervantes tale and must be Shakespeare's own idea. But the main similarity is to the late plays, especially *Cymbeline*: the wronged heroine, the reconciling of young and old in a family reunion, the opposition of court and country, and the key role given to music. It is a great pity that the play is lost because of the fascinating possibilities offered by the meeting of Shakespeare and Cervantes, the progenitor of the modern novel.

While *Cardenio* and other pieces were in rehearsal for the royal wedding celebrations, Richard, the most elusive member of the Shakespeare family, died. He was thirty-eight. All three of William's younger brothers had now gone. None had married, left children or lived to a good age. The four Shakespeare boys did not turn out to be good family makers. By Tudor standards, an unusual family. And more intimations of mortality.

The Blackfriars House: A Mysterious Purchase

In spring 1613 Shakespeare was back in London. On the morning of 10 March he signed the deeds to buy the gatehouse at Blackfriars, adjacent to the indoor theatre. The owner of the Mermaid, the vintner John Jackson, was a witness.

Many questions still surround the purchase of this property. It was a place long known to the government's thought police as a Catholic safe house – its warren of tunnels had been the despair of Elizabeth's priest-hunters. So why did Shakespeare buy it so late in his career, and after he had retired to Stratford? Was it just an investment, or was there something more to it?

The poet's will, drawn up in early 1616, mentions a John Robinson living in the house at that point, and someone of that name appears as a witness of the will, although he did not sign it in person. It would seem that Robinson was a London man, but his identity is still a mystery. The surname appears among the stewards of the Fortescues, the former owners, who were obstinate recusants, but it is also the name of a young Catholic priest, who was living in London at that time and later became a Jesuit. The house appears in the poet's will among the property conveyed to his daughter Susanna but with special conditions attached, and two years after his death it was conveyed to John Greene and Matthew Morris 'in accordance with the true intent of Mr Shakespeare's will'. Stranger still, one Sunday years later, a floor in the main upstairs chamber of the adjacent building collapsed, killing a Catholic priest and ninety of his 300-strong congregation, among them Warwickshire folk, including a Tresham. So the place was still a secret mass house, just as it had been in Elizabeth's day. Shakespeare was a cunning and discreet person: the purchase of the Blackfriars gatehouse and its later history may yet throw new light on his business dealings, and perhaps his religious sympathies, at the end of his life.

HEALING THE WOUND OF ENGLAND

Now, right at the end of his career, we come to a move that is intriguing in its implications. Early in 1613 the King's Men put on a play based on the tale of Henry VIII – the split with Rome, his divorce from Katherine of Aragon and relationship with Anne Boleyn. It was to be performed in the Blackfriars, where Henry's ecclesiastical court had sat, in its days as a monastery, to hear the divorce case. In this room, then, the schism had begun. What a theme to choose – and what a place to play it!

Shakespeare sets out the way he wants it to be understood in an enigmatic prologue, another example of his cunning:

> I come no more to make you laugh: things now
> That bear a weighty and a serious brow,
> Sad, high, and working, full of state and woe,
> Such noble scenes as draw the eye to flow,
> We now present. Those that can pity here

> May, if they think it well, let fall a tear;
> The subject will deserve it. Such as give
> Their money out of hope they may believe,
> May here find truth too ....

On the surface it might be thought that such a theme would have to be developed in an anti-Catholic way. Not at all: the key message is one of reconciliation. Henry is oafish; Katherine of Aragon, the mother of Queen Mary, the heroine.

Any play concerned with the controversies of Henry VIII's reign had, of course, been impossible to stage in Elizabeth's lifetime. And although this one is often looked on as an anti-climax to Shakespeare's career, it is fascinating that he should now complete his cycle on English history with the instigator of the great schism. Over eighty years on, the scars were healing. For a comparison, one would have to go to Calderón's great *Love after Death*, about the suppression of Moorish culture in Spain, written seventy years after Philip II's edict against Muslim customs. The wound of Spain, as this was of England.

Henry VIII was one of the most repellent rulers in English history, and he isn't airbrushed in the play. But it is Shakespeare's treatment of Katherine, one of his great women's roles, which most clearly reveals his approach. Her defence speech – a mirror of Hermione's in *The Winter's Tale*, right down to her citing of her father's rank – leaves a strong impression of the nobleness of the old generation of Catholics. Castigating the 'hearts crammed with arrogancy' of her accusers, Katherine appeals in 'the name of God' in the most plain and measured language:

> Sir, I desire you do me right and justice;
> And to bestow your pity on me: for
> I am a most poor woman, and a stranger,
> Born out of your dominions; having here
> No judge indifferent, nor no more assurance
> Of equal friendship and proceeding. Alas, sir,
> In what have I offended you? what cause
> Hath my behaviour given to your displeasure,
> That thus you should proceed to put me off,
> And take your good grace from me?

Once more, we hear the stranger's case. And remember, this was delivered in the very hall where it had happened seventy years before. Is there a sense here that history has moved on – the clock cannot be turned back? As in *The Winter's*

Tale, *Pericles* and *The Tempest*, the theme now is recognition and forgiveness; here, however, it is not in fiction but in English history. The way is prepared immediately after her trial by the boy singing a beautiful Johnson song on Orpheus, and then fully expressed in the mystical scene of Katherine's dying vision, when to 'sad and solemn music' she falls asleep to see, in one of Shakespeare's longest stage directions, six angels descend 'clad in white robes, wearing on their heads garlands of bays, and ... branches of bays or palm in their hands ...'. Neo-Platonist balm applied to the wound of England.

At the end, as in other late plays, a baby is brought on stage to be the agent of reconciliation. This one is Elizabeth herself. But that scene, with its slightly nauseating eulogy of the golden time she would inaugurate (in marked contrast to the tight-lipped epitaph, if such it is, in Sonnet 124), was written by his collaborator, Fletcher. With that, Shakespeare backs gently out. But, as always, he keeps his cards close to his chest. We call the play *Henry VIII* today, as the Folio editors chose to do. But this is not the author's title. Through the mouthpiece of his stage chorus, in a typical sleight of hand, Shakespeare gives us the most teasing of all his titles: *All Is True.*

It was during a performance of this play, on 29 June 1613, that the Globe burned down. Henry Wotton saw it happen:

> The kings players had a new play, called All is true, set forth with many extraordinary circumstances of pomp and majesty .... Now ... certain chambers [cannon] being shot off ... some of the paper, or other stuff, wherewith one of them was stopped, did light upon the thatch, where being thought at first but an idle smoke, and their eyes more attentive to the show, it kindled inwardly, and ran round like a train, consuming within less than an hour the whole house to the very grounds. This was the fatal period of that virtuous fabric ....

The Globe would be rebuilt, but perhaps for Shakespeare the fire drew a line under the era. It has been conjectured that at this point he sold his share in the company. The physical fabric could be restored, but what of time?

'Bear Us Like the Time'

From that same time comes Shakespeare's last known work – another collaboration with Fletcher. The new piece was called *The Two Noble Kinsmen*, and was based on Chaucer's *Knight's Tale* – but maybe with a nod to Euripides, who had long been available in Latin translation. Chaucer was much admired by Shakespeare's generation of writers: 'I know not whether to marvel more,' wrote

Philip Sidney in his *Defence of Poesie*, 'either that he in that misty time could see so clearly, or that we in this clear age walk so stumblingly after him.' Since then, Shakespeare had taught his age how to walk.

Was *The Two Noble Kinsmen* hastily written for the new theatre? In his prologue Fletcher mentions 'Our late losses' and suggests that there will be 'better plays in the future', as if to acknowledge that this one had been hastily cooked up. The theme is the ambiguous and irrational power of Eros, echoing earlier plays (especially *A Midsummer Night's Dream*). In the nineteenth century, Thomas de Quincy thought the sections by Shakespeare the greatest poetry in English literature. Not all have agreed with him since, but even so, no one then or since could have written this – even if the language is so knotty that at times it obscures the meaning:

> O my petition was
> Set down in ice, which by hot grief uncandied
> Melts into drops; so sorrow wanting form
> Is press'd with deeper matter

So what was the last stage verse he wrote? Prospero's elegiac valediction, much as we would like to think so, may not be Shakespeare's farewell to the stage and may not represent his state of mind towards the end of his life. It has even been suggested that the bitter satire *Timon of Athens* was the script left on his desk at the end. But a much more likely alternative is that the final speech of Theseus in *The Two Noble Kinsmen* is the last thing he wrote. Fittingly, it is an address to the inscrutable gods:

> Oh you heavenly charmers,
> What things you make of us! For what we lack
> We laugh, for what we have are sorry, still
> Are children in some kind. Let us be thankful
> For that which is, and with you leave disputes
> That are above our question. Let's go off
> And bear us like the time.

From his last plays we can see that Shakespeare remained interested and engaged in the ideas of his day, as one might expect from a man whose friends were in the artistic avant-garde, widely travelled and knowledgeable about foreign cultures. Shakespeare's books were those of a professional writer of the Renaissance with wide interests in European humanism and a working knowledge of several languages – back in Stratford, we know that New Place had 'a study of books'. So we can be sure that at the end of his life he could retire there to read: if, that is, his sight was still holding up, after years of writing by candlelight in the ordinaries of Bishopsgate and Southwark. Unfortunately, the time to read books, to supervise his landholdings and to cultivate his garden would be all too short.

STATE OF MIND: THINKING OF DEATH

In the new year of 1616 Shakespeare dictated the first draft of his will. He may have been prompted to do so by the imminent marriage of his younger daughter, the surviving twin Judith. But usually in those days people drew up their will when they felt they had not long to live, and while, at fifty-one, Shakespeare was not that old, his younger brothers were already dead and his own health may have been deteriorating. There is a tale of a fever brought on by a drinking session with the Warwickshire poet Michael Drayton and his old sparring partner Ben Jonson. Some have even suspected that Shakespeare had syphilis; this is not impossible, since he had lived the life of a single man in London for all those years, and there is an apparent reference to venereal disease at the end of the sonnets – the 'strange maladies' caught in his 'hell of time' in the late 1590s. Others have drawn attention to the signature, which could be regarded as shaky for a man of only middle age. Writer's palsy? Were his eyes indeed going? Or had the tavern life in London taken its toll? Actors today are high on the list of 'drinking professions', and perhaps they were then, too.

BELOW: *Shakespeare's signature on his will, March 1616. The pronounced deterioration in his handwriting in the previous four years suggests a degenerative illness, perhaps alcoholism.*

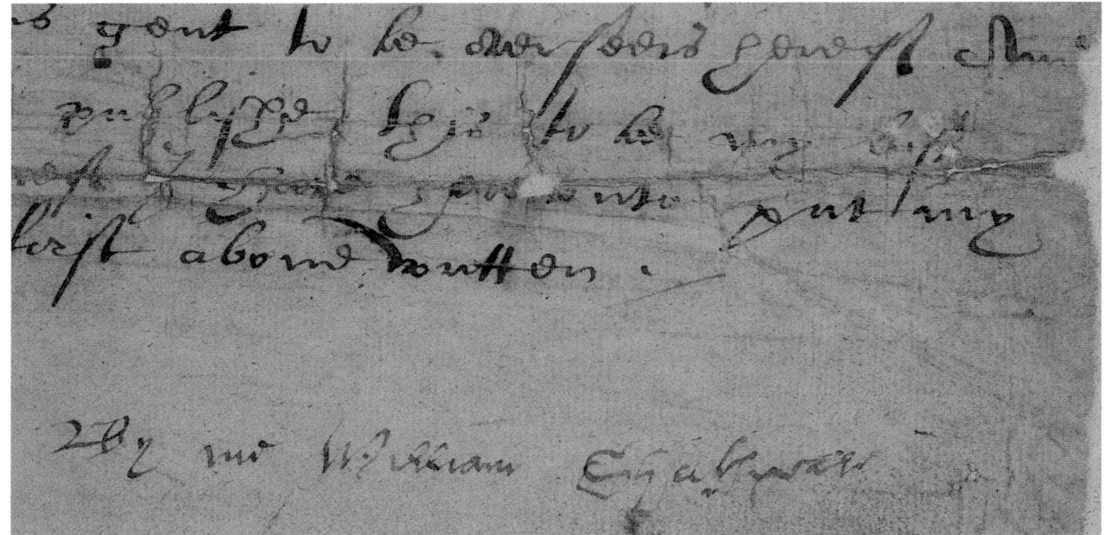

Consider the evidence: a life lived in theatres; the heavy consumption of ale as a normal part of the sixteenth-century diet; nights on his own in London for over twenty years; eating and drinking by himself; writing alone at night. It takes us back to the old tale that his death was brought on by drinking.

It is not the fate of all great writers to end up disillusioned, of course; but not all of them reach middle age with equanimity. Tolstoy, at the same point in his life, had also lost a small son. His earlier novels had taken a cool, calm view of death, whether in war, on the scaffold, in poverty or on the estates of the rich. But when he reached the age of fifty this rationality left him, for he knew his own death was coming closer. He wrote to his brother, 'It is time to die – that is not true. What is true is that there is nothing else to do in life but die. I feel it every instant. I am writing, I am working hard … but there is no happiness for me in any of it.' Then, in a curious parallel with Shakespeare's activities in this sphere, Tolstoy, already the owner of large estates, concluded that making futher land deals was the only way to prevent thoughts of death getting an intolerable grip on him. It was on a journey to finalize such a purchase, staying in a country inn, that he had a classic death dream in which his room became a tomb. 'All told me the same story – there is nothing in life, nothing exists but death – and death should not be!' Then he wrote that great exploration of death and dying, *The Death of Ivan Ilyich*.

Was it like that for Shakespeare? A case could be made: the long decline in productivity; the late collaborations, which started even before he was fifty; then the continued compulsive purchasing of land and property that he had begun much earlier. Was all this an earthy substitute for his airy art? All through his career his keen intelligence had been concerned with the limitations of his art. In his sonnets he was obsessed with memorializing and with the possibilities of language while admitting the ultimate inadequacy of art, language and metaphor: 'We are such stuff as dreams are made on'; 'The best in this kind are but shadows.' In his last plays, especially in the tortured syntax of *The Winter's Tale*, he had taken language as far as he could. The dense, clotted verses in the collaborations with Fletcher might suggest he had reached the point where it was not of interest to him to write more.

Or was it not like this at all – did he just end his days happily in his garden among the rosebushes, his granddaughter Elizabeth laughing on her swing? As always, we search for clues, and impose on him what we will.

Family Scandal

Early that spring, after the first draft of her father's will had been prepared, Judith Shakespeare became caught up in a sex scandal. It was not the first

unpleasantness involving the poet's daughters. Three years earlier her sister Susanna had been slanderously accused of adultery and of being infected with gonorrhoea. That was all quickly dealt with to the Shakespeare family's satisfaction; this time it would not be so easy.

In February Judith married the vintner Thomas Quiney, son of John's friend Richard, in Stratford. But a month later the couple were excommunicated for having married in Lent without a special licence. This was a huge public humiliation for the family. Then came the revelation that Quiney had got another woman, Margaret Wheeler, pregnant; she died in childbirth, along with her baby, at about the same time. Documents preserved in the archives of the ecclesiastical 'bawdy courts' in Maidstone, Kent, show that Thomas was then summoned to appear in his local church court on a charge of moral delinquency. On 26 March he duly confessed to 'carnal copulation' with the poor deceased woman. It's like a scene from one of the plays: this, after all, is what Claudio is condemned for in *Measure for Measure*.

It must have been a painful further humiliation for both Judith, now thirty-one and almost beyond marriageable age in those days, and her father, especially given his deep-rooted ambivalence about sex. The court imposed an embarrassingly public penance on Thomas, which the family managed to have commuted to a fine.

This was the background to Shakespeare changing his will. The previous day he had brought in his lawyer, Francis Collins, from Warwick and altered it to protect Judith and to impose conditions on her husband. All this anxiety must have hit William hard. The latest signature on the will, some have thought, shows signs of illness. A tiny detail sticks out in the original document: in the line 'whereof I have hereunto put my Seale', the word 'Seale' is struck through and replaced by 'hand'. In 1810 a ring was found in a field close to Holy Trinity churchyard. A beautiful, big, heavy gold signet ring, it was certainly Elizabethan, of the kind treasured by its owner. On it were entwined the initials WS. Had Shakespeare dropped his signet ring after Judith's wedding a few weeks earlier?

BELOW: *Shakespeare seems to have lost his seal ring early in 1616: this was found near Stratford church in 1810.*

The ceremony had taken place in February, the coldest month of another very cold winter. He might well have been wearing gloves. He was perhaps already ill, and might have lost weight; the ring could have been loose. Outside the church, after the service, perhaps he took his gloves off to shake hands with an old acquaintance. The ring would easily have fallen, unnoticed, and been lost. Your seal is an emblem of yourself. To lose it is a blow.

And still the slings and arrows continued to hit the family. Shakespeare's brother-in-law William Hart, husband of his sister Joan, died and was buried on 17 April. 'Nothing 'gainst Time's scythe can make defence.'

His Wife Anne: The Mystery of the Second-best Bed

So it was during these crises that the poet made the final alterations to his will. There were gifts to many friends and neighbours; £10 to the poor of his home town; money to his old fellow actors in London, Hemmings, Burbage and Condell, with which to purchase remembrance rings. He faithfully remembered the old recusant friends and neighbours Hamnet Sadler and William Reynolds, and his godson William Walker. After the bequests to Judith, most of the estate went to Susanna and John Hall.

But what about his wife? Anne had brought up their children, and must have looked after his business affairs in Stratford all these years as Tudor wives were expected to do. Yet we know next to nothing about her. Many husbands put words of affection for their spouses ('my dear wife') in their wills. But William's is devoid of such phrases, and for Anne there is only a last-minute addition scribbled by his lawyer: 'Item to my wife the second best bed...'

A vast amount of ink has been spilt on these few words. Most wills of the day, it has to be said, are matter of fact, but in the desperate search for the poet's feelings much has been read into this laconic bequest. Some interpret it as cruelty or hatred. Others have seen in it a discreet reference to the marriage bed, remembered sentimentally at the last minute, and specified over and above the one-third of his estate that fell to his widow as a matter of course. Recently a new theory has been argued from the minutiae of medieval English customary law: that on his deathbed William was making a tacit admission that he had been unfaithful in marriage and had broken their 'bed vows'. In so dry a document it would be a metaphorical twist almost worthy of him; but this seems strained. The solution may well be altogether simpler, though not without its own poignancy.

At the time of its alteration the will would have been read to Anne, who knew she would get her widow's third portion and continue to live at New Place with her daughter and John Hall. So was it *she* who wished the bed to be specified? And if so, why? The answer lies, perhaps, in her father's will. Back in 1581, the summer before she married William, her father made a curiously specific stipulation about two beds in her old home, Hewlands Farm in the village of Shottery: 'Item, my will is that ... the two joyned-beds in my parlor, shall continue and stand unremoved during the natural life or widowhood of Joan my wife and the natural life of Bartholomew my son, and John my son, and the longest liver of them.'

The beds, then, were heirlooms; they meant something to the Hathaways. Their descendants lived in the house until the nineteenth century, and two late sixteenth-century 'joyned beds' (four-poster, framed beds) remain there today. But in the inventory of Anne's brother Bartholomew in 1624, only one 'joyned bed' is mentioned. So the year after her father died, when she had married her teenage lover, had Anne brought one of the family's 'joyned beds' from Hewlands Farm to Henley Street, but on condition that it should eventually go back to the family? If so, it would eventually need to be singled out in her husband's will.

This is only speculation, of course: the fact is that with the second-best bed, as with so much else, he left us a mystery. Tudor marriages were generally based on companionship and partnership, not on romantic love. But Shakespeare was a man who believed in the ideal of love, and for all we know, despite the beautiful boy and the broken 'bed vow', he loved Anne till the end and still felt as he had on their marriage day, that she had 'sav'd my life'.

Ars Moriendi: The Art of Dying

We have no idea what Shakespeare's last illness was; presumably he was tended by his son-in-law Dr Hall. Unfortunately, only one of Hall's two casebooks survives and it begins the next year, in 1617. Maybe the other will turn up one day and give us a bedside account of the poet's last days, but until then we must imagine.

When you knew you were dying you disposed of your goods, paid off your debts and readied your mind for the end. Tudor people prepared for death, and there was a plethora of self-help books available to guide them. Shakespeare had used one for Claudio's famous speech in *Measure for Measure*.

But what of Shakespeare himself? In his lifetime many of the things by which English people had lived their lives for so long had been swept away. The tiny, old-fashioned and provincial England of the mid-sixteenth century had been transformed out of recognition in terms of population, culture and world view; in the beginnings of colonization and empire; and even down to the homely detail of pewter on the table, consumer goods and all those chimneys. And, of course, a once-Catholic country was now a Protestant one. The role of his generation had been to live through, and to shape, a remarkable time.

The idea that you play your part on the stage of history was a contemporary commonplace. In the 1560s' English version of Thomas More's *Utopia* there is a prophetic tract for the times expressed in those same guiding metaphors of the Tudor age:

> What part so ever you have taken upon you, play that as well as you can, and make the best of it: and do not therefore disturb and bring out of order the whole matter, because that another that is merrier and better cometh to your remembrance .... You must not forsake the ship in a Tempest, because you cannot rule and keep down the winds .... But you must with a crafty wile, and subtle train study and endeavour your self, as much as in you lieth, to handle the matter wittily and handsomely for the purpose, and that which you cannot turn to good, so order it that it be not very bad ....

And wittily and handsomely Shakespeare had handled it. But what of his final allegiance when he died on 22 or 23 April 1616 in Stratford? In his greatest work he had dramatized the tensions of a world that had lost the comfort of religion. Whether he himself turned back to such comfort at the end – as people often do even now – we cannot know for certain, but the testimony of Richard Davies, a seventeenth-century Gloucestershire clergyman, is unequivocal: 'William Shakespeare,' he says, 'dyed a papist.'

Davies had no reason to lie, and plenty of reasons to know. He is not a primary source, but it would be incredible if such a story should have surfaced had the poet been a conforming Protestant. What the story means, of course, is another matter entirely. All we can say is that Davies had heard that the poet received the last rites from a priest according to the Catholic faith.

His modern biographers have argued this case and others beside: an outward conformist but with inward regrets; a reverent agnostic; a humanist who found greatest solace in the pagans. But he was, after all, a man who drew on more than one tradition to animate his imaginal world. Like many people who had lived through the Elizabethan age, he probably eschewed certainties and no longer held any deep sectarian conviction. But he remained a Christian; the Bible was still his book; and from 'incertainties which now crowned themselves assured' it may be, as Davies records, that he was drawn to his childhood certainties at the end. And if he did go through that last ancient rite of passage on his deathbed, was it perhaps as much in loyalty to the past, to his parents and ancestors, and to the spirits of England, which to many of his generation had been 'leased out like to a pelting farm'?

His funeral took place at Holy Trinity, where his father and mother, his son Hamnet and other family members had all been buried. As a tithe holder, he was entitled, unlike them, to be buried inside the church. The inscription on his tomb, according to an early authority, was composed by him. It is the kind of doggerel he had written at the drop of a hat for friends and neighbours,

the sort of old poetry of Christianity still to be seen crumbling on the guild chapel wall:

> Good friend for Jesus sake forbeare,
> To digg the dust encloased heare:
> Bleste be the man that spares thes stones,
> And curst be he that moves my bones.

ABOVE: *The burial register of William Shakespeare, 'gentleman', 25 April 1616. By then he was a pillar of the local community. Later the story surfaced that he had received the last rites as a Catholic. If true, it would be typical of the torn loyalties of so many of his generation.*

His wife, it was said, requested to be buried with him when her time came; but the curse proved stronger, and Anne was interred close to him near the altar, where their graves may be seen today, along with those of their daughters and their in-laws John Hall and Thomas Quiney. In the end the Shakespeare family made their way back from John Shakespeare's troubles: New Place, old Clopton's house, the landholdings at Welcombe and Bishopton, and a prime position in the place where Stratford folk had worshipped, and been buried, for 900 years.

And what of Shakespeare's works? To our eyes he had been shockingly negligent about the preservation and publication of his scripts. He is said to have disparaged the pretensions of Ben Jonson, who had already collected his 'Workes' into a grand folio volume (several contemporaries jokingly suggested that Jonson had forgotten the difference between 'work' and 'play'). Unsettling as the thought is, he may not even have cared about his works being handed down. Instead it was his friends who published his plays in 1623, prefaced by these words:

> We have but collected them, and done an office to the dead ... without ambition either of self-profit or fame, only to keep the memory of so worthy a friend and fellow alive as was our Shakespeare ... And there we hope, to your diverse capacities, you will find enough both to draw and hold you; for his wit can no more lie hid than it could be lost. Read him, therefore, and again, and again, and if then you do not like him, surely you are in some manifest danger not to understand him.

If it were not for the efforts of Hemmings and Condell, half of the plays would never have seen the light of day. Among other tributes was one from Ben Jonson, Shakespeare's cantankerous colleague, who still couldn't resist a last jibe about his 'small Latin and less Greek'. But Jonson was generous enough to recognize that his old rival had surpassed even the greatest of the ancient Greeks and Romans: 'He was not of an age, but for all time.'

MR. WILLIAM
SHAKESPEARES
COMEDIES,
HISTORIES, &
TRAGEDIES.
Publiſhed according to the True Originall Copies.

LONDON
Printed by Iſaac Iaggard, and Ed. Blount. 1623.

EPILOGUE:

What's Past Is Prologue

The Glory Everlasting of the Pen

In the twenty-first century most countries are no longer traditional societies, or will soon cease to be. England was the first to go through such a great cultural and psychological transformation, and the struggles that began there in the sixteenth century were a harbinger of those that have been fought in many parts of the world since. By its very nature, of course, modernity destroys tradition, the 'givenness' of the past. Like archaeologists, today we sift through the wreckage, examining texts and physical remains to reconstruct an idea of our history; but what is most exciting and valuable is to find a living continuance of the past that is still meaningful in the present. It can still be seen in surviving traditional societies, such as in south India, for example, where it is possible to wander out of a high-tech computer block in Bangalore into a temple and see and hear the same rituals and language in the same building that people have used for 1000 years.

And what is the analogy for us in Britain? It is certainly not religion. The language of King James's Bible or the Book of Common Prayer is no longer thought to be comprehensible, or even relevant, and has almost vanished from our lives. Where these texts are still spoken in public, they come in a modern translation drained of its poetry and numinous power. Today there is only one part of sixteenth-century English culture still expressed in the original language as a regular public performance or ritual: Shakespeare's plays. His is the one case where the authentic language and thought of that time is still seen as integral to the national culture. And his is also the one case where sixteenth-century texts are still taught in their original language at the core of the national school curriculum.

The religious language of the sixteenth century is gone; the tremendous words of the 'Great Sentence' for the dead have faded away. But *Hamlet* is still here.

This tells us something about the nature of the English Reformation and its 400-year aftermath in which we still live. The texts at the centre of the Tudor government's conception of the national culture have no place today. Yet the texts of a popular mass medium, which frequently questioned the ways of authority and asked people to think for themselves, still matter to us. It is Shakespeare's plays that are our living contact with the people of his time.

Our modern world began in the sixteenth century. Caught between tradition and modernity, religion and magic, state absolutism and individual conscience, even ordinary people glimpsed the beginning of the end, not only of the institutional structures but also of the ideas that had ruled people's lives for so long. For some, all religion was revealed as the construction of men, all sacred texts merely as human works. In Queen Mary's day Devon villagers held a marriage ceremony for a goose; others turned to atheism. People no longer knew what to think. Although he remained a Christian and a Bible reader, Shakespeare was deeply involved in all this questioning, evolving his own new world of words to mediate 'the revolution of the times'.

In his parents' day England had been a traditional society, a land of rood screens and female saints, holy wells and incantation magic, church ales and painted devils. Like many of his generation, Shakespeare knew that lost world through his parents. His tales exist on a profound psychological level, transcending language in their portrayal of character, love and friendship, power and suffering. Across cultures they have the entertaining and educative power of the fairy tales they often shadow. But they work on other levels too. His background enabled Shakespeare to incorporate into his drama the beliefs, the active mythology and the imagery of the pre-Reformation world: his characters are its kings and queens, priests and witches, mothers and fathers, clowns and fairies. This no doubt helps explain his great popularity in the eyes of his own audience, but it also helps us understand his continuing relevance today. He brings back to life the world we have lost. This will perhaps become even more apparent in the twenty-first century, as, through globalization, our past accelerates away from us at an ever faster rate. The changes we are now going through may turn out to be even more profound and far-reaching than those experienced by his contemporaries. Like the paintings in the guild chapel with which this story began, humanity's encoded memories are being erased everywhere across the planet. But it is perhaps for this reason that, rather than diminishing in relevance, Shakespeare's humanity, his language, his humour and his toughness of mind will become all the more valuable to us as our own 'revolution of the times' unfolds.

FURTHER READING

This book argues that an important key to Shakespeare's thought world is the traditional society of Warwickshire and the conflicts engendered in it by the Tudor Reformation. The Reformation has been subject to major revision by historians during the last thirty years; the corollary, of course, is that the life of Shakespeare will need to be rethought too.

First, then, for the broad sweep: Susan Brigden, *New Worlds, Lost Worlds* (2000), a very readable survey of the Tudor era with a rich bibliography; C. Haigh, *English Reformations* (1993); Eamon Duffy, *The Stripping of the Altars* (1992) and *Voices of Morebath* (2001), a study of one community in Devon, a model of the kind of change revealed in Warwickshire sources (see next paragraph). See also K. Thomas, *Religion and the Decline of Magic* (1971); Patrick Collinson has written an important short study of Shakespeare's religious background in his collection of essays *Godly People* (1983).

Next the Warwickshire background, the old society of Shakespeare's parents and grandparents that shaped his first twenty years and beyond. A good introduction to Stratford is *The History of an English Borough,* ed. Bob Bearman (1997), with essays by Alan Dyer and Anne Hughes; on material life in Stratford, Jeanne Jones, *Family Life in Shakespeare's England 1570–1630* (1997) is a fascinating survey based on wills and house inventories, which is especially useful as a teaching aid. *The Victoria County History* is a great resource on individual parishes, and is now going online. On the politics and social life of Tudor Stratford, the starting point is the town council's books *Minutes and Accounts*, Dugdale Society, 4 vols, ed. Savage and Fripp (1921–9); Vol V, ed. Levi Fox (1990) takes the story up to 1598. The crucial evidence of the survey of priests (see pages 35–6) is in Vol III (1926); the priests' replies are in *Warwickshire Ecclesiastical Terriers,* ed. D. M. Barratt, Dugdale Society (1955). The most valuable compilations of source material for the Forest of Arden are J. Rylands, *Records of Rowington,* 2 vols (1896, 1922) and *Records of Wroxall Abbey and Manor* (1903); also *The Register of the Guild of Knowle,* ed. W. Rickley (1894). Further leads may be found in earlier writers, such as Charlotte M. Stopes, *Shakespeare's Warwickshire Contemporaries* (1897) and *Shakespeare's Family* (1907), and in E. Fripp, *Shakespeare's Stratford* (1928), *Shakespeare's Haunts* (1929) and *Shakespeare Studies* (1930). Mark Eccles, *Shakespeare in Warwickshire* (1961) adds more detail. On family and neighbours in the religious courts (including the poet's daughter Susanna), E. R. C. Brinkworth, *Shakespeare and the Bawdy Court of Stratford* (1972) is essential.

On the defacing of the guild chapel described in my prologue, the key text is J. G. Nichols and Thomas Fisher's *Ancient Allegorical Historical and Legendary Paintings* (1838) along with Clifford Davidson, *The Guild Chapel Wall Paintings at Stratford-upon-Avon* (1988). On John Shakespeare's business dealings, especially his career as a brogger, the background is in P. J. Bowden, *The Wool Trade in Tudor England* (1962). The remarkable brogger's account book quoted on pages 42–3 is *Warwickshire Grazier and London Skinner, 1532–1555,* ed. N. W. Alcock (1981). Extracts of the town book of Warwick were edited by Thomas Kemp as *The Book of John Fisher* in around 1899 for Warwick Corporation; a full publication is desirable. On Coventry: C. Phythian Adams, *Desolation of a City* (1979) and 'Ceremony and the Citizen' in *Crisis and Order in English Towns, 1500–1700*, ed. P. Clark and P. Slack (1972); on village life in sixteenth-century Warwickshire, N. W. Alcock, *People at Home* (1993). The interviews in the Cotswolds on page 18 are from H. J. Massingham, *Where Man Belongs* (1946). The interview on page 44 comes from *The Dillen*, ed. A. Hewins (1981).

On Shakespeare biography the indispensable starting point is the brilliant Samuel Schoenbaum's *Shakespeare's Lives* (1993 edition); the key documents are summarized in Samuel Schoenbaum, *Shakespeare: A Documentary Life* (1975), also in compact paperback edition; D. Thomas, *Shakespeare in the Public Records* (1985); and Bob Bearman, *Shakespeare in the Stratford Records* (paperback, 1994). E. K. Chambers, *William Shakespeare* (1930) is still very useful for its transcription of sources. Park Honan's recent *Shakespeare: A Life* (1998) is a very enjoyable survey by a literary scholar; K. Duncan-Jones, *Ungentle Shakespeare* (2001) is a challenging tilt at what she sees as the myth of 'gentle' Will. These last two titles both contain many fresh insights.

On Tudor childhood and education there is a vast literature: see David Cressy, *Birth, Marriage and Death: Ritual, Religion, and the Life Cycle in Tudor and Stuart England* (1997) and *Literacy and the Social Order: Reading and Writing in Tudor and Stuart England* (1980); on Shakespeare's knowledge of the curriculum the definitive work is T. Baldwin's forbidding *William Shakspere's Small Latine and Lesse Greeke*, 2 vols (1944). On Ovid see *Shakespeare's Ovid,* ed. A. B. Taylor (2000) and Jonathan Bate, *Shakespeare and Ovid* (1993); the Ovid translation used in my text is by A. D. Melville, Oxford World Classics (1986). On Seneca (see pages 56–7) I am indebted to J. Lever, *The Tragedy of State* (1971) and on the Coventry mysteries to Diana Whaley's 'Voices From the Past: A Note on Termagant and Herod' in *Shakespeare Continuities: essays in honor of E. A. J. Honigmann*, ed. J. Batchelor, T. Cain, C. Lamont (1997).

On the question of the Shakespeares' Catholicism, controversy still rages; for background Eamon Duffy's *The Stripping of the Altars* (1992); a useful introduction to sources is R. N. Swanton, *Catholic England* (1993). On the family there is much useful material in the older literature, such as John Semple Smart, *Shakespeare: Truth and Tradition* (1928); J. H. de Groot, *The Shakespeares and the 'Old Faith'* (1946); H. Mutschmann and K. Wentersdorf, *Shakespeare and Catholicism* (1952); and Peter Milward, *Shakespeare's Religious Background* (1973). On John's testament the main facts are laid out in Samuel Schoenbaum, *Shakespeare: A Documentary Life* (1975); in Patrick Collinson's view, *Godly People* (1983), it is 'virtually certain' that the testament is genuine; Bob Bearman, however, in *Shakespeare Survey* (forthcoming 2003) suggests an eighteenth-century forgery is still possible, but it is hard to explain how that might have come about. For a parallel, William Bell's testament and autobiography (see page 75) was composed in 1587 and published at Douai in 1633.

On the Jesuit missions: T. McCoog, *The Reckoned Expense* (1996); R. Simpson, *Edmund Campion* (1896); Henry Foley, *Records of the English Province of the Society of Jesus* (1875) is an essential collection; Tom McCoog has also published an alphabetical directory of Jesuits in Tudor and Stuart England. The publications of the Catholic Record Society are also a mine of information in these matters.

On the 'lost years' E. A. J. Honigmann, *Shakespeare: The Lost Years* (1985) is full of fascinating detail about Shakespeare and Lancashire, but with no smoking gun; Honigmann was followed recently by Anthony Holden's enjoyable *William Shakespeare* (1999), but the Shakeshafte theory has not survived closer scrutiny: see now Bob Bearman in *Shakespeare Quarterly*, Vol LIII, No.1 (2002). On his Lancashire patrons: Barry Coward, *The Stanleys, Lords Stanley and Earls of Derby 1385–1672* (1983); and J. J. Bagley, *The Earls of Derby* (1985).

On the theatre in London: E. K. Chambers, *The Elizabethan Stage* (1923); Andrew Gurr, *The Shakespearean Stage, 1574–1642* (1992 edition) and *Playgoing in Shakespeare's London* (1987); Herbert Berry, *Shakespeare's Playhouses* (1987); *Shakespeare's Globe Rebuilt*, ed. J. Mulryne and M. Shewring (1997); Julian Bowsher, *The Rose Theatre* (1998); and a very interesting look at the material remains and their analogues, Jean Wilson, *The Shakespeare Legacy* (1995).

On the plays I have consulted both the new Arden editions and the handy and user-friendly Oxford editions. On the broader questions of play and text, R. Proudfoot, *Shakespeare: Text, Stage and Canon* (2001) and David Scott Kastan, *Shakespeare and the Book* (2001) are informative, enjoyable and highly recommended. The Oxford Shakespeare Topics series, ed. Stanley Wells, offers an interesting crop of handy paperbacks, such as Robert Miola, *Shakespeare's Reading* (2000) and Steven Marx, *Shakespeare and the Bible* (2000); other topics include women, masculinity, race, and film.

On Shakespeare's early years in theatre there is still controversy. Again, there is much of value in E. K. Chambers' *Elizabethan Stage* (1923). The money now is on the Queen's Men, on whom see S. McMillin and S. MacLean, *The Queen's Men and Their Plays* (1998); E. A. J. Honigmann, *Shakespeare: The Lost Years* (1985) favours Strange's Men. As a portrait of his creative process, Emrys Jones, *The Origins of Shakespeare* (1977) is still, to my mind, the most exciting read of its kind. Peter Thomson, *Shakespeare's Professional Career* (1992) looks at the life of a working dramatist; P. Levi *The Life and Times of William Shakespeare* (1988) is good on the working poet; D. and B. Crystal, *Shakespeare's Words* (2002) is an invaluable dictionary of his extraordinary vocabulary; Frank Kermode, *Shakespeare's Language* (2000) is essential for anyone interested in the poet, or, for that matter, in poetry.

Many connections remain to be explored: one is Catholic poetics. Alison Shell, *Catholicism, Controversy and the English Literary Imagination* (1999) opens up fascinating paths of inquiry: I owe my knowledge of 'I C' to her (see pages 270–1), and I am also indebted to her unpublished paper 'Why didn't Shakespeare write religious verse?'. The Southwell connections also await close attention. Astonishingly he is not indexed in any recent Shakespeare biography. Till we get a full-length study, F. W. Brownlow, *Robert Southwell* (1996) is a handy guide; see too C. Devlin, *The Life of Robert Southwell* (1956) and Pierre Janelle, *Robert Southwell the Writer* (1935). Devlin's *Hamlet's Divinity* (1963), written from the Catholic side, gives vivid and suggestive accounts of topics such as the poisoning of Lord Strange, the Babington Plot and the sinister Topcliffe.

London: from an immense literature, pride of place goes to John Stow's *Survey* of 1598; on the inns: John Taylor, *The Carriers Cosmographie* (1637); on the streets: A. Prokter and R. Taylor, *The A–Z of Elizabethan London* (1979) and R. Hyde, *The A–Z of Georgian London* (1992); on the location of the public and private theatres: E. K. Chambers, *Elizabethan Stage* (1923).

Many parish registers are now published, including St Helen's and St Botolph's, Bishopsgate; St Botolph's, Aldgate, and St Mary's, Aldermanbury; a transcript of St Olave's, Silver Street, has been deposited by Professor Alan Nelson in the Guildhall library.

The Middlesex and Southwark Court Sessions and the records of the guilds and livery companies are another rich source of local detail. My account of the 1603 plague in Muggle Street, for example, is taken from *Annals of the Barber Surgeons* (1890). In addition to these sources, for my maps I used: *The London Surveys of Ralph Treswell*, ed. John Schofield (1987); David Mander, *More Light, More Power: An Illustrated History of Shoreditch* (1996); and M. Carlin, *Medieval Southwark* (1996), which has revolutionized the view of fifteenth- to sixteenth-century Southwark; histories of individual London wards and parishes include Sir John James Baddeley, *Cripplegate* (1922); and the unrivalled photographic archive of the National Monument Record in Swindon and the London search room, which are open to all researchers.

Foreign visitors: there are many anthologies. My quote about blank verse on page 122 is by Samuel Sorbière, whose seventeenth-century *Voyage en Angleterre* was published in English in 1709. See also F. M. Wilson, *Strange Island* (1955).

On censorship: Janet Clare, 'Art Made Tongue-tied by Authority', *Elizabethan and Jacobean Dramatic Censorship* (1999 edition).

On the Herbert family: M. Brennan, *Literary Patronage in the English Renaissance: The Pembroke Family* (1988). C. Burrow, *The Complete Sonnets and Poems* (2002) came out after my draft was completed but supports the dating of the sonnets adopted here, with one surprising caveat – a perplexing hint that the Dark Lady poems might be the earliest in the sequence. I assume a statistical quirk here, as Burrow appears to do – most of the poems to the woman are surely from the same period of the later 1590s? Stephen Booth, *Shakespeare's Sonnets* (1977) offers a rich commentary, as does Katherine Duncan-Jones, *Shakespeare's Sonnets* (1997), and I have gratefully profited from both. Mary Wroth's sonnets are in *Woman Poets of the English Renaissance*, ed. M. Wynne-Davies (1999). On Emilia Lanier there is now a full-scale study by Susanne Woods, *Lanyer: a Renaissance woman poet* (1999). Some of William Herbert's poetry was published in *Poems Written by the Rt Hon William Earl of Pembroke…* (1660).

On the Jews: James Shapiro, *Shakespeare and the Jews* (1996) has a wealth of references. On the Bassano family: D. Lasocki and R. Prior, *The Bassanos* (1995).

On Simon Forman there has been a recent flurry of interest, including Barbara Howard Traister, *The Notorious Astrological Physician of London* (2000); A. L. Rowse, *Sex and Society in Shakespeare's London* (1973) has more on the poet's circle. On sex, cross-dressing and gender: Stephen

Orgel is typically challenging in *Impersonations* (1996). On the book industry: Peter Blayney, *The Bookshops in St Paul's Churchyard* (1990). Blayney also wrote the indispensable *The First Folio of Shakespeare* (1991).

For the War of the Poets: James Bednarz, *Shakespeare and the Poets' War* (2001) is a fascinating detective story on which I have relied for the chronology. On the tragedies and Greek translation I am indebted to Louise Schleiner, 'Latinized Greek Drama in Shakespeare's Writing of Hamlet', *Shakespeare Quarterly*, Vol XLI (1990), whose version of the Latin *Orestes* I have adapted on page 223. Stephen Greenblatt, *Hamlet's Purgatory* (2001) looks at the changing relationship between the living and the dead in the sixteenth century. On *Othello*, E. A. J. Honigmann's new Arden edition (1999); on Elizabethan black people in general Nabil Matar, *Turks, Moors and Englishmen* (1999), and *Shakespeare and Race,* ed. Catherine M. Alexander and Stanley Wells (2000).

On Ireland: C. Highley, *Shakespeare, Spenser and the Crisis in Ireland* (1997). On *Macbeth*: Gary Wills, *Witches and Jesuits* (1995). On *King Lear*: F. Brownlow, *Shakespeare, Harsnett and the Devils of Denham* (1993), to which I am indebted on pages 275–8. See too J. Murphy, *Darkness and Devils* (1984). Two valuable older critical works are John Danby, *Shakespeare's Doctrine of Nature* (1949) and Philip Edwards, *Shakespeare and the Confines of Art* (1968).

On revision and collaboration: K. Muir, *Shakespeare as a Collaborator* (1960); John Jones, *Shakespeare at Work* (1995); in *King Lear: Division of the Kingdoms,* ed. Gary Taylor and Michael Warren (1983); in *Othello*: E. A. J. Honigmann's Arden edition (1999). B. Vickers, *Shakespeare Co-author* (2002) came out too late to be used here, but bears out the view of his collaborations adopted in this book.

New finds: the widely publicized recent 'finds' have all proved illusory. The famous *Funeral Elegy,* which now appears in many editions of the collected works, including the Norton and Riverside, is clearly not by Shakespeare at all, but by John Ford; the poem 'Shall I Die?' has not found acceptance; nor, sadly, has Peter Levi's seductive party piece for Alice Strange; but hopes of finding more Shakespeare are not yet over. The most likely recent Shakespeare find is printed in W. A. Ringler and S. W. May, 'An Epilogue Possibly by Shakespeare', *Modern Philology* (1972): found in the commonplace book of a member of the Hunsdon household, it is an epilogue spoken to the queen 'by the players, 1598' which closely resembles Puck's epilogue in *A Midsummer Night's Dream.* A throwaway, but this looks like the real thing.

On the culture of James I's reign: James Doelman, *King James I and the Religious Culture of England* (2000). On the late plays: Simon Palfrey, *Late Shakespeare* (1997) is good on the language. Contexts: *The Tempest and Its Travels,* ed. P. Hulme and W. Sherman (2000) and G. de Sousa, *Shakespeare's Cross-cultural Encounters* (2002); Catherine Belsey, *Shakespeare and the Loss of Eden* (1999) on statues coming alive, child death, and dismembered families. On the late music: J. P. Cutts in *Music and Letters,* Vol IIIVI (1955) and *Musique de la Troupe de Shakespeare* (1959); Johnson's music is transcribed in *Ayres,* ed. I. Spink (1974).

For children: Michael Rosen, *William Shakespeare* (2002) and Andy Gurr's very breezy photographic re-creation *William Shakespeare* (1995) are highly recommended. For younger children there are Marcia Williams's irresistible comic book versions. Novels include Geoffrey Trease, *Cue for Treason* (1940) and Susan Cooper, *King of Shadows* (1999). A. Claybourne and R. Treays, *The Usborne World of Shakespeare* (2001) is especially recommended, with over fifty links to that 'fantasticall Engine, call'd Internet…'

Finally, the afterlife: Stanley Wells, *Shakespeare For All Time* (2002) is a typically readable and humane survey; and John Gross, *After Shakespeare* (2002) has many gems; future editions might also include Michael Madhusudhan, a Bengali writer I first encountered nearly twenty years ago from the mouth of a wandering holy man one midnight on the burning ghats in Calcutta. A typical Bengali polymath, Madhusudhan was familiar with an incredible range of world literature, from Latin and Greek to Persian and Sanskrit; but in 'The Hindu and the Anglo-Saxon' (1856) he argues that English literature is the greatest, and Shakespeare the jewel in its crown. His favourite was the wonderful scene between Falstaff and Hal in the Blue Boar in *Henry IV* Part 1: Madhusudhan would trade it all for 'Banish plump Jack and banish all the world'. So would this author.

ACKNOWLEDGEMENTS

Any work on Shakespeare is a collaborative venture and in writing this book, and making the films, my debts are unusually great.

In Stratford At the Birthplace Trust: Roger and Marion Pringle, Josephine Walker, Anne Donnelly, Susan Brock, Mairi McDonald, Lorraine Finch; Jon Colton and the staff at Henley Street; Richard Morris and everyone at Wilmcote; Charles, Gail and all at Shottery; Ann Kenyon and the Halls Croft staff; Mary and all at Nash's house. Thanks too to Bob Bearman for chewing over many knotty problems; and Stanley Wells who was prepared to be a sounding board and, with the typical generosity he shows towards all students and seekers, read my final draft: needless to say any errors of fact interpretation remain mine. Thanks to Liz Flowers, our wonderful fixer. Others in Stratford-upon-Avon include Richard Edgington and all the town council; Martin Gorick, vicar at Holy Trinty; Tim and Iwona Moore-Bridger, and all the staff, boys and parents at King Edward VI Grammar School; Keith Wilmot, the Latin master; and special thanks to Perry Mills for his wonderful support at all times, especially in putting on sections of *Ralph Roister Doister* and *Poetaster.*

The players Our first and greatest debt is to the Royal Shakespeare Company, starting with Adrian Noble who first supported the project and put us in touch with Greg Doran, who made it all possible. Greg's enthusiasm, knowledge, humour and skill was an inspiration to us all, and it is fitting that our shows went out in the year he received an Olivier award for achievement in the theatre. The excerpts were performed by Tony Sher, Harriet Walter, Jane Lapotaire, Julian Glover, Mal Storry, Estelle Kohler, Alex Gilbreath, Ray Fearon, Des Barrit, Gerald Kyd, Jo Stone Fewings, Nancy Carroll, Steve Noonan, Rob Whitelock, Adrian Schiller and Simon Trinder – and if one could bottle what they have one would make a fortune. On the road with us were Linda Hood, Vic Cree, Pip Horobin, Stuart McCann and Brenda Leedham; thanks too to Roger Mortlock and Lynda Farren at the RSC and all the staff at the Swan Theatre. Thanks also to Mark Rylance, Claire Van Kampen, Sherri Plant and Rowan Walter-Brown and the Globe Company as well as Anthony Arlidge from the Middle Temple for a truly memorable performance of *Twelfth Night*. Also 'The Comedy Store Players' who helped us imagine Shakespeare's comedy: Jim Sweeney, Paul Merton, Josie Lawrence, Lee Simpson, Neil Mullarkey, Richard Vranch and Andy Smart.

The scholars Stanley Wells, Andy Gurr, Peter Blayney, Frank Brownlow, Richard Wilson, David Cressy and Imtiaz Habib gave freely of their expertise; so too did Alexandra Walsham and Marion Wynne-Davies; Alison Shell and Siobhan Keenan who generously helped me with their unpublished research. To Alan Nelson I owe Cordelia Taylor and the anatomisings (page 275). Nat Alcock, Peter Davidson, Judith Mossman, Tim Wilks and David Crankshaw kindly answered my questions. My thanks too to Pam Willis at the Priory of St John; David Trendell for the Byrd Mass; Philip Burden; the Liverpool Archaeology Unit; Robin Whittaker and the Worcester Record Office; the Bishop of Worcester; Dereck Maudlin, the Warwick town clerk; John Schofield at the Museum of London; Peter Milward, Tom McCoog and the English Society of Jesuits; the John Rylands Library; Dr Christine Hodgetts and the Record Offices in Warwick, Nottingham, Birmingham, Norfolk, Hampshire and Stoke; Jan Graffius at Stonyhurst College; Helen Clish and Lancaster University Library; Guy Hutsebaut and the Plantin-Moretus Museum in Antwerp; the London Guildhall Library; David Beasley and the Goldsmiths; Ian Murray, Alan Eastburn and the Company of Barber Surgeons; Robin Myers and the Stationers' Company. At the National Monument Record: Anna Eavis, Anne Woodward, Ian Savage and Tony Rumsey. I am especially indebted to Jan Piggott at Dulwich College and Ian Dejardin and the staff of Dulwich Picture Gallery; Sir Paul Getty and Bryan Maggs at the Wormsley Library and Georgiana Ziegler at the Folger. Among many archives my greatest debt is to David Thomas at the PRO for his tremendous help; thanks also to Hugh Alexander and the rest of the staff for allowing us behind the scenes; and at the British Library thanks to Hugh Cobb, and the staff of the Departments of Western Manuscripts and Printed Books.

Descendants, eye witnesses and practitioners I would like to thank William Hunt and the staff of the College of Arms; Sir Bernard and Lady de Hoghton; Christopher Allen and Gill Godfrey at Ede and Ravenscroft; Mark Booth, David Meredith and the National Trust staff at Rufford and Sutton House; Alan Longstaff and his helpers who were so generous at Baddesley Clinton; Sir Edmund Fairfax Lucy at Charlecote; Lord Montague of Beaulieu; the Herbert family at Wilton House; the Derby family at Knowsley; the Earl of Rutland; Hedley Duncan at the House of Lords; David Schwarz and all at St Winifrid's Well; Mark Beabey; Nick Pank; Bill Turner; Alan Fiddes; Leslie Winfield; Nicole Ryder; Billy McKeen; Peter Shakeshaft; Peter McCurdy; Anne Payton; Marc Meltonville and the experimental archaeologists at Hampton Court; Billy Purefoy and Paula Chateauneuf for the wonderful Cardenio music; Crispins of Shoreditch; Rev Brian Lee at St Botolph's, Aldgate; Wendy Harrington and all at the New Inn in Gloucester; the staff at Leicester Guildhall; the Tower of London and Hampton Court Palace.

The film makers At Maya Vision Rebecca Dobbs was the producer who cheerfully held it all together, Sally Thomas was the wonderful line producer and Barbara Bouman did a huge amount of rare picture and textual research; John Cranmer as usual was the computer wizard and Kevin Rowan the accountant. The director was David Wallace who with Peter Harvey and Neil Lacock swapped the Andes and the Hindu Kush for the M40. Thanks too to Dave Scott, Jeff Baines and Peter Eason as well as Lucy Wallace, Rosa Rogers, Nicol Smith and all the FT2 trainees who worked on the films. Our fantastic editor Gerry Branigan whose contribution as always goes far beyond the editing of pictures and Sally Hilton who stepped in to help at very short notice; Howard Davidson who did the music and the graphic artists Dave McKean and Chris Krupa. Thanks also to Lavinia Trevor and Kevin Sim. At BBC Books my thanks as ever to Chris Weller, Sally Potter, and Shirley Patton; Martin Redfern and Linda Blakemore who did a great job on the book; Pene Parker; Esther Jagger who performed the heroic task of reducing and editing my huge original text. Thanks too to all those in BBC Television who have been involved in the films: Laurence Rees who first supported us and whose advice is always valued by we programme makers, Jane Root for commissioning the series, Krishan Arora our Executive Producer and Adam Kemp in BBC Independent Commissioning. In the States Leo Eaton, Executive Producer for PBS, was our rock as always; thanks too to Jacoba Atlas and all at PBS, including John Wilson, Jack Dougherty, Sandy Heberer and Jim Guerra for their support, not forgetting Kathy Quattrone for setting the ball rolling.

Friends and family I would like to thank the many friends, going back over forty years to my school and college days, with whom I acted in Shakespeare's plays. Also Richard Cottrell and Jonathan Miller, and Jonathan James-Moore and members of the Oxford and Cambridge Shakespeare Company. But above all my thanks go to the two inspiring teachers who first taught us Shakespeare in Manchester in the 1960s, did plays and took us by bus to Stratford in the days before the motorway to see the great productions of that time – among them Hugh Griffith and Paul Rogers doing 'Banish plump Jack'. Few gifts are more precious and it is with the deepest gratitude that the names of Bert Parnaby and Brian Phythian are inscribed at the front of this book

My greatest debt as always is to my family: to my daughters Mina and Jyoti and my wife Rebecca, who with her insight and support has contributed more than she will ever know to this book and who bore with great patience my relationship with the man from Stratford. This book is really as much hers as mine; and my debt to her goes beyond what can be put into words.

INDEX

Page numbers in *italics* refer to illustrations. WS stands for William Shakespeare.

PICTURE CREDITS

BBC Worldwide would like to thank the following for providing photographs and for permission to reproduce copyright material. While every effort has been made to trace and acknowledge copyright holders, we would like to apologize should there be any errors or omissions.

AKG London: 110–111, 169, 284–5; Antiquarian Images: 174–5; Barber Institute/University of Birmingham: 253; Trustees of the Berkeley Will Trust. Photo: Photographic Survey, Courtauld Institute of Art: 158; Birmingham Central Library, Local Studies Department: 90; Bodleian Library, University of Oxford, Arch Ge. 81 (2): 149, 151; Bodleian Library, University of Oxford, MS ASHM. 226. fol. 201r: 198; Bonhams, London/Bridgeman Art Library: 196–7; Boughton House, Northamptonshire/Bridgeman Art Library: 236; By permission of the British Library: 153, 178, 199, 215, 242–3, 262, 268; British Library/Bridgeman Art Library: 255; Clive A. Burden Ltd: 112–115; Special Collections, Case Library, Colgate University Library: 84t; The Master and Fellows of Corpus Christi College, University of Cambridge: 121; The Conway Library, Courtauld Institute of Art, Neg No. 348/35(29): 34; Dulwich Picture Gallery, London/Bridgeman Art Library: 257b; Reproduced by permission of English Heritage/NMR: 32, 128–9, 249; Dennis Field, under the direction of William Hunt, Windsor Herald: 167; Fitzwilliam Museum, University of Cambridge/Bridgeman Art Library: 147; By permission of the Folger Shakespeare Library: 16, 23t, 76, 126, 172–3b, 179, 188, 216, 239, 247, 251, 273, 329; Guildhall Library, Corporation of London, UK/Bridgeman Art Library: 171; Hermitage, St Petersburg/Bridgeman Art Library: 58–9; Hulton Archive: 51, 176, 301, 305; Reproduced by kind permission of the Huntington Library: 206, 342; Mansell/Timepix/Rex Features: 226; Reproduced by permission of the Marquess of Bath, Longleat House, Warminster: 137; Mary Evans Picture Library: 10, 88, 170, 287; Maya Vision International Ltd/David Wallace: 8, 29, 82, 116, 143b, 209; Board of Trustees of the National Museums and Galleries on Merseyside (Walker Art Gallery, Liverpool): 68; Museum of London: 143t; The National Archives: 235, 335; National Portrait Gallery, London: 12, 93, 180, 221, 257t, 265; Oxford Picture Library/Chris Andrews: 23b, 26t, 53; From the Collection at Parham Park, West Sussex: 307; Pepys Library, Magdalene College, Cambridge: 106; Private Collection/Bridgeman Art Library: 18t; Royal Collections © 2003, Her Majesty Queen Elizabeth II: 309; The John Rylands University Library of Manchester: 133; Scottish National Portrait Gallery: 100b; Scottish National Portrait Gallery/Bridgeman Art Library: 258; Shakespeare Birthplace Trust: 3, 9, 24, 30, 40–1, 54, 103, 159, 288, 337; Shakespeare Birthplace Trust/David Wallace: 341; Shakespeare Globe Trust/John Tramper: 228, 229; By kind permission of the Trustees of Stonyhurst College: 73, 152; V&A Picture Library: 2, 18b, 45, 67, 84b, 98, 192, 245, 266, 325; Reproduced by kind permission of Viscount de L'Isle from his private collection at Penshurst Place: 186–7; Warwickshire County Record Office: 100t; The Warwickshire Museum: 14; Woburn Abbey, Bedfordshire/Bridgeman Art Library: 232.